SOME CALL IT UTOPIA

SOME CALL IT UTOPIA

The Origins, Doctrine and Implications of
the World's Most Misunderstood Ideology

Thomas R. Fair

Bartleby Press
Washington • Baltimore

ISBN 978-0935437-64-5
ISBN 978-0935437-65-2 (ebook)
Library Of Congress Control Number: 2023939830

Bartleby Press
JACKSON WESTGATE PUBLISHING GROUP
PO Box 858
Savage, MD 20763
800-953-9929
BartlebythePublisher.com

Printed in the United States of America

10 9 8 7 6 5 4 3 2 1

Contents

Socialism • "Fairness" is Being Treated the Same, Not Getting the Same • Ameliorating Poverty is Fundamentally Different than Equalizing Wealth • It is Both Just and Fair to be Rewarded That Which is Deserved • No Two People are Exactly Alike, Attributes Naturally Vary Among Individuals • The Less Fortunate • Competition, Cooperation and Compassion is the Natural State of Human Affairs • Socialism's Very Essence Conflicts with Religious Beliefs and Human Spirituality • Judeo-Christian Ethical Tradition vs. Socialism • Socialism and the Catholic Church

PREFACE

Writing any book, much less a book on the history and consequences of communism, was never my life's goal. While I had lived through the Cold War, read world history and much about political philosophies over the years, actually writing my own thoughts about history and what the ascent of utopian ideologies portends was not something I had ever aspired to do. So why me, why this particular topic, and why now?

In December of 2013 my wife and I took a trip to Southeast Asia. We cruised from Hong Kong to Singapore with stops in Vietnam and Thailand. Following that experience, we ventured off on our own to Cambodia primarily to visit Angkor Wat, the vast ruins of a now vanished civilization, definitely a bucket list item for me. We had hired a local guide for five days to facilitate our visit.

Over those days with many hours in the car, our guide responded carefully, but forthrightly, to my many questions about life in Cambodia. He was a child of the Pol Pot era who had experienced the horrific nightmares of the Killing Fields with family members among the millions who were slaughtered. He had been taken to a forced labor camp as a mere youth to work the fields, and sometimes had to sneak back into those same fields by moonlight to capture rats and snakes to just stay alive. And yet, despite all the horrors he had experienced, his peaceful nature and optimism trumped even his utter contempt for remnants of the

Khmer Rouge regime and became an inspiration for me, as well as a source of valuable insights.

Upon returning home, I could not get our conversations out of my head. What began as a modest effort to merely capture the results of my own reflections, thoughts, and soul-searching gradually grew into an extensive research project encompassing many years. I became more and more curious and had to find out where each of the various forms of communism and socialism around the world had their origin. I began to reflect in earnest on my memories of: the loss of a cousin in the Korean War long before I had any awareness of the implications of ideology, my visit to the Berlin Wall and East Berlin many years later, the oppression in Hungary that had affected a good friend's family, the Cuban Missile Crisis and the experiences of Cuban exiles whom I came to know well while working in Miami, the Vietnam War which so affected my generation, the collapse of the Union of Soviet Socialist Republics, and more recent events in Venezuela, Nicaragua, and China.

How did the citizens in each of these and other countries get sucked in and allow such an ideology to take root, grow in power, and become an enemy of freedom, including even killing those who resist its control? Answering that question became a ten-year quest I could not set aside.

The result of that unshakable curiosity is now contained in these pages.

Despite having drawn upon many ideas from many sources, some well-deserving of fame and others of disrepute, as the author, I am solely responsible for the content of this book, in whole and in part, including the views taken and any mistakes it may contain. While that is true, I received a great amount of help and encouragement from others. I have been incredibly fortunate to have well-educated friends and colleagues who agreed to read, edit, and critique early drafts of the manuscript, contributing ideas and advice that improved the work. I am particularly indebted to: Dr. Martin Smith, a longtime friend and somewhat of a maverick like me, without whose encouragement and many contributions this work would not have been completed, Roberto Denis, who as a child experienced the revolution that brought Castro to power, Charles Merk and Gary Lavine, each of whom provided very valuable advice, the accomplished author Christopher Sandford who was very generous with tips on writing, Jeremy Kay and his staff at Bartleby Press, who spent three years working with me on the text, and lastly my very insightful and talented wife of over forty years, Mary, and my daughter Allyson who has a very keen eye for the written word.

Please note that I am a reasonably well-educated but obscure person who lacks honorific prestige, particularly the kind conferred by academia. I have labored at this book more diligently than any other undertaking of my life, save that of attaining several advanced college degrees and supporting my family. And, while I greatly respect those who have managed to truly master a discipline, I expressly reject the notion that any self-ordained, often ideologically driven intellectual aristocracy which attempts to claim monopoly access to the telling of truth and imparting wisdom (be it the news media, academia, government bureaus, or other organizations) has any exclusive mandate to interpret the world to the rest of us. Much less can they be trusted to prescribe what needs to be done to improve upon the human condition. All such people are subject to the same human failings as the rest of us; for example: sloppy thinking, hubris, blindness to facts and truth that do not conform to our presuppositions, emotionally driven biases, some degree of dishonesty, and self-righteousness. They may indeed have important things to say, but if we do not think freely and reason for ourselves using facts and logic, and instead cave into the false security of following dubiously proclaimed "thought leaders" we will be lost.

While this is not a completely novel work in its constituent parts, taken as a whole, I believe it is a warning and a full story not seen before, which I fervently believe needs to be communicated to and understood by the many for whom the fundamental cause and realities of the "Cold War" and utopian experiments of the 20th Century are a fading or non-existent memory. Those who are too young, or who have simply let such memories fade may be unable to recognize warning signs of the reemergence of utopian thinking and politics from the detritus of the past.

As an unabashed polemic with sharp-edged honesty, this work may offend some. I make no apologies at all for that. The truth one discovers is often uncomfortable to confront because it does not conform to heartfelt preconceived notions. Rather than slipping your feet into your favorite pair of well-worn shoes, it sometimes takes you in bare feet across the "rough gravel" of realism. And it can be horrifying at times. This work is not, however, intended to demonize those liberals, progressives or socialists who are sincere in their humanitarianism. No one can truly know for certain the thoughts and feelings another has within their heart. Actions are what matter, not the political label one may assume, unless the label is part of a deception.

As I delved more and more deeply into what socialism truly is, I came to realize that no one field of knowledge by itself can adequately explain socialism within just the confines of its framework and each necessarily has its own biases in interpreting reality. Therefore, I have woven together many facts and ideas from dozens of works of history, ethics, economics, political philosophy, and other branches of knowledge in laying out as honestly as I could this account of socialist utopianism's "monumental debauch" of humanity in the 20th Century, the rise of messianic socialism before that, and the broader problem of militant utopian ideologies which continue to plague humanity.

However, this work should not be taken as a call to ignore or take lightly other perils that curse humanity. Chief among those are the rise of racism, both a political disintegrating and negative organizing ideological force, and militant theocratic Islam. Both racial and radical Islamic ideologies appeal to base human passions disguised as virtuous, and unbridled by Reason.

My hope is that some persons who are in consciousness-shaping roles will read this. But if not, I will at least have met the challenge I gave myself nearly ten years ago to commit my thoughts to writing in order to find out if I had anything worth saying on the subject of utopian political creeds. You the reader will have to be the final judge of that.

For those of you who do not believe what is written here, as well as those who do, I leave you with this simple message: Check for yourself! Do your own research, the deeper and more thorough the better. Delve carefully through source works while considering your own moral compass, then draw your own conclusions. If you do so I am confident you will share my outrage.

INTRODUCTION

How could anyone possessing even the least shred of human decency ever accept for a moment the political legitimacy of an ideology responsible for the systematic State-directed slaughter of millions upon millions of helpless men, women, and children through horribly cruel forms of torture, slave labor, forced starvation, bullets, axes, hanging, freezing, and other equally gruesome means? Let me be very clear. This is not the death toll from revolutions and wars. These are the deaths from conscious decisions taken by socialist utopian regimes after they gained political control; this is murder in one form or another of their own people! This immense slaughter was an unprecedented, entirely human-caused global catastrophe that had its origins in "mad scribblings" of arrogant ideologues and intellectuals – horribly bad ideas that like a pestilential disease quickly spread through time and space until almost no part of the planet was left uninfected. Though the utopian creed of socialism has now resurfaced and begun to challenge for political power and even in some corners find favor, questions about the inherent immorality of its ideology (not just the impracticality of its doctrines) are rarely asked or answered in public debate. It is a deafening silence that speaks of a great lie, a lie we must refuse to meekly submit to and accept, as though the true cause of the great suffering and death of those millions of human beings is not well known, is of no interest, has no one or nothing to blame, or is utterly lacking in significance for humanity today.

Again, let me be clear. The story that follows is not about the massive military casualties and enormous collateral civilian death toll caused by the two World Wars of the last century, nor the uniquely horrific Nazi industrialized genocide of Jews known as the Holocaust, nor other episodes of genocides before and since, as incredibly horrible as all that is. It is about something entirely different. The sinews of history, of course, interlace the World Wars and Holocaust with the utopian ideologies described in this book. I am referring particularly to the devil's embrace of Hitler's ruthless race-based, pan-Germanic Nazi movement with Karl Marx's equally totalitarian, hate-based socialism, first implemented by Vladimir Lenin's Bolsheviks then replicated by his and Marx's fanatical followers across the globe. However, Hitler's totalitarianism was based on different ideology than Lenin's, though their two systems share much in common. Utopian movements within nations have different origins than warfare between nations. Such movements have been with us throughout history in one form or another, and are not the direct result of war, even though wars often create social chaos and the "detritus" that allow nascent utopian movements to gain large followings. Various utopian movements can be distinguished from one another, even though their methods, aims, and evil consequences are not dissimilar. Using Nazi and communist utopian visions as examples, though different in their ideological concept, both gained a political foothold and then spread from the same disease-infected Petri dish of imperfect human nature, resulting in the same savage, pitiless, totalitarian methods and mass murder.

Utopian tyrants and their acolytes have sought not just to reshape their own nations, but to take all humanity down a violent, previously untraveled path to an utterly dystopian world, using their power to create a new order consistent with their vision of what the future ought to be. Indeed, in the past century, the world came to see that the very nature of utopian power necessitates that it continually multiply itself until nothing is left outside of its ambit, and increasing such power becomes an end in itself regardless of horrific consequences for those ruled by it. Ideology driven by utopian zeal thus became a primal force shaping human affairs in the past century. The one hundred million deaths attributed to it have shown that ultimately, even life itself hangs in the balance when truth is twisted, the words and syntax of language are debased, and beguiling promises that are in reality nothing but impossible utopian dreams take hold. Then Reason slumbers, releasing the ever-restless monsters always lurking within the lower regions of the human psyche.

After a quiescent period of only several decades, certain utopian ideologies have again resurfaced. Adherents of political theories thought to be largely discredited have begun to regain favor in today's public discourse. The question of likely consequences is rarely even asked, much less addressed. As a prime example, socialism was thought to be dead and buried following its dismal failure in every form during the past century. But defying reason and all historical experience, it has once more become politically popular in many places, especially among those ignorant of socialism's history. Despite being utterly discredited in the 20th Century as a social, economic, and moral catastrophe, socialism rises again like a vampire of lore. Resting until the night of ignorance or forgetfulness descends, it emerges to suck the blood of our freedom and prosperity. A new generation of true believers has lately been created, boldly promoting socialism with pious zeal in our educational systems, news media, and cultural institutions, which, to quote Alexandr Solzhenitsyn, have been "carried-away by shallow, worthless ideas." Now these new believers are again seeking to control the levers of government, not only in Asia, but in parts of Europe, Latin America, and North America as well.

The warning signs are clear though socialism was thought by many to have been irretrievably consigned to history's ash heap with the dissolution of the Soviet (Union of Soviet Socialist Republics) Empire and freeing of Eastern Europe at the end of the Cold War. Consider the results of a 2016 survey of 2,300 people conducted by the Victims of Communism Memorial Foundation and reported in "Annual Report on U.S. Attitudes Towards Socialism." Among "Millennials" 42 percent did not know of Mao Zedong (aka Mao Tse Tung), and among the mere 33 percent who said they were familiar with Vladimir Lenin, 25 percent had a favorable view of him. One-third of Millennials surveyed believed more people were killed under former President George W. Bush than Joseph Stalin. (Historians believe upwards of 20 million people were killed under Stalin's regime, including 98 of his comrades in the Communist Party's Central Committee who were ordered executed by Stalin personally.) Perhaps of greatest concern, almost half of survey respondents then 18-22 years of age said they would vote for a socialist. It is no unusual thing that young people begin with the belief that the world is "all screwed-up" and that they have a moral obligation to change it. Many youth, especially those who are alienated from religion, community, and patriotism, and those who have little involvement in the market economy, tend to be susceptible to socialism's beguiling message, thinking it to be nothing more than a form of justifiable wealth redistribution by a benign, protective welfare state. But the truth is much, much different.

Most readers know that as a result of World War II, the Nazi regime was not only militarily vanquished, but both it and its ideology, Nazism, were universally condemned, especially following revelation of the full extent and true nature of the

Holocaust. This was over 75 years ago. Yet, other regimes based upon Marx's socialism have never been similarly vanquished and held to account by any international tribunal for their vast crimes against humanity. Notwithstanding being discredited as a failure with the collapse of the USSR and its Stalinist puppet states, and leaving a trail of oppression, atrocities, and death on an almost unbelievable scale, at the beginning of the new millennium the cause of "building socialism" has been taken up by a new powerful standard-bearer, Communist China, and growing number of apostles and radical acolytes within Western institutions.

Socialism as an international revolutionary movement received an enormous boost as WWII ended with Stalin's victorious Soviet regime becoming a nuclear superpower dedicated to challenging the Western democracies, and championing Marxist revolutions across the globe. During the 45 years of the "Cold War," aided by the Soviet Union and then China, socialist ideology extended its reach and became deeply entrenched in places including Indochina, North Korea, and parts of Africa and Latin America, such as Ethiopia, Zimbabwe, Cuba, and Venezuela. As a result, the Cold War concluded not with a surrender of those who had led these criminal states and their henchmen, nor a reckoning like the Nuremberg trials, but with only a whimper of dimming significance to present generations. These newer generations may remember the destruction in 1989 by joyous Berliners of that infamous symbol of oppression, the Berlin Wall, and perhaps also the dismantling of an Iron Curtain that had kept Eastern Europeans captive for 45 years. But how much do they know of the utopian ideology that built these instruments of oppression, and has wreaked havoc in other parts of the world?

My research on ideological utopianism in its different forms inevitably led to what one might call today's "unfinished business" of the Cold War. The so-called victory in the Cold

War was at best partial, at worst delusional for the "victorious" West. This book attempts to lay out in non-academic style the origin and true nature of modern socialism, an ideology often interchangeably referred to in the literature and by its theoreticians and activists as Marxism and communism, what socialism is, and what it is not, its doctrines, practices and consequences, and the reasons for its failure and counter-factual revival. This work is intended as an urgent admonition to free people everywhere that to the extent socialism makes gains politically, it constitutes a very real threat to our freedom and way of life, indeed to everything we hold dear. I believe it to be a sinister threat of greater significance and immediacy than militant Islamic Fundamentalism with its theocratic vision of ruling the world according to Sharia law. Warning signs abound that socialism is again becoming politically respectable in the democratic West even the United States, despite socialism's unmistakable record of broken promises, gross inhumanity, and economic dysfunction. Not just human progress and prosperity, but the entire Western liberal democratic political tradition is at stake. There will be incalculable consequences, if we allow the truth about socialism to be forgotten, ignored, or twisted.

Living by lies starts with allowing language to be debased in public discourse by those who would use censorship and personal attacks to control freedom of speech, and by those who substitute clever lies and propaganda for reality. Those who can discern the truth must defend and proclaim it lest it be drowned out by malevolent demagoguery. As the great Russian hero of freedom Alexandr Solzhenitsyn observed, we need not "live by lies."

CHAPTER ONE
The Evolution of Utopian Ideologies

"Utopia is not only a dream...it is a dream that wishes to be

realized."

—French philosopher Paul Ricoeur

W hat is Utopianism, and what is its connection with socialism?

As in John Lennon's famous lyric, just imagine a world without poverty, avarice, war, envy, hate, or crime, filled instead only and always with the love of people for one another. A very appealing vision indeed!

Utopia reaches for such an imagined ideal. It promises a vastly superior way of life for those within its ambit, a new social order that is a dramatic break from a present imperfect and messy world shaped as much by humans' frailties as by their positive attributes. It provides an easily understood, though often simplistic, explanation of what's "wrong" with the world, combined with an alluring vision of how all people could live much better under a new order not burdened by undesirable human behaviors. But there is a catch; a large number of people must en masse buy into the vision of wiping the slate clean in order to create something shiny, new, and pure. This must include ignoring the moral dilemmas that inevitably arise in wiping the slate. That is where power-seeking agents of utopia enter with ready plans for overturning and replacing the existing political

7

system and placing a gloss of imagined morality on their actions, regardless of how harsh they may be. Indeed, the gathering of power is a requirement for establishing utopia.

Let us then focus on the meaning of the word "power" for a moment. In the literature one can find numerous definitions of power. For the purpose of this writing, I define power simply as the ability to dictate the terms of another's existence. While there are many facets to it, and degrees of it, that is its essence. For instance, power over others can obviously come from direct means such as a slave-master's whip, the barrel of a gun, or physical control of a person's sustenance. Yet power also comes from indirect means such as financial control over others, the issuance of decrees requiring obedience under threat of punishment, and the ability to influence what is taught, publicly printed and said, and what ideas are deemed acceptable or condemnable. In the political realm, power is often referred to as the ability to create the law the state will enforce, as well as controlling its means of enforcement.

The process of constructing utopia entails creation and use of power by the governing agents to steer society toward a predetermined outcome. However, initiation of utopian social change does not involve prepossession of the full power of dictatorial authority from the start, spanning across all segments of society. In preparation, such power must be acquired by first "seeding fertile soil" so it can rapidly grow and then become focused on carrying out a program of political action. Seeding begins with utopian true believers colonizing institutions that shape public consciousness, particularly self-interested institutions which give wide latitude to those with a strong sense of self-virtue and superiority. This colonization is driven by a craving for the power to influence public opinion and attitudes and thus politics according to their utopian world view. What ideas, what turns of phrase, what promises, will rally people to the cause? These institutions then become recruiting centers. In the past century, it has been well learned that in order to be successful, organizing political action requires inspirational ideology, the close cousin of utopia. Ideology is where the "ism" comes in.

If we look at definitions of the term "utopia" and its use in the English language, we find that "utopian" and "utopianism" refer to idealism put into action. One scholar defined utopianism as "a conception of social improvement either by ideas or ideals themselves or embodied in definite agencies of social change."[1] Agencies of course require human agents for purpose and direction.

Agents of utopianism at first consist of a self-chosen few who see themselves as a visionary vanguard attempting to design and implement the perfect governmental system and culture that supports it. Their ultimate aim is to transform current reality into the "ideal" human society at least from their viewpoint, even if that would require altering human nature itself. The utopian model is meant to assure that the "common good," or perhaps "the greatest good for the greatest number," will reign supreme even though what is considered "good" is an inherently normative judgement not subject to logical deduction, shaped by individuals' desires and their cultural milieu. If this flawless world will not arise spontaneously, it must be made the product of human resolve. As one Chinese Communist Party newspaper put it while describing their infallible leader Mao Zedong's Great Leap Forward, "The human will is the master of all things."[2]

Why shouldn't such ideals become the basis of concerted human action? The Nobel Prize-winning British philosopher Sir Bertrand Russell argued that "A Utopia, if seriously intended, obviously must embody the ideals of its creator."[3] Ideals, though formulated by individual persons, unlike mundane objects of desire, do not pertain to just that single person. Instead, the idealist wishes that everyone else desires the same something that he or she does. But people can have very different desires and, therefore, different wishes about what everybody *ought* to desire. That is where controversy begins and is why overcoming the differences in human desires and ideals is the fundamentally intractable problem of Utopianism.

Furthermore, abstract ideals, when acted upon in the arena of human affairs, often become warped and impure. Ideals that are subject to compromise in a political process are no longer ideals where the rubber meets the road, i.e., in controlling the machinery of government as well as other aspects of society. That is why to create the actual utopia, or close to it, the utopian must exhibit complete self-assurance, an iron will, and be able to wield sufficient political power that compromise is unnecessary, to the point of even killing others who may stand in the way.

Thus, to reach the goal of building such a society the utopian activist must possess enough power to completely extinguish other ideals and competing opinions that do not conform to his or her utopian proposition. Such crusaders are impatient in bringing about the transformative changes in attitudes and opinions they believe are necessary. They are willing to proselytize by threat of force those who are old enough to resist. It is perhaps axiomatic that the more massive the social changes sought in each time period, the stiffer the resistance, the more brutal the measures required to achieve the goal, and the more likely unforeseen consequences will arise.

Utopian theorists who write the grandiose script for those pulling the strings reflecting an unshakable belief in the power of the human will to shape reality, have tended to treat human society, and human nature itself, as subject to design, manipulation and direction according to a master plan, as if human societies can be designed like a clockwork produced by an expert watchmaker to predictably operate with complete unitary order according to the laws of physics.

Using another analogy, ambitious idealists who zealously embrace such theories crave to drive others to the truth as they see it. They and those they rally to their cause aspire to be puppeteers of a sort; that is, one of those with the power to pull the strings from a position on high in a fully scripted idealized world, so that the pseudo-human drama of life proceeds in the exact manner intended by these omniscient masters smiling down with great pride on their creation like gods from Olympus above.

The essence of this analogy is not the drama itself, but rather the control of the puppets' lives by such secular "gods," (the master puppeteers). Regardless of the individual role each of their followers plays in influencing events, they proudly become part of a collective undertaking bigger than themselves. It can be a compelling proposition. From their societies' commanding heights, they convince their followers that because they are "servants of the gods," they are soon to become "masters of the earth"[4] sharing in their glory.

Not surprisingly, we find that in practice the demand for public adoration of deified supreme leaders is often a prominent part of secular utopian systems, for example: Lenin, Stalin, Hitler, Mao Zedong, and Kim Il-sung, to name a few.

Then there are the intrusive behavioral dictates and sanctions established by rulers of utopian theocratic states. They are convinced that if only everyone adhered to the requirements of *their* government-enforced religion believers in the one true creed would become "masters of the earth," and the world would be perfect.

Let us set aside for the moment the factual history of mankind's repeated misadventures with various utopian schemes. On a philosophical level, the assumption of certain influential 18th and 19th Century intellectuals that human societies can be "engineered" as if they were a "closed," deterministic, and predictable physical system analogous to Newton's physics and Leibniz's calculus, was completely discredited in the 20th Century. New paradigms for understanding self-adapting and pluralistic "open" social systems have consigned the mechanical clockwork and master puppeteer paradigms to the list of many other discarded social science theories. It is now clear there are no mechanics of the human universe to be discovered enabling political activists to launch society on a set trajectory toward a certain orbit, nor any "scientific laws" of history. Furthermore, the notion that there is a certain predictable "arc of history" that assures continuing human progress must be considered nothing but a hope-filled, feel-good fantasy, given the many horrendous events of the past 100 years, and looking ahead, the plausibility of a nuclear holocaust at some point in the future as such weapons proliferate, and their use is threatened by ruthless dictators. A pessimist could make the case that "might" stands an equal chance of triumphing over "right."

Nothing concerning worldly human affairs is completely certain except the individual's cycle of birth, life and death, and capacity for both good and evil. Nonetheless, knowledge of the material world has steadily accumulated. While we can add to our store of knowledge by studying science, society and history, that understanding should not be confused with an ability to accurately predict, much less control, the making of "future history" according to some design, or to alter human nature itself for better or worse. Neither does mankind's accumulation of information and broader knowledge necessarily correspond to greater wisdom or inevitable moral improvement in human affairs. The truth is quite obvious, simple, and straightforward: the human condition cannot be bettered by attempts at engineering societies or human nature itself, notwithstanding the pretentious social blueprints of utopians. We know this instinctively, as confirmed by logic, personal experience, and the hard lessons of history.

Mankind has, however, succeeded in innovating and gradually improving organizations and institutions in free nations, although the road to improvement has not been an altogether smooth one. Real lasting progress is rarely quick and easy or free from muddling, as history proves. In sharp contrast to the failures of frustrated utopians, such learning has led to dramatic improvements in global prosperity in the past 200 years.

On a more pleasant note, utopias, without a call to political action can simply be benign and even beneficial imaginings. They may encompass comforting (if perhaps unrealistic) visions of a better world, such as an "ecotopia" in which everyone freely chooses to live in "harmony with nature." Utopian visions may also be spiritual, such as the Buddhists' Nirvana or the Paradise of Christianity and Islam. These utopias include moral codes to guide human behavior toward goals like eternal life or divine enlightenment and can lead to human betterment so long as they do not become temporal dictatorships through fire and sword.

Still other utopias represent purely imaginary societies often described in science fiction; for example, the advanced society of the supra-intelligent Krell in the 1956 film *The Forbidden Planet,* or the powerful 1927 film *Metropolis* depicting a hellish futuristic city divided into two separate worlds, with manipulated worker slaves underground supporting a pampered "utopia" of planners and industrialists above – both works based on inherently flawed visions of "perfection;" just two of many such imaginary worlds found in literature and film. Works of fiction based upon imaginary utopian visions may not include a call to transform society but may warn of the delusional and dystopian nature of the worlds so envisioned; the totalitarian regimes of Aldous Huxley's *Brave New World* and George Orwell's *1984* come to mind.

Fictional utopias may provoke thoughtful refection

revealing real opportunities for bettering human societies, or merely entertain the reader by providing a temporary escape from a reality that is not always nice and neat into an imaginary dreamlike one in which everyone is always happy, satisfied and completely secure. The reader may be transported from a messy world of muddling along and the compromising of diverse ideals into a world conforming throughout to a unitary vision, in which everything is always in its right place, all parts of it function together harmoniously without fail, and human frailties and conflicting norms are non-existent. In the abstract such visions may be quite appealing. And what is wrong with any of this? Nothing, of course, assuming such utopian constructs do not morph into disastrous real-world ideological crusades.

The Curse of Ideological Utopianism

There is nothing wrong in imagining how the world might be made better. Indeed, such dreaming about what may be possible is necessary for progress. But utopian theory can be dangerous, especially when it is ideological and put into action. Some may think that ideology simply defines how power is to be utilized. But for utopian ideologues it is a grand theoretical explanation of life's purpose that determines not only the use of power for constructing the ideal society, but also the means to acquire and continually increase it.

In the past century, it has been well learned that successfully organizing political action requires inspirational ideology, the close cousin of utopia. Ideology is succinctly defined as "a form of social or political philosophy...a system of ideas that aspires both to explain the world and to change it."[5] For some the attraction of the system when vitalized by a political movement is so strong that they may end up abandoning morality in exchange for the gratification gained from the feeling of empowerment to "make things right" for themselves and others, thus fulfilling a higher purpose. In this noble undertaking, such activists continually seek to acquire the power needed to sweep aside any who resist, so they can reliably shape the course of events according to their uncompromised vision of what *ought* to be.[6]

Typical utopian ideology claims to be the key that will unlock history and the universal laws of nature and man within its appealing, though unproven, system of abstract ideas. Those ideas demand human action in the real world aimed at their fulfillment. With its demands, it becomes a political weapon used by activist utopians who insist their philosophy be adopted as the official national doctrine all are obliged to accept. Once a utopian idea becomes an ideology it becomes a weapon to be used against certain people who express different ideas and ideals, as its followers become committed to acting on its central idea and exiling or crushing those who oppose its implementation, including even their imprisonment or murder.

Utopian ideologies are those that take on the messianic political militancy of a "cause," a movement to design and construct an entirely new and better world based upon a set of ideals that are largely incongruent with reality. The new world cannot be superimposed on that which already exists. That world must be burned down and destroyed. Those who defend "the system" must be attacked and done away with, in order for the new and better world to be brought into being.

In addition, a utopian ideology may become itself a belief system of certitude, which proclaims infallibility, often makes moral claims, and has the power to animate the passions of adherents. These "believers" take on the missionary purpose of organizing and gaining power over others in order to bring their utopian vision to reality in their own society as far as their power can reach and then propagate it around the globe --mounting a crusade to fundamentally change their society and others around it. The utopian crusader, often with delusions of omnipotence, believes the world should be shaped entirely by the human will, starting with words and persuasion, but also using deceit and commands backed by force when necessary.

In seeking total societal transformation, utopian ideology must exist on an even higher plane than mere observable facts, religious traditions, the law, and an independent judiciary, otherwise truly transformative change is impossible. Through their actions, declaratory assertions, and exhortations we find that secular utopian crusaders share a common trait; that is, a belief that they possess undeniably virtuous insights and superior intelligence that will benefit society as a whole, and that they therefore have a natural right to be exempted from strictures, moral and otherwise, that apply to the "average" person. Once in power, their version of "freedom" is that those who occupy society's most lofty positions are at liberty to act however they will, but the masses must be instructed in the right way and submit to being told what to do by such "exceptional" elites so they might enjoy the "collective freedom" that is prescribed for them. Thus, written laws reflecting timeless wisdom and moral principles applicable to all become mere scraps of paper with little or no influence on those running things and those subject to their power.

It is important to recognize that ideas take shape through words and are shaped by them. Hence, words are the raw material from which ideologies are created, and ideological manipulation of words leads to control of thoughts, and consequently of beliefs, and ultimately actions. This is particularly the case when carefully crafted words are repeatedly transmitted to large audiences of impressionable people with the potential to become eager followers. Such words do not have to resemble reality to be ideologically effective, and often do not. In George Orwell's *1984* the main character, Winston Smith, is employed by the "Ministry of

Truth" altering the records of the past to conform to current policy, a process known as Newspeak. Control of what is taught and what words may be used in public discourse are essential aspects of utopian ideology.

Ideologically driven organizers take delight in the thought-shaping *effects* of their propaganda, instead of in any kernel of *truth* that might be in it. To transition words into a cause and then an organized movement, it is essential that the *ideology* be stripped of intellectual trappings and reduced to a stirring slogan that captures attention and excites the emotions of potential recruits.

Ideological Utopians endeavor to remake and direct an imperfect world into an invented future that ensures perfect order. They see themselves as change-agents in sole possession of legitimacy, zealously spearheading societal transformation, often through violent political action when voting won't work, in order to capture and use government's ability to command others through enforcement of decrees. Sadly, history shows many people are willing to accept the dictates of a domineering government, particularly if disobedience and opposition come with significant risk and uncertainty.

"Might makes right" tyrannies possessing the power to demand full obedience of their subjects are not a new thing. Tyrannies that spanned generations date back to the dawn of recorded history, as amply documented by archaeological research of ancient civilizations in the Near East and elsewhere, and more recent recorded historical experiences. Submission to, rather than struggle against such power was the norm until diffusion of the revolutionary idea that self-determination and freedom *from* tyranny should be the natural state of human affairs.

Regrettably, despite this real progress in the struggle for freedom, in modern times there are examples of long-lasting collective submissiveness driven by perverse customs reinforced by fear in ruthless police states (for example: North Korea, Cuba, Iran, China, and the former Soviet Union) in which people have been quietly "disappeared" and sentenced to a dungeon or prison camp, tortured, or publicly "tried" then hanged or shot by firing squad. In North Korea when a home catches fire and burns, the family may have to choose between rescuing their most valuable possessions or the picture of deceased supreme leader Kim Il-Sung which hangs in every loyal citizen's living room and which the state demands be honored and protected! While the inhabitants of such dominions may become accustomed to unquestioning obedience, pervasive fear of arrest and severe punishment is nonetheless essential to their rulers' power to govern.

Of course, fear of punishment for political "crimes" cannot come into play until power has been seized, and/or a revolution is underway. Initially, an ideology must be appealing to potential followers. For some it is the system of ideas comprising the ideology, for others it is simply the utopian vision. Very often, background experiences play a critical role.

Those who become activists, i.e., those who get their hands dirty and often take sizable risks in the push and pull of politically disruptive actions, are not always themselves members of the cultural or academic elite. Those who are susceptible to recruitment to the cause can come from varied backgrounds. Many players in the utopian drama often begin a journey toward political activism with seeds of resentment from perceived mistreatment in their youth. Perhaps they were alienated from their family and society at large or suffered as a result of personal misfortune or social unrest; they may feel stuck in the lower ranks of society through no fault of their own, burdened with feelings of injustice, powerlessness, and frustration they desperately want to overcome.

Others, regardless of class origin, are simply fervent idealists seeking virtue in a just and righteous cause. Few who have followed their heart's feelings into social activism start out having thought through a comprehensive formula for creating a perfected social order to replace the existing system which they find immoral and intolerable, much less considered the actions required and full consequences.

Some may carry the psychological scars of injustices, maltreatment, envy, and resentment from cumulative slights experienced by themselves or family members, which they blame on those in positions of wealth and power or simply the "system" as a whole. Still others may be imbued with a cause inherited from parents or teachers who zealously indoctrinated them, much like, and often a substitute for, the intergenerational transfer of religious beliefs.

Depending on how well they are presented, utopian ideas and ideals can provide the incendiary spark to the kindling of individuals' background experiences. For those without a strong predisposition, it is not until they encounter a utopian vision as either a student, a worker, or from within some other peer group, that they develop a sense of outrage; outrage that can only be assuaged by commitment to a cause and joining hands with others to mobilize collective action. In the works and exhortations of utopian theorists, presented as wholly credible and admirable, they find a coherent and seemingly plausible set of beliefs that explain the causes of the world's failings and provide an uncompromising formula for its betterment. All that is then needed to make the necessary transformative changes is willful leadership and a path to political power. That requires expanding the circle peacefully or by revolution.

Those who are most uncomfortable with uncertainty in their lives tend to be susceptible to utopian ideology because it confidently promises a dependable future better than the present, instead of one of continuing unpredictability in which chance plays an important role in determining social status.

Such a vision, when plausibly presented, can be very appealing. Despite the impossibility of any experiential evidence to prove the ideology will produce the desired result, the utopian peddles belief in his or her holistic "blueprint," propped-up by claims of inevitability and infallibility. People who succumb buy into the plausible explanation of harsh realities, and simply want to believe in the confidently presented promise of a secure and better life, content to place their faith in charismatic strong-willed people projecting certainty.

Of course, there are always skeptics who raise objections and ask questions difficult to answer. A utopia cannot be a utopia if there are discontented troublemakers within it. In order to "move forward" the social engineer must turn a deaf ear to any critics and dissenters, have the power to suppress them, and eventually "reeducate" or destroy those who resist. The amount of arrogance and malevolence required to pursue such a path is indeed breathtaking!

Utopian schemes often seem to be rooted in two wishful concepts of human nature. The first is that humans in a natural state uninfluenced by society are intrinsically benign. According to Karl Marx, human beings are nothing but a malleable product of social relations. Change the social relations and you fundamentally alter human nature. "All history is nothing but a continual transformation of human nature," he wrote.

Accordingly, a person's capacity to commit evil actions comes about solely from unjust social conditions that distort and suppress one's underlying benign nature, rather than an individual's needs and desires, natural impulses, will, and moral agency playing a role; in other words, those things we normally consider important determinants of our behavior, and not just the "social environment," or how we respond to the actions of those around us.

The second, corollary premise is that prolonged

manipulation of socio-economic conditions can alter human nature itself in a purposeful way; through an empowered act of human will together with broad control of socio-economic conditions, people can be reprogrammed for the better. At birth humans are just a blank sheet of paper yet to be written on, a "tabula rasa." With full and firm social control of our lives and our environment from cradle to grave, we will regain our undistorted natural virtue and harmlessness, resulting in a new and better model human who, depending on the decision of a higher authority, becomes either like the drone that must accept its predetermined role and fate in the beehive of propagating the collective whole, whilst its food is provided by the "worker bees," or like the servient worker bee who exists simply to take care of the others in the hive, including drones and the queen.[7] Eventually, the need for governmental authority will simply vanish when hive-like total harmony is achieved. In order to create this improved type of human being, this "New Man," not just indoctrination by the state from early childhood, but extreme tools like eugenics, compulsory "re-education," and selective murder are sometimes employed to rid society of undesirables and dissenters while on the road to fulfilling their formula.

Despite any intellectual trappings, what animates the utopian cause is not logic, superior knowledge, experience, or discernment, but instead subconscious passions and desires presented by its activists as virtuous idealism. The motivation is often a desperate craving for power. Those who stand in the utopian's way toward such progress are not just disagreeing because they hold differing opinions; they are in effect defending social evils, and, therefore, must themselves be evil. Such people, and those who belong to a group encompassed by utopians' assertion of collective guilt, may be treated as subhuman or eliminated entirely in order to create utopia. The psychologist Steven Pinker has noted that utopian ideologies summon forth our "inner demons" by justifying unlimited violence in pursuit of unlimited good, overriding reason. Science has conclusively shown that these demons are from our evolution, which according to Pinker "has permanently saddled our species with many irrational and destructive traits."[8]

Solzhenitsyn felt that the dividing line between good and evil goes through the middle of everyone's heart. Contrary to utopian beliefs, man's inner demons cannot be *erased* from the human heart by acts of human will and social pressure. They may only be *kept under control* by individuals with the help of institutions and laws reflecting social norms, which humans have invented over time for that purpose. These harness both positive self-control and the deterrent fear of punishment.

But is the dream of an earthly utopia itself inherently bad and dangerous? Dreams are not necessarily bad; however, as French philosopher Paul Ricoeur once noted, "Utopia is not only a dream...it is a dream that wishes to be realized."[9] Of course, as a mere idea, utopia has no determination of its own and cannot realize itself. It is the inevitable nexus of utopian ideology with political power, particularly with individuals possessing what Nietzsche terms the "Will to Power," that sparked the catastrophes of the past century. So, while not all utopias are ideological, all ideologies from their inception contain the extremely dangerous "seed" of utopianism, that appeals to humans' susceptibility to being ruled by their feelings and thus to clever manipulation by those possessing a ruthless resolve. To repeat, it is not simply from abstract doctrines, but in their attempted realization that the danger arises. Ascendant totalitarian dictators may present themselves as "prophets of the inevitable,"[10] but of course such "inevitability" depends on the way actual events play out. It is not until some turn of events allows such would-be dictators to take control of the machinery of government (including its potential for unimpeded use of their power against their political competitors and those they deem to be enemies) that idealistic utopian visions capable of capturing human imagination and inciting passionate feelings override reason and mutate into a living nightmare. One thing is abundantly clear from history: the more a utopian ideology spreads and gains the upper hand to control a society's culture and politics, the deadlier it becomes.

Another question is whether utopian idealism could otherwise be a force for good in the right benevolent hands. One is tempted to say yes, because imagining the betterment of the world has value by informing and guiding society's collective decisions, particularly concerning the creation of human institutions. However, the normative and often moral judgments of what is "better" must be grounded in the free actions and open expressions of those whose lives would be affected positively or negatively. In other words, without decisions made by free people acting freely it is impossible to respect the natural right of all to an equal say in their own government, and to achieve genuine improvement morally, as well as increased material benefits.

Any utopian social system, either old or recently conceived, must be viewed as superior to all others; if not perfect, better able to comprehensively serve the common interests of all members of society than any other system, and as such, be the universal avenue to achieving advancement of the human condition. But then, who has the right, or who can take it upon themselves to make such judgments? Despite the infinite complexities of humans and the societies they form, utopia designers must have foreknowledge of everything affecting human wellbeing and be convinced that their brand of ideology will produce in practice a better world. Unintended consequences cannot be possible, or they must be suppressed with a strong authoritarian response.

For the utopian, what more noble calling could there be

than to pursue the power to control the "cosmic levers" of cause and effect necessary to create a perfect human society that will provide the greatest good for all? Since a utopia represents imagined perfection, it follows that its believers cannot accept the possibility that different systems of government can meet the needs of members of those societies just as well or better than the utopian system...at least once the utopian system is fully and faithfully implemented. Of course, implicit in the utopian construct are profound value judgements concerning the *common good* and the morality of the actions needed to ultimately achieve and perpetuate the desired social structure.

To achieve a flawless world, the vanguard of those seeking to create a utopian society must first take whatever steps are necessary to replace the existing power structure. Next, they must find the means to counteract any who cling to "backward" and "reactionary" social thinking or competing ideas about the future of society. Logically, utopia represents the one true creed and perfect social order, or as Pyotr Stepanovich, the sinister conspirator and revolutionary character in one of Dostoyevsky's masterworks, put it: "Apart from my solution of the social formula, there can be no other."[11]

All competing claims, whether inside or outside a given utopian society must be illegitimate, ignoble and false. Any opposition must arise from errors of faith, fact and logic, or from greed and undue privilege. Choices and honest analysis are not required. All would-be opponents must be threatened, denounced, and their resistance criminalized. Criticism of any new structure by the proponents of old customs would undermine progress, endangering fulfillment of the utopian vision. Contrary ideas and beliefs, be they political or from other sources, must therefore be attacked and eliminated if the utopian vision is to be achieved and sustained. This of course requires creating a permanent political monopoly that cannot be challenged through a democratic electoral process.

As noted above, ideological utopianism, as the "dream to be realized," also requires that the system be brought into being and led by morally superior, wise, and beneficent ruling elites. Self-selected "change-agents," who presume to know what is best for all within their utopia's ambit and are willing to do whatever necessary to achieve what they believe is, by definition, the "ideal."

The dream must be realized even if it involves tough sacrifices (mostly on the part of others) and radical moral compromises. It follows that, since the masses and rabble who inhabit democracies cannot be trusted to think for themselves, ideologues and their followers find it imperative to "colonize" government agencies, news media, academia, and other key institutions in order to shape public opinion. They present their cause as morally superior to any other and themselves as selfless agents on the right side of history, but when such peaceful means fail to dominate, these crusaders soon resort to threats, intimidation, violence, and even terror to prevail over those who resist. As Michael Novak stated: "In the name of a single vision of humanity, inhumanities are often justified."[12]

Utopia's disciples harness the primal forces of fear, envy, and hatred to pit religion against religion, or race against race, or engage in class warfare in a violent, if not barbaric contest for supremacy, working as masters or overlords to impose their ideal of a superior world. They believe themselves justified in possessing and using irresistible power to rule others and must also confront the inescapable question of how to control "them." Ever the master of condescending metaphors, China's murderous supreme leader, Mao Zedong neatly phrased it.: "We [members of the Communist Party] are the 'seeds' and the masses are the 'soil'."[13]

Nobel Prize winning author Alexandr Solzhenitsyn spent years in the Soviet Gulag prison camp system. His crime? He wrote derogatory comments to a friend about the way Stalin was conducting the War. He was arrested in February 1945 at the front lines where he was serving as a decorated officer in the Red Army. Interrogated by the NKVD at the infamous Lubyanka prison, he was then sent away. In the *Gulag Archipelago* he compares literary characters of the past, to the true believers of his day:

> "Macbeth's attempts at justification were weak – and his conscience gnawed away at him. Even Iago is a little lamb. The capacity for fantasy and the inner strength of Shakespeare's villains were worn to a frazzle by a dozen or so corpses. Because they did not have an ideology. Ideology! – this is what provides the desired justification for villainy and fortifies the villain for the long haul... it is thanks to ideology that it fell to the lot of the twentieth century to experience villainy on a scale of millions."[14]

History records three major and distinct types of aggressive utopian ideologies. In the modern world,[15] those at the forefront of these political movements seek to not only end freedom as we know it, but to extinguish the concept of it in thought and literature as well. The word "freedom" itself loses meaning while morphing into a conforming servitude to a totalitarian state intolerant of pluralistic values, beliefs, and thought. Lies become "truth" for the wretched subjects in such regimes through language manipulation, ceaseless indoctrination, intimidation, terror, and other instruments of human oppression. The three major types of ideological Utopias I am referring to are theocratic, racial, and social.

The Theocratic Master Creed Utopia

The belief that the primacy of following a single formula or particular religion will lead to a perfect world order can be described as theocratic. Of course, most religions are typically based on belief of a one true faith and derive inspiration from the transcendent, often through chosen representatives on earth. This much is common among the world's religions. What differentiates a theocratic utopia is its insistence on conformity through secular political authority, not voluntary conversion. In the past, the assertion of an exclusive divine mandate for rule of *secular* societies was used to justify hereditary monarchies which conjoined religious with temporal authority, just as it was by Aztec and Incan emperors, Egyptian pharaohs, Japanese and Chinese emperors, and Islamic Caliphs.

A recent example of theocratic utopianism is the single-minded interpretation of Islam as the sole and unchallengeable source of both spiritual life *and* temporal rule espoused by Muslims attempting to create a new "Caliphate" and rule the world according to Sharia law. In this utopia, the Caliph, the unchallengeable absolute authority, is divinely anointed. Examples of wannabe Caliphates are the Islamic Emirate of Afghanistan, (a.k.a. the Taliban), al Qaeda, ISIL, (a.k.a. ISIS or Daesh) organized and led by the late Abu Bakr al-Baghdadi; and the theocratic dictatorship of Iran led by "Supreme Leader" the Shia Muslim clergyman, Ayatollah Khamenei, who rules the country by decree. In addition to the well-known terrorism and massacres of thousands by the followers of al Qaeda and ISIL, there is the reported mass execution of some 30,000 political prisoners in 1988 on the order of Khamenei's predecessor, Ayatollah Khomeini. One of the perpetrators, Hamid Nouri, then a member of Iran's "Death Commission," is now on trial in Sweden where he was arrested for his part in this crime against humanity.[16]

Iran's theocratic regime is seeking to create an Islamic utopia by force and through fear, purifying the peoples they are able to bring under their control, and murdering those who resist, especially *"infidels"* (non-believers). It has pledged to spread its Islamic revolution beyond its own borders, beginning with the Near East, and not stopping until "a single world community is formed."[17] Iran's messianic Shia Muslim dictators ascribe to and eagerly anticipate an apocalypse that would wipe-out other civilizations, abolish nation-states, and create a theocratic world government under the rule of the Mahdi for whom they will have paved the way. This is very similar to ISIS's goal of a Sunni caliphate with dominion over the entire world, to be attained by a grand holy war ("jihad") in which all the secular states that stand in its way are abolished, non-believers eliminated, and Sharia law is universally applied. Iran's imminent possession of long-range nuclear weapons and potential for their suicidal use by its religious fanatics makes the threat of an apocalypse engulfing at least a part of the globe all the more palpable and frightening. There is no doubt that the Ayatollahs' purpose for developing weapons of mass destruction goes far beyond mere defense against the "forces of Satan." Their unspoken message may soon be "Submit to the will of Allah as we proclaim it, or we, the righteous ones, will incinerate your cities. We are prepared for martyrdom."

When asked to whom he would leave his empire, a dying Alexander (the Great) of Macedonia is said to have answered, "To the strongest." Today, few believe that a God directly and divinely appoints emperors and kings, although some believe God permitted certain rulers to rule in order to accomplish divine purposes. Rather, most would argue that past kingdoms and empires arose either by a contest of strength and will or from conquest and permanent subjugation. The assumption of authority can come by the actions of so-defined "Stationary Bandits" described by Mancur Olson in his 1993 article *Dictatorship, Democracy and Development*,[18] by Rousseau's violent progression of inequality and power concentration,[19] by selection of tribal or clan regional chieftains in an ascending territorial hierarchy, or by a militarily organized force deriving its power through community protection.

Notwithstanding the origin of their political authority, rulers throughout history happily appropriated and perpetuated the concept of a divine mandate sanctioned by religious authorities that gave them the unquestioned right to rule their subjects with absolute power. And regardless of how they may come to power, those who head theocratic states proclaim that theirs is the only true, divinely mandated creed and path to paradise, which they then zealously spread until no non-believers remain. All mankind must ultimately recognize their theocratic rulers' moral superiority in all matters. In a theocracy, non-believers at best face persecution and harsh taxation, and at worst torture and death. Any alternative belief systems are suppressed by a theocratic State, like the ayatollahs' rule in modern Iran. Such claims of justice through infallible divine authority justify intolerance of any who differ in their creed, including even their annihilation.

Understand also that the individualism of non-believers will not be accepted in a Theocratic Utopia, since it is disruptive to the ruling order. James P. Cain, former U.S. Ambassador to Denmark, wrote after the 2016 Islamist suicide attack in Brussels that killed his son-in-law: "This fight is not against America and Europe, and it is not against Christianity. It is a fight against the individualism, reason and independence of thought that began during the Enlightenment over 350 years ago...This freedom is now under attack by henchmen of the Dark Ages wherever they detect it..."[20]

Certainly, religion is most often a force for good as defined by nearly universal moral precepts. Nevertheless, history demonstrates it can also be easily misused. In areas which were until recently controlled by the Islamic State, people were beheaded and burned alive as unbelievers in horrific scenes straight from the Dark Ages. Alas, such religious hatred is still being taught in many parts of the globe as this fanatical brand of Islam continues to work its terror. Just as theocratic regimes of the past attempted to justify political murder, fanatics today justify terrorist attacks directed at infidels including Christians, Jews, Kurds and many other groups. History tells us that theocratic utopianism has produced dreadful despots, never a utopia.

The Master Race Utopia

Another form of utopianism is based on the belief that ethnicity should be the governing determinant of hierarchical social structure in the world; that race is the natural and primary organizing force of society. In this context, the words "race" and "racial" are used non-scientifically, to include ethnic, tribal and cultural groupings of people of shared ancestry. This ideology might also be called "racial determinism," or the belief in the superiority of a race destined through "*natural order*" to rule. It led the "Aryan" Nazis to devise and carry out their hideous "final solution" against the Jews, and seek the destruction of homosexuals, the disabled and others. Even those groups who were not slated for destruction, Slavs for example, were still to be considered inferior to the Nazi Aryan race and could be disposed of when they hindered Aryan expansion. Another version of this morally repugnant doctrine, colonial imperialism, was used throughout the centuries to justify enslavement, imperialistic conquest, exploitative rule, and attempted destruction or subjugation of "backward" peoples.

Racial determinism, like racism itself, is by no means confined to the white race in the western world. The concept of racial superiority with its irreconcilable differences and grievances is deeply ingrained in many tribal societies in Africa resulting in tragedy such as the 1994 Hutu – Tutsi Rwandan genocidal conflict. It was this belief that allowed the Japanese to brutalize Koreans, Chinese, Filipinos, and other East Asian peoples without qualms, the Turks to destroy much of the Armenian population that inhabited a part of Asia Minor, and long ago, the Muslim sultans to slaughter entire cities of Hindus during their conquest of India. In recent times we see the unmistakable signs of the same tribal animosity in wretched episodes of "ethnic cleansing" in the Balkans, the Near East, and Africa.

The Nazis' "National Socialism" is a special case because of its well-documented totalitarian ideology that targeted Jews, and later its policies of exterminating all Jews and others deemed to be inferior or undesirable in the racial hierarchy they sought to establish. In its founding, Nazism was an aberrant form of socialism; Hitler's party was named the "National Socialist German Workers' Party," or NSDAP. While the Nazi state intervened in the German economy and began militarizing, it did not appropriate German industry but rather controlled it fully through decrees. The Nazi program initially sold to the people sounded a lot like socialism jazzed-up with Pan-Germanic Nationalism. As a branch of socialism, it too was collectivist, anti-capitalist, and antireligious, but with a particular insistence on achieving national racial homogeneity as a precondition to pursuit of social equality.

During the mid-1920's and early 1930's Hitler and his infamous propaganda chief Joseph Goebbels venomously attacked capitalism, and publicly laid claim to the socialist label for the Nazis. Goebbels effusively praised the Russian Bolshevik leader Lenin as a great man until instructed by Hitler to stop. By attacking prosperous Jews whom he scapegoated for the Great Depression of the 1930's, Hitler was able to politically fuse class envy with racial antipathy. In Hitler's rise to power he blamed a punitive WWI Versailles Treaty forced on Germany by its enemies, principally the Anglo-Saxon powers (Great Britain and America), the ineffectual Weimar Republic, and an ethno-religious group, the Jews, (characterized by the Nazis as parasitic capitalist "moneymen") for the economic hardships being experienced throughout Germany instead of the bourgeoisie class who were being blamed by the Left (Social Democratic and Communist Parties). During this crucial time period of the early 1930's the Nazis and communists were considered by many to be "...interchangeable in ideology. Nazis, the joke went, were brown on the outside and Moscow red on the inside. Both wanted to fight Jewish capitalists."[21]

The Nazis sought to eliminate individual freedom and concentrate all power and resources, especially over military-related industrial production, under the absolute rule of the "Fuhrer." Initially downplayed was the savagery of Nazi policies for the racial "purification" of Germany and subjugated non-Aryan conquered territories through extermination of all Jews, and enslaving and dominating "inferior" Slavic peoples, including Poles and Russians. Notably, the National Socialist doctrine of inevitable "us" versus "them" conflict of races, or "Rassenkampf,"[22] has its counterpart in the antecedent socialist doctrine of inevitable class conflict, or "Klassenkampf,"[23] formulated by Marx in the 1800's. Hitler's political genius was in deftly merging the two to broaden the Nazis' popular appeal. The Nazi's goal was to begin creating a utopia for people of "pure" Nordic ancestry that over a century or more would become a new world order, a "thousand-year Reich," based on racial superiority and domination, replacing liberal democratic nation-states and all other forms of government through a Darwinian contest for survival of the fittest. His utopian society would become egalitarian in a socialist sense, but must first be made racially homogeneous. This vision required that "inferior" races be either subordinated into slavery or exterminated on the path to the future he planned to create.

Historians have also noted that like the Bolsheviks, Hitler's totalitarian regime also sought to suppress religion. He launched a gradual but increasingly aggressive and widespread campaign against Christianity, which was deeply rooted in German culture at the time, seeking to displace it in Germans' hearts with devotion to Nazism. This was based on his view that its passivistic and non-violent ethical teachings weakened the German nation as he was preparing to pursue Rassenkampf and wage wars of annihilation against any who would oppose him. There can be no competing belief systems in a truly totalitarian state. They must be outlawed then rooted-out if they go underground. This is a policy that can be called "Kirchenkampf," struggle of religions. In this case, a secular pseudo-religion versus a spiritual one. Those who resisted Hitler's antireligious policies were persecuted; some were sent to concentration camps, while others, including the Lutheran pastor and author Dietrich Bonhoeffer, were simply executed.[24]

By inciting and then fusing racial hatred with the class hatred borrowed from Marx's revolutionary socialism, Hitler created a politically powerful ideology I refer to generically as Racial Socialism. "All who are not of good race in this world are chaff," Hitler wrote in his manifesto *Mein Kampf (My Struggle)*.[25] In, *Origins of Totalitarianism*, written shortly after WWII, Hannah Arendt points out that Hitler forwarded a concept of world politics which transcended the nation-state with "an enlarged tribal consciousness as a basis to unite peoples of similar folk origin."[26]

Rulers such as Hitler believe that ethnic groups are naturally differentiated by intelligence, technical and economic advancement, and physical attributes. Members of the Master Race, being superior to all others, have a natural Darwinian predatory right to rule over those they deem inferior peoples. They may do so under the guise of beneficence, (as in "the white race continuing its civilizing mission throughout the world") or they may feel they have license to destroy, enslave or otherwise exploit inferior peoples as they choose. In short, members of a Master Race believe it is their undeniable evolutionary destiny to rule.

Such thinking did not originate with the Nazis, nor did it die with Hitler. As early as the 1840's pseudo-scientific theories of anti-Semitic racial superiority had formed in Europe and had begun to evolve into a discernable ideology through the works of self-proclaimed race theorists in France, Germany, and Great Britain.[27] Such thinking had penetrated Russia as well; in 1918, shortly before Hitler wrote *Mein Kampf*, the Russian literary icon Maxim Gorky told a story in *Untimely Thoughts* about a leaflet he had received, published in Moscow by the Central Committee of the Union of Christian Socialists. It decried the "false principles of equality and brotherhood of all peoples and races" and argued that "the Aryan race is a positive type from a physical as well as moral viewpoint; the Jews are a negative type, standing on a lower stage of human development."[28] Such anti-Jewish thinking reflected the historical progression of socialist antisemitism exemplified by the writings of French intellectuals such as Pierre-Joseph Proudhon (1809-1865), Pierre Leroux (1797-1871), Charles Fourier (1772-1837), the Russian socialist Mikhail Bakunin (1819-1904),[29] as well as by those of Karl Marx. Sadly, humanity is a long way from extinguishing such racial, tribal thinking. As we can see today, "Jew-hating" can often be considered the principal ideology not only among some Muslim states, but also among certain Left-leaning Western political action groups.

In the Master Race Utopia, one's ethnic group identity rather than individual ability is paramount. If you are a member of a lower ranking ethnic group your fate is sealed at birth, and your individual ability counts for nothing other than immediate usefulness to your masters. If you are unable to provide a service desired by your superiors, you are merely dirt beneath their feet and a superfluous mouth to feed. Great hatred is thus kindled on the part of the downtrodden, which then requires utter ruthlessness on the part of their rulers to suppress. Arendt expressed grave concern that accepting the idea of history as a natural contest of races would "signal the end of Western man."[30]

What About Fascism?

Let's spend a moment on the much overused and misused term "Fascism" brought to prominence by the Italian dictator and former Marxist, Benito Mussolini in 1915. Mussolini's Italian Fascism is the archetype that defined the term. The story of fascism is a complex one, which I have distilled into a brief summary here so that we can see where it fits within our ideological framework.

Fascism (its symbol of a bundle of rods is of Roman origin also used during the French Revolution) is sometimes conflated with the Nazism, despite lacking the racial animosity and aims that are central to the latter. In fact, even though they had borrowed from it, the Nazis drew sharp distinctions between their ideology and Italian Fascism, as did Mussolini. Although both were ultra-nationalist in outlook (the Nazis were actually pan-Germanic rather than focused just on the German state), and both had "personality cult" dictators, a militarized society, and an utter distain for democracy, German Nazism and Italian Fascism were driven by different ideas, and it is a very serious error to use these labels interchangeably in public discourse.[31] Nor does fascism easily fit within socialism, despite there being a hereditary connection and significant ideological overlap with it.

Mussolini, brought up a fervent Marxist by his father, was at one time a radical Leftist leader in the Italian Socialist Party and editor of its paper *"The Class Struggle."* Mussolini's deviation from socialism was largely a result of his insistence on wedding nationalism to socialist doctrines. He doubted that class conflict is the primary driver of history, and he disagreed that socialism must be a unified international movement to succeed. When in 1914 he advocated for Italy's intervention in WW I, he was expelled from the Socialist Party, but nonetheless insisted that he continued to believe in socialism and the Revolution of the working class. He and other like-minded socialists favoring intervention splintered off and gathered new members to form a political movement called *Fascio d'Azione Rivoluzionaria* (Fasces of Revolutionary Action) in 1915, the forerunner of the Italian Fascist Party.

With its origin in Marxist theory, its revolutionary aims, and its egalitarian appeal to "the workers," fascism might best be characterized as yet another (recall the origins of Nazism) heretical offshoot of socialism. Despite its origins, two years after the Marxist Bolshevik victory in the Russian Revolution of 1917 which shocked conservative elements in Western Europe, the former Marxist Mussolini opportunistically sought to broaden his party's political appeal by declaring his newly formed (1919) Fasci Italiani di Combattimento (renamed the National Fascist Party in 1921) to be anti-Marxist!

For the political economist Joseph Schumpeter, the defining attribute of fascism is that once its leader is installed, he cannot be evicted by political means, a criterion that equally applies to Nazism and Marx's Socialism. Without political competition, the leader readily accumulates dictatorial power not possible in a democracy in which people are free to run for office and free to vote as they desire for those who will represent them. Here again, the lack of true democratic elections is a commonality with socialism, but with neither the messianic world vision nor intrusiveness into every aspect of life that is characteristic of socialist doctrine.[32] Whether fascism can be considered utopian is debatable at best. While its origin to some extent reflects Marx's ideological utopian seed, its primary emphasis on installing a military-oriented dictatorship for the purpose of national aggrandizement, rather than on pursuing a top-to-bottom purification of society according to a universal dogma, differs substantially from ideologies of utopian intent.

When fascism is unwrapped one finds that it consists of little more than an authoritarian dictatorship that promises to make the nation prouder, fairer, and stronger, extending its dominion by conquering weaker nearby states. In practice, under Mussolini's dictatorship his Fascist Party used the State to control many facets of society in the public sphere and intervened heavily in the economy. However, despite his Marxist roots, unlike Russia's revolutionary Lenin, when Mussolini rose to power he neither possessed nor implemented a plan for the complete overhaul of Italian society. In fact, he was taken aback by the bloody excesses of Lenin's Bolshevik Party.

Tapping into national pride, Mussolini sought to amplify the unity, nationalism and martial fervor of the Italian nation-state by resurrecting the long-past imperial glories of the Roman Empire, including claims of racial superiority to justify the conquest of parts of North Africa and Greece. To solidify his support by labor unions in the 1930's, Mussolini professed his sympathy with socialism and spoke of equality and social justice for all Italians. He defined social justice as the guarantee of work, fair wages, decent homes, and the hope of more – he would help labor triumph over capitalism, a promise he did not fulfill.

Although, like Nazism, Mussolini's Fascist program was superficially socialist in some ways, such as its egalitarian appeal to the Italian working class, it did not in practice embrace the key Marxian socialist principle of Klassenkampf. Despite his anti-capitalist revolutionary rhetoric, he did not attempt an actual revolution to destroy the bourgeoisie. His Fascist party instead sought to destroy Marxist and socialist political factions in Italy, which were rivals competing with it politically for the hearts and minds of Italy's working-class masses. However, after taking the reins of government he reverted somewhat to his socialist roots in order to save the largest and most vulnerable Italian banks and heavy industries from failure during the Great Depression, and from practical necessity in preparing for war, using state-funded financial institutions created for that purpose. This was very similar to the USSR's New Economic Policy of so-called "state capitalism" instituted by Lenin's Bolsheviks in 1922 to revive the Russian economy following its post-Revolution collapse. Mussolini's Fascists thus gained the ability to centrally plan, control, and comprehensively direct Italy's economic production and resource allocation in accordance with their political desires.

Mussolini's Fascist credo of power concentration, summarized as "Everything within the State, nothing outside the State, nothing against the State,"[33] while also ultra-nationalist, is essentially different from Hitler's racialism-based global vision in *Mein Kampf* that is prominent throughout the Nazis' literature and speeches, and of course, gave rise to their horrific plans for the Holocaust. Historians agree that *race* is "the big thing" that distinguishes Nazism from other ideologies and which makes its ideology so utterly and uniquely repulsive. In contrast to Nazism, Mussolini's regime did not terrorize or attempt to "purify" its own people, nor create a system of gulags to first imprison, then destroy Jews and other racial "inferiors." Mussolini was also careful to maintain a modus vivendi with the Church, as opposed to warring against it. Despite his regime's neo-colonial attitude toward Slavs and Africans, Mussolini's doctrine of absolute nationalism did not center on a global contest of races nor did it plan for inevitable world domination by an Italian "master race."

Mussolini proclaimed his sympathy for the revolutionary Marxism of his youth, and utterly rejected racism, mocking those such as the Nazis, who insisted on racial purity:

> "I had been infuriated by the sorrows of my parents; I had been humiliated at school; to espouse the cause of the revolution gave hope to a young man who felt himself disinherited. It was inevitable that I should become a Socialist ultra, a Blanquist, indeed a communist. I carried about a medallion with Marx's

head on it in my pocket. I think I regarded it as a sort of talisman.

"What do you think of Marx now...? 'That he had a profound critical intelligence and was in some sense even a prophet.

"Do you believe now that racial unity is a requisite guarantee for vigorous nationalist aspirations? 'Of course there are no pure races left; not even the Jews have kept their blood unmingled. Successful crossings have often promoted the energy and beauty of a nation. Race! It is a feeling, not a reality; ninety-five per cent, at least, is a feeling. Nothing will ever make me believe that biologically pure races can be shown to exist today. Amusingly enough, not one of those who have proclaimed the 'nobility' of the Teutonic race was himself a Teuton. Gobineau was a Frenchman; Houston Chamberlain an Englishman; Woltmann, a Jew; Lapogue, another Frenchmen...National pride has no need of the delirium of race...Italians of Jewish birth have shown themselves good citizens, and the fought bravely in the War. Many of them occupy leading positions in the universities, in the army, in the banks.'[34]

Mussolini was something of a contradiction. Notwithstanding his Marxist background, in the end he veered away from Marxism's dogmas, but remained sympathetic to its ideals. Although he scorned the Nazis' racial tenets, he became a close ally of Hitler. Mussolini's influence was strong enough that his Italian Fascism, a third type of dictatorship different from that of Germany's Nazism and Russia's Socialism, became emblematic of strongman nationalistic rule but without the aim of reshaping mankind. He was a dictator with uncontested rule over the Italian State. But despite his fascist credo and use of the word "totalitarian," unlike Hitler and Stalin, in action his rule fell short of being totalitarian, according to how that term is defined by historians and exemplified by the Soviet Union, Nazi Germany, Mao's China, the Kim's North Korea, and the Khmer Rough Cambodian regime.[35]

Much the same can be said of Francisco Franco's regime in Spain, Antonio Salazar's in Portugal, and several other similarly partly-fascist regimes in pre-WWII Eastern Europe, such as in Austria, Hungary, and Romania, and in post-War Latin America.[36] As bad as they were, the fascist states fell far short of the absolute and highly intrusive control of every aspect of life that defines "totalitarianism." Only after Mussolini became allied with Hitler's Nazi regime did his fellow Blackshirts adopt the racial policies that made it more closely resemble Nazism. In the end, as Arendt points out, despite a military alliance between the two dictators, Hitler and Mussolini, there really was no single ideology of the "Right" called fascism that dominated Europe during WWII.

All this aside, fascism was and remains an abhorrent system totally at odds with liberal democratic values. As is clear from the archetypal Italian experience of Mussolini, it may be regarded as the ugly offspring of an even uglier parent: Marx's socialism. Unfortunately, its influence is still reverberating long after Nazism has faded. From what we see evolving today out of failed socialist states, it is certainly possible that Peter Drucker and Frederick Hayek were correct in 1944 when they argued that fascism, with its concentration of unrestrained power in the hands of one person or party, and its corrupting influence on industrial enterprises, is likely to become the awful but "natural" successor to failed socialist regimes, inheriting both disenchanted socialists and their pre-established apparatuses of State power. Witness the fascist characteristics of the current regimes in Russia, Belarus, and Venezuela.[37]

Arendt focused not on fascism but on the much greater threat of totalitarian racial ideology resurfacing, with its immense capacity for destroying mind, body and spirit, explaining that when politicized, race is an exceedingly potent force that quickly undermines the restraining counterforces of liberal laws and institutions, leading to "ethnic cleansing," genocide, and racial oppression. The defeat of the Nazis, along with the passing of colonialism and imperialism into the ash bin of history, has meant that regimes built upon appeal to a particular ethnic identity face a daunting challenge if they attempt to use race as a controlling force extending much beyond the geographic nucleus of their ethnic heartland. A vast ethnic cleansing such as attempted by Hitler may be unthinkable today. Nonetheless, within large, ethnically diverse democratic societies, the restraints posed by civilizing laws, institutions, and traditions can still be undermined by "activist" demagogues. Seeking the pathway to power, they can dangerously stoke ethnic animosities to disunify society, leading to the formation of perverse racial and ethnic political identity groups pitted against one another.

Thus, the threat of racial politics to democracy in multi-ethnic nations is quite serious. People who are organized into mutually hostile political camps by activists, each with its own race-based rallying cry, become focused on their social, cultural, and economic differences rather than on a shared values, visions, and interests. A "contest of races" is unleashed, a centrifugal force that destroys the social cohesiveness and trust needed for democracy to function. Each identity group, with antipathy toward others, promotes its own myths and engages in a struggle for political power, favoritism, wealth, and privilege. To borrow again from Arendt, such weaponizing of racial diversity for political gain undermines the very foundation of pluralistic nations built upon the Western liberal idea that racially neutral Reason, put to the test in democratic political processes, should rule over the raw impulse of racial animosity. The disintegration of nation-states along ethnic lines is a major source of political instability and human suffering in our world today and should be of grave concern to all. Arendt's admonitions against allowing ascendancy of racial identity-based politics are as valid today as they were when she penned them over 60 years ago.

The Socialist Master Class Utopia

A totalitarian form of government based on achieving a paradise of universal justice through a class struggle in which the so-called "Proletariat" or "workers" (i.e., the exploited victims of class-based oppression) have seized and continue to hold all political power. The aim is to wrest political power, property, and the means of production from their propertied and privileged oppressors, the hated "Bourgeoisie." This struggle can entail either a paroxysm of revolutionary violence or a gradual asphyxiation of freedom by a self-selected ruling class claiming to represent the "working class."

In this workers' paradise, society is to be totally transformed over the long run from capitalism into what the new rulers believe it should be, namely a "classless socialist State" in which business is collectively controlled if not owned by the State, and everyone is satisfied and happy because they are at the same level in all respects. Society will then have been perfected into an earthly paradise, and the old, class-based State itself will simply wither away, no longer having any purpose to serve!

In addition to abolishing private property and other evidence of self-determination, there is also no room whatsoever for theistic religion or spiritual beliefs. In fact, all forms of religion that might compete with socialism for dominance of the human conscience must be suppressed and ultimately abolished. Religious groups might challenge its policies and edicts, and since socialism is a totalistic belief system that cannot tolerate organizations of any kind with competing thoughts and norms, that could undermine its ability to direct people, i.e. such organized groups must be suppressed and eliminated. Shutting down churches and otherwise suppressing if not actually killing or imprisoning pastors, priests and nuns are but a few of the priorities when the "new religion" replaces the old.

Socialists hold that theirs is the only source of eternal truth and hope for redemption; thus, only their dogma should drive the thoughts and actions of mankind. In their view, religion is a source of superstition, and its institutions were created by the bourgeoise to control the proletariat. Since traditional religions are usually intertwined with the existing hierarchical social structure, they must be totally rooted out. Socialist leaders can then become "high priests" monopolizing the "commanding heights" of society.

Man's actions under socialism will be governed only by the passion and hatred summoned forth by the new god he has come to worship. In *The Tragedy of Russia*, written when the communists had been in control for a mere fifteen years, Will Durant explains: "The proletarian dictatorship does not mean as the uninitiated suppose, government *by* the proletariat; it means that the new Church, [i.e. the socialist government], will rule *for* the proletariat...He [socialism] is a jealous God, Who will not have other gods before Him; to deny or question Him is a mortal sin, a capital crime for which the sinner will be excommunicated, and sentenced to Hell – Siberia – or death."[38]

Karl Marx, the indisputable architect of modern socialism (along with Friedrich Engels) and author of its "holy scriptures," *The Communist Manifesto, Das Capital,* and other works, was an atheist but also a moralist. He felt the need to assign blame for the world's ills, concluding the bourgeoisie were the source of all manifestations of evil, and he thus demonized an entire social class, urging his disciples to unleash their predatory instincts in a "class war" of annihilation. This is the "Klassenkampf," or Socialist antecedent to the counterpart Nazi "race war" doctrine of "Rassenkampf." The result was like utopian constructs based on race or religion; namely, the necessity of hate, torture, and even murder of people without qualms based simply on social class identity.

No matter the original socialist utopian purpose, terror progresses, rights and due process are eliminated and "show trials" replace legitimate attempts at establishing whether individuals persecuted are guilty of any real crime.

Marx and Engels's call to arms: "Workers of the world unite!" transformed socialism almost overnight from a theory into an ideology, an explanation of reality that is also a call to radically transform the world into what it "ought" to be. Thereafter, under the righteous banner of "equality for all," socialists became focused on seizing political power to control the State for the benefit of some and to the detriment of others – this instead of the State's role consisting of working for overall betterment and only providing help to those in need. Uniting the so-called "working class" also meant eliminating competing political parties and ideas based on the appeal of freedom, lest they someday attract a following able to effectively resist and even undo the socialists' coercive redesign of society. Of perhaps even greater significance is that in calling on workers to unite with mutual aid and cooperation in a class struggle for their "fair share," Marx's Manifesto led socialism into the realm of electoral politics for the first time, with the immediate aim of forcing wealth redistribution.

It must be noted that the process of achieving Marx's Socialist Utopia is not so rigid as to preclude a more gradual, less violent transition to a socialist society in circumstances where conditions are not ripe for severe social upheaval but would still yield to an organized movement taking step-by-step political action stopping short of violent revolution.[39] This is where so-called "soft power" comes into play. The goal in either case though is to create a "dictatorship of the proletariat."

Whether the path to power is through a bloody revolution or through deceit, subversion, and other subtle, more gradual means, the new system will espouse the same tenets and have the same tendencies that have characterized all socialist movements. Over time, radical policies alien to free societies will be enforced, in which government owns or otherwise commands all the important means of economic production, confiscates property, distributes wealth, and sets prices and wages so as to attain complete social equalization.

In the utopia of equality promised by socialists, the realm of the economy cannot be separated from all other aspects of life. The natural variety of human tastes, traits, talents, ideas, and aspirations must be brought to a common uniform level much like a butcher making sub-standard sausage from a variety of lowly, spoiled meat scraps. Eventually it is fed to everyone because that is all there is to eat. The natural diversity that causes the growth and creativity of a free society is forcibly annulled to establish intellectual, cultural, and economic homogeneity. Rather than benefiting all, socialism instead centers on the simplistic and numerically popular policy of appropriating wealth from a minority of people targeted for being successful, doled out as ongoing reparations to "victimized" classes presumably to the point at which wealthy peoples no longer exist.

By killing essential motivation and emulation, such a "butcher's economy," fixated only on distribution, results in stagnation and decline of society's ability to produce what people want and need, discouraging innovation and growth that benefits all. It also means eliminating free markets for the exchange of goods and services, beginning with the broadest and largest sectors, such as health care and energy.

Before its social equalization policies can be implemented, the State first must be sure to have its people fully under control, including all forms of public expressions, the news media, all education, all products of labor, and individual actions. It must also be able to preemptively silence all dissent from its newly created victims whose wealth is confiscated for redistribution. Of course, because such radical transformation of a society will not happen naturally, strong intervention using the irresistible enforcement power of the State is required. Basic human rights and morality take a back seat, or are completely ignored, because the ends will justify the means. A statement some attribute to Vladimir Lenin, the founder of the Union of Soviet Socialist Republics, is that "You have to break eggs in order make an omelet."[40]

Socialist doctrine will be implemented through whatever strategies and tactics achieve the desired results. The beginning strategy is typically one of obfuscation. The advent of the new "socialist man" will be extolled, drowning the dangers in a sea of good intentions, a vision of social utopia with compassionate promises of fairness, justice, and equality. If that fails, simply ignoring that any peril might exist may work.

The lofty socialist mission is to rescue humankind from all the alleged dangers and injustice of capitalism. Solzhenitsyn observed: "Modern society is hypnotized by socialism. It is prevented from seeing the mortal danger it is in. And one of the greatest dangers of all is that you have lost all sense of danger, you cannot even see where it is coming from as it moves swiftly toward you..."[41]

The approach of socialism will be quite frightening to those who are more observant and have an awareness of history. They will easily recognize the Marxist/Leninist tactics used to fracture society into irreconcilable camps and pit them against each other, including:

- Harnessing envy to foment class and ethnic hatreds
- Encouraging and supporting groups who see themselves victimized and oppressed
- Using violence and intimidation to stifle freedom and free speech
- Trafficking in clever lies and character assassination
- Imposing censorship rules and acceptable ("politically-correct") speech, standards, and slogans

- De-legitimizing and ridiculing unifying patriotic or religious symbols and practices as "symbols of class oppression"
- Infiltrating, then taking control of the main education, media, and entertainment organizations
- Creating agitation-propaganda incidents for use by media stooges
- Demonizing all political opponents and political opposition

It is important to point out that the terms "Socialism," "Marxism," and "Communism," the Left's Unholy Trinity, were used almost interchangeably by Marx, Engels, and their many so-called theoreticians and disciples, including Lenin, Stalin and Mao Zedong, and by most observers. These three "isms," in fact, represent a singular essence and concept, thus the trinity metaphor. A brief look at communism and its modus operandi as a form of socialism is warranted here.

The roots of communism as a revolutionary socialist movement can be traced back to the French Revolution in the late 18th Century, which overturned the monarchy of Louis XVI along with its feudal system of inherited privileges and landed aristocracy.

In many ways, the French Revolution was a harbinger of the Russian and Chinese Communist revolutions more than one hundred years later. Of course, there are also more recent examples of uprisings to overthrow brutal despots, colonialist rule, and military juntas, but since the Russian example, the communist technique of installing a socialist State is the version that has defined what the world considers a complete revolution.

Despite being fueled by opposition to existing injustice with noble-sounding goals, most such movements then and now have tended to eschew any moral boundaries to their own use of force. Those who are the most ruthless take power by eliminating their more moderate competitors, as the Bolsheviks did in Russia. They then establish the means to take command of people's lives: transforming law enforcement institutions first into a politicized police and courts that investigate and punish opposition leaders as criminals, and next into a secret police network with firm control of all public information, achieved through media indoctrination of adults and use of educational institutions to indoctrinate youth. Business enterprises are then appropriated and used to reward and punish employees and suppliers depending on their party loyalty, and civil liberties are suspended when attacking remaining political opponents.

What follows thereafter is wide-ranging imprisonment, often in a system of forced-labor camps, and murder on a large scale, torture, and sometimes even withholding of food supplies to starve those considered reactionary or disloyal, quashing dissent through censorship and terror. Incredible as it may seem, these are not the aberrant behaviors of a few rogue regimes, they are the hallmarks of the socialist utopia consistently manifested across the globe as demonstrated in chapters that follow.

Socialism is in many important respects a throwback to the absolutism of emperors for whom "no aspect of human life was the protected domain of personal freedom."[42] To paraphrase Dostoyevsky, starting from the promise of unlimited freedom, such socialist movements soon conclude with unlimited despotism.[43] A fatal flaw is the contradictory need for authority separate from "the people," leading to a new ruling class, a la Plato's "Guardians,"[44] who take on the trappings of the ruling class they just destroyed. In more modern times this is by the barrel of a gun[45] instead of a sword. Socialism could also be called a "Master Class" Utopia.[46]

As Bertrand Russell described it: "Marx's Socialism is a doctrine of a dictatorship of the Master Class instead of Master Race, with his final stage of development, complete political and economic harmony, like the Second Coming; in the meantime, there is war and dictatorship, and insistence on ideological orthodoxy."[47]

Most ironically, the dream of a classless Socialist Utopia necessarily leads to a new master class of totalitarian elites, whether they be faceless unelected bureaucrats at their desks or their vicious masters whose criminal actions are treated reverentially by the media lapdogs they control with a tight leash.

The three fundamental utopian ideologies, theocratic, master race (Nazi and colonialism), and master class (Socialist), though distinguishable from each another are not mutually exclusive. As one might expect, elements of each have at times been melded together to amplify the power, fervor, and following to be gained from a broadened appeal. Incitement of the populace can often more easily be achieved by combining a message of racial ethnic superiority or victimization with socialist class hatred and envy, and in other cases by mixing militant theocratic beliefs with that of ethnic/tribal ascendancy and empowerment. For example, the Nazi Party was formed by appropriating and blending elements of socialism with its dominant doctrine of pan-Germanic racial supremacy.

In a present-day inverted variant of Hitler's Nazi formula that might be called "Tribal" or "Racial Socialism," claims of ethnic superiority are replaced by real or imagined ethnic grievances based on claims of systemic racial privilege, which are inflamed, appropriated, and brought under a political banner of class oppression and conflict, producing an explosive mixture. This type of socialist strategy is very different from that promoted in an ethnically homogeneous socialist nation, where the emphasis is put on economic differences among classes. Rather than focusing primarily on class economic differences, in ethnically mixed societies such exploitation of racial group antagonisms extends the Marxist divide-and-conquer strategy from classes to races. By combining a "struggle of classes" with a "struggle of races," Tribal Socialism becomes a much more powerful, violent, and perhaps an even existential threat that can tear apart multi-ethnic nations like the United States.

There are other nasty combinations as well, such as the mixing of militant theocratic beliefs with those of ethnic supremacy. This is exemplified in the case of Japan's "divine" Emperor's role in overseeing his "ethnically-superior" people's quest to dominate other peoples in Asia. Japan's militaristic leadership was duly instilled with the goal of extending their God-Emperor's regime to ultimately "cover the eight corners of the world," as supposedly "commanded by Heaven" thousands of years earlier. The utopian vision of a "Greater East Asian Co-Prosperity Sphere" gave rise to an ambitious campaign of ruthless conquest of "inferior" peoples, like the Chinese and the Koreans, which engulfed most of Asia and the Pacific starting in the 1930's.

None of the utopian ideologies in either a pure or "hybrid" form have given rise to anything like a true utopia. Nor could they ever do so. History has proven them all to be the opposite: utterly hollow, hellish dystopias, for without cruelty, suppression of freedom, and murder based on the victims' religion, race, class or mere political viewpoint, their grand utopian design could not possibly be fulfilled. Moreover, utopian ruling elites endeavor to destroy all who do not willingly submit within their own borders and often those beyond who are deemed an ideological threat. As Friedrich Hayek observed, "Those who are most anxious to plan society are of necessity the most intolerant of the planning of others, further noting that it is but a step to go "from saintly-minded idealist to fanatic."[48]

Truly, history proves the road that often leads from idealism to fanaticism, from fanciful utopia to real dystopia, is a very short one. The three militant utopian movements described above have been shaped and led by messianic self-selected, supreme leaders who, in assuming complete authority rejected any moral restraints and happily set ablaze the dry kindling of the world surrounding them. They let nothing stand in their way while they burned society to the ground. Ruthless yet charismatic, they always have an unshakable belief in themselves and their vision, exemplifying Nietzsche's Will to Power, and employing force whenever necessary to seize governmental control when social order breaks down. You've heard their names. They were men such as the French Revolution's Maximilien Robespierre and Georges Danton, Russia's Vladimir Lenin and Josef Stalin, Germany's Adolf Hitler, China's Mao Zedong (aka "Tse Tung"), Cuba's Fidel Castro, Cambodia's Pol Pot, and today's Middle Eastern footnote, ISIL's self-proclaimed caliph, Abu Bakr al-Baghdadi.

It is certainly not necessary to profile at length the accession to power of these infamous figures and the roles they and their followers played in history. That has been done quite well and in detail by numerous scholars. It is enough to note here that militant utopianism at its ideological core begets real flesh and blood monsters, and not just those of the Freudian or metaphorical kind. These human monsters served as a utopian vanguard, exploiting war and other socio-economic crises and the resulting disorder as an opportunity to supplant an existing regime and redesign society. While fomenting public indignation, resentment, and internal conflicts in the short term in order to create crises, they despised disorder (see V. I. Lenin's *Socialism and War*[49]). They wished only to use social upheaval strategically as the open door for gaining control of the levers of state power, which they then used to punish, delegitimize, and otherwise quash all political opposition. Thus, disorder and crises are useful to the socialist in gaining power, but once in power they will use a pitiless "iron fist" to reestablish order on their terms, stifling dissent and unrest as they drive society toward their utopia.

Dostoyevsky was profoundly influenced by incipient revolutionary events and literature of 1860's and 1870's Russia. He was so troubled by such socialist and revolutionary ideas that he wrote his masterwork, *Demons*, as an attack on the immoral foundation of that entire way of thinking. In creating the characters in *Demons*, he is known to have drawn upon *Catechism of a Revolutionist*, an 1869 nihilistic Russian pamphlet written by Sergei Nichaev which presages the Bolsheviks: "The Revolutionist is a Doomed Man. He has no private interests, no affairs, sentiments, ties, property nor even a name of his own. His entire being is devoured by one purpose, one thought, one passion – the revolution." He "feels no pity for anything... He hates and despises the social morality of his time... Everything which promotes the success of the revolution is moral, everything which hinders it is immoral."[50] Nihilism is the rejection of all religious and moral principles, often driven by the belief that life is meaningless.

According to the French historian Stephane Courtois in *The Black Book of Communism*, Nichaev's pamphlet further anticipated and may have inspired the credo of Lenin's Bolsheviks, arguing that revolutionaries should divide the whole of society into two categories: "those to be killed immediately," and the second, individuals "allowed to continue life for a while...[to] accelerate the inevitable uprising of the people."[51]

In contrast to the godless nihilism of socialism, with an opposite utopian premise theocratic utopian movements are based upon overwhelming pseudo-religious zeal, religious intolerance, and on a demand for indifference to the pain they inflict upon non-believers. The rise of theocratic Islamic fundamentalism should therefore be of special and continuing concern because of its unique brand of fanatical intolerance, extreme cruelty, violence directed at non-believers, cultural destructiveness, global aspirations, and a value system antithetical to the liberal traditions of the Western world. Examples in the Middle East, Africa, and some Western cities include: suicide attacks to kill masses of unarmed people in public places; attacks on places of worship; the beheading of non-Muslim captives; the kidnapping, rape, and enslavement of non-Muslim women; and destruction of ancient archaeological sites and irreplaceable artifacts that date back thousands of years. However, while Islamic fundamentalism may be a growing influence among the youth in traditionally Muslim populations, it has otherwise very limited appeal to non-Muslims because it is the antithesis of civilization itself; it symbolizes an intolerant, medieval belief system at odds with freedom, basic human rights, economic progress, science, and modernity. It represents a belief system which seeks not just to conquer, but to destroy. Treating the violent manifestations of radical Islamic beliefs as a problem subject to a military solution has led to Western failure after many years, much blood, and huge lost investment, and unintended geopolitical consequences. Following 9-11 and other terrorist attacks, the West invaded Afghanistan, Iraq and Libya to destroy the perpetrators. After drawn-out armed conflicts, before their withdrawal the occupying Western forces succeeded only in decapitating targeted terrorist organizations and toppling governments but failed in "nation-building" to establish stable, peaceful democratic states, and to win over the indigenous Muslim populations to political ideals mistakenly believed by Western foreign policy elites to be of universal appeal, and thus "on the right side of history."

Violent Islamic fundamentalism stands in markedly sad contrast to the glorious centuries of enlightened Islamic civilization, which is the true legacy of Islam today, not just for its believers but for the rest of the world as well. I expect that the majority of modern youth in non-Muslim communities are more likely to be seduced by the arguments and promises of socialism than by Islamic jihadism, especially a chameleon-like socialism forever shapeshifting under the cover of misleading labels. Nevertheless, "lone wolves" continue to be enlisted by radical Islamists to commit acts of terrorism.

Despite such continuing threats, a recent very encouraging sign of non-violent Islamic renewal is the Kingdom of Saudi Arabia's support for the Muslim World League's 2018 Charter of Makkah. The Charter is a pan-Islamic declaration dedicated to furthering peace and understanding among the world's religions, opposing religious extremism, hate, and violence. Its stated principles supporting religious and cultural diversity and promoting unity and global coexistence were unanimously endorsed by a group of the world's leading Muslim scholars, gathered for a four-day conference in the Holy City of Mecca. It has now been endorsed by Islamic leaders from 139 countries.

History has shown that militant utopian movements, whether religiously inspired or not, often are stimulated by a fanatical sense of moral superiority and inevitability among their adherents, which paradoxically unleashes morally unbounded savagery that pays no heed whatsoever to the natural rights of human beings. Today, except perhaps for the segment of the Islamic world that insists on following a severe interpretation of Sharia law, there is near universal rejection of Theocratic Utopianism. With a few, mostly symbolic exceptions (such as the small African country of Eswatini – until 2018 known as Swaziland – the continent's last remaining absolute kingdom), and a sprinkling of hereditary kingdoms in Europe, the Middle East and Asia, the dictatorial monarchies and their nobility that gave rise to socialist class-driven movements of the early 1900's are today in many cases considered an anachronism for their failure to adapt their political systems to modern life in a way that truly reflects the aspirations of their people.

So too are largely gone the human plagues of Nazism and colonial imperialism (the idea of a utopian world mission defined by Hans Kohn, an expert on political ideologies, as "ordering human society through unified dominion and common civilization."[52]), along with slavery and apartheid which engendered blazing hatreds in both the oppressor and the oppressed. Claims of racial superiority are now universally condemned, although racism itself certainly persists to some extent wherever different races cohabitate, and vestigial traces of slavery sadly can be found, especially in Africa, in Chinese and North Korean "re-education"/labor camps, in Chinese Communist genocidal persecution of its Uyghur minority, and in human trafficking by criminal gangs, all tragic situations in which people are imprisoned and treated as either a malleable or disposable commodity.

It is in the former case that the practice of "modern" slavery has emerged; modern in the sense that it is characterized by widespread use of advanced technologies by the state to continuously track behaviors, auto-evaluate them for obedience, trigger arrests and imprisonment, and coerce people on a mass scale with terror and violence when necessary. These modern tools augment huge walled prison compounds in which forcible "reeducation" takes place. The only difference from the slavery of the past is that individual slaves are not bought and sold. However, their lives are "owned" by an all-powerful state that dictates the terms of their existence. The purpose of this slavery has remained unchanged from millennia past, that of directly forcing some against their will to work for the benefit of others. That is, indeed, one of the greatest ironies of socialism!

There is some evidence, therefore, that all three versions of utopian ideology could be in decline. Wisdom gained from historical experience with successful models of social and economic organization is apt to become accepted when repeatedly proven and disseminated and not distorted or blocked by vested interests. One would hope that the human condition will continue to improve over the long run from the development, evolution and diffusion of liberal social structures grounded on principles of freedom, including tolerant pluralism and representative democracy, and equal justice through courts that peacefully resolve disputes based on laws rather than group identity and the arbitrary whim of the powerful.

However much we would like to believe in human progress, the calamitous events of the past 100 years (two World Wars, murder of many millions by totalitarian regimes, genocide and ethnic cleansing, Islamic religious "cleansing" and terrorism) should disabuse even the most ardent optimist of the notion that a new and improved model of "man" has come onto the scene. Instead of being permanently vanquished and consigned to the ashbin of history, the evils of the past are only imprisoned in the depths of the human subconscious, biding their time, awaiting historical amnesia and a lapse of Reason to enable their escape into the present.

Institutions such as the United Nations, though very imperfect, are necessary and helpful because by highlighting such evils, they are a constant reminder to all of the continuing need for vigilance lest once-vanquished evils and new ones arise and spread to wreak havoc on humanity. However, it is highly unfortunate that, lacking a clear and consistent moral compass, at times the UN has been discredited as an honest decision-making body by caving into the pressures brought by powerful member states who are hostile to freedom and democracy.

Socialism's illusory goal of reshaping human nature itself became the most widespread and fastest growing ideology during the past century. In a relatively short span of time, it spread across the globe, despite its abject failure to deliver on its promise of equality and prosperity, and regardless of its institutionalization of terror and political violence on a mass scale. Nevertheless, socialism with its allure of a "workers' paradise," its sanctimonious talk of man's "freedom from want," "justice for victims of oppression," and its "zero-sum" mentality remains a pestilence upon the earth in danger of resurgence.

Despite suffering significant setbacks in 1989-91 with the collapse of the USSR and its Eastern European empire, and the resulting loss of political momentum, it is much too soon to write the final chapter of the history of socialism. Later I will lay out the reasons why a resurgence of socialism, although characterized over sixty years ago by the American former Communist writer and political activist leader Max Eastman as a discredited antique "system of wishful thinking,"[53] is not only possible, but likely. With that in mind, I will now devote the rest of this book to the menace of socialism, the most dangerous of the three utopian ideologies, and with its many millions of followers, the most likely to rise from the shadows of the past to regain the power over people it lost in the century before.

Notes

1. Hertzler, Joyce. O., *History of Utopian Thought*, George Allen & Unwin, Ltd., London, 1922, Chapter One, "Introduction," pp. 2-3.

2. Quote taken from "China: A Long March into Night", by Jean-Louis Margolin in *The Black Book of Communism: Crimes, Terror, Repression*, p. 488 edited and authored in part by French historian Stephane Courtois, co-contributors Nicholas Werth, Jean-Louis Panne, Andrzej Paczkowski, Karel Bartosek, and Jean-Louis Margolin, Consulting Editor Mark Kramer, Harvard University Press, 1999. I used this quote because it perfectly represents the arrogant utopian belief in the ability of "man" to totally reshape and control his world, including the reshaping of human nature itself in accordance with some kind of planned outcome, or perhaps one that is believed to be historically inevitable, but only needs a little helpful "push" along the way. Imperfect men are supposed to be able to engineer perfected humans! In such a world view man is supreme. There is no place for belief in God. Morality is only what those in power

say it is. In *The Black Book,* the source of this quote is footnoted as Domenach, *Origins of the Great Leap Forward,* p. 152.

3. Bertrand Russell, *A History of Western Philosophy, And Its Connection with Political and Social Circumstances from the Earliest Times to the Present Day,* 1945, Simon and Schuster, Ch. XIV "Plato's Utopia," pp. 115-116.

4. Paraphrase of an ode by Horace, quoted on p. 9 of *"Virgil"* in Encyclopedia Britannica, Ed. Robert Deryck Williams, Ap version. In his epic poem, *The Aeneid,* Vigil wrote of Rome's divinely appointed destiny being that of conquering, then civilizing the known world according to its way of life; i.e., its customs and precepts. Virgil considered such a quest noble, if not heroic. His poem has had incalculable influence over the ages.

5. Maurice Cranston, Encyclopedia Britannica; "Origins and characteristics of ideology," page 1 of e-version, attributed to the French philosopher A.-L.-C. Destutt de Tracy at the time of the French Revolution): "In the loose sense of the word, ideology may mean any kind of action-oriented theory or any attempt to approach politics in the light of a system of ideas. Ideology in the stricter sense stays fairly close to Destutt de Tracy's original conception and may be identified by five characteristics: (1) it contains an explanatory theory of a more or less comprehensive kind about human experience and the external world; (2) it sets out a program, in generalized and abstract terms, of social and political organization; (3) it conceives the realization of this program as entailing a struggle; (4) it seeks not merely to persuade but to recruit loyal adherents, demanding what is sometimes called commitment; (5) it addresses a wide public but may tend to confer some special role of leadership on intellectuals. In this article the noun ideology is used only in its strict sense; the adjective ideological is used to refer to ideology as broadly defined."

6. To gain a deeper understanding what the term "ideology" means I refer the reader to Hannah Arendt *Origins of Totalitarianism,* Second Edition, Meridian Books, The World Publishing Company, 1958, p. 159, and Alexandr Solzhenitsyn, *Gulag Archipelago,* Chapter 4 "Bluecaps," ebook version, p. 216 of 1099. The dictionary offers a definition of "ideology" as simply "a system of ideas and ideals." However, as used in the socio-political realm it is much more than that. I would request the reader to carefully consider the following descriptions of it by Hannah Arendt and Alexandr Solzhenitsyn

Hannah Arendt on Ideology:

"ideologies…systems based upon a single opinion that proved strong enough to attract and persuade a majority of people and broad enough to lead them through the various experiences and situations of an average modern life. For an ideology differs from a simple opinion in that it claims to possess either the key to history, or the solution for all the "riddles of the universe," or the intimate knowledge of the hidden universal laws which are supposed to rule nature and man.

Few ideologies have won enough prominence to survive the hard, competitive struggle of persuasion, and only two have come out on top and essentially defeated all others: the ideology which interprets history as an economic struggle of classes, and the other that interprets history as a natural fight of races [Marxism and Nazism respectively]. The appeal of both to large masses was so strong that they were able to enlist state support and establish themselves as official national doctrines. But far beyond the boundaries within which race-thinking and class-thinking have developed into obligatory patterns of thought, free public opinion has adopted them to such an extent that not only intellectuals but great masses of people will no longer accept a presentation of past or present facts that is not in agreement with either of these views.

The tremendous power of persuasion inherent in the main ideologies of our times is not accidental. Persuasion is not possible without appeal to either experiences or desires, in other words to immediate political needs. Plausibility in these matters comes neither from scientific facts, as the various brands of Darwinists would like us to believe, nor from historical laws, as the historians pretend, in their efforts to discover the law according to which civilizations rise and fall. Every full-fledged ideology has been created, continued and improved as a political weapon and not as a theoretical doctrine."

Alexandr Solzhenitsyn on Ideology:

"Ideology—that is what gives evildoing its long-sought justification and gives the evildoer the necessary steadfastness and determination. That is the social theory which helps to make his acts seem good instead of bad in his own and others' eyes, so that he won't hear reproaches and curses but will receive praise and honors. That was how the agents of the Inquisition fortified their wills: by invoking Christianity; the conquerors of foreign lands, by extolling the grandeur of their Motherland; the colonizers, by civilization; the Nazis, by race; and the Jacobins (early and late), by equality, brotherhood, and the happiness of future generations.

Thanks to ideology, the twentieth century was fated to experience evildoing on a scale calculated in the millions. This cannot be denied, nor passed over, nor suppressed. How, then, do we dare insist that evildoers do not exist? And who was it that destroyed these millions? Without evildoers there would have been no Archipelago.

7. Maurice Maeterlinck, an essay, *The Life of The Bee*, 1901, published translation by Alfred Sutro in 1914; in this work Maeterlinck reflects on human life metaphorically, including "the spirit of the hive" by which all individuals

are reduced to eternally prescribed roles, achieving perfect community order without even the least glimmer of freedom or personal attachment to others.

8. Steven Pinker, *The Blank Slate: The Modern Denial of Human Nature* (Penguin Books 2002, 2016), and his interview by Rainer Zitelmann in Forbes Magazine, March 2, 2020 "Steven Pinker: 'Evolution Has Saddled Our Species With Many Irrational and Destructive Traits'."

9. From the French philosopher Paul Ricoeur's 1975 *Lecture Series on Ideology and Utopia*, published in 1986 by Columbia University Press; see Part II "Utopia," Chapter 16 Mannheim, p. 273.

10. Hannah Arendt's *Origins of Totalitarianism*, "The Totalitarian Movement," p. 349, enlarged Second Edition Meridian Books, The World Publishing Company, 1958.

11. Fyodor Dostoyevsky's 1872 masterpiece *Demons (aka "The Devils,"or "The Possessed")*, Part Two, Chapter 7 "With Our People," translation by Maquire, p. 446; also found at p. 1801 of 3260 in Vintage iBook version, translation by Pevar and Volokhonsky, 1994.

12. Charles Krauthammer quoted in *National Review* article by Matthew Continetti, April 22, 2019 "Why Krauthammer Matters," and Michael Novak *The Spirit of Democratic Capitalism*, "The Ideal of Democratic Capitalism," Madison Books 1982, 1991, p. 66.

13. *Quotations From Chairman Mao Tse Tung* (aka "Zedong"), his famous "Little Red Book" published from 1964-1976, p. 299, quote taken from "On the Chungking Negotiations" (October 17, 1945), Selected Works, Vol. IV, p. 58.

14. Alexandr Solzhenitsyn, *The Gulag Archipelago*, vol. 1, p.181; Solzhenitsyn was arrested by the NKVD in 1945 at the front lines despite being a decorated soldier, for correspondence with a former school friend critical of the Soviet socialist regime's handling of the War, and saying that the regime should be replaced. He was interrogated by the NKVD at its infamous Lubyanka prison in Moscow, then sent to the labor camps with an eight-year sentence. He wrote several books about his experience in the Soviet Gulags as they came to be known, and was awarded the Nobel Prize in literature in 1970.

15. By "modern world" I am referring to the period identified by the British historian Paul Johnson in chapter 1 of his book by the title (*Modern Times*, Harper Perennial, 1983, revised 1991). According to Johnson, Modern Times began as the 20th Century was dawning, with Einstein's theory of relativity, the First World War, and Russian Revolution, and of course extend to the present. Obviously, some of the roots of these major events (for example the writings of Karl Marx) can be traced back to the mid-1800's and even earlier. It is often said that to understand the present we must have knowledge of the past.

16. Euronews article by Senabargh Zahedi, May 11, 2021, "The world should be watching Hamid Nouri's trial in Sweden."

17. From Daniel Yergin, *The New Map: Energy, Climate, and the Clash of Nations*, Penguin Press, 2020, p. 209; see footnote No. 6 on p. 209, and No. 5 on page 222; Penguin Press, 2020; Yergin cites Pierre Razoux's *The Iran-Iraq War*, and Ray Takeyh's *Guardians of the Revolution: Iran and the World in the Age of the Ayatollahs* among his sources. It is believed the Mahdi will emerge at the End of Days to establish universal peace and justice.

18. Mancur Olson 2000 book *Power and Prosperity: Outgrowing Communist and Capitalist Dictatorship*, Basic Books, 2000, and September 1993 journal article *"Dictatorship, Democracy, and Development"* (American Political Science review, Vol. 87, No. 3) Mancur Olson describes why and how anarchistic "Roving Bandits" may evolve into tyrannical "Stationary Bandits" who become more or less permanent rulers.

19. This concept is explained in detail in Jean-Jacques Rousseau's 1754 *Discourse on the Origin of Inequality, Part II*, pp. 60-81 and "Notes to Part II," pp. 107-109, found in *Jean-Jacques Rousseau: The Basic Political Writings*, Hackett Pub. Co., Inc., 1987.

20. James P. Cain, former U.S. Ambassador to Denmark, in the Wall Street Journal Opinion Section *"Alex Sascha and the Toll of Islamist Terror"* April 11, 2016.

21. L. K. Samuels, *Killing History: The false Left-Right Political Spectrum, and the Battle between the 'Free Left' and the 'Statist Left'*, pp. 322-323, Freeland Press, 2019.

22. Three sources: Ludwig Gumplowicz, *Der Rassenkampf*, Hannah Arendt *Origins of Totalitarianism*, and Adolf Hitler *Mein Kampf*, "Nation and Race," can give the reader a full understanding of the meaning of the term "Rassenkampf." Also, according to historian Paul Johnson in *Modern Times*, Harper Perennial, 1983, 1991 (p. 120) "the Marxist German racial theorist, Ludwig Woltmann... transformed the Marxist class struggle into a world race struggle and advocated the arousal of the masses by oratory and propaganda to mobilize the Germans into the conquest needed to ensure their survival and proliferation as a race." Woltmann, an anthropologist, wrote a number of influential pieces on "race theory" which presaged Hitler's National Socialism, including among others the *Darwinian theory and socialism* (1899), *Marxism and race theory* (1905), and *Klemm and Gobineau* (1908). Another who is often mentioned by historians is the British antisemite Stewart Chamberlain, who was influenced by the Gobineau's race theory, and wrote *The Foundation of the Nineteenth Century* (1899). These so called "theorists" and others of the same ilk were concerned about racial "pollution" of superior races by those they deemed inferior.

23. Karl Marx, *The Communist Manifesto*, 1848 co-authored with Friedrich Engels; the first sentence is "The history of all hitherto existing society is the history of class struggles." "No. 1, Bourgeois and Proletarians," p. 473 of *The Marx Engels Reader, Second Edition*, Edited by Robert Tucker, 1978.

24. L. K. Samuels, *Killing History: The false Left-Right Political Spectrum, and the Battle between the 'Free Left' and the 'Statist Left'*, pp. 407-410, Freeland Press, 2019.

25. Hitler devoted a lengthy chapter of *Mein Kampf* (Chapter XI, Nation and Race) to his anti-Jewish theory of an ongoing struggle for racial supremacy, and basis for the Darwinian Rassenkampf driving National Socialism.

26. Hannah Arendt, *Origins of Totalitarianism*, Chapter eight: "Colonial Imperialism: the Pan-Movements," pp. 223-224 and footnote 10. According to Arendt (p. 222) the 19th Century tribal racist movements of Pan-Germanism and Pan-Slavism influenced and were appropriated by Nazism and Bolshevism respectively. We may be seeing similar misuse of race by the Chinese Communist Party and its leader Xi Jinping attempting to exert its less than benign pan-Chinese influence through diaspora émigré communities throughout the world, as a pretext for expansion and dominance in East, South and Southeast Asia, and in the CCP's campaign to suppress Tibetans, and the China's Uyghur minority.

27. As early as the 1840's pseudo-scientific theories of racial superiority had formed in Europe and began to evolve into an anti-Semitic ideology. Prominent in the early development of race theory were the works of Arthur de Gobineau, such as his 1853 book *An Essay on the Inequality of the Human Races;* also, note the development of "race theory" by Ludwig Woltmann (see end note #20 above), and the influence of Paul Lagarde, known for a later anti-Semitic essay, *Jews and Indo-Germanics* (1887).

28. Maxim Gorky, *Untimely Thoughts: Essays on Revolution, Culture and the Bolsheviks 1917-1918, No. 106*, June 2, 1918, 1995 Yale University Press.

29. L. K. Samuels, *Killing History: The false Left-Right Political Spectrum, and the Battle between the 'Free Left' and the 'Statist Left'*, pp. 298-304, Freeland Press, 2019; to the early socialist Proudhon has been attributed the vicious statement: "The Jew is the enemy of humankind. It is necessary to send this race back to Asia, or exterminate it..." (this quote is taken from *The Two Souls of Socialism*, a pamphlet by the Marxist writer, Hal Draper, p. 11, 1960).

30. Hannah Arendt, *Origins of Totalitarianism*, Meridian Books: The World Publishing Company, 1951, 1958 second edition, Part II: "Imperialism, Chapter Five The Political Emancipation of the Bourgeoisie," III "Alliance Between Mob and Capital," p. 157.

31. Stanley G. Payne *A History of Fascism 1914-1945*, University of Wisconsin Press, 1995, Part I "History," Ch. 6, "German National Socialism," subheading "German Nazism and Italian Fascism," pp. 208-209; echoing Hannah Arendt in her Origins of Totalitarianism, Payne presents the critical ideological differences between German Nazism and Italian Fascism, many of which I touch upon in my brief overview. Payne concludes that "sharp differences were noticeable from the start, differences so profound that the two regimes can be grouped together only at a very general level of abstraction. When viewed closely, the differences were frequently more striking than the similarities..." While highlighting such crucial distinctions, Payne, nonetheless disregards his own arguments by characterizing (p.468) Hitler's regime as "the most extreme expression of generic fascism," an unexplained contradiction in his own account, and a conclusion that is not supported by historical fact. Mussolini's National Fascist Party, which preceded Hitler's National Socialist Workers Party into power on the world stage by more than 10 years (1922 vs. 1933), invented "fascism" and of course in doing so defined what it stood for, thus becoming the referent for it in any scholarly typology of ideologies. While it was influenced by both the Italian's fascism and Bolshevik's socialism, Nazism stands on its own as a distinct ideology of racial determinism. That is its defining attribute, combining racial Darwinism, genocidal ethnic cleansing of its own citizens and those of states it conquered, and true totalitarian rule. Its totalitarian and anti-capitalist tendencies also give it an affinity with Marxism-Leninism. But, its core belief in racial struggle for supremacy and aspiration of racial dominance sets it dramatically apart from the other regimes Payne considers fascist.

32. Joseph A. Schumpeter, *Socialism and Democracy*, 1942, Harper 2008 edition, "The Consequences of the Second World War," p. 404, footnote 37, and p. 272 in Part IV "Socialism and Democracy," Ch XXII "Another Theory of Democracy, I Competition for Political Leadership."

33. Hannah Arendt, *Origins of Totalitarianism*, Meridian Books: The World Publishing Co., 1951, 1958 second edition, Chapter Eight: "Colonial Imperialism: The Pan-Movements," pp. 257, and Chapter Ten: "A Classless Society" No. 1 "The Masses," pp. 308-309 and footnote 11; this description of the Fascist slogan is also found Paul Johnson's *Intellectuals*, 1988, Harper & Row, Chapter 1 "Jean-Jacques Rousseau: An Interesting Madman," p. 25.

34. Benito Mussolini, interviewed by the German journalist, Emil Ludwig, titled *"Talks With Mussolini,"* published in 1932, p.p. 37, 38, 69 and 70, transl. into English by Eden and Cedar Paul, Little Brown and Company, Boston, 1933.

35. Hannah Arendt, *Origins of Totalitarianism*, Chapter Eight: "Colonial Imperialism: The Pan-Movements," pp. 257, and Chapter Ten: "A Classless Society" No. 1 "The Masses," pp. 308-309 and footnote 11. Writing in the 1960's

Arendt, perhaps the world's most prominent authority on totalitarianism, considered Hitler's Nazism and Stalin's Communism with its satellite Stalinist clones in Eastern Europe, and possibly also Mao's China, as the only truly totalitarian regimes which had emerged by that time (see "Preface to Part Three, Totalitarianism," pp. xxiii-xxviii; she excluded fascist dictatorship (pp. 308-309), writing of their relatively gentle treatment of dissenters, and that recurring terror, permanent internal instability and elimination of all group solidarity are requisites of totalitarian domination. If she was still alive, I believe she would consider the regimes of North Korea, Cambodia under the Khmer Rouge, possibly Cuba, and Iran further examples of totalitarianism. Also see Brzezinski, Zbigniew, *Ideology and Power in Soviet Politics, Dictatorship and Totalitarianism*, ed. Betty Brand Burch (New York: D. Van Nostrand Co., Inc., 1964), p. 180; Brzezinski's definition of totalitarianism is the following: "Totalitarianism is a system in which technologically advanced instruments of political power are wielded without restraint by centralized leadership of an elite movement for the purpose of effecting a total social revolution including the conditioning of man, on the basis of certain arbitrary ideological assumptions proclaimed by the leadership, in an atmosphere of coerced unanimity of the entire population." The reader may also wish to consult Hans Kohn's *Political Ideologies of the Twentieth Century*, Harper and Row 1949, 1966 edition. Kohn describes Nazism as a form of fascism, but nonetheless devotes seperate chapters to Nazism and Communism, treating them, but not fascism, as the definitive examples of a totalitarian socio-political order.

36. Stanley G. Payne, *A History of Fascism 1914-1945*, Part I "History," Ch. 8 "Four Major Variants of Fascism," pp. 245-290; Payne highlights the nations I mention in the text.

37. Frederick Hayek, "The Great Utopian" p. 33 in *The Road to Serfdom*, 1944 echoes Peter Drucker in *The End of Economic Man* (1939) p. 230; "Fascism is the stage reached after communism has proved an illusion, and it has proved as much an illusion in Stalinist Russia as in pre-Hitler Germany." It is difficult to rid a nation of absolute rulers where such regimes have been in place for generations. This observation was made centuries earlier by Etienne de La Boetie in his 1553 *The Politics of Obedience: The Discourse of Voluntary Servitude* in which he asserts that "while liberty is the natural condition of the people, servitude is fostered when people are raised in subjection. People are trained to adore rulers. While freedom is forgotten by many there are always some who will never submit." Hence the regime's need for ongoing repression.

38. Will Durant, *The Tragedy of Russia, Impressions from a Brief Visit*, Simon and Schuster, 1933, "Religious Revolution," p. 115-116, and Will and Ariel Durant, in *The Story of Civilization, The Age of Napoleon*, Chapter VI, II "The New Morality,"* 1. "Morality and Law," p. 129; in a work titled *Social Democracy*

versus Communism (written in the early 1930's and first published as a book in 1946 after his death), the Marxist theoretician, Karl Kautsky, used some of the same words to describe the Bolshevik "new gods" of socialism in Russia:

"Like the God of monotheists, the dictator is a very jealous god. He tolerates no other gods but himself. Those in the party who do not believe in his divine infallibility provoke his fierce hatred. Lenin demanded that the entire working class submit meekly to his leadership. Those in the party who were inclined to show more confidence in other leaders or to defend opinions of their own were regarded by Lenin as the worst possible enemies, to be fought with any and all means. Hence it was impossible for Lenin, as it is impossible for anyone who would be dictator of a party, to work together with comrades who occasionally differed from him. Hence the impossibility of working at all for any length of time on a level of equality with comrades of character and independence of thought."

39. Karl Marx 1872 speech *The Possibility of Non-Violent Revolution;* Marx's actual quote is: "...we do not deny that there are countries like America, England...where the workers can attain their objective by peaceful means. But such is not the case in all other countries." In *Social Democracy* Karl Kautsky interpreted this to mean the following:

"Where democracy exists, it is not necessary for the working class to resort to armed force as a means of attaining power... under conditions of adequate freedom the workers could by their own efforts lift themselves to a high enough level to be able finally to achieve political power not through 'civil strife and foreign wars' but through the class struggle waged by their political and economic mass organizations. The condition prerequisite for such a struggle is an adequate measure of political freedom. Where this is lacking, where it has yet to be won, 'civil strife and foreign wars' may be necessary to achieve democracy as essential to the rise of the working class."

Nonetheless, permanent political dominance by the working class, not power shared by all classes must be achieved in order for the state, directed solely by representatives of the working class, to institute the Marxist formula of collectively owned and managed production assets, and evenly distributed wealth in a fully planned economy. What is the chance that the bourgeoisie would passively accept such disempowerment and economic rape?

40. This statement is pregnant with meaning. It is an analogy attributed to Lenin that trivialized the atrocious means he claimed the Bolsheviks had to use to accomplish their goal of building a socialist society – the omelet. You must first irrevocably destroy what is there in order to create an entirely new society free from the pathologies (feudal aristocracy being one, religion being another) embedded in the old. This analogy is also akin to Cortez burning his

ships, because it is irreversible – one cannot re-assemble the broken eggs. In a revolution you are forced to press on. There is no turning back. According to L. K. Samuels, "Actually, Maximilien Robespierre is credited with coining this metaphor in 1790, in his attempt to justify earlier executions during the Reign of Terror, saying: 'One can't expect to make an omelet without breaking eggs.'" (see Samuels' *Killing History*, 2019, Note #167, p. 90). It is quite possible that Lenin knew of and used this same metaphor, having been a student of the French Revolution. Others attribute the metaphor to Robert Louis Stevenson in 1897.

41. Alexandr Solzhenitsyn, *Warning to the Western World, BBC Radio Broadcast March 24 1976*, pp. 43-44.

42. Cambridge professor of History, F. J. C. Hearnshaw *A Survey of Socialism: Analytical, Historical, and Critical*, McMillan and Co. 1929, p. 26.

43. Same as endnote #11; Fyodor Dostoyevsky's 1872 masterpiece *Demons (aka "The Devils," or "The Possessed")*, Part Two, Chapter 7 "With Our People," translation by Maquire, p.446; also found at p. 1801 of 3260 in Vintage iBook version, translation by Pevar and Volokhonsky, 1994.

44. Plato, *The Republic*, circa 375 BC; see Chapter XIV "Plato's Utopia;" also see Book One: "Ancient Philosophy," Part II. "Socrates, Plato, and Aristotle," in Bertrand Russell's *A History of Western Philosophy*, 1945, Simon and Schuster pub., pp. 108-119.

45. Mao Zedong is said to have originated the phrase "Political power grows out of the barrel of a gun." during an emergency meeting of the CCP on 7 August 1927 at the beginning of the Chinese Civil War, and also used it on 6 November 1938 in his speech at the sixth Plenary Session of the CCP's sixth Central Committee. Source: www.en.m.wikipedia.org; Significantly, Mao included this statement in his 1964 *Little Red Book* "*Quotations from Chairman Mao Tse-Tung*," (p. 121) which says "Every Communist must grasp the truth 'Political power grows out of the barrel of a gun.'" The context of this statement in his Chapter 5 "War and Peace" (p. 115) is Mao's discussion of the Von Clausewitz's famous axiom that "War is the mere continuation of policy by other means" found in the classic work *On War*, Chapter I, "What is War?" p.119, Ed. by Anatol Rapoport, Penguin Books Ltd., 1968. Mao, however, applied this doctrine to internal war between classes and between political groups, not just to war between nations, saying that war must continue until every obstacle to the Party's political aims has been swept aside, otherwise its permanent peaceful rule cannot be assured. In other words, a complete and ongoing cleansing of any dissent is necessary to assure that the revolutionary dictatorship can build socialism in China.

46. The phrase "Master Class Utopia" is used by Paul Johnson in *Modern Times* revised edition, 1991. "Master Class" also appears in discussion of Marx's

doctrine by Bertrand Russell in *A History of Western Philosophy* (1945), Chapter XXVII., "Karl Marx," p. 790.

47. Bertrand Russell, *A History of Western Philosophy* Simon and Schuster, 1945, Chapter XXVII., "Karl Marx," p. 790.

48. F. A. Hayek, *The Road to Serfdom*, University of Chicago Press, 1944, Chapter 4, "The Inevitability of Planning," p. 62.

49. V. I. Lenin and G. Zinoviev pamphlet *Socialism and War*, Geneva, August 1915, p. 17 referring to the Basle Manifesto which was issued by The International Socialist Congress in 1912.

50. Russian pamphlet authored by Sergei Nichaev in 1869 titled *Revolutionary Catechism* referred to by H. Arendt *The Origins of Totalitarianism*, at p. 330, footnote 55. In his 1866 work *Revolutionary Catechism* the famous Russian anarchist/revolutionary socialist Mikhail Bakunin had written a passage very similar to that of Nichaev, read by the prosecutor at the trial of a of a Russian Nihilist in 1871: "The revolutionist is a man under a vow. He ought to have no personal interests, no business, no sentiments, no property. He ought to occupy himself entirely with one exclusive interest, with one thought and one passion: the Revolution...he has only one aim, one science: destruction...He despises and hates existing morality. For him everything is moral that favors the triumph of the Revolution. Everything is immoral and criminal that hinders it...Between him and society there is war to the death, incessant, irreconcilable..." from *Contemporary Socialism*, by John Rae, Charles Scribner's Sons, Second Ed. 1891, p. 275. Thus, the link between Bakunin's troubled Russian Nihilist philosophy and Marx's revolutionary socialist theory is quite clear. Its wholesale violation of moral principles has been embraced by Lenin and the socialist revolutionaries who followed his example across the globe.

51. French historian Stephane Courtois in *The Black Book of Communism: Crimes, Terror, Repression*, 1999, Harvard University Press, "Conclusion – Why?" p. 730, quoting from Nichaev's pamphlet, *Revolutionary Catechism*.

52. Hans Kohn, *Political Ideologies of the Twentieth Century*, Chapter VIII "Imperialism," p. 119, 1949, Third Edition, Harper & Row, 1966.

53. Former Communist Max Eastman *Reflections on the Failure of Socialism*, "Biographical Introduction," p. 12, Devin-Adair pub., 1955.

CHAPTER TWO
The Origins and Spread of Socialism

Early Socialist Thought

The idea of a utopia ruled by righteous supermen is not new. Indeed, the intellectual inspiration for modern Socialism dates back millennia and has been augmented over the centuries by a host of righteous do-gooders grimly determined to rescue humanity from its imperfections and eliminate all unhappiness.

In his book *The Origins of Socialism*, historian George Lichtheim asserts that "the spell of utopianism" had its beginnings in ancient philosophy.[1] In Plato's philosophical treatise *The Republic*, a wise and virtuous "Philosopher-king" and elite communistic "Guardians" rule Plato's idealized state and direct all human affairs to achieve universal wellbeing and harmony. Nearly 2,000 years later, Thomas More wrote a religiously-inspired work he initially named "Nusquam," a Latin word meaning "nowhere and on no occasion." More was an English intellectual, churchman, and political advisor to King Henry VIII. Penned in 1516, the work was later retitled *Utopia*, which when translated from Greek, also means nowhere.[2] The Greek origin of "utopia" is two-fold and thus ambiguous: on the one hand eutopia, which means good place, and on the other outopia which means no place. In *Utopia*, More described his idealized vision of a physical place, an island roughly the size of Britain, inhabited by "Utopians" governed by a virtuous King and a selected elite group of Guardians. Together, King and Guardians would assure an orderly society in which all its parts operate like clockwork, in total harmony with one another.

The famous Marxist Karl Kautsky, writing in 1888 considered *Utopia* a work of true genius that identified the fundamental problem of the political and economic inequality of social classes and foresaw the basic outlines of Marx's "scientific socialism" required to solve it.[3] Surely More hoped that at least some of the educated class (who could read his Latin text) might take his observations about feudal class injustice to heart. As to his utopian remedy, his intent and expectations seem far less certain, especially considering the name he chose for the work.

More's austere vision of a divinely inspired kingdom (but with slaves!) in which everything is freely shared is believed to have been influenced in no small part by his reading of Augustine of Hippo's influential *The City of God*. Written in the early 5th century, *The City of God* sets forth the conflict between the Earthly City (the secular City of Man) and The City of God where people are guided by eternal truths. In Augustine's world, all of history and human life is the manifestation of this struggle between good and evil, God and the Devil. Augustine did not accept that humans and human institutions could attain perfection. According to the historian of political thought, Larry Sidentrop, Augustine held that "Human weaknesses and vices beset all Earthly Cities. All were subject to the vicissitudes that follow from the [inescapable] weaknesses of human nature."[4] One must wonder what More might have thought about the possibility of anyone ever trying to construct his or any other Utopia upon such a weak foundation.

It is important to note that for More, *Utopia* was essentially an abstract thought experiment, not a blueprint for real government or restructuring of real-world human societies. Nor did it invite revolution. Moreover, *Utopia* has been interpreted by some to be a satire, a critique of then prevailing political mores in Europe and not a prescription for government. It is perhaps fair to conclude that both Plato and More's grandiose, idealized visions for humanity are essentially socialist constructs long before the term was invented and may have influenced later social philosophers. Western history going back centuries is replete with aborted attempts to create socialist utopias that suppressed individuality, were anti-religious, eliminated private property, and encouraged the sharing of everything, even women and children. Then there are the radical reformers such as Thomas Muntzer, the German preacher and theologian, and his Peasants uprising of 1524-25, which was considered by some socialist theoreticians (e.g., the 19th century Marxists, Frederick Engels, and Karl Kautsky) as prefiguring the French Revolution of 1789, and later modern social-political revolutions. It may also have led Marx and Engels to incorporate the likelihood of spontaneous insurrection by the proletariat into their doctrine. Generally, such anti-feudal movements were considered heresies by both Protestant and Catholic authorities, and because they threatened both theocratic and secular authorities, were met with severe punishment, including military action to prevent their spread.[5] In the case of the German Peasants War it is estimated that approximately a third of the 300,000 followers, and Muntzer himself, were slaughtered during its suppression by authorities in Central Europe.

Revolutionary and Messianic Socialism

The inspiration for the bloody French Revolution which, in turn, inspired Marx and anti-monarchical revolutionary movements of the early 20th Century, did not directly stem from Plato, Thomas More, or other stillborn utopian models from centuries past. Rather, it flowed from the highly influential pen of Swiss-born Jean-Jacques Rousseau, the author of *Discourse on the Origin and Basis of Inequality Among Men, Principles of Political Right,* and *Of the Social Contract.* In those works, written between 1754 and 1762 and perhaps inspired by sketchy knowledge at the time of primitive societies known for freely sharing food and land, Rousseau argued for the perfectibility of human nature, writing in *Discourse* that man is naturally good, and only by institutions is he made bad.[6] Rousseau believed that the pure natural soul of humans starts to become corrupted as soon as it is influenced by competition, self-interest, ownership of property, and other "evil" manifestations of human nature present in all societies.

In stating "you are lost if you forget that the fruits of the earth belong to everyone, and the earth to no one," Rousseau foolishly ignores the various circumstances that involve acquiring fruit: time, energy, talents, skills, ideas, tools, industriousness, division of labor, and willingness to take measured risks. Rousseau then contends that the right to own private property is inherently evil because its ownership implies inequality of wealth. However, even in prehistoric times, the trade that naturally occurred among peoples required properties owned (and possession defended!) by kinship groups, tribes and individuals that could be exchanged for mutual benefit. In this he further ignores humans' natural, survival-driven behavior of acquiring for one's exclusive use necessities such as food, shelter and tools, and the sources of same. Indeed, humanity's invention and diffusion of agriculture and animal husbandry is associated with permanent human settlements and tilled property, giving rise to what we call civilization. The concept of property (land) belonging to some and not others extended to the political borders between nations, however such geographic divisions might be defined and defended!

Food obtained and stored for one's own consumption for survival is indeed private property, because its use is inherently exclusive; i.e., what one person consumes or is using another cannot, as are the land tilled for one's sustenance, the shelter one occupies, and the tools one makes and depends upon. From the beginning of time the trade that naturally occurred among hunter-gatherers, and later among agricultural communities, required surplus property ("goods"), either acquired or produced, that could be exchanged for benefit of the owners.

It is also well recognized that people are only inclined to invest their labor and savings in maintaining and improving the productivity of the property they own or otherwise possess rights to for an extended period of time, so that they reap the resulting benefits, and not in collectively-owned "public property" they may randomly share or temporarily use. Commons subject to use by anyone as they might see fit are soon ruined from misuse and overuse, such as the dumping of waste, and unsustainable extraction of living or non-living resources, rewarding for a limited time only the most aggressive users. This is not a newly discovered truth. Aristotle observed that "what is common to the greatest number receives the least care."[7] In natural resource parlance this is called "The Tragedy of the Commons."[8] True commons are distinguishable from the realm of privately-owned property by their indivisibility. Resources such as breathable air, drinkable water, and the oceans' fisheries which all must draw upon to sustain life are natural commons. Commons must be managed collectively to avoid despoliation and depletion, by means of specific protective agreements among users, governmental regulation, or public investment. This is very similar to inherently public functions such as military defense, highway and public drinking water systems, and urban waste management, which I will discuss later on.

Of course, there have always been bandits and invaders who choose to forcefully take from others that which they do not produce for themselves, or which simply adds to their wealth, often subjugating and enslaving, or displacing, if not massacring those they take from. We also know that tribal claims to territorial hunting grounds were fought over from time immemorial, as were water sources in arid areas. With the advent and diffusion of animal husbandry and agriculture, competition for the right to control access to sustenance-producing property extended to pastoral and tillable lands as well. As a natural survival-driven instinct, such territoriality can lead to violence and war. Since ancient times more powerful imperialistic states have waged wars of conquest against those weaker. Yet, as with other instincts that become dangerous when given free reign, it is subject to control by human reason, willpower, incentives, and defensive deterrents; also by established customs, agreements, and where governmental authority is present, laws that account for it.

We see an early example of this in the ancient Biblical injunction against coveting another's possessions. Laws protecting property ownership exist to minimize disputes and prevent those that do occur from becoming violent and destructive, thus enabling beneficial investments of time, energy, and saved wealth that make such properties and the human efforts applied to them increasingly productive. Socialists would have us believe that laws defining and protecting property rights were invented by oppressors who forcefully impose them as a means to control the spoils from their earlier aggression. But the desire to control property, including land and the resources it contains, is not vested only in certain individuals. Rather, as Donald Brown points out in *Human Universals*, "the concept of property ownership, distinguishing what belongs...to the individual, or group, from what belongs to others," is part of our human nature.[9] It is not, as Rousseau implies, simply a social construct invented long ago in the mists of time and imposed by greedy individuals.

None of this is to say that vast landholdings stemming

historically from absolutist monarchical regimes with a feudal origin, worked by tenant serfs and peasants but owned and enjoyed by an aristocracy, bear any resemblance to a fair and reasonable distribution of the earth's natural assets. They are instead an unjust "might makes right" anachronism predating modern democracy, often reflecting monarchy and its feudal-era social hierarchy, that is subject to political reform. Those who can will often migrate from rural to urban areas in search of a better life, or emigrate to another nation with better living standards, higher wages, and opportunities to acquire and own property. Such lopsided division of productive agricultural lands with exploited tenants helped stoke the fire of revolutions during the last few centuries that repudiated monarchy together with its aristocratic land barons, as a form of government.

We must not lose sight of the most basic property right, that of ownership of the product of one's own labor. If the product of one's labor is owned not by that laboring person, but instead by the state, then that person is but a slave to the state. In addition to the crimes of physically abusing slaves and stealing their freedom, slave owners also commit the equally grave crime of stealing the labor of their victims. This is obviously true whether the enslaved or their "masters" are Caucasian, African, Asian, or any another race or ethnic group.

For this reason, over millennia, societies everywhere have developed rules regarding ownership of property and punishment of those who steal it. This is a primary reason for the existence of governmental authority: laws, police, and courts. In the same vein, we have come to regard slavery as an abhorrent form of theft of both one's freedom and one's property. Did Rousseau, in seeing private property ownership as evil, not see the connection between loss of the right to property a person enhances or creates with their efforts and slavery?

Nearly a century after Rousseau, the Germans Karl Marx and Friedrich Engels drew on his legacy in their 1848 *The Communist Manifesto*.[10] They prophesied the coming of socialism and issued a call for abolition of private property via a workers' revolution and class war. ("Workers of all countries, unite!") In its call to replace the boogeyman "Capitalism," the *Manifesto* is considered "the birth cry of modern socialism."[11] But it was Rousseau's earlier writings about the "General Will" of a virtuous State, human rights, property, and use of the State as the instrumentality to achieve greater equality of living conditions that inspired history's first national revolution. This was a revolution influenced by what would later be termed "Socialist" utopian ideas and ideals: The French Revolution of 1789 that replaced the monarchy of Louis XVI.

For Rousseau's devotees following the example spawned by the Revolution, the indisputably virtuous collective interest of the state divined by an enlightened few must predominate over the rights, freedom, and even the very existence of any individual citizens. This line of Rousseau's thinking carried forward into socialism. Essentially, every citizen's primary role in society is to serve the interests of the state, rather than the state existing to serve the interests of the individual citizens who comprise it.

Based on Rousseau's correspondence with and views of his contemporaries, and other historical evidence concerning his at times villainous behaviors, British historian Paul Johnson postulated that Rousseau was "a man of little character and honesty, full of envy, self-pity, resentment, and hate, who, because of his talent and notoriety as a writer, may have deemed himself above the "strictures imposed by Reason and disciplined thought."[12] In short, Rousseau lacked good character.

How sadly ironic it is that such a person's delusional thoughts about the supposed pure goodness of humanity in a state of nature would gain wide acceptance and have such a strong influence long into the future on people and events that shaped history! It was Rousseau who also provided the arrogant, self-righteous excuse for Robespierre, his fellow Jacobins, and socialist dictators of the 20th Century whom they inspired. In justifying their seizure of power, these tyrants argued that "the spirit of the people" (the "General Will") resided in an enlightened minority who consequently had "the right to act for the political advantage"[13] The Jacobin Robespierre no doubt believed his own arrogant statement that he did what he did because "France demanded it."[14] The 20th Century's most prominent revolutionary communist dictators Vladimir Lenin and Mao Zedong are both known to have absorbed Rousseau's works.

One might seek to excuse Rousseau in not foreseeing that his ideas would unleash real-world ideological monsters and give rise to the radical Robespierre and the moral implosion in France known as "The Reign of Terror." Rousseau was a product of the so-called "Enlightenment" and considered himself a rationalist looking down on society from atop a philosophical Mount Olympus. On the other hand, with the depth of his observation and thinking about human nature, and his own self-centered amorality, how could he have missed an essential truth: while there is good in humanity, there is also a dark side of our nature. I speak of the primitive "red in tooth and claw"[15] subconscious impulses that overtake our conscious lives when aroused by the feelings of envy and hatred of "them," or from our survival instinct

Later in the mid-20th Century, Cambodia's Pol Pot, who had become a devotee of Stalin and Mao Zedong after becoming a Marxist-Leninist in Paris, admitted to being inspired by the French Revolution.[16] No doubt Pol Pot, like Robespierre and Lenin before him, was utterly certain that the "construction of socialism" he envisioned demanded the pitiless cruelty he and his fiendish Khmer Rouge henchmen inflicted upon millions of countrymen, women, and children in his infamous Killing Fields

The French Revolution of 1789 and Reign of Terror

In modern times, systematic widespread use of political murder of a government's own subjects – any who might stand in their way – did not become a prominent ideological feature until the ascent of ruthless regimes in Russia, China, Germany, North Korea, Cuba, Vietnam, and Cambodia. However, it is possible that historians will mark the true beginning of ideological terror and mass murder with the Jacobins' execution of over 40,000 "enemies of the revolution" during the French Reign of Terror from June 1793 to July 1794, and with the preceding attempt to exterminate much of the Catholic royalist "counter-revolutionary" population in the Vendee region of France.

It is well worth a brief look at the Vendee experience as a particular case in point. Some historians believe that the Robespierre-led Committee of Public Safety's total war on the rebelling Vendee peasants, killing from 50,000 to well over 100,000 civilian men, women and children[17] (the orders were "Leave nobody and nothing alive"), was an act of barbarism that paved the way for Lenin and Stalin's atrocities against demonized "bourgeoisie" segments of Russian society such as the "kulak" farm owners. This was not simply the action of a rogue, out-of-control military unit. Rather, it represented the wishes of the Revolution's leaders. The Revolution's Committee on Public Safety was established in 1793 ostensibly to defend the new Republic and oversee its government. The Revolution's General Francois J. Westermann ("the butcher of the Vendeens") reportedly boasted to the Committee in Paris "There is no Vendee, Republican citizens. It died beneath our free sword, with its women and children. ... Following the orders you gave me, I have crushed the children beneath the horses' hooves, massacred the women...who will bear no more brigands. I do not have a single prisoner...I have exterminated them all."[18] A friend of the fallen out of favor Georges Danton, Westermann was later guillotined by the Committee despite his zealous loyalty to the Republican cause. Another more moderate Republican general in the Vendee, Jean-Baptiste Kleber, was given only slightly less draconian orders "to destroy the peasant forces and devastate all regions supporting them."[19]

Before long, Robespierre's Revolutionary dictatorship which had instituted a policy of terror turned on its own and became "like Saturn...devouring its own children."[20] Marie-Jeanne P. Roland, who was purged by her fellow revolutionary Robespierre, painted a picture of the widespread horror. While awaiting the guillotine in August 1793 she wrote, "France has become a vast Golgotha of carnage and arena of horrors, where her children tear and destroy one another...Never can history paint these dreadful times, or the monsters that fill them with their barbarity."[21]

Tragically, a history of ideological terror far deadlier and more grotesque than the living nightmare experienced by Mme. Roland, would be written in the 20th century by an even worse generation of megalomaniacal monsters whose ideological bloodline is traceable back to France's revolutionary socialist utopian intelligentsia and leaders.[22]

In the case of France, Robespierre, the radicals, and the henchmen of the Reign of Terror were in turn deposed and radical factions pushed aside as France became fully militarized under emperor Napoleon Bonaparte. In the end, the glorious Revolution had fully embraced Egalite, but sacrificed much of the other two ideals of its slogan, Liberte and Fraternite.

Finally, after suffering several more spasmodic turns of the wheel of history, which included a brief uprising by the socialist Paris Commune in 1871 and France's military defeat by

Prussia, France finally became a democratic republic. The same cannot yet be said for the denouement of the later, 20th Century revolutions in Russia, Asia, and parts of Latin America and Africa, revolutions which borrowed the worst from Rousseau's proto-socialist philosophy, the methods of France's Terror, and the teachings of Marx's *Manifesto*.

Following Rousseau, a series of thinkers and writers and a succession of radical activists greatly influenced the next 150 years. These included the influential French philosophers, Helvetius and Condorcet, who shared Rousseau's delusion about the perfectibility of the human species, and politically inclined thinkers such as Henri Saint-Simon, Francois-Noel (aka "Gracchus") Babeuf, Philippe Buonarroti, Francois Fourier, Louis Blanc, Etienne Cabet, Auguste Blanqui, Pierre-Joseph Proudhon, Moses Hess, and last but not least, Karl Marx, who struck up a friendship with Friedrich Engels at Paris' famous Cafe Regence in 1844. At this time, according to Lichtheim, Marx himself was becoming a communist after taking the measure of Proudhon, Cabet and other French activists, and intensive study of "the French Revolution and the radical movements to which it had given birth."[23] Events of that period constituted a "crucible" for the formation of the tenets of modern socialism, which because of the French Revolution "taught men to think in terms of seizing power."[24] Note that the legacy of the French Revolution is explicitly acknowledged in the Soviet Communist International's (a.k.a. the Comintern) 1919 manifesto, which states "We Communists...consider ourselves the direct continuators of the heroic endeavors and martyrdom of a long line of revolutionary generations [starting] from Babeuf."[25]

It is interesting that during the French Revolution a group of ex-Jacobins even proposed the violent overthrow of the Revolutionary Directory itself because it wasn't radical enough! Called "Babouvistes" after their executed leader, Gracchus

Babeuf, they formed what we might consider the first modern Communist movement. It was Babeuf who asserted that to fulfill its promissory slogan "Liberte, Egalite, Fraternite" the new state founded by the Revolution would need to assure the equal condition of everyone within it. The Babouvistes' planned assault on private property was far more extreme than anything other radical contemporaries had put forward. They proposed a new Reign of Terror during which all private property would be nationalized and an equal distribution of goods provided to each citizen. Taking Rousseau's political theories a step further, they argued that "Miseries and slavery are consequences of inequality, which is itself the result of property. Property is therefore the greatest scourge on society; it is a veritable public crime. All differences in wealth are unearned – they accrue by the exploitation of others, or by the accident of naturally endowed strengths and talents – and therefore are undeserved."[26]

The Babouvistes were the logical consequence of Rousseau's assertion that private property, not the frailties of human nature itself, is the root of all society's evil. The early Communists were eager to justify taking whatever they wanted from others on the premise that all private property is undeserved. Marx, Lenin, Castro, Pol Pot and others inherited the Communist revolutionary ideas of Babeuf and his co-conspirator Phillipe Buonarroti, as well as Rousseau's flawed thinking.

The boiling pot of French radical socialism led to a series of political upheavals in 1830 and 1848, and finally to the Paris Commune of 1871. The Commune was a short-lived radical socialist revolution triggered by Emperor Napoleon III's military surrender to the Prussians and the following widespread social upheaval. Although the Commune succeeded in governing Paris for only 72 days until suppressed by the regular French army, it would influence all future socialist revolutions. It resulted in tens of thousands killed or exiled. The words of the militant anthem of socialism, "The Internationale," were written by a member of the Commune, Eugene Poitier that same year.

In the somewhat sarcastic words of Martin Malia, the short-lived Paris Commune was "a glorious failure that would live on as a beacon for future socialist revolutions."[27] According to Malia, the Commune was fortuitous for Marx, because, although he was wrongly blamed by European governments for it, the Commune succeeded in making both him and communism famous, enabling Marx to thereafter dominate the socialist movement. Both Marx and Lenin later wrote influential political pamphlets about the Commune, the words of which have been spread far and wide.[28]

Marx proclaimed that "workingmen's Paris with its Commune, will forever be celebrated as the glorious harbinger of a new society. Its martyrs are enshrined in the great heart of the working class. Its exterminators' history has already been nailed to that pillory from which all the prayers of their priests will not avail to redeem them." Despite such high praise for the Commune, he criticized the revolutionary Communards' "magnanimity" in not promptly and ruthlessly finishing the job with its armed National Guard.

While the Commune issued decrees confiscating church property, and abolishing levies on workers, its leaders failed to take control of the Bank of France and seize industries, another mistake pointed out by Marx. Forty years later, in 1911, Lenin paid tribute to it: "The Paris Commune was the first step...The cause of the Commune is the cause of the social revolution, the cause of the political and economic emancipation of the workers. It is the cause of the proletariat of the whole world. And in this sense it is immortal."

One of the key lessons socialist revolutionaries like Lenin drew from the Communards' debacle was that "The absence of a disciplined, well-knit leadership both prior to and after the establishment of the Commune spelled disaster at the outset."[29] Another was that revolutionaries must be prepared to unhesitatingly go all the way, regardless of the human cost. Paris' reputation as an international haven for radicals continued into the 20th Century when expats such as Russia's Leon Trotsky and Vladimir Lenin, China's Zhou Enlai and Deng Xiaoping, Vietnam's Ho Chi Minh, the future leader of the Khmer Rouge, the butcher Pol Pot, also a member of the French Communist Party and the Cambodian Cercle Marxiste resided in Paris during the early 1950's. They, and many others who well absorbed the philosophy of Rousseau, teachings of Marx, and lessons of the Commune spread their socialist ideology to many parts of the globe, established their communist connections and bona fides in the City of Light.

Various socialist and communist parties continued to play a prominent role in polarizing French politics until the collapse of the Third Republic when Nazi Germany invaded in 1940 and the collaborationist Vichy government was formed. Even today, the Socialist Party of France, an ideological hybrid originally founded in 1902 by merger of the Marxist French Workers' Party and Blanquist Central Revolutionary Committee, has remained a major force in French politics (25-35% of popular vote since the 1980's). Like Germany, France's Socialist Party now benefits from the support of labor unions, its acceptance of democratic elections, distancing itself from earlier violent revolutionary rhetoric, and alignment with the power-seeking environmental movement. It is noteworthy that the Green movement is also on a crusade to increase the power of government so it can issue diktats that will force humanity to save itself from the ravages of capitalism. Thus, the Greens are a natural part of the Left.

Dating from the time of the Revolution of 1789, Paris has been the acknowledged home of radical political movements and remained the world's breeding ground for future socialist intelligentsia and revolutionaries, as well as a haven for the future theocratic dictator of Iran, Ayatollah Khomeini. By incubating and nurturing the seeds of a revolutionary model of socialism and by birthing its ideological offspring, communism, portions of the intelligentsia in one of the West's great cultural centers have persisted in ignobly debasing themselves and their wonderful city. To grasp the full extent of the dreadful tragedy one need only look at the consequential fate of many millions of Russians, Eastern Europeans, Latin Americans, Africans, Chinese, Koreans, Vietnamese, Cambodians and others in each of the more than dozen criminal regimes that at one time had encompassed much of the globe.[30] Inspiration from the French Revolution and the cabal of early French Socialists produced a mixed legacy not just for France but for the whole world, and the aftermath of the French Revolution remains a source of endless analysis and debate by historians on both the Left and Right.

"Left" and "Right" is Wrong

It is well to note here that referring to political factions as "Left" or "Right" (their seating locations in King Louis' National Assembly) gave rise during the French Revolution to an outdated but still widely used political syntax of dubious validity in today's world. These labels are a misapplied and at times harmful political legacy created by the French Revolution. While in democratic societies the "Left-wing" is an identifiable political carry-over from the Revolution that still strives to push societies across the globe toward socialism, there nowhere remains a corresponding "Right-wing" political entity composed of aristocratic nobles defending, much less seeking to restore a king's rule under a hereditary monarchy. The "Right" today is instead the home of liberals in the truest sense of the word—those who fear and oppose the tyranny of any government or elite ruling class.

Underlying our present-day confusion of Left and Right-wing labels is the careless mis-adaptation of a simplistic, 200 plus-year old political model to modern times, positioning the ideology of socialism/Marxism/communism at one extreme of a continuum (the once and future Left-wing), but replacing supporters of hereditary monarchy (the historical Right-wing) with Nazi and fascist ideologies at the other extreme. Because they were opponents of socialists/communists in the Spanish Civil War and fought against the Soviets in WWII, the Nazis and Italian Fascists became labeled "Right-wing," thereby indicating their political opposition to socialism. Consequently, many political commentators have since fallen into the trap of the Left's false dichotomy, simplistically characterizing all those who most vigorously oppose socialism, even in democratic societies, as "Right-wing," and therefore also having fascist or Nazi tendencies.

The labels "Right wing," "Fascist" and "Nazi" are today often being misused to smear and discredit anyone who has the temerity to publicly oppose socialism and the Left. Smearing with pejorative labels is a favorite tactic used by Leftist front organizations and their fellow travelers in the news media to sow discord in democratic societies. Hitler and Stalin both considered the highly successful capitalist democracies of the West as the principal adversaries they had to destroy to achieve the world domination they envisioned. During the War the USSR conducted extensive espionage in the U.S. and Great Britain. Once Nazi Germany was defeated, Stalin redoubled his efforts to: create a Soviet-style socialist empire encompassing all of Eastern Europe, subvert the capitalist democracies, and support Third-World "liberation movements" in impoverished non-Western nations which would pave the way for Marx's prophesied worldwide socialist revolution, causing what became known as the Cold War.

Because the USSR engaged in a death struggle during

World War II with its then principal rival for control of Eurasia, Nazi Germany, it has been easy for modern day pundits to overlook the many commonalities of Nazism and socialism. After the Nazis double-crossed Stalin by invading Russia, the Western democracies deliberately chose to ignore Stalin's 1939 bilateral non-aggression pact with his counterpart dictator, Hitler, an agreement to divide Eastern Europe into respective spheres of control. This agreement gave the green light to the Nazi's initial campaign of conquest. With its territorial aims, the Nazi-Soviet Non-Aggression Pact was very different from the temporary "allies of convenience" arrangement Stalin later entered with the democracies to defeat Hitler's regime. Both regimes were anti-religious, anti-capitalist, totalitarian police states controlled by iron-fisted dictators, who, absent the true democratic processes they abhorred, could not be removed from office by popular vote, and both were fully militarized, expansionist, and incredibly brutal. They each used similar means to control their people, and embraced the indiscriminate principle of collective guilt, ruthlessly extending punishments, including death and imprisonment in slave labor camps, to all blood relations and ethnic group members.

Such means included establishing vast concentration camp systems modeled on Lenin's Gulags to essentially enslave and then do away with large numbers of dissenters and certain types of people (such as "kulaks" in Russia and in the case of the Nazis, the extermination of all the Jews of Europe). Paramilitary forces were created to intimidate and suppress domestic opposition. News, education, and cultural institutions were converted into propaganda organs, and arbitrary force was employed by secret police to terrorize vilified groups as well as any individuals who might be labeled an "enemy of the State," together with their entire families. Millions were condemned to great suffering and death because of what they were, not for anything they had done.

Both the Nazi's racial ideology and Marx's socialism reject the moral precept of individual guilt or innocence for those designated enemies of the State. They instead incite primitive hatred of certain groups of people whom they blamed collectively for the ills of society, then dehumanized and sought to destroy them by any methods no matter how brutal; by gassing, by starvation, by bullets, by axes, or by hideous forms of torture, it matters not. Both are anti-individualistic, insisting upon uniformity of beliefs, habits, and outlook, to create the unity of a homogeneous, centrally controlled beehive-like nation. Nazism's roots in socialism are clearly stated in the sample of remarks by its propaganda minister, Joseph Goebbels (see sidebar).

With benefit of hindsight it is easy to see that in actual practice, modern socialism, including communism, has a great deal in common with Nazism, and lesser with fascism which is populist, but neither a class nor race based ideology. However, in a broad sense all of the collectivist ideologies, including fascism, share from their genesis certain strands of ideology found in Western Europe's 19th Century Socialism which give them an underlying affinity, particularly the alluring promise of national redemption and prosperity for everyone achievable only if society is organized and controlled by an omnipotent central state. In the cases of socialism and Nazism, the path to fulfilling their divergent utopian visions is determined by a revolutionary vanguard politically organizing and mobilizing the proletarian power base to transform or destroy all pre-existing societal institutions, and once in control, becoming a dictatorship willing to use the most horrific means to root out all people deemed "enemies of the state." For these ideologies, violence directed at dissenters became a sacred duty, a necessary step towards establishing a new way of life for humanity.

The Nazis' enthrallment with socialism ended as the

Great Depression of the 1930's set in and parties representing political extremes, including the Nazis, made significant gains among the electorate. During these turbulent economic times the German socialist parties became the Nazi's principal political rival for the support of those Germans who were disenchanted with the democratic Weimar Republic which had been established in 1918 following the abdication of Emperor William II. By 1933 the Nazis had gained control of the German government. In 1935 the Nazis' propaganda chief began denouncing Russian Bolshevism and the propaganda and espionage of the Communist International ("Komintern") at every opportunity, saying that "Bolshevism is not merely anti-bourgeois; it is against civilization itself," and accused it of: acts of terror, hostage murders, experiments in agricultural collectivization resulting in mass starvation, plunder and arson, armed risings, sabotage, espionage, and world propaganda in pursuit of a world revolution.[32] Although his remarks were correct, instead of being concerned with spreading truth, Goebbels' aim was to attack international and domestic communism because it challenged the Nazi's power.

Goebbels accusations aside, in addition to their many superficial similarities, at a fundamental level, both Nazism as a racial movement and the modern socialist movement of Marx and Engels represent millennial "secular religions arising from the arrogant endeavor of man to transform religious promises directly into worldly reality," and that "project into the past a vision of what never was, conceive of what is in terms of what is not, and the future in terms of what can never be." Taken from a comparison of communism and Nazism by Frederick A. Voigt,[33] these quotes refer to the utopian vision of an incorruptible communist system that peacefully transitions from the socialism that supplants capitalism, producing the mythical Age of Innocence, a classless society of eternal peace and joy. In the case of Nazism, it was elevation of humanity

Joseph Goebbels on Nazi Socialism[31]

• Lenin is the greatest man, second only to Hitler, and that the difference between Communism and the Hitler faith is very slight.

• Germany will become free at that moment when the thirty millions on the left and the thirty millions on the right make common cause. Only one movement is capable of doing this: National Socialism, embodied in one Führer – Adolf Hitler.

•To be a socialist is to submit the I to the thou; socialism is sacrificing the individual to the whole.

•Socialism is the ideology of the future."

• You and I [speaking to socialists], we are fighting each other but we are not really enemies. By doing so we are dividing our strength, and we shall never reach our goal.

•That is why we place ourselves alongside Russia as equal partners in the struggle for this freedom which means everything to us."

• The bourgeoisie has to yield to the working class ... Whatever is about to fall should be pushed. We are all soldiers of the revolution. We want the workers' victory over filthy lucre. That is socialism."

•We are socialists, because we see in socialism, that means, in the fateful dependence of all folk comrades upon each other, the sole possibility for the preservation of our racial genetics and thus the re-conquest of our political freedom and for the rejuvenation of the German state."

• We are not a charitable institution but a Party of revolutionary socialists."

•The socialist worldview begins with the folk and then goes over to things. Things are made subservient to the folk; the socialist puts the folk above everything, and things are only means to an end."

by race, and only eventually by eliminating wealthier classes. However, both promise and aim to bring the real world as we know it to an end.

It is overly simplistic to assert that Hitler merely grafted a struggle for racial superiority onto socialism, but perhaps Tribal Socialism is the frightening synthesis of these two abhorrent ideologies in multi-ethnic societies and another of Hitler's awful legacies. Regardless, it is indisputable that dictatorships, whether Nazi, socialist, or fascist, whether theocratic or oligarchic, are the antithesis of democracy. Failed socialist states seem prone to morphing into corrupt fascist-style dictatorships; shall we point to Putin's Russia, with his messianic appeal of national redemption, and former Soviet satellites such as Belarus, Castro's Cuba, or Maduro's Venezuela?

On the flip side, even popular revolutions that oust fascists or military juntas can quickly morph into socialist police states run by dictators rather than establish liberal democracies. In such unhappy circumstances, one form of brutal dictatorship is essentially exchanged for another even worse as any latent peace-loving democratic reformers are swept aside. Some have argued, as did the British former socialist MP, Ivor Bulmer-Thomas, that "From the point of view of human liberties there is little to choose between communism, socialism, and national socialism [Nazism]. They all are examples of the collectivist or totalitarian state...in its essentials not only is completed socialism the same as communism but it hardly differs from fascism." [34]

Returning to the modern labels of Left and Right, one might ask, now that despotic monarchies are long gone and we have a better historical perspective, shouldn't our model of ideologies cluster the 20th Century's most noteworthy forms of anti-individual state-centered dictatorship at one end of a continuum, and individual freedom-centered democracy, which barely existed at the time of the French Revolution, at the other end? Shouldn't we place on the Left, near one another, socialism, Nazism and fascism, (and perhaps radical Islam), each a self-proclaimed implacable enemy of classically liberal democratic capitalism? Shouldn't we then place on the Right liberal democracy in the form of representative republics, with decentralized, bottom-up power and freely formed, open markets that help restrain government from becoming tyrannical? This would include those forms of government in which the people elect and peacefully replace those who govern, determine their own laws, have independent courts and competing political parties?

Both philosophically and empirically, socialism, Nazism, and fascism, each a form of tyranny, have much more in common with one another than with democratic capitalism. One could argue that a "freedom continuum," which places democracy with its individual freedom and rights at one end (the true liberal "Right") set against the authoritarian rule of the single-party central State or oligarchy at the other (the true "Left"), capture the most fundamental ideological difference of the political movements of our time far better than a maladapted, fuzzy, and now misleading syntax carried over from the French Revolution that history has emptied of meaning.

In the West, those who consider themselves political "Conservatives" are labelled "Right-wing" by Left-wing politicians, media and academicians so that they can be tarred with the fascist/neo-Nazi brush, notwithstanding that conservatism, if it even qualifies as an ideology, is obviously far closer to liberal democracy than to any form of tyrannical ideology. It is probably more correct to think of conservatism as an "anti-ideology." Broadly speaking, conservatives believe that beyond assuring the nation's continued existence by defending against external threats, it is not the province of government to guarantee a particular future for each of its citizens, only an opportunity to pursue their own happiness using the gifts they are endowed with; the future is created by the nation's citizens themselves, their free actions restrained only by law and respect for one another's rights.

Conservatives generally espouse: 1) restraining government, by limiting its size and power so as to protect the freedom and rights of its citizens, 2) opposition to socialism, Nazism, fascism, and oppressive government of any other kind, including defending the nation against these ideologies, 3) demanding consistent, non-discriminatory treatment of all people, including enforcement of laws that treat all citizens equally and thus guarantee equal citizenship, 4) promoting realism, acknowledging unvarnished facts, and applying common sense in political discourse instead of politically correct "narratives" spun from utopian desires, 5) collectively providing life-sustaining support for those unable to care for themselves, while emphasizing individual versus governmental responsibility for one's relative prosperity, 6) espousing peaceful assembly and freedom of speech to display and express dissent, while opposing lawlessness, rioting, and violence that increase mistrust and division among segments of society, 7) fostering a culture which embraces patriotism, respect for law, and strong shared moral values (sometimes scornfully ridiculed by Leftist media and intellectuals as Neanderthal "traditionalism"), and lastly 8) respect for the human wisdom embedded in traditions and values over the idea that a past not completely comporting to the Left's notions is automatically detrimental or of little value, and must be reinvented from new "facts" creating a history that never was, but is consistent with their ideology.

Contrary to what some would claim, conservatives are not altogether against change while the Left is for change. Conservatives do not believe in a status quo unchanging world. Far from it. Instead of centralized State planning by self-anointed puppet masters, they believe in continuous improvement through the liberty that releases creativity, better ideas and industriousness, and the discarding of failed policies. It is democratic capitalism, not socialism, that has produced the many astounding benefits for humankind in all social strata and thus transformed the world. Rather than a static status quo, it is the auto-adaptive dynamism of democratic capitalism that conservatives wish to conserve! Such liberating dynamism contradicts the very idea of socialism. That is why conservatives are hated by socialists of every stripe. The socialist doctrine is not only destructive and evil, but has also been rendered pointless, unnecessary, and hopelessly outdated from the innumerable adjustments and adaptations made by free people in prospering capitalist democracies across the globe.

Later in this book I will amplify on the intellectual and historical background preceding ill-fated attempts made in the 20th Century to create egalitarian utopias, which, instead of bringing Heaven down to Earth created a Hell on Earth for large portions of the world's population. One "catch" undermining socialism is that human societies do not behave like the clockwork I wrote of earlier. The ongoing struggle between Left and Right philosophies, however they may be characterized, proves that human society is by nature inherently messy and unpredictable. It is subject to infinite complexity resulting from the continual interactions of: 1) diverse individual human capabilities, desires, viewpoints, free will and creativity, 2) all sorts of individual and collective transactions and undertakings, 3) the ramifications of unforeseeable new technologies, 4) the social influences of people upon each other, 5) the natural preoccupation with one's own life and family, 6) frequent irrational behaviors, 7) diverse cultures and belief systems, and, sad to say, 8) the criminal tendencies of some.

Reason would argue that social systems do not obey

deterministic scientific principles that can be used to control and mold them to perfection. They are not, "problems" to be solved, despite the delusional notions of both the French revolutionaries and followers of Marx. Moreover, when driven by humble commonsense realism of the kind propounded by the American philosopher Reinhold Niebuhr in his 1940 anti-utopian essay "An End to Illusions," reason will lay bare the ambiguities of human nature and history, as well as the limited but crucial role played in human affairs by knowledge, logic and discernment. As the noted American professor of psychology Steven Pinker pointed out:

"Enlightenment [and] endorsement of reason must not be confused with the implausible claim that human beings are perfectly rational agents. Nothing could be further from historical reality...The deliberate application of reason was necessary precisely because our common habits of thought are not particularly reasonable," given "our irrational passions and foibles."[35]

In his 1759 work *Theory of Moral Sentiments*, Adam Smith further highlighted the foolishness of individuals enamored by the theoretical beauty of their utopian plans:

"The man of [utopian] system. . . seems to imagine that he can arrange the different members of a great society with as much ease as the hand arranges the different pieces upon a chess-board. He does not consider that the pieces upon the chess-board have no other principle of motion besides that which the hand impresses upon them; but that, in the great chess-board of human society, every single piece has a principle of motion of its own, altogether different from that which the legislature might choose to impress upon it."[36]

While people of honorable intention can have very different views of the best way of governing, of fair laws, of justice, of behavioral norms, and of moral restraints on imposing their views on others, these differences can be resolved through democratic processes provided there is tolerance for compromise and dissent, and human rights are respected. This is a cornerstone and promise of democracy, and why, absent a freely shared commitment to such values that enables a coherent "we" to exist, democracy is unsustainable.

Conversely, utopianism is about government enforcing the perfect ordered society, which much resembles "puppeteering," and not at all about accommodating the differing desires of free persons within society. Let us ask then the Socialist Utopian, "Who can lay claim to being superior among his or her fellow human beings? Who can justify crowning themselves as the self-anointed leader with the one true answer and absolute authority to create their version of Heaven on earth? Who can play the Grand Puppeteer? What if instead of Plato's benign "philosopher king,"[37] an evil despot seizes power through revolution, terror, and political murder, turning men into obedient monsters who pitilessly spread terror that ends up producing Hell on earth?

The world has come a long way from the time of the French Revolution, the Reign of Terror, Karl Marx, and the birth of modern socialism. But more than a century of socialist-induced global misery has apparently not been enough. Though thought by many to have been irretrievably extinguished at the end of the Soviet Empire and freeing of Eastern Europe in the late 1980's, socialism's embers are smouldering still. Like the fabled vampire Nosferatu, who eludes a reckoning in this world, it has not been possible for free people to drive the stake of Liberty through the heart of socialism. The undead vampire rises and hunts for its victims while Reason sleeps or is silenced by intimidation. After a brief period of dormancy, protected within the ideological excrement of the past century, socialism is now on the march again at universities, in street demonstrations, at political rallies, in entertainment, and in communications and mass media. Neo-socialist organizations with deceptive names are sprouting like poisonous mushrooms out of decayed institutions. In these forums its doctrine is being revived not to be studied as a disproven theory that has left a dark stain on human history, but as a newly repaved road to utopia.

Utopian Holocaust of the 20th Century

Given the historical record, it cannot be denied that Marx's Socialist State became the "Molech"[38] of modern times, a false idol created and worshiped by man, with an insatiable appetite for the sacrificial slaughter of the helpless. In their feverish delusions, the powerful high priests of this modern Molech proclaimed the slaughter necessary for mankind's salvation from worldly evil. Yet, driven by such a moral contradiction its toll on humanity has been undeniably catastrophic. The promise of a paradise on Earth is worth killing many people for, is it not? As Virgil pointed out in his epic poem describing the founding of Rome, *The Aeneid*, nothing glorious can be achieved without considerable human cost. But what is the ultimate price of such a grandiose undertaking, not only in victims' lives, but also in the killers forsaking their own humanity? It matters not if it is predestined by the gods.

The "butcher's bill" of socialist barbarism that spanned 70 years in the 20th Century is estimated at nearly 100 million human beings executed outright or systematically killed by torture, starvation, forced labor and consequential disease. (See Appendix Tables 1 & 2.) Courtois et al. have extensively documented the results of more than a dozen such criminal regimes that at one time spanned much of the world, and you can easily reference *The Black Book of Communism* to grasp the full extent of the catastrophe. The very immensity of the slaughter across three continents and the massive efforts undertaken by criminal socialist regimes to eliminate witnesses and evidence make it difficult for historians to fully document the magnitude of this global human holocaust. However, despite the systematic liquidation of millions of potential witnesses, often including entire families, a great many human beings remain alive today who managed to survive its horrors and have borne witness with their testimonials.

I am not the only one to compare socialism to the worship of Molech, the ancient god-idol who required the sacrifice of children into its flames. Dialogue in a recent Russian documentary film series entitled "Trotsky" contains very similar wording and also refers to the Marxist State created by Lenin as "eating its own children," a scene metaphorically depicted in the famous Francisco de Goya painting of Saturn devouring the son who would otherwise challenge to take his place.

The millions sacrificed to the modern Molech does not include the millions consumed by the genocidal "Final Solution" carried out against Jews during Nazi Germany's twelve-year reign of terror begat from Hitler's racial utopian vision. It is the other holocaust of modern times, a transnational and ideological holocaust equal in brutality and malignancy to its ideological cousin National Socialism (Nazism), but longer-lived and engulfing fully one-third of the planet. Given its breadth, magnitude and methods, it seems entirely appropriate to label the institution of Marx's modern socialism the "other Holocaust" of the 20th Century, as did Courtois et al.[39]

That is not to say that either Nazism or communism is the greater of the two totalitarian evils. Hardly so. Does mankind need a scale for comparing absolute evils so vast and heinous? Indeed, such a level of evil defies moral ranking. The evil of Hitler's unimaginable but real industrial extermination camps and genocidal vision is truly unprecedented and unique in all of history. It is incomparable and evokes infinite revulsion in the human soul. The devastating consequences for humanity had Hitler prevailed and thus been able to take his Master

Race ideology to its hideous conclusion is hard to imagine. But could not the same be said of Stalin's gulags? There the bitter cold, starvation, and sometimes the executioners' axe blades or bullets did the same demonic work as Hitler's bullets and poison gas. However we may come to terms with these two revolting demonstrations of man's inhumanity to man, Lenin, Stalin, Mao, the Kims, Castro, Pol Pot, their indoctrinators, acolytes and enablers, each and every one richly deserve a seat next to Hitler and his Nazi operatives at Satan's feet in Hell. There, surrounded by the shrieks and groans of their many millions of innocent victims, may they remain unconsumed in the agony of eternal flame and despair!

In the short span of forty years following the Russian Revolution in 1917, Karl Marx's ideological synthesis of socialist beliefs, labelled "Communism," spread like a rat-borne pestilence from Europe, where it had its genesis and first infected political thought, into Russia, and thence into Asia, Africa, and Latin America.

The Russian Empire Becomes the Union of Soviet Socialist Republics (USSR)

The 1917 Revolution in Russia overthrew the highly autocratic, cruel and incompetent Czarist monarchy, along with its widespread poverty and long-simmering discontent. It was triggered by domestic unrest caused by the costly and humiliating battlefield failures of the Czar's army early in WWI. At the time of the Revolution, Vladimir (aka "Nikolai," born V. I. Ulyanov) Lenin's Marxist revolutionary organization – he insisted it be called the "Bolshevik (word meaning "majority") Party" – consisted of only between 20,000 and 40,000 members, a miniscule percentage of the total population of Russia. The Bolsheviks' clever revolutionary slogan promising "peace, land, and bread" led to the Party's growing popularity among the Russian peasantry and workers who, already unhappy with their status, were disdainful of the Czar's war efforts, and being subjected to famine and social chaos.

However, the Bolshevik Party (officially the "Russia Social-Democratic Labour Party") was never really meant to be comprised of urban workers and rural peasants representing the common man, the "proletariat" it purported to champion. Lenin himself only briefly held a real job. He quickly became a full-time political activist and organizer, and finally the "iron fist" of socialism. At the time the Bolsheviks fully seized power in October 1917, at Lenin's insistence, Party membership had been limited to only Leftist intelligentsia turned professional revolutionaries, with some murderous henchmen thrown in for good measure. Nonetheless, to gain legitimacy amongst the masses, by a political slight-of-hand Lenin equated his Bolsheviks with Marx's "proletariat class," never acknowledging the Party's entirely different origin and makeup.

The Bolsheviks came to power by quickly and ruthlessly eliminating all competing political parties, and later, all remnants of the Czarist regime. Only the socialist doctrines of Marx, as interpreted and implemented by his disciple Lenin, would rule. At Lenin's insistence, this Marxist "Bolshevism" was soon proudly relabeled "Communism." The Bolshevik (now "Communist") Party transformed itself into the one and only permanent governing body (not subject to being rejected in elections), unaccountable to the public.

The Bolsheviks became the model socialist revolutionaries that future dictators would look to for forcefully concentrating all power in the hands of a very small group of those most hardened who easily sweep aside moderate factions that lack their ruthlessness. It was a model followed by every subsequent Marxist-inspired revolution. In the end, the "big tent" that is needed to sell broad support for the revolution becomes a very small and exclusive tent for governing, as those who are most radical with power concentrated in their hands call all the shots and do as they will with anyone who resists.

Lenin had complete disdain for democracy and the common man. Borrowing from the example of the French Revolution's 12-member "Committee on Public Safety," from the beginning he wanted an unchallengeable revolutionary dictatorship led by a small fanatical vanguard of educated elites, rather than council leaders chosen by proletarian workers and peasants - Marx's oppressed class! - whom he despised and distrusted. Despite their very small numbers, through ruthless use of force, Lenin and his band of Bolshevik followers had managed by 1922 to place the entire Russian Empire of over 130 million under the yoke of the Union of Soviet Socialist Republics (aka Soviet Union) and thus subject to the will of a single man, V. I. Lenin.

The outcome is staggering. Before his death in 1924, Lenin is known to have issued directives resulting in the murder of over two million fellow countrymen, women and children, not counting the deaths from starvation of combatants during the civil war he and Trotsky waged to gain total control of the country.[40] It was at Lenin's direction that a massive system of prison labor camps was initially established by his Cheka secret police to do away with "counterrevolutionaries" and any who might dissent from the Bolshevik onslaught. By 1921 Lenin, like a high priest of Molech, had in two short years established 84 such camps, a number that would exceed 400 under comrade Stalin. Lenin's secret police soon became an extension of his iron fist, a ubiquitous source of terror. But Lenin was just a preview of the coming horror; before its final demise at the end of the Cold War, the Soviet experiment in Socialist Utopianism had snuffed out the lives of over 20 million of its own people.[41]

To lead his secret police in carrying out the terror that quickly eclipsed that of the Czar's secret police, Lenin selected Feliks Dzerzhinski, whom he considered a "staunch proletarian Jacobin." Dzerzhinski was succeeded in the Stalin era by the equally brutal and much feared: G. Yagoda, N. Yezov, and L. Berea. The Extraordinary Commission on Counterrevolution and Sabotage, the infamous "Cheka" formed by Lenin in 1917, evolved into the equally infamous GPU and OGPU in 1922 and 1923, then the NKVD in 1934 and finally the KGB, organizations which proved the Lenin maxim: "One man with a gun can control 100 without one." This instrument of organized terror not only tortured and summarily executed millions, but it also fed many millions more into its hellish "Gulag" slave labor camp system in which a vast number were eventually worked to death or perished from starvation, disease, and exposure.

Once he had consolidated the Bolshevik's power in Russia, Lenin founded the "Third International" (aka "Comintern" which stands for Communist International) in 1919 as the successor to much weaker international socialist organizations dating back to the First (socialist) International formed in 1864 in London, followed by the broader and more successful Second (aka "Socialist") International in 1889. In alignment with orthodox Marxism, Lenin and Josef Stalin, his protégé and successor, always held that socialism had to be an international movement. Having become the acknowledged leader of the socialist cause worldwide, Lenin gave the newly revitalized organization a strong sponsor in his newly formed Soviet State, the USSR. But with that support came his total control of its activities and those of its loyal member parties around the globe.

Lenin's purpose for forming the Comintern was to direct and support increasingly aggressive revolutionary activities of communist parties and subversive organizations worldwide from Moscow. The Comintern operated as a highly secretive organization under the centralized control of the Cheka (later the NKVD). It was used by Lenin and then Stalin with the aim of furthering the cause of Marx's worldwide socialist subversion and revolution to create communist "dictatorships of the proletariat" wherever possible. This involved using armed underground rebel groups it sought to covertly establish under the communist party in each country. It would direct local conspiratorial political and revolutionary tactics, and funnel in weapons, money, and agents to surreptitiously carry out destabilizing activities, then take advantage of the resulting social unrest to overthrow existing governments.

Some of the Comintern's earliest efforts in the 1920's were focused on destabilizing governments in Germany, Eastern Europe and the Baltic region. Lenin also sent Comintern agents into China in 1920 to help form the Chinese Communist Party, and set up two front organizations, the Sino-Russian News Agency, and a foreign-language school as a cover for Communist recruiting activities.[42] It is worth noting that the Chinese Communist Party has recently taken a page out of the Comintern's playbook in establishing of a network of "Confucius Institutes" at Western universities.

The Comintern's tentacles reached into Yugoslavia in the late 1920's, and then into France and Spain in the early 1930's. It always worked through "domestic" communist parties in each country which submitted to its orders from Moscow. The Kremlin also directed the Comintern to covertly undermine stable democratic capitalist governments in the West, such as the United States in 1920's, and Great Britain, through extensive espionage, spying, and infiltration of their key institutions (much as China is now doing in the United States and elsewhere). For example, the Communist Party of America (CPUSA) was formed in 1919 as an offshoot of the Socialist Party then headed by Eugene Debs who declared in his February 1919 article titled "The Day of the People" published in *The Class Struggle* "From the crown of my head to the soles of my feet, I am a Bolshevik, and proud of it." It recruited mainly from radical immigrants, the unemployed, labor union members, and poor Blacks subject to racial injustice whom it sought to radicalize with a promise to reconstruct society on a socialist basis to even the score. By the mid-1920's the CPUSA was under the control of the Comintern, having formed both an above-ground and an underground covert arm at Moscow's direction.

It is noteworthy that almost twenty years prior to Stalin's invasion of Poland at the start of WWII, Lenin sent the Red Army into Poland to extend the reach of his Socialist regime to the borders of industrial Europe, which he believed held the lynchpin to initiating Marx's dream of a worldwide revolution of the proletariat. It was a military invasion that turned into a debacle for the Bolsheviks, as the Red Army was soundly defeated in 1920 near Warsaw by a Polish army under General Jozef Pulsudski.[43] For a while thereafter comrades Lenin and later Stalin would have to bide their time and depend upon espionage. Toward the end of WWII, the retreat of Hitler's Wehrmacht again gave the Red Army the opportunity to invade and occupy all of Poland as well as all of Eastern Europe's borderlands, but the Western World owes a debt of gratitude to those forgotten heroes of history, Pilsudski, and the brave Poles who fought beside him, who succeeded in keeping Stalin and the horrors of messianic socialism at bay for 25 years.

Speaking of Lenin's protégé the megalomaniacal Josef, aka "Koba" Stalin (born Ioseb Jughashvili), there is ample reason to call him "The Monster," the name given him by the former gulag inmate and Nobel Prize-winning author Alexandr Solzhenitsyn. Under Stalin's forced collectivization begun in the 1920's, a peasant family who owned more than 37 acres, had three head of cattle, or had two or more hired hands was automatically considered wealthy and an "anti-Soviet element." Such peasants were worthy of being arrested and sent to a labor camp in Siberia and their land and other property seized. The story of one of an estimated eight million of these so-called "kulaks," a man executed in 1937, is told in an article by James Marson in the December 17, 2016, edition of the Wall Street Journal titled "A Russian Fights for Stalin's Victims." It is a story worth reading for its vivid description of the Soviet application of Socialist Utopianism.

In the "Soviet Republics" of Ukraine and Kazakhstan (and later in China, Cambodia, North Korea and other places), communists especially targeted the political control of all farmlands and food supplies in order to "socialize" the production and distribution of food by brutally forcing family farms into "communes" or "collectives." Through this approach, in which all land and food produced are owned not by individual farmers but by the State, authorities could then confiscate and control the distribution of food where and when it served their purposes. These calamitous policies induced episodes of intentional mass starvation that killed many millions. Hunger is, to be sure, a most powerful tool of totalitarian rule. When all food is controlled by the government it can be withheld from those suspected of resistance, bringing them to their knees as surely as if a gun were pointed at their head. The ruthless Bolshevik Leon Trotsky candidly stated (after he had been exiled by Stalin) "In a country where the sole employer is the State, opposition means death by slow starvation. The old principle 'Who does not work shall not eat' has been replaced by a new one: 'Who does not obey shall not eat.'"[44]

The Monster Stalin did not stop at starvation. According to a *New York Times* citation in Robert Conquest's book, *The Great Terror: A Reassessment*:

> "At the eve of World War II in early 1939, at least one in 20 of the population of Stalin's communist Soviet Union had been arrested. Some eight million innocent people were being held in prisons and camps, where 90 percent of them would soon perish. Two million inmates had died in the previous two years, and one million people had been shot. The overall vic-

tims of this particular episode of Stalin's terror would eventually number over 10 million. Worse still, other episodes of arbitrary executions and induced starvation earlier in the decade had destroyed over 14 million, and the total number of victims was rising."[45]

Recall that from its inception under Lenin the Soviet-controlled Comintern was dedicated to overthrowing the capitalist democracies and replacing them with socialist states that could be manipulated by Moscow to realize the cherished goal of World socialism. Although Stalin announced its dissolution in 1943 in order to appease Russia's wartime allies, America and Great Britain, and mute any criticism in the West of the vast amount of war material the USSR was being given by the Roosevelt Administration, the dissolution was a fraud. Stalin merely shuffled some papers and continued his deliberate spreading of the socialist pestilence by other means. These included subversion of existing governments by his vast army of covert operatives, arming indigenous revolutionaries, armed invasion of formerly independent nations by his vast military machine, and military occupation of areas surrendered by the Nazi and Japanese armies.

Russia's suffering was on an enormous scale indeed. But while it was the first, it was not the bloodiest example of imposed socialist utopian doctrine. A greater, almost unimaginable death toll ensued due to socialism's spread from Soviet Russia into China, Southeast Asia, Eastern Europe, Africa, and Latin America, thus far consuming the lives of an estimated 100 million victims in total. In some places Lenin, Stalin and Mao succeeded in spreading their deadly doctrine, but in others like Spain, they failed.

In the Spanish Civil War the Socialists Lose to the Fascists

Marxian Socialism had its first run at seizing power from within Western Europe and establishing an indigenous socialist "dictatorship of the proletariat" during the abortive Paris

Commune of 1871, which was quickly put down by French troops. Then came the Spanish Civil War. It is estimated that, separate from battlefield casualties, the Spanish Civil War of 1936-38 led to the outright murder of several hundred thousand non-combatant Spanish citizens by fascist, Republican, and communist factions, in addition to numerous other atrocities.

The history of Spain in modern times illustrates that once the "Dogs of Hell" are unloosed by ideologues willing to torture and murder others and willing to chance being killed themselves, there is no neat, peaceful and moral way to transition from despotism into a just civil society. Because of underlying injustice, different segments of society may become susceptible to polarizing ideologies - in this case fascism and socialism - that then lead to widespread social disintegration and conflict. In the end, most people, yearning for peace, order, and security, will usually accept whichever physical authority prevails however repugnant its underlying ideology.

During the 1800s, Spain's political structure underwent several convulsive changes as it lumbered into the modern age. The people of Spain suffered from a corrupt monarchy and land-based oligarchy of feudal origin ruling over the largely agrarian economy, many parts of which were very poor. The fissures in Spanish society grew wider at the dawning of the 20th Century. Socialist ideas began to spread, and trade organizations formed and gained sufficient power to contest the status quo. In 1931, the Spanish monarchy gave in to popular pressure and established an elected "Republican" central government. Following the election of many Republicans and Socialists the King fled the country. With a weak central government, Spain became increasingly polarized as it experienced more and more political murders and reprisals, and the country began to fracture into armed camps. Socialist factions, including labor unions and communists under Russian control through the secret activities of the Comintern and NKVD, each sought to institute their own regional or local brand of property "socialization" and abolish existing authority and open markets. In certain districts this even extended to controlling acquisition and distribution of all food.

During the 1930's, Stalin's agents became active in Spain's political unrest, providing significant military, organizational and financial support to the Communist Party there. The Party planned to use this aid to supplant the Republicans in the effort to achieve victory over German and Italian-supported Spanish fascists, and establish a Soviet puppet regime. In Barcelona and Catalonia where the central Republican government was powerless, the anti-clerical anarchists and communists managed to infiltrate, to "colonize," the majority of governmental functions, seizing and collectivizing a large part of the economic activity of the city and countryside.[46]

The NKVD ran Moscow's operations in Spain for Stalin. In Catalonia the NKVD cell camouflaged itself with the name "Unified Socialist Party of Catalonia." One of its directives from Moscow was to recruit and organize a Comintern/Communist Party-controlled army in the form of an "International Brigade" that would be able to increase the ideological polarization of the conflict, eliminating any possibility for compromise, and assuring Moscow's policies would be followed. Through the Comintern, Moscow directed communist parties in the U.S. and throughout Latin America to aid the effort in Spain with military recruits, arms, funds, and supplies.[47]

With Spanish societal unrest reaching a boiling point in 1936, part of the military staged a revolutionary coup toppling the hapless Republican government. Factions from outside Spain soon began to participate in the violent civil war that followed between the socialist/communist "Republicans" and the fascist/loyalist "Nationalists," who eventually prevailed. The so-called Republicans drew military and financial support from Stalin's Soviet Russia, Socialist Mexico and to some extent from France, while the Nationalists were supported by Hitler's Nazi Germany and Mussolini's Fascist Italy. In the end, the Nationalists prevailed.

Though there had always been disagreements, there was a great escalation of confrontations between the labor unions and the communists during the spring of 1937. In Madrid, the communists overseeing public order were accused of maintaining secret prisons to hold Republicans, anarchists, and socialists who had not submitted to NKVD control, and blamed for either torturing or executing them as traitors. Again, socialism was "eating its own children."

The Spanish Civil War is highlighted here for its moral ambiguities and contradictions, and sheer savagery, and for its far-reaching geopolitical significance. First, considering the actions of the rival factions and their allied fascists and communists, neither side was worthy of support from those who champion freedom, yet the War seduced many idealistic volunteers into its lethal vortex to fight on the pseudo-Republican side either for socialism or against fascism or both. Second, the War began as a coup to overthrow an elected but questionable Republican (actually socialist) government that was attempting to redistribute property to address legitimate grievances stemming from an unjust feudal society with its inherited privileges and wealth. In so doing, the government had failed to prevent certain elements from taking much more radical actions in several regions of the country. Third, radical socialist/communist elements also transformed Spain's revolutionary political movement into a murderous anti-clerical campaign, much as in Jacobin France 143 years earlier. Fourth, both sides engaged in widespread atrocities against those who sympathized with the opposing side. Lastly, the Spanish Civil War transcended Spain itself, and presaged the vast global conflagration now known as World War II. Spain became both an ideological battleground in a global contest and a geopolitical prize of such importance to rival utopian ideologies that the outcome continues to reverberate to this day.

For some socialist sympathizers who flocked to the Republican cause, such as George Orwell, later author of the books *1984* and *Animal Farm*, along with other Western notables, the Spanish Civil War represented a personal journey from idealism to horrified realism. Stalin's order to NKVD operatives in Spain to imprison several of Orwell's socialist comrades, plus revelation of Stalin's Great Purges in Russia during the 1930's, and then finally, and impossible to ignore, the shocking revelation of the 1939 Nazi-Soviet Pact to divvy-up Eastern Europe, all contributed to opening Orwell's eyes to what happens when Marx's ideology is followed. However, despite these shocks and his hatred of totalitarian government, he remained hopeful to the end that a workable form of "democratic socialism" would emerge following WWII.

With access to the Soviet archives becoming available in the 1990's, today it is clear Stalin did indeed seek to establish a communist puppet regime in Spain under his control, similar to those he later imposed in Eastern Europe through force of arms and duplicity in the immediate aftermath of WWII. A victorious Marxist revolutionary regime in Western Europe would have given the USSR and the cause of spreading international socialism considerable prestige. Spain was a prize with enormous geopolitical implications as well. With Spain as a base and control of the Straits of Gibraltar Stalin would have been able to project Soviet power over the Mediterranean, Middle East and Eastern Atlantic regions.

Apart from the war casualties themselves, the Spanish Civil War of 1936-38 led to numerous atrocities on all sides and the outright murder of several hundred thousand innocent, non-combatants by fascists and socialists. Spain thus witnessed the devastation that would shortly thereafter be repeated on the Eastern Front during WWII when communists and Nazis were again at each other's throats as rivals for supremacy over a vast part of the Eurasian land mass. The experience in both cases gives testimony to the monsters unleased in the clash of two totalitarian utopian ideologies.

Socialism Spreads into China, North Korea and Southeast Asia

It is now also known from Soviet archives that in the 1920's, following through on an earlier initiative by Lenin, the cunning Stalin dispatched Soviet Comintern agents to infiltrate a restive China in the throes of a chaotic, drawn-out revolution aimed at overthrowing the sclerotic vestiges of its despotic millennium-spanning monarchy.

Intervention in China's revolution at first by Lenin and then by Stalin's operatives during the 1920's and 1930's, initially supporting the Nationalists, then the emergent Chinese Communist Party (the "CCP "founded in 1921), led to the rapid rise of the Chinese counterpart to Stalin; namely, the ruthless, diabolical and sadistic Mao Zedong. Through treachery, torture and political murder on a vast scale, and the force of arms in a civil war that raged sporadically for over a decade, Mao became the absolute ruler over China's hundreds of million (now billion plus) inhabitants. As described by Samuel Huntington in his book *Political Order in Changing Societies*,[48] Mao followed Lenin's example to gain support of the citizenry, shrewdly shifting focus from the urban proletariat to China's rural peasantry after carefully researching it.

In rural China the margin between life and death was often precariously thin. Much of China's vast rural population was consigned to wretched poverty and did backbreaking work over long hours with primitive technologies to produce meager amounts of food for themselves. Even by standards of the day, their living conditions were nothing but atrocious. These poor farmers wanted land reform and were suffering greatly from the chaos caused by Japanese military incursions, roaming bandit gangs, and rapacious warlords. Such conditions made fertile ground for seeding the socialist message of land confiscation and redistribution by the CCP. Mao recognized that the grinding poverty, unjust landlordism, insecurity, and constant political turmoil in rural China would, with a focused organizational effort, allow the CCP to greatly broaden its base of popular support, and swell the ranks of its political cadres and revolutionary Red Army.[49] While the Soviet-backed Chinese Communists' Red Army under Mao's control was battling the competing Nationalist Chinese Kaomin-tang (KMT, aka Guomindang) Army for political supremacy, the Soviets were able to capitalize on the widespread chaos following Japan's WWII defeat to promote Mao. Stalin surreptitiously provided the funding and the political and military support necessary for Mao to eliminate his internal Communist Party rivals in the 1930's and ultimately triumph over the Nationalist Chinese army on the battlefield in 1948.

Would the CCP's victory usher in a new humanitarian era of greater caring for China's oppressed poor? Not including battlefield casualties, over the course of his 28-year rule and until his death in 1976, "Great Helmsman" Mao and the Chinese Communist Party killing machine he led were responsible for upwards of a mind-numbing 60 million Chinese deaths from direct murder (10 million), gulag "laogai" labor camps (20 million), and ideologically-induced famines, such as Mao's utopian "Great Leap Forward" (38-46 million). Bloodthirsty comrade Stalin was no doubt envious of Mao's cavalier attitude toward the deaths of so many. "It [the Great Leap Forward] was a fantastic dream, and it led to catastrophe for millions of people as famine followed euphoria."[50] Recall the aforementioned statement Mao wrote in his Little Red Book that members of the Party are the "seeds" while the common people are the "soil." Indeed, under his directives the common peoples' lives were crushed with just such arrogant and incredibly callous distain! Mao is reported to have blithely said in 1957 "We are willing to sacrifice 300 million Chinese for the victory of the world revolution," and in 1958, "...half of China may well have to die. If not half, one-third, or one tenth —50 million die,"[51] Mao's record of mass murder makes these chilling quotes all too credible.

Then there is Korea. During the late 1940's, Stalin backed another hand-picked ruler, the ruthless Kim Il Sung in formerly Japanese-occupied northern Korea thus beginning what would become a murderous North Korean communist family dynasty, which continues to this day despite, apart from the Korean War, killing as many as two million of its own people. The Korean War pitted the Stalin-backed North Korean army allied with Mao's People's Liberation Army against the South Korean Army and its Western allies deployed under UN auspices, most notably the U.S.

The Korean conflict was an opening salvo of the hot "Cold War" fought to contain and prevent communism from consuming all of Asia. It succeeded in preventing the total conquest of Korea by communist force of arms, ending in a military stalemate that eventually enabled a new democratic capitalist nation to become established and dramatically flourish in South Korea, but a nation that is still under threat from the dangerous totalitarian regime in the North. Today, nowhere on the planet can one find a clearer, more stark comparison between the systems of Marx's socialism and that of democratic capitalism. The Korean Peninsula's very heavily fortified 150-mile DMZ (Demilitarized Zone) roughly following the 38th parallel (38 degrees latitude), marks the division of the peninsula into the two entirely separate Koreas. Indeed, the north and south are two entirely different universes; one totalitarian and very poor, the other, free and very prosperous. The DMZ is a very deadly East Asian version of the USSR's now defunct Iron Curtain that separated Eastern Europe and its peoples from Western Europe. Essentially, it is a physical barrier with armed patrols that prevents escape southward from a state that is a vast prison. One need only look at the night satellite images of the Korean Peninsula from space to see the obvious contrast in how well people live under the two systems. North Korea, The Kims' "Democratic Peoples' Republic of Korea" (DPRK), is truly the epitome of a dark dystopia. The harrowing stories of those few who have been able to escape from North Korea and describe life there underscore the Kim regime's unlimited capacity for totalitarian evil.[52]

Soon following the end of WWII and the Japanese military occupation, the Vietnamese Communist Party, under the leadership of Ho Chi Minh (born Nguyen Sinh Cung), began a war to drive the French colonial era government from Vietnam. Decades earlier, at the conclusion of WWI during the 1919 Versailles peace talks Ho had sought self-determination for the Vietnamese people in what was then called French Indochina. Ironically, Ho became a communist in France in 1921 after becoming imbued with Marxist revolutionary fervor in that wonderful "City of Light" Paris. After his return to Vietnam, and with the defeat of Japan, his revolution against French rule gained the support of both the Soviet Union and China.

Ultimately, Ho Chi Minh and his successors were able to drive out the French in 1954, and in 1976, the United States which was seeking to "contain" the threat of communism spreading throughout Southeast Asia. The loss of Vietnam to communism in the 1970's was regarded as a major setback for the U.S. in the Cold War. With the continuing Soviet threat hanging over Europe, in following its global strategy known as "containment" in Vietnam, as in Korea, the U.S. sought to prevent the further spread of an ideology inherently hostile to democracy and freedom, not to supplant the French or Japanese as another imperialist colonial ruler.

As the former 60's radical David Horowitz points out in his autobiography, *Radical Son*, The American Left's opposition to the Vietnam War arose more from its antagonism toward America, than from any real desire to help the Vietnamese people, though its members claimed otherwise. Some truly wanted a Marxist regime to prevail, while others simply wanted the U.S. to lose in order to aid their goal to turn American politics, especially in the Democratic Party, radically leftward, a goal their aging remnants and a new generation of disciples continue to pursue.

In retrospect, the Vietnam War, waged in a limited fashion by a U.S. under poor leadership, and hamstrung by political opposition to it within the U.S., was perhaps as much or more a struggle for national unity and independence for the Vietnamese, than it was a significant event for the West in the 45-year contest of ideologies – the Cold War. Installation of the communist regime nevertheless triggered an exodus from the areas it had conquered as it began a campaign to round up and "re-educate" those sympathetic to the losing side. Note that the term "re-education" has very sinister implications; you may be tortured, shot, hacked, bludgeoned or starved to death, or perhaps buried alive if you do not totally submit. The hundreds of thousands of fleeing refugees in this infamous episode became known as the "Boat People." Vietnam has steadfastly remained a one-party communist controlled enterprise ever since, seeking to build its own brand of socialism, but, unlike North Korea and Cuba, its government has undertaken many pragmatic economic and social reforms leading to growth and greater opportunity for its people.[53]

The Failed Communist Coup Attempt in Indonesia

In 1965 and 1966, communism was ruthlessly suppressed

after a coup attempt in Indonesia, a large nation of 6,000 inhabited islands with over 250 million inhabitants. Some 85 percent of the population is Muslim, but the nation is otherwise very diverse both ethnically and linguistically.

Indonesia's paroxysm of violence ultimately resulted in the virtual annihilation of the PKI, the Indonesian Communist Party. Large-scale violence followed the seizure of certain Muslim-owned lands by communists and the brutal murder of six high-ranking generals in the Indonesian army. But the communist coup attempt failed when a general named Suharto seized the reins of government from the communist-sympathizing Sukarno in a countercoup. Sukarno had previously led the country's struggle for independence against the colonialist Dutch and British. Soon after the counter coup a combination of the Indonesian military, Islamic groups, and local paramilitary units scattered throughout the islands began the indiscriminate murder of communists in much the same manner as the Bolsheviks and Chinese Communist Party had murdered political rivals when seizing power. It is believed that the anti-communist purge resulted in at least 500,000 killings, and perhaps as many as a million or more.

By way of background, the Indonesian Communist Party was founded in 1914 by a Dutch European Indonesian attempting to import the revolutionary Marxist ideology of Lenin and the Russian Bolsheviks. The PKI never counted more than about three million Indonesians among its members or less than 2% of the population. Nevertheless, Lenin's Bolshevik example of the 1917 Russian Revolution opened the possibility of a small but ruthless and determined communist vanguard seizing control of a large country, particularly one experiencing widespread poverty, hunger, and social unrest. This was the situation during the colonial period and later under Sukarno's rule.

By 1965, with Sukarno's help, the PKI had penetrated

much of the national government, finally leading to Suharto's counter coup. Like the Spanish Civil War, the Indonesian upheaval drew in world powers representing contesting ideologies, but this time with only their indirect, non-military involvement. The PKI was supported politically by Mao, while Suharto and the military faction drew support from Western powers, including the U.S.

No one will ever know what terrible actions the communists would have taken to transform Indonesian society into a socialist state had their coup succeeded. The calamity of Stalin's Russia and Mao's China had already become widely known by the 1960's. It is difficult to justify, in any moral sense, a military coup as the lesser of two evils. However, the violent reaction to and suppression of the communists in Indonesia during that brief period undoubtedly avoided the specter of a much worse, longer-term fate for the nation and its citizens.

The Killing Fields of Cambodia

Unlike the outcome in Indonesia, Mao's support during the early 1970's enabled the barbaric Pol Pot (born Saloth Sar), leader of the Khmer Rouge, to become the communist totalitarian ruler of Cambodia. It was in Cambodia that the socialist beast demonstrated its greatest potential for butchery in a four-year orgy of executions and deliberate starvation. Between 1975 and 1979 Pol Pot and his fellow butchers instituted a massive campaign of death today known as the infamous "Killing Fields," which wiped-out an estimated one to two million or more of their countrymen, women and children.[54]

This amounted to the deaths of one-quarter to as much as one-third of all Cambodians at the hands of the Khmer Rouge! On a personal note, it was after meeting a survivor of the Killing Fields that I decided to expand my inquiry into that horrendous episode of Hell on Earth, and then to write this book. Among other things, this survivor related the fate he and his family had suffered, including beatings, forced starvation, and outright murder, and reminded me that whether openly or from the shadows, communists still control China, North Korea, Cambodia, Vietnam, Laos, and other countries in which attempts at political opposition to one-party rule are crushed by police state apparatuses.

Stalin Outwits His Western Counterparts During World War II

During the final phases of World War II from 1943-1945, Stalin had millions of "boots on the ground" in Eastern Europe as a result of the Soviet Army's campaign to defeat, drive out and supplant Germany's Wehrmacht as an occupier. He was able to charm, outwit, and outmaneuver his Western Ally counterparts, the arrogant, and physically depleted American President, Franklin Roosevelt, along with Harry Truman, and Winston Churchill, at the critically important Allied conferences in Tehran, Yalta, and Potsdam that would shape the post-War World. On the geopolitical stage, none of them were a match for the guile, skillful planning, and ruthless intransigence of Stalin. Sympathetic with Stalin's demands, and seemingly convinced he could elicit his good will by being solicitous, Roosevelt sold out Poland (which had been raped twice-over by Stalin and Hitler) and numerous other Eastern European nations to ultimate Soviet control. He barely made any attempt at all to negotiate for their future. Instead, his feeble and maladroit actions sealed the fate of many millions of Eastern Europeans for generations until the USSR finally collapsed. Given carte blanche to his aggression by Roosevelt at Tehran and Yalta, Stalin gained iron-fisted control not only over the eastern half of a defeated Germany, but also over a vast part of Eastern Europe stretching from the Baltic to the Black Sea.

In addition, Roosevelt's famous "Lend-Lease" program,

originally sold to Congress as aide for Great Britain, was quickly and quietly converted by him into a blank check giveaway Stalin eagerly used to obtain nearly endless quantities of top-grade military supplies, fuel, industrial machines, and blueprints for secret proprietary technologies from the United States. Many American-source tanks, airplanes, trucks, jeeps, small arms, and other supplies were not just used against Germany, they were also used by the Soviet Red Army to overrun, occupy, and enforce Soviet rule on Eastern Europe. An ultimately unanswerable question is whether Stalin's Red Army would have been able to expand its footprint and control to such an extent without America's capitalist largesse placed at its disposal.

As though Roosevelt's and Harry Hopkins' (his top aide and closest confidant) unrestrained sympathies for Stalin's communist regime were not bad enough (a generous but less plausible interpretation of the record is that they were living in denial), we now know that the Roosevelt Administration was laced with high-placed, influential agents reporting to Stalin's NKVD. We also know that several scientists in the U.S. Manhattan Project were communist-sympathizing spies who stole technical Atomic bomb secrets for the Soviet Union, hastening its development of nuclear weapons with which it could, and did, challenge the West. Regrettably, an addle-brained, careless, and Left-leaning Roosevelt Administration helped midwife a communist Soviet superpower during WW II that became a menace to America and the rest of the Free World, having never softened its self-proclaimed Marxist-Leninist hostility toward the capitalist West[55]

To briefly digress from the European outcome, of perhaps even greater and longer lasting . geopolitical and human significance was the consequence of the Roosevelt Administration's negotiation malfeasance for East Asia. At the final wartime Allies' Conference in Potsdam the U.S. and Great

Britain were designated to take the surrender and oversee the repatriation of Japanese occupying armies in the southern halves of Korea and Vietnam respectively. The Soviet Union, a last second entrant into the war against Japan, was given control of the Japanese surrender in Manchuria and northern Korea, and the Chinese, under Chiang Kai-shek, titular control of northern Vietnam. With his nose thus under the tent, Stalin proceeded to invade and loot Manchuria and provide vast military supplies he had recently seized from the defeated Japanese to Mao's Chinese communist army (ironically relabeled the "Peoples' Liberation Army"), which were of particular importance in turning Mao's civil war with Chiang Kai-shek's forces in his favor. As it had in Europe, in Manchuria Stalin's Red Army left a trail of massive war crime atrocities in its wake.

The War's endgame had created a military and political vacuum on the world stage the U.S. political leadership was ill-prepared to deal with, but the hardened communists led by Stalin and Mao, were all too eager to fill. For Korea and Vietnam, Potsdam had left unresolved the tricky questions of unification, ending French colonial rule (in Indochina), and the formation of legitimate civilian governments. Consequently, these geographic divisions set the stage for bitter drawn-out military conflicts to follow in those two nations, both involving the U.S., as indigenous communist forces with the strong military and political backing of Stalin's USSR and Mao's CCP (fresh from his military victory over Chiang Kai-shek in 1948) established communist governments whose armies soon launched attacks against Western backed non-communist forces in the south.

To this day the world is living with the consequences of war-time agreements and decisions orchestrated by Stalin and botched by American and British government leaders. The assertion of a total victory by the Western Allies in achieving their World War II aims has largely gone unquestioned in

Western history texts. It is based on the utter defeat and post-War democratization of the Axis nations, Germany, Italy and Japan, and the subsequent de-colonialization of politically repressed and exploitative European and Japanese "colonies" which had been the product of imperialist conquest. No one should question the significance of that achievement. However, as significant as it was, it is in no way a sufficient basis for a realistic full accounting of the global struggle between the forces of freedom and democracy, and those representing totalitarianism.

With insights drawn from archival sources, and aided by the passage of time, historians are now better able to dispassionately assess how the geopolitical outcomes negotiated and fought for affected the fates of vast numbers of people in China, Indochina, and Eastern Europe, not just those in the Soviet Union and so-called "Free World." Regrettably, in the post-war era contest of ideologies the global cause of "building socialism" so near and dear to Stalin's heart, and which he had relentlessly fought for, spread around the globe, and placed the cause of freedom for all peoples on the defensive. In the Cold War decades following WWII the cause of creating a socialist world by revolution, originally sparked by the words of Karl Marx and Friedrich Engels in their mid-Nineteenth Century *Communist Manifesto*, and first put into real life practice by Lenin and Stalin in the Soviet Union, led to the rise of a line of brutal dictators who studied and followed their example in Asia, Africa and Latin America, as well as Europe.

Stalin's Long Shadow and the Denouement of the Soviet Socialist Empire

Until the implosion of the USSR in 1991, the many nations then behind Stalin's Cold War "Iron Curtain" (the enforced line of military and political control dividing the communist East from the free democratic West) were forcibly cut off from contact with the West by Moscow-controlled puppet regimes.

Within this vast geopolitical prison compliance of the puppet regimes with Soviet demands was enforced by Stalin's agents and the menacing Soviet military machine standing ready to invade, as it did in East Germany (1953), Hungary (1956) and Czechoslovakia (1968).

Stalin installed the Leninist model of totalitarian government in these subjugated countries, a process described comprehensively in *The Iron Curtain*.[56] This authenticated history was written in 2012 by Anne Applebaum, who was able to access both Soviet and Eastern European archives unavailable to historians before 1990. For example, in her book we learn that to terrorize the populace into compliance by purging any opposition, in 1948-1949 Stalin ordered a major wave of arrests in Poland, Romania, Czechoslovakia, and the Baltic states comparable to his Great Terror in the USSR of 1937-1938. The wave of atrocities killed approximately 700,000 people and imprisoned many more. Also, pitiless mass deportations of large ethnic populations in these subjugated countries were carried out as soon as Soviet occupation began, pulling hundreds of thousands out of their traditional homelands, along with the uncompensated loss of all their property. To further ensure the imposed Socialist society would never be challenged, the communists took complete control of the most valuable institutions, even rewriting history textbooks and hand-picking teachers, and suppressing all religious institutions in these ancient Eastern European nations.

In the 1950's, Soviet Communists further extended their influence into Latin America, Africa and the Middle East, sometimes secretly, and at other times by overtly fomenting and arming revolutions. Their goal was to overthrow corrupt dictatorial regimes in the so-called "Third World" and replace them with communist dictators. They succeeded in Cuba, Nicaragua, Angola, the Congo, and several other countries. Soviet funds and arms were used in the effort, and at times,

Cuban soldiers. Before its yoke was thrown off by massive, spontaneous civil disobedience in Eastern Europe and the USSR, the ideological monster of socialism therefore spread misery and despair across much of the globe, with proliferation of secret police, gulags, and Killing Fields. A planetary human catastrophe of unimaginable scale had been created in less than half a century!

As word leaked out of Soviet Russia concerning Stalin's enormous atrocities, and as he dragged Eastern Europe into the giant maw of a totalitarian regime at the end of World War II, the West was forced at last to acknowledge the awful nature of the monster, a monster at least partly of its own creation considering the pivotal and inspirational role played by the historical precedent of the French Jacobins and the writings of Karl Marx. Awakened to this utopian threat to freedom and democracy, the West fought the forty-five-year Cold War to contain the further spread of Marx's socialism and Stalinist and Maoist clones. This included military conflicts in Korea, Vietnam, Cambodia, Laos, Cuba, and Nicaragua, and Soviet military incursions into East Germany, Hungary, Czechoslovakia, and Afghanistan. Only through the monumental efforts of the Western powers, the unbending commitment to human freedom, and the meeting of force with force was the further global spread of the murderous socialist holocaust halted.

The end of the Cold War was initiated by a groundswell of freedom beginning in the early 1980's in Poland that burst forth fully in 1989. Ironically, it was Marx's "oppressed workers" themselves who challenged the authority of the communist overlords. In a word, the Soviet empire imploded. The dysfunctional socialist regimes in Eastern Europe and the Soviet Union were abruptly dismantled by their own citizenry and the socialist leadership pushed into the shadows.[57]

Faced with growing public dissatisfaction over its domestic and foreign failures, and without a Stalin on hand, the Soviet

Communist Party leadership had lost some of its ruthlessness, making it incapable of the sustained brutality and internal terror needed to crush growing dissent and keep the diseased socialist empire it had created alive. Nevertheless, despite the rapid collapse of socialist regimes in Eastern Europe, the dissolution of the so-called Union of Soviet Socialist Republics between 1989 and 1991, and the cataclysmic geopolitical sea change that resulted, reports of communism's final demise have been highly exaggerated and premature. The ruthless totalitarian zeal of Socialist Utopianism remains undiminished among many remaining adherents whose hands are still around the throat of the peoples of China, North Korea, Vietnam, Laos, and Cuba. In the past 20 years alone, socialism's tentacles have also spread through Castro's agents into Venezuela, just as they did into several other Latin American countries in the 1970's and 80's, most notably Nicaragua. More recently Mexico, Uruguay, Ecuador, Peru, and Bolivia have shown signs of socialists' growing political power.

Like a deadly virus that spreads silently and cannot be seen or felt until it is too late, blind faith in the promises made by socialist leaders persists in many places, and therefore socialism itself may prove impossible to eradicate completely despite it being thoroughly debunked in both theory and practice. Free people everywhere must therefore be forever vigilant and steadfastly confront the Monster each time it rises anew like an insidious phoenix from history's ashes to regain control over the lives of millions both in societies where it had been vanquished and in many new places. Were that to happen, it would inevitably empower a new generation of ruthless dictators coveting absolute power above all else. Mankind must never again allow Reason to slumber, otherwise monsters from the dark side of human nature will again wreak havoc on the world.

Revolution, Right or Wrong?

Causes and Confounding Difficulties

Considering the forgoing history and prospects of continued contagion, we must inquire as to the preconditions that set the stage for the socialist-inspired revolutions and civil wars that resulted in such an immense human toll.

It is obvious that much of the reason for the rise of socialism can be traced to a legacy of unjust governments in many parts of the world – governments in which political power was concentrated in the hands of a privileged few who had inherited wealth and vast landholdings, and who treated many of their citizens arbitrarily and unjustly, repressed freedom, and showed little if any regard for individual rights and the general public well-being. It has long been observed that revolutionary movements do not often have their origins or spontaneously arise in healthy, just societies in which widespread discontent has not been fostered. In truth, Louis XVI's 1780's France was a swamp of poverty, oppression, and anachronistic feudal privilege. The Jacobin leaders of the French Revolution were perhaps the first who sought to justify organized political murder and mass terror on the basis that it was necessary to achieve the noble utopian end of social and economic justice. But it would be events of the early 20th Century that would fully reveal to the world the vast scale of absolute evil made possible by the moral contradictions inherent in utopian political movements.

In his famous Long Telegram of 1946, the U.S. statesman George Kennan prophetically wrote: "World Communism is like a malignant parasite which feeds only on diseased flesh."[58] Indeed, it was the spread of truly liberal values during the first half of the 20th Century, and consequently, recognition that monarchism and colonialism with their manifold injustices were illegitimate and collapsing, that provided much diseased flesh for communism to feast on. What was not foreseen at the time by Kennan or others, was the inevitable decay and collapse of the socialist states created by the Communist Party, and this only 70 years after the founding Bolsheviks had feasted on the rotting Russian monarchy.

Winston Churchill wrote his classic work *The River War* in 1905, a dozen years before the Russian Revolution. The book concerned the conflict involving the British, Egyptians and the Arabs of the Sudan in the late 1800's. Churchill, always the astute observer of human affairs, eloquently describes the explosive preconditions of injustice and oppression that allowed the fanatical Mahdi to seize power and institute his brand of Theocratic Utopia:

> Few facts are so encouraging to the student of human develop-
> ment as the desire, which most men and all communities manifest
> at all times, to associate with their actions at least the appearance
> of moral right. However distorted may be their conceptions of vir-
> tue, however feeble their efforts to attain even to their own ideals,
> it is a pleasing feature and a hopeful augury that they should wish
> to be justified. No community embarks on a great enterprise with-
> out fortifying itself with the belief that from some points of view
> its motives are lofty and disinterested. It is an involuntary tribute,
> the humble tribute of imperfect beings, to the eternal temples of
> Truth and Beauty. The sufferings of a people or a class may be
> intolerable, but before they will take up arms and risk their lives
> some unselfish and impersonal spirit must animate them...The
> French Communists might plead that they upheld the rights of
> man. The desert tribes proclaimed that they fought for the glory
> of God. But although the force of fanatical passion is far greater
> than that exerted by any philosophical belief, its sanction is just
> the same. It gives men something which they think is sublime to
> fight for, and this serves them as an excuse for wars which it is
> desirable to begin for totally different reasons.[59]

Churchill was convinced that misery and feelings of powerlessness helped trigger the bloodshed of the Mahdi, not just religious fanaticism alone. Similar preconditions set the stage for utopian catastrophes of immense scale in the 20th Century. Revolutions feed on injustice, unpopular wars, social disorder and widespread hunger. There is a saying that has been attributed to the French Revolution "No bread equals no laws, equals no liberty." Understandably, desperate people will sacrifice their freedom for the promise of food. Pre-industrial agrarian societies in which legacy ownership of farmland was highly concentrated in huge estates, and non-owner peasants treated like feudal serfs working the land in grinding poverty were ripe for revolution. As Kennan confirmed in 1946, much of the rise of socialism during the past century can be traced to a legacy of unjust governments – governments in which political power was concentrated in the hands of a privileged few, with little opportunity for gain in social status for all others. Arguably, such conditions still exist in certain corners of the world today and must be remedied lest they give rise to a repeat of the morally barren and disastrous socialist experiments of the past century.

It is also true that nations which suffered humiliating military defeats and/or foreign colonial occupation and rule became fertile ground for revolutionary activity. Such is the history of Russia with the complete defeat of its Czarist military early in WWI; harsh penalties imposed on Germany by the Versailles Treaty that ended WWI; China with its sovereignty compromised by its weak emperor and subject to exploitation by European powers; Southeast Asia long subjected to exploitative French colonial rule; monarchical Ethiopia conquered by Fascist Italy; and so on.

Frustrated and resentful, the well-educated elites in these countries often became the vanguard in organizing revolution. They found in Marx's socialism and Lenin's and Stalin's derivative works an animating message of revolution to restore national pride and achieve greater social justice on their own terms, free from foreign domination. Lenin well understood

126 ■ Some Call it Utopia

this to be a weakness of the European powers of that time, and cleverly wrote a book titled *Imperialism, the Highest Stage of Capitalism* in 1916, in which he characterized territorial colonialism as an inevitable by-product of the so-called "Great Power's" capitalism, as a result of which they were attempting to divvy-up and enslave the "have-not" nations of the world. Lenin's ready solution for those subject to such exploitation was of course revolutionary socialism, which later under Stalin became a principal export of the Soviet Union along with weapons to arm the revolutionaries, guerrilla warfare advisors, and intelligence gathered by his NKVD/KGB spies.

Unjust monarchies, exploitative colonial empires, and other forms of despotic governments that abused their subjects have made fertile seed beds for the rise of ruthless and cunning political movements. Sadly, those seeking to supplant such governments with utopias usually are no less despotic and tend to be far worse in other ways. Nature abhors a vacuum, and thus totalitarian utopians feed on social disorder. Revolutionary organizations find it easy to attract and impassion with righteous indignation a large following among society's alienated and disaffected, particularly those who believe they have nothing to lose. If only we could have justice...If only everyone were equal...If only we were in control...These are the things they are willing to commit increasingly violent acts to achieve. These are the emotions socialists can exploit with their simple-sounding, seemingly noble promise to equalize society and ensure an equal share for everyone. Such was case before the revolutions in Russia, China, Cuba and elsewhere, as well as the Spanish Civil War.

Victor Hugo, author of the classic *Les Miserables* stated: "When dictatorship is a fact, revolution becomes a right." Yet, as John Adams warned in 1818 after reflecting upon the American Revolution, "Revolutions are no trifles...they ought never to be undertaken rashly; nor without deliberate

Consideration and sober Reflection; nor without a solid, immutable eternal formulation of Justice and Humanity; not without a People possessed of Intelligence, Fortitude and Integrity..."[60] Unfortunately, these conditions rarely ever exist, which is a dilemma. Absent them, violent revolutions lead to widespread mob violence, gangsterism, executions, and dictatorship by those most ruthless in taking power and imposing their version of the ideal social order. So, when can revolution be the right path?

Denial of the universal rights of man, such as self-determination, freedom from enslavement, and freedom of speech and religion, can justify overthrowing an un-democratic, oppressive regime, particularly one that fails at least to keep its people from starving. Revolution is the process of causing a dramatic forcible change of governmental structure into a new system that presumably better serves the general welfare, and there have been many armed revolutions, revolts, coup attempts, and civil wars throughout history. In just the past 250 years, revolutions against European monarchical colonial rule in the Western Hemisphere, Asia, as well as monarchies in Europe gave birth to new societies with new systems of political order on those continents, many of which are today democratic and free. However, the validity of John Adams' admonition was amply demonstrated in the 20th Century by the outcomes of revolutions led by a merciless communist vanguard seeking to overthrow moribund monarchies in Russia, China and Cambodia. There have been numerous other revolutions in modern times that also failed to bring freedom and prosperity to the people. The 1950's revolution led by Fidel Castro in Cuba that replaced the corrupt dictator, Fulgencio Batista, with a communist regime is an example. More recently, one can point to the disappointing results of the 2010 "Arab Spring," and Daniel Ortega's rise to dictatorship years after a civil war was fought in Nicaragua.

But revolution is not an end in itself, notwithstanding Leon Trotsky's and Mao's doctrines of continuous revolution. In addressing the question of "revolution, right or wrong?" it must be recognized that one cannot replace something (existing structure and authority) with nothing, unless the goal is perpetual chaos. Critical follow-up questions must then be answered: Who will lead the revolution and decide to what end it is striving, and how does one know the true aspirations of the people affected by the revolution? Will those bent on seizing power embrace the seductive but intellectually arrogant Hegelian notion that the world can be designed according to their will's desire as opposed to honestly representing the will of the people? As described by Lichtheim in *The Origins of Socialism*, Hegel maintained first that "the material world can be completely understood" and thus "can and must be transformed by human direction, so that it is a creation of the human spirit" and second, that rather than communities benefiting from individuals who behave reasonably, "in order to determine what is beneficial to individuals...the ultimate truth about history, society, man and nature" grasped by a select few must guide everyone's actions because "the whole [society] is greater than the sum of its parts."[61] Given obvious human limitations, Hegelian preconditions for an ideal community are impossible to fulfill, and so, too often in a revolution does the will of a select few "guide" the people into a disaster far worse than their previous condition.

Like "just war" theories, the moral issue of "revolution, right or wrong?" must also consider both means and ends, both during revolution and afterward. This raises yet additional questions. With what moral principles is the revolution carried out? Is the process itself, though violent, just, or will it stop at nothing: looting, property destruction, political murder, torture, arbitrary arrest and imprisonment? What form of government of greater efficacy and morality, more respectful of its citizens' right to basic freedoms and self-determination, will supplant the previous regime or will there simply be anarchy and terror?

Sadly, once passions are inflamed to the point of undertaking violent revolutionary action, Reason may recede and thus fail to keep in check the human impulses toward predatory envy, arbitrary and excessive force, vengeance, and concentration of power. Such impulses further enable a self-selected few to dictate the terms of existence for all those brought under their sway after sweeping aside those who are pacific by nature and believe in constitutional law and democracy.

The pessimistic and all too often accurate view of what revolutions may produce is represented by the Russian dissident Vladimir Bukovsky:

> Revolutions usually occur when real poverty and deprivation of rights are long gone, but accumulated hatred and mistrust of the authorities render every reform unacceptable and insufficient. In such circumstances an indecisive or inept government is a sure guarantee of revolution.
>
> Expecting justice or freedom from a revolution is incredibly naïve. Every social upheaval brings the worst dregs of society to the fore, and 'those who were nothing, will become everything.' A revolution promotes the most cruel, ignoble, bloodthirsty people with strong despotic personalities. Predatory chieftains. After a fierce civil strife the most ruthless and cunning of them concentrates all power in his hands. That is, revolutions always end in tyranny, not freedom and justice.[62]

It is difficult for even well-intended revolutionary leaders not to become morally compromised as they seek the power to first prevail and then maintain their hold on the apparatuses of government. As the French philosopher Andre Glucksmann aptly noted, a revolution to overthrow an existing authority requires more centralization of command, greater secrecy, greater discipline, and greater ruthlessness than the regime it seeks to destroy, spawning power-seeking "Doctor Strangeloves all over the planet, even in the remotest townlets of Asia and Africa."[63] Moderate elements are usually less willing to either concentrate power and/or act with total ruthlessness, and so are seldom able to keep from being swept aside or eliminated by radical violent elements willing to make the most alluring but empty promises. Reflecting on his disenchantment with the Bolsheviks he supported, the socialist author Maxim Gorky was prophetic in 1917 when he wrote in *Untimely Thoughts*:

> Lenin and Trotsky, and all the others who are accompanying them to their ruin in the quagmire of reality... dishonor the revolution and dishonor the working class by forcing it to organize bloody slaughter and by inciting it to outrages and the arresting of innocent people...Imagining themselves to be the Napoleons of socialism, the Leninists rant and rave, completing the destruction of Russia. The Russian people will pay for this with lakes of blood.[64]

In the Introduction to his book *Reflections on the Failure of Socialism*, the former prominent communist Max Eastman wrote:

> Armed seizure of power by a highly organized minority party, whether in the name of the Dictatorship of the Proletariat, the Glory of Rome, the Supremacy of the Nordics, or any other slogan that may be invented, and no matter how ingeniously integrated with the masses of the population, will normally lead to the totalitarian state. 'Totalitarian state' is merely the modern name for tyranny.[65]

Comparison of the American and French Revolutions

Mankind can certainly be thankful to the American and French Revolutions for inspiring new and better modes of civilization. These revolutions spawned democracy, egalitarianism, and freedom from monarchical rule through signal statements such as the American colonies' Declaration of Independence, the United States' Bill of Rights, and France's Declaration of the Rights of Man and Citizen. These declared that a nation's citizens naturally possess equal rights. However, there were significant differences in revolutionary outcomes, as their similar statements of human rights were treated very differently in the two societies.

In America, under the English tradition, the rights to life, liberty, and pursuit of happiness were enshrined in a written constitution to protect individual citizens from political interference in their lives, and much autonomy was left in the hands of each of the now unified colonial states. What had motivated the colonists to come to America in the first place with all the risks the migration entailed? Perhaps it was as much to escape interference by political power in their lives, including their religious beliefs, as the opportunity for betterment. Checks and balances preventing concentration of power in a single authority was a key principle in their formula for self-determination. While in France, Rousseau's chimera of natural human equality beckoned irresistibly to discontented, nascent revolutionaries, together with a simple promise of bread for those of lowest station. Rather than rights of its citizens being a restraint on collective authority, the Revolution's central government in Paris assumed an affirmative duty to ensure the equalized welfare of all, which led it to bring all of France and all Frenchmen firmly under its sway, in some cases by use of deadly force; no less a concentration of power than under the deposed Monarch, Louis the XVI.

Nonetheless, unable to satisfy the wants of the masses, its national Constituent Assembly was soon cast aside as democratic debate and consent of the governed yielded to the radical Jacobins, their leader Robespierre, and the Reign of Terror under the crushing weight of intractable economic realities. As the Polish historian and philosopher Leszek

Kolakowski posits in *Main Currents of Marxism,* "objective economic laws cannot be overruled by decrees and violence. An example of this is the Jacobin dictatorship...regarded [by Marxists] as a dictatorship of the proletariat. The Terror was supposed to smash profiteering and keep up the revolutionary enthusiasm of the masses, but it only brought fear and disillusionment."[66]

To explain such sharply different outcomes in America and France it must first be recognized that prerevolution economic conditions in the two countries were very different. The relatively egalitarian American colonies had fertile land for the taking (from indigenous peoples), and with their legacy of citizens' rights and common law had come to enjoy a widespread prosperity that resulted from the freedom to pursue opportunities, in contrast to the hand-to-mouth conditions, medieval social stratification, and tenant agriculture common in France and throughout continental Europe. Paradoxically however, in France popular discontent was rising while its common people were becoming more prosperous in the decades before its Revolution. Perhaps, as Tocqueville concluded, ironically, a time of gradual improvement is the most perilous for government.

Secondly, as Hannah Arendt observes in her wonderful 1963 history *On Revolution,* pre-revolution America was governed by the British form of limited monarchy, whereas the French labored under a millennial legacy of absolute rule. She argues that this much different political starting point helps explain the absolutist direction the French Revolution took.

Thirdly, there were basic differences in the Revolutions' animating ideas and ideals. Rousseau had had a profound effect upon the intellectual class of France. Those who spearheaded the French Revolution were without a doubt highly influenced by the conception of society Rousseau so eloquently presented, whereas their American counterparts, men such as Thomas

Jefferson, John Adams, Benjamin Franklin, and Alexander Hamilton, drew their inspiration more from the branch of the Enlightenment liberalism represented by David Hume, John Locke, and Adam Smith. As I explained earlier in discussing socialism's origins, Rousseau's theories asserting that: a) the evils of society are caused by property ownership and social influences rather than innate human frailties and instincts, b) all people have not just equal rights, but a natural right to an equal share regardless of the inequality of what they produce, and c) a "general will" of the nation exists not determined by vote, set the stage for Robespierre, the Jacobin Reign of Terror, anti-religious fervor, and the rise of a proto-socialist dictatorship in France.

Fourth, there were cultural differences, not all of which are Rousseau's influence. I refer here to the difference between the essentially Anglo-British culture adapted to the colonies, and that of the French people and their institutions. For example, the largely Protestant American colonists were devoted to freedom of religion, whereas during the Revolution the French embraced freedom from religion including the Church as an institution. Although it can be manipulated to a degree in the short term, the persistent influences of culture on political institutions and outcomes, including its ability to ride through turbulent times, can easily be underestimated.

Fifth, in America government had always been decentralized, whereas in France whoever ruled Paris, ruled all of France, and of course taking control of Paris and ruling from that seat of power was the key to its Revolution. Paris had grown to become the commercial as well as cultural and administrative center of all France – the sun all planets orbited around. In contrast, without a dominant power center, the United States was formed democratically as a union of separately governed colonial states. From the very start this curbed the formation of a dominant central government. Its states together covered a geographic area considerably larger than France, most of which was outside of its coastal cities, sparsely populated, and for all practical purposes, a terra incognita inhabited mainly by indigenous peoples, except for a scattering of pioneer settlements.

Sixth, France was subject to military threats from hostile states at its borders, whereas America enjoyed the geographic buffer of the Atlantic Ocean, and a sparsely populated Canada to the north. The British had to twice learn that projecting power across that expansive water body to subdue the upstart American republic whilst preoccupied with their European rivalries was a bridge too far.

Clearly, these widely differing, pre-existing economic, political, cultural, and geo-political conditions must have had a great deal to do with the dramatic contrast between the American and French Revolutions, particularly their immediate political outcomes.

Leaders of the American Revolution succeeded in establishing a new nation and new form of government for their colonist citizens based on the principles of liberty (including especially religious freedom given their Protestant background), equal rights and justice through the rule of law, and consent of the governed with democratic checks and balances on the use of power to prevent government from doing its tyrannical worst. However, the American Revolution did not directly lead to the abolition of slavery and acceptance of Blacks as equal citizens, thereby leaving a large population in its midst unable to protest and escape its unjust misery. Nor did it account for indigenous peoples, the Native Americans, who after being ravaged by disease, were being dislocated by a flood of immigrants in a war of overwhelming numbers and technology they could not win. In that sense the American Revolution failed to fully satisfy its stated ideals, notably for those of its inhabitants who were oppressed or otherwise excluded from citizenship.

We should, however, bear in mind the historical context in which the political ideals of freedom, self-determination, and equality were being framed for the first time in human history. In the year of the American Revolution, 1776, and for millennia before that, worldwide, personal freedom as we know it was very much the exception, while slavery and other forms of human exploitation such as indentured servitude and serfdom were the rule for most human beings. Real freedom, where it existed at all, was the rare exception. Democracy based upon equal human rights, was only just beginning to emerge in a very limited manner. Slave trading involving people of all races had had a very, very long history in Europe, the Near East, Asia, and Africa. Various indigenous peoples of the "New World" were also known to have slaves, typically captured in warfare, and were at times themselves enslaved by European colonists. Moreover, at the time of the American Revolution, slavery involving importation of captured Africans had become widespread within the Western Hemisphere, especially in the Caribbean islands and Brazil, for work at sugar plantations, and in other parts of colonial Latin America, in addition to the American South. Great Britain, France, Spain, Portugal, and the Netherlands all had a hand in importing African slaves into the colonies. Because it was so extensive and lucrative, the practice of slavery was not completely outlawed in the Western Hemisphere until the mid to late 1800's.

In America it took a very bloody civil war, three constitutional amendments in the mid-1800's, and finally enactment of legislative reforms in the mid-twentieth century to establish equal citizenship for America's Blacks. It cannot be denied that the product of Black slaves' labor, like that of slaves everywhere, was stolen by those who "owned" them or otherwise profited from their enslavement. Instead, like slaves from time immemorial, they were treated as mere "property" with economic value, not persons, which could be bought, sold, and abused. All the while that slavery was perversely cloaked in false "legality" (until adoption of the 13th Constitutional Amendment in 1865), such theft of labor was a source of illicit wealth which former slaves who lived through that era did not recover. Nor was there any compensation forthcoming after their emancipation for the abuses they had suffered. With no savings, education, or property, but only the skills they had acquired as slaves, most were left to fend for themselves, taking whatever jobs they could find.

Did the American Revolution and subsequent Civil War result in a utopian paradise full of virtue and unstained by sin? No, far from it, but it did create a dynamic system of debate, self-reflection, and improvement around its principles and constitution, and with the general prosperity it created became a magnet for those seeking freedom and a better life. As observed by historian Arthur Schlesinger Jr., America is still on a journey from racial exclusion toward its ideal of inclusion, an ideal once, beyond question, that, alas, is now being challenged by those who seek a society permanently splintered along racial and ethnic cultural lines.

In sharp contrast to the American Revolution, and presaging future socialist revolutions, under the Jacobins the French Revolution took a decidedly anti-religious turn, attacking the central position of the Catholic Church in French society based upon its association with the monarchical status quo and extraction of wealth from the populace. Indeed, it marked the beginning of the Left's ongoing war to destroy religion and planted the seeds of the anti-religious secular state that has arisen in modern times, one that mocks and suppresses religion.

In France, where dehumanizing deprivation and hunger among the lower class at times threatened life itself, the Revolution succeeded in abolishing an unjust and oppressive feudal monarchy and its landed aristocracy, a first in recorded history and its pivotal achievement. Although land ownership among those previously landless had been rapidly spreading in the decades before, in causing the further break-up the great estates of feudal origin and abolishing their unjust levies on farmers, the Revolution drew a number of rural French peasants to it. Broader land ownership coupled with reduction of onerous fees on those who worked the land created an all but irreversible social change. Slavery, far less consequential in France than in the U.S., was abolished in 1794 following the successful slave revolt in Haiti, many years before the American Republic did so. Sadly though, vestiges of slavery persist in the island nation of Haiti.

The French Revolution was understandably driven more by hunger and the resentment by its peasant class of aristocratic privileges (particularly the incendiary Parisian "sans culottes" as they were called), and a demand for equal treatment (Egalite!), than by its other aspirational ideals of liberty and the brotherhood of man. Despite failing to establish a stable democratic government responsive to all its citizens, France's Revolution, with its denouement of Jacobin dictatorship, became an inspirational model for revolutions ever since to overthrow oppressive aristocratic regimes, under the flag of improving the living conditions and political representation of the poor.

While in that respect it was a positive inspiration, sadly, on the other hand, its Jacobin example prefigured revolutions in the twentieth century that proved disastrous for many millions across the globe. It is fair to say that the Revolution's Reign of Terror with its dictatorship and summary execution of thousands of "counter-revolutionaries" cracked open the door to future generations of socialist revolutionaries committing profoundly evil crimes whilst seizing and exercising power, particularly political mass murder, all in the name of equality and justice.

As I outlined earlier, Paris, the epicenter of the French Revolution, subsequently became the world's breeding ground for future socialist intelligentsia and nihilist revolutionaries possessing the Will to Power and a passion for use of force. As Dostoevsky is said to have observed, the legacy of the West's so-called "Enlightenment" has a dual face, a dark side as well as a side of light. George Lichtheim wrote in *The Origins of Socialism* that events of that 1790's revolutionary period formed a "crucible" for forming the tenets of socialism, which particularly through the French Revolution, "taught men to think in terms of seizing power."[67]

Charles Krauthammer concluded, "Indeed the French Revolution was such a model for future revolutions that it redefined the term." Some have said the American Revolution, though successful, has been treated as incomplete because it lacked "the messianic, bloody-minded idealism of the French. The French Revolution failed, argues Shama [in Simon Shama's book *Citizens*] because it tried to create the impossible: a regime both of liberty and of 'patriotic' state power. The history of revolution is proof that these goals are incompatible. The American Revolution succeeded because it chose one, liberty. The Russian Revolution became deranged when it chose the other, state power. The French Revolution, to its credit and sorrow [emphasis added] wanted both."[68]

Tocqueville wrote:

> By the time their ancient love of freedom reawakened in the hearts of the French, they had already been inoculated with a set of ideas as regards the way the country should be governed that were not merely hard to reconcile with free institutions but practically ruled them out. They had come to regard the ideal social system as one whose aristocracy consisted exclusively of government officials and in which an all-powerful bureaucracy not only took charge of affairs of State but controlled men's private lives...The nation as a whole had sovereign rights, while the individual citizen was kept in strictest tutelage; the former

was expected to display the sagacity and virtues of a free race, the latter to behave like an obedient servant.[69]

With the French Revolution as their model, socialists since the time of Marx have incessantly preached the need for overthrow and destruction of the existing social order through a radical political activism, and failing that, a fully violent, bloody revolution, to create a social tabula rasa on which they can build their perfect system. Never do such utopian activists honestly portray the ugly godless reality they are pursuing, nor its dreadful human toll. As a former Khmer Rouge official said looking back at the derailment and demise of their Cambodian socialist utopia that was to replace a corrupt French controlled monarchy, "The train was going too fast. No one could make it turn."[70]

A rather prosaic explanation for having instituted, among other things, the infamous "Killing Fields" on their left turn toward the Khmer Rouge's dreamed of utopia. Shades of Mao and Stalin, and their utter disregard for human life! Use of such a shockingly trite metaphor in talking about the estimated one-and-a-half to two million lives extinguished by his Khmer Rouge bespeaks a profoundly sociopathic ideology.

In every revolution there are participants who are able to foresee what might happen to the train they are on but are powerless to stop it before it derails. Usually, their communications are either destroyed or simply lost in the mists of time or the chaos of revolution. However, one such warning we have in the historical record concerning the political embrace of utopian idealism is just as valid today as it was when written two-hundred and thirty years ago. In 1792, before the Reign of Terror, there were indeed some in the proto-socialist French Revolution who understood and raised dire concerns about what the messianic secular movement they birthed would ultimately lead to. Quoted below is the text of a particularly prophetic letter written by a "liberal" Girondist,

Salle, to a fellow liberal, Edmond Louis Alexis Dubois-Crance, a respected soldier and elected member of the French Republic's National Convention, in which he states his grave concerns:

> The principles [a perfect 'natural order' that would bring about universal happiness], in their abstractness and in the form in which they are constantly being analysed in this society - no government can be founded on them; a principle cannot be rigorously applied to political association, for the simple reason that a principle admits no imperfection; and, whatever you may do, men are imperfect. I say more: I make bold to say, and indeed, in the spirit of Rousseau himself, that the social state is a continuous violation of the will of the nation as conceived in its abstract relationships. What may not be the results of these imprudent declamations which take this will as a safe basis; which, under the pretext of full and complete sovereignty of the people, will suffer no legal restriction; which, present man always in the image of an angel; which, desirous of discovering what befits him, ignore what he really is; which, in an effort to persuade the people that they are wise enough, give them dispensation from the effort to be that!...I would gladly, if you like, applaud the chimera of perfection that they are after. But tell me, in divesting in this way man of what is human in him, are they not most likely to turn him into a ferocious beast?[71]

During the 20th Century, communist/socialist revolutionaries crusading under the populist banner of equality for all did indeed create many ferocious beasts, leaving an almost unimaginably vast legacy of human suffering, enslavement, and death. Wherever their ideology took root, communist tyrants accreted government power to themselves through systematic imprisonment, torture, and outright murder of all who might stand in their way. Victims were almost always branded as "enemies of the people," "reactionaries," or "counterrevolutionaries" to help justify their harsh treatment.

Contrary to Marxism, it became obvious there was no spontaneous class warfare as political power was being seized; it was simply a matter of the emerging socialist State in a calculated way eliminating large numbers of its own citizens individually and in targeted groups. In the end, this kind of "warfare" did not lead to compassionate welfare states. It led to police states. The violence of these police states was so irresistible and on such a colossal scale as to evoke terror in those not yet subject to it, thereby weakening any incipient resistance to imposition of the socialist utopian pseudo-paradise.

Supreme leaders of such "gone wrong" revolutions (e.g., Lenin, Stalin, Mao, Pol Pot, and Castro) were successful in seizing control through armed uprisings, murder of competitors, and widespread campaigns of brutality and terror. They were able to maintain their grip on power, not by providing for the welfare of their citizens, but through ruthlessness and a paranoia that prompted them to use extrajudicial secret police to hunt down, torture, imprison, or murder their opposition. This they saw as necessary and acceptable means for achieving their version of a "just" society.

Vilification and dehumanization of whole classes of people, a tactic the Nazis used to destroy their political opponents and the Jews, made it easier for their radicalized followers to justify all manner of atrocities. And once charismatic revolutionaries such as Lenin and Mao consolidated their power and gained control of the police, military, and legislative and judicial apparatuses of government, they often stopped bothering with even token attempts to create the promised utopian welfare state. These tyrants then unleashed destruction upon their own people, limited only by their whims.

The carnage in the Soviet Union, China, North Korea, Cambodia, and parts of Africa was similar in purpose, but longer lasting and more widespread than the labor camps and horrific industrialized extermination of European Jews by Hitler's Nazi Germany. Indeed, many of Stalin's atrocities actually preceded the genocidal endeavors of the Nazis, and

Hitler is said to have initially modeled the Nazi system of concentration camps on the Soviet gulag system instituted by Lenin and expanded by Stalin, but then added the capacity for the unprecedented, industrialized extermination of human beings. Stalin had used more "old-fashioned" ways of murdering large numbers of "enemies of the state."

To their everlasting discredit, since the 1960's Vietnam War, the West's Leftist intelligentsia have championed the cause of revolutionary Marxist movements across the globe by viciously attacking those who attempt to raise awareness the horrible realities of Marx's socialism in practice, with the effect of creating a demoralized political paralysis that stymies any help to less than perfect democratic factions fighting for their freedom. Reflecting on the fate of the Cambodians and Vietnamese under victorious Communist regimes, the famous former radical leftist, David Horowitz, observed "Looking back on the left's revolutionary enthusiasm...we have painfully learned what should have been obvious all along: we live in an imperfect world that is bettered only with great difficulty, and easily made worse, much worse."

Political Revolutions of a Different Kind

Thus far we have been discussing modern era Marxist-style revolutions that further the international movement of "building socialism." What about revolutions to oust failed or failing socialist regimes? Henry Kissinger pointed out in his 1985 book *Observations* (p. 48) that "The joke of history is that the only spontaneous revolutions in industrialized countries have been *against* Communist governments" [emphasis added]. The spontaneous upheavals between 1989 and 1991 that resulted in throwing off the shackles of communism throughout Eastern Europe, and then dismantled the Union of Soviet Socialist Republics were surprisingly brief and nearly bloodless. Despite their immense geopolitical significance, as I discuss below, these upheavals hardly qualify as "revolutions" in the way the term is normally thought of; that is, a form of armed civil war. But, that seismic series of events, widely considered as marking the end of the Cold War, was in fact preceded by violent popular uprisings against several socialist regimes in Eastern Europe behind the infamous Iron Curtain created by Stalin.

The earliest was the 1953 insurrection in East Germany. Following a labor strike, over a million East Germans throughout the country revolted against increased work quotas, poor living conditions and unpopular Sovietization policies, seeking to replace their Stalinist East German government. The revolt was quickly suppressed with brute force by Soviet troops armed with tanks.

Another example of insurrection to gain freedom from domineering socialism is the Hungarian Revolution of 1956 against policies imposed by the USSR through a Stalinist puppet regime. Again, the tanks rolled in. Far bloodier than the East German revolt, it too was violently repressed by Soviet troops.

Third is the Soviet-led Warsaw Pact invasion of Czechoslovakia in 1968 to snuff out democratic reforms (the so-called "Prague Spring"), but having done so, it led to fracturing of support in the socialist camp for use of such brutal measures. While it would be overly simplistic to characterize these incipient revolutions as ideologically driven by "anti-socialist" democratic sentiment, in heroically endeavoring to topple or drastically reform their socialist systems against overwhelming odds the insurgents clearly demonstrated that in modern times people have a limited tolerance for single-party socialism that seeks to force its "square" fallacious economics into the "round" hole of true human nature, particularly when that system is not indigenous in origin, but rather has been imposed from outside through force. Indeed, a fear of such popular uprisings is one of the main reasons why socialist regimes maintain the extensive, extra-judicial secret police operations they use to imprison or otherwise silence political dissidents.

To present the full range of arguments in support of or against revolution under various scenarios is far beyond the scope of this book. The noted political scientist Samuel Huntington presents a full treatment of the nature of modern revolutions in the chapter "Revolution and Political Order" of his 1968 book *Political Order in Changing Societies*.[72] For purposes here, it is perhaps sufficient to note that for human betterment, a revolution must not be usurped by those who would reject any moral boundaries, such as the aforementioned Dostoyevsky nihilist revolutionary, or by those who would hijack its justice-seeking intent and merely supplant one evil regime with another equally evil or worse.

In advocating for support of revolutions to replace non-socialist authoritarian regimes with socialism, Leftists always claim their actions are driven by wanting "to be on the right side of history." But contrary to the Left's belief in discredited Marxian historicism with its "scientific" laws, in his 2014 memoir the former U.S. Secretary of Defense and veteran National Security advisor Robert Gates reflected on then President Obama applying pressure that ousted Egyptian President Hosni Mubarak in February 2011 during the "Arab Spring." Mubarak's ouster led to a series of dictatorial regimes less friendly to Western liberal values, in fact, quite the opposite. Echoing other observers cited in the pages above, Gates had asked "how can anyone know which is the 'right' or 'wrong' side of history when nearly all revolutions, begun with hope and idealism, culminate in repression and bloodshed? After Mubarak, what?"[73] The same question applies to the West's ouster of the Libyan dictator Muhammar Qaddafi at about the same time, leaving a power vacuum Islamic radicals were all too ready to fill. Another earlier example of no-win revolutions is the 1979 ouster of the corrupt Nicaraguan dictator, Somoza, by Daniel Ortega, the leader the Left-wing Sandinista rebels, and now President of an increasingly oppressive and undemocratic regime hostile to the U.S. But to see how terribly badly things can go during the chaos of revolution, one need only look at the consequences of President Carter having pulled the rug out from under the Shah of Iran in 1979 during an incipient Islamic revolution, which gave rise to an implacable enemy of the West, the Islamic Republic of Iran, a nation now ruled by religious fanatics. Iran has become a textbook case of what not to do, but it's very unpleasant lessons have not been publicly acknowledged, much less understood and absorbed by the left-leaning foreign policy establishment in the U.S. and Europe.

Then there have been numerous anti-government protest movements which have taken place around the world from the late 1980's to the present, referred to as the "Color Revolutions," which have stopped short of civil war. The beginning of these mass protest movements can be marked by the 1986 People Power (aka "Yellow") Revolution in the Philippines that ousted Ferdinand Marcos, and the anti-communist 1989 "Velvet Revolution" in Czechoslovakia. One is tempted to add to the list the non-violent 1989 Tiananmen Square student protests which were forcefully suppressed by the PRC's People's Liberation Army. The Arab Spring is also considered part of this "quasi-revolution" trend.

Although the news media have used the word "revolution" to describe these movements, most of them pressed their cause through street demonstrations rather than violent attacks on government institutions, planned coup d'etats, or political assassinations. Nor were they driven by a desire for a complete overhaul of society that would conform to a particular ideology. Some were anti-communist, some have been anti-authoritarian, while others were driven by ethnic or religious separatism. Most were animated at least to some extent by a desire for real democracy and freedom from tyranny. Some were widespread and succeeded in causing regime change or reforms. Others were repressed by authorities and failed. Were these protest movements true revolutions? Mostly no, not in the sense I have been writing about. While my main concern in this section of this book is to consider armed uprisings with plans for a comprehensive overhaul of society, to avoid confusion, I briefly mention the Color Revolutions to point out use of the term revolution by some more broadly, to include impassioned protest movements disruptive enough and at a scale that make them impossible for authorities to ignore.

Unfortunately, the historical record shows that in an armed revolution widespread violence and ensuing chaos is likely to open the door in unpredictable ways to well-organized and ruthless agents of totalitarianism emerging from the dark recesses of society. Revolutions are less likely to convey power to humanistic liberals, as naively wished for by Western idealists. Historicism's fantasy of a deterministic path to enlightenment, justice, and peace (or any other utopian vision; i.e. the "arc of history") vanishes like the ephemeral rainbow when the drops stop falling or the sun is hidden behind clouds.

Radical fringe revolutionaries, following Lenin's and Mao's example, have no interest in martyrdom. They are quite determined to avoid the fate of the Paris Commune by being utterly ruthless in destroying all obstacles on the path toward power and their imagined Utopia. Consider Lenin, Stalin, Mao, Kim Il-sung, Castro, and Pol Pot, and others of their ilk who have risen to power during gone-wrong revolutions and coups who left a record of terror, ruin and death in their wake as they "built socialism." Humanity can never know what the fate of these nations would have been had an evolutionary path of gradual political reform been taken instead of revolution.

Notes

1. George Lichtheim, *The Origins of Socialism*, published by F. A. Praeger, 1969, Part Two Critics of the Industrial Revolution, Chapter 7, The New Commonwealth, p. 111.

2. Thomas More, *Utopia*, 1516.

3. Karl Kautsky, *Thomas More and his Utopia*, 1888, Part III "Utopia," Chapter V "The Aim of Utopia;" this work by Kautsky was first published in English in 1927 by A C Black, Source: Marxist Internet Archive, transcribed by Ted Crawford, 2002; In addition to a discussion of More's work, Utopia, Kautsky examines European Christianity and Monarchism in the feudal era through the lens of orthodox Marxism.

4. Augustine of Hippo, *The City of God*, written in 413-426, see Larry Siedentop's commentary in *Inventing the Individual: The Origins of Western Liberalism*, Penguin Books, 2014, "The Weakness of the Will: Augustine," pp. 108-109.

5. Igor Shafarevich, *The Socialist Phenomenon*, Harper and Row, 1975 provides a thorough account of Socialism's pre-modern origins, history, suppression, and many definitions.

6. Jean-Jacques Rousseau, *Discourse on Inequality, Principles of Political Right, and Of the Social Contract* between 1754 and 1762. He was no doubt inspired by sketchy knowledge at the time of primitive societies known for freely sharing food and land. Despite man's evolution over millennia bequeathing us with unalterable natural instincts for survival, acquisitiveness, covetousness, and fear of those who might threaten, in his *Discourse* Rousseau naively argued for the perfectibility of human nature, for example, doing away with the universal desire to own property. His fundamental view of human nature was that "man is naturally good, and only by institutions is he made bad" Ironically Rousseau cited the Caribs as an example of an unspoiled primitive people. However, it is known that the Caribs waged wars to conquer and exterminate other tribal groups as they spread among the Caribbean islands, and practiced cannibalism at times.

7. Bertrand Russell, *A History of Western Philosophy*, 1945, Simon and Schuster, Part II "Socrates, Plato and Aristotle," Ch. XXI "Aristotle's Politics," p. 188.

8. Garrett Hardin, *Tragedy of the Commons*, in *Science* 162 (1968) p.p.1242-1249.

9. Donald E. Brown, *Human Universals*, 1991, 2017, Chapter 6, "The Universal People," location 3012 of 6032 in Kindle version; also see Brown's extensive list of universal human traits catalogued by Steven Pinker in *Blank Slate: The Modern Denial of Human Nature*, Penguin Books, 2002, Appendix p. 455-459.

10. Karl Marx, in *The Communist Manifesto* co-authored with Friedrich Engels, 1848, found in *The Marx and Engels Reader*, Ed. Robert C. Tucker, W.W. Norton & Company, 1978, p. 469.

11. John Spargo, *Socialism: A Summary and Interpretation of Socialist Principles*, 1906, Chapter III. "The Communist Manifesto and the Scientific Spirit," p. 116 of 796 in e-version.

12. Paul Johnson, *Intellectuals*, Harper & Row, 1988, Chapter 1 "Jean-Jacques Rousseau: An Interesting Madman," pp. 5, 10 and 18.

13. Jean-Jacques Rousseau, *On the Social Contract* (1762) Book I, Chapter VI "The Social Compact," found at pp. 148 and 158 in *The Basic Political Writings of Jean-Jacques Rousseau*, 1987, translated by Donald A. Cress, Hackett Publishing Co. Rousseau asserts that a disembodied "spirit of the people" exists as "the general will" apart from government. "The people making the law for itself cannot be unjust. Therefore, the general will is always righteous." Also see Paul Johnson, *Intellectuals*, Chapter 1 "Jean-Jacques Rousseau: An Interesting Madman" p. 24. In this and Rousseau's *Discourse on Inequality* we see the seeds of socialist totalitarianism. Robespierre and his Jacobin revolutionaries adopted Rosseau's ideas that Man is by nature only good, rather than having any evil tendencies; he becomes corrupt through unjust institutions and laws set upon him by others, rather than from his own willed behaviors, and thus is a slave to injustice caused by such people, who must break his chains to become free.

14. James Michael Egan, *Maximilien Robespierre: Nationalist Dictator* (New York: Farrar, Straus & Giroux, 1978), p. 11; this source footnote is found in an academic paper by Scott McLetchie from 1983-1984 entitled *Maximilien Robespierre, Master of the Terror*.

15. Will and Ariel Durant, *Rousseau and Revolution*, Simon and Schuster, 1967, in the series *The History of Civilization, Vol. X*, p. 23.

16. Philip Short, *Pol Pot: Anatomy of a Nightmare*, 2004, Chapter 2 "City of Light;" Pol Pot, became a Communist while studying in Paris in the early 1950's. Before becoming politicized, in his youth, through French colonial education in Cambodia, he became familiarized with the ideas of Jean-Jacques Rousseau, the French Revolution of 1789, and Robespierre. In his 1950's Paris days, as a

member of the Marxist Circle (the "Cercle Marxiste," a group of revolution-minded anti-colonial Cambodian ex-pats), his political development was most heavily influenced by the Russian anarchist, Pyotr Kropotkin's 1893 book *The Great French Revolution 1789-1793*, which was based on the French Revolution and its socialist principles, by Stalin's 1939 *History of the Communist Party (Bolshevik)*, and Mao's 1940 piece *"On New Democracy* [socialism]."

17. A description of the Robespierre-led Committee of Public Safety's total war on the rebelling Vendee peasants ("Leave nobody and nothing alive") can be found in "The Vendee War of 1773-1799 – the Loire Valley During the French Revolution" in *Social History in the Touraint – Central France*, March 6, 2012, and Secher.

18. Secher, Reynald, *A French Genocide: The Vendee*, University of Notre Dame press, 2003, p. 110.

19. Will and Ariel Durant, *The Age of Napoleon* in Vol. XI of the series *The Story of Civilization*, Ch. 4, "The Convention," Simon and Schuster, NY, 1975, p. 72.

20. A Girondin sentenced to the guillotine by the Revolutionary Committee on Public Safety during France's 1793 Reign of Terror said "The Revolution is like Saturn devouring his own children." Quote taken from page 66 of *The Age of Napoleon* in Vol. XI of *The Story of Civilization*, by Will and Ariel Durant, 1975; from Lamartine, Alphonse de, Histoire des Girondins, III, pp. 36-37.

21. Will and Ariel Durant, *The Age of Napoleon*, Chapter IV "The Convention," in Volume XI of *The Story of Civilization*; from Roland, Mme, "Private Memoirs, 105," written on August 28, 1793, pp. 66-67.

22. George Lichtheim, *The Origins of Socialism*, "Part One. Heirs of The French Revolution," and illustrated by the chart "Bloodlines of Modern Socialism" included in this book.

23. George Lichtheim, *The Origins of Socialism*, Frederick A. Praeger, 1969, Part Three "German Socialism," Chapter 10 "The Marxian Synthesis," p. 197.

24. George Lichtheim, *The Origins of Socialism*, Frederick A. Praeger, 1969, Part One, "Heirs of the French Revolution," Chapter 2 "The Egalitarians," p. 18 .

25. Joshua Muravchik, *Heaven on Earth: The Rise and Fall of Socialism*, Encounter Books, 2002, quotes the 1919 founding manifesto of the Soviet Comintern (aka "The Third International") in "Beginnings," Chapter 1 "Conspiracy of Equals," p. 25.

26. Francois Noel (Caius Gracchus) Babeuf (1760-1797) "A Society of Equals – A Manifesto of the Equals, Analysis of Babeuf's Doctrine," Article VI, from *French Utopias: An Anthology of Ideal Societies*, pp. 255, The Free Press,

Collier-Macmillan Ltd., 1966, ed. Frank Manuel and Fritzie Manuel, 1966. The radicalizing influence of French intellectuals and Left-wing Parisian political activists upon future socialist revolutions and totalitarian dictators is abundantly clear from many testimonials in the historical record. The case of the future Khmer Rouge monster Pol Pot is described by Philip Short in Chapter 2 "City of Light" in his book *Pol Pot: Anatomy of a Nightmare* "Since the time of Beaumarchais and Voltaire, Paris has called itself, with fine indifference to the intellectual claims of other European centres, La Ville Lumiè re, the source of light and of enlightenment for the rest of the civilized world. At times that has been a mixed blessing. It was in Paris, not in Moscow or Beijing, that in the early 1950s Sâr [aka Pol Pot] and his companions laid down the ideological foundations on which the Khmer Rouge nightmare would be built. That this occurred was not—as Sihanouk and his French advisers liked to pretend—because their minds were warped by the Stalinist vision of the world then being propagated by the French communists, the country's largest political party; nor was it due to the influence of Mao Zedong, whose writings the young Cambodians encountered in France for the first time. Stalin and Mao both had their part in the making of Pol Pot's Democratic Kampuchea. So did the Vietnamese and the Americans. But the foreign intellectual legacy which would underpin the Cambodian revolution was first and foremost French."

27. Martin Malia, *Soviet Tragedy: A History of Socialism in Russia, 1917-1991*, p. 41 of 576 in e-version, The Free Press, 1994.

28. Alexander Trachtenberg, *The Lessons of the Commune*, International Pamphlet No. 12, International Publishers, NYC, 1934 in which he quotes Marx and Lenin; pp. 10 and 31; Trachtenberg was considered the "Cultural Commissar" of the U.S Communist Party, responsible for political education.

29. Ibid., p. 5.

30. Courtois et al. the entire book *The Black Book of Communism: Crimes, Terror, Repression*, 1999, English trans. Harvard University Press, 1999.

31. Wikiqoute.org: Joseph Goebbels, Nazi politician and Propaganda Minister (1897-1945); the origin of each of Goebbels' quotes for the decades of the 1920's and 1930's which were selected and transcribed in the Sidebar is identified here, referencing various books, speeches, and correspondence.

32. Joseph Goebbel's 13 September 1935 speech at the annual congress of the Nazi Party is one example of Goebbel's attempts to distinguish "National Socialism" from Bolshevik socialism. Also see "Weimar Republic" in Encyclopedia Britannica.

33. F. A. Voigt, *Unto Caesar*, 1938, p. 45 quoted by the philosopher John Gray in his book *Black Mass*, pp. 65-66. For readers seeking a fuller analysis of the

similarities of Communism and Nazism, I commend this difficult to find but very rewarding volume by Voigt published by G.P. Putnam's Sons, NY, 1938.

34. F. A. Hayek, *The Road to Serfdom*, 1942, University of Chicago Press, 1994 edition, "Preface 1956," pp. xlii and xliii; Hayek footnotes a quote from Ivor Thomas's 1949 book *The Socialist Tragedy*, pp. 241 and 242, Latimer House, 1949.

35. Steven Pinker, "Dare to Understand" in *Enlightenment Now: The Case for Reason, Science, Humanism, And Progress*, Penguin Books, 2018, pp. 8-9.

36Adam Smith, *Theory of Moral Sentiments*, 1759, Part Six, Section II: "Of the Character of the Individual, so far as it can affect the Happiness of other People," Chapter II: "Of the order in which Societies are by nature recommended to our Beneficence," p. 769 of 1140 e-book version.

37. Plato, *The Republic*, 375 BC, see Part III. (Books V, 471 c-VII) "The Philosopher King," pp. 175-179 in *The Republic of Plato*, translated by Francis MacDonald Cornfield, Oxford U. Press, 1941.

38. Moloch (also called Molech, Milcom, or Malcam) is the biblical name of a destructive Canaanite god and subject of idol worship associated with forbidden child sacrifice through fire or war; *Book of Leviticus* (18:21, 20:2, 20:3, 20:4, and 20:5).

39. The "other Holocaust" of the 20th Century, is a controversial use of the term, but it seems to me a quite accurate characterization of the vast globe-spanning crimes of Communist states, summarized by Stephane Courtois in *The Black Book of Communism: Crimes, Terror, Repression, Introduction*, Harvard University Press, 1999, p. 4, and described in great detail for each country in the subsequent chapters.

40. The number is found in *Impressions of Soviet Russia* by Charles Sarolea, E. Nash & Grayson Ltd., pp. 81-82, 1924, and *Survey of Socialism* by Hearnshaw.

41. Estimates of the Soviet death total of 20 million or more can be found in Courtois, et al *The Black Book of Communism*, Part I "A State against Its People: Violence, Repression, and Terror in the Soviet Union," Harvard University Press, 1999, *The Great Terror: A Reassessment*, by Robert Conquest, Oxford University Press, 1990, and *The Soviet Tragedy: A History of Socialism in Russia, 1917 to 1991*, The Free Press, by Martin Malia et al.

42. Jonathan D. Spence, *The Search for Modern China*, "The Comintern and the Birth of the CCP," pp. 296-297, Third Edition, W. W. Norton & Company, NY, London, 2013.

43. Paul K. Davis, *100 Decisive Battles: From Ancient Times to the Present – The World's Major Battles and How They Shaped History*, Oxford University Press, 1999; "Warsaw" 16-25 August 1920, pp. 368-372.

44. In *Socialism: An Economic and Sociological Analysis*, 1951 Ludwig von Mises quoted the then exiled but ruthless Bolshevik Leon Trotsky "In a country where the sole employer is the State, opposition means death by slow starvation. The old principle: who does not work shall not eat, has been replaced by a new one: who does not obey shall not eat." Mises paraphrases this Trotsky quote in *Human Action*, "The Market," p. 277 "A world-embracing socialist state would exercise such an absolute and total monopoly; it would have the power to crush its opponents by starving them to death." Footnoted to a 1937 Trotsky statement quoted by Hayek in *The Road to Serfdom* (London, 1984) p. 89.

45. Robert Conquest, *The Great Terror: A Reassessment* ; Quote taken from NY Times May 13, 1990 article *"Now It Can Be Told, Even In Russia"*

46. See "The Comintern in Action" and "Shades of the NKVD in Spain," in Courtois et al *The Black Book of Communism*, Harvard University Press, 1999, pp. 271-332, and pp. 333-352. This work is based on the Soviet archives opened in 1991, which reveal, among many ugly facts, the Comintern's relentless espionage across the globe.

47. Stephane Courtois et al, *The Black Book of Communism, World Revolution, Civil War, and Terror,* "The Shadow of the NKVD in Spain," Harvard University Press, 1999, p. 335-337, and *Secret Cables of the Comintern 1933-1943*, Ch. 4 "The Spanish Civil War," by Firsov, Klehr, and Haynes, pp. 86-87. This latter work corrects the historical record by showing the hard evidence from the Comintern archives themselves that for many decades the members of the American Communist Party clandestinely acted on behalf of the Soviet-Union as its agents through the Comintern, which was entirely a creature of Lenin and Stalin. Those documented facts are in sharp contrast to the revisionist history of American Communism propounded by Leftist academicians for the past 60 years that have portrayed American Communism as nothing more than a radical but benign part of normal electoral politics rather than the subversive element it is.

48. Samuel Huntington, *Political Order in Changing Societies*, Yale University Press, 1968, "Revolution and Political Order, Peasants and Revolution," p. 295.

49. For the story of Mao's approach to recruiting support among the rural peasantry see Nathan D. Spence, *In Search of Modern China*, Ch. 16 "Communist Survival," pp. 362-370, 3rd Edition, W. W. Norton Co., NY, 2013. In this Chapter Spence also includes a detailed account of the CCP's celebrated "Long March" to the north by which it escaped the Guomindang army and was able to successfully regroup under Mao's then consolidated leadership.

50. Ibid, "Introduction to Part IV, War and Revolution," pp. 394-395.

51. Jung Chang and Jon Halliday, *Mao The Untold Story*, 2005, "Part Five – Chasing the Superpower Dream," Ch. 40 "Half of China May Well Have to Die" (1958-61), p. 431; ; also see *Memoirs of Nikita Khrushchev: Volume 3: Statesman [1953-1964]*, edited by Sergei Khrushchev, 1999, Pennsylvania University Press 2007, translated by George Shiver, p. 436, where from memory Khrushchev quotes Mao as saying in a speech at a 1957 international conference of Communist and Workers' Parties: "If imperialism imposes a war on us, we have 600 million people, and if we lose 300 million of them, what of it? After all, that is war. Years will pass, and we will raise up a new batch of people and restore the population to its previous numerical strength."

52. An excellent example is the autobiography of a young North Korean woman, pen name Hyeonseo Lee, with David John, entitled *The Girl with Seven Names: Escape from North Korea*, Williams Collins pub., 2015.

53. Vietnam's economic and political policies, and a critique of capitalism differentiating it from a market economy, are outlined in broad terms by Dr. Nguyen Phu Trong, General Secretary of the Central Committee of the Communist Party of Vietnam, in *"Vietnam's path to socialism: Theoretical and practical issues,"* October 29, 2021, posted on CPUSA website at www.cpusa.org.

54. Paul Johnson, *Modern Times*, Harper Perennial, 1991, see pp. 654-57 for a brief summary of the enormous atrocities that took place, and several other books for a fuller account: *Cambodia: The Country of Disconcerting Crimes*, by Jean-Louis Margolin, in *The Black Book of Communism*, (see *First They Killed My Father: A Daughter of Cambodia Remembers* by Loung Ung, *Alive in the Killing Fields* by Nawuth Keat, and *Stay Alive My Son* by Pin Yathay for survivors' accounts. See *Pol Pot: Anatomy of a Nightmare*, by Philip Short for a deep biographical dive into Pol Pot's background, ideological evolution, and history of his infamous Khmer Rouge.

55. Sean McMeekin, *Stalin's War: A New History of World War II*, see Chapters: "Tehran and Cairo," "Moscow and Yalta: Unfinest Hour of the Anglo-Americans," "Booty," and "Red Star Over Asia," pub. Basic Books, 2021, at p. 510. McMeekin's chapter note #46 ties back to certain official American papers documenting the Tehran Conference located in the FDR Library under "Hopkins Papers." The scope and nature of American "Lend-Lease" support of the USSR is vividly illustrated in the March 29, 1943 Special Issue of *Life Magazine*, "USSR," which featured a flattering portrait of Joseph Stalin on its cover, and at p.29 called Lenin, "The Father of Modern Russia - Perhaps the greatest man of modern times...Lenin was the rarest of men, an absolutely unselfconscious and unselfish man who had a passionate respect for ideas, but even more respect for deeds...Lenin did not make the Revolution in Russia, nor did any organized group of men. But, he made the Revolution make sense and saved it from much of the folly of the French Revolution." This delusional

eulogy reads like Soviet propaganda! Lenin was indeed prophetic. Useful idiots abounded in capitalist countries, and shaped the news fed to American public about the Soviet Union until the realities of the Cold War sunk in. In his memoir, *White House Years*, Little, Brown and Company, 1979, Henry Kissinger sums up Roosevelt's bumbling naivete (or worse, ideological sympathy) toward the Stalin regime by relating a statement made by his trusted White House advisor Harry Hopkins to the author Robert Sherwood following the Yalta Conference in 1945: "The Russians had proved that they could be reasonable and farseeing and there wasn't any doubt in the minds of the President or any of us that we could live with them and get along with them peacefully for as far into the future as any of us could imagine. But I have to make one amendment to that —I think we all had in our minds the reservation that we could not foretell what the results would be if anything should happen to Stalin. We felt sure that we could count on him to be reasonable and sensible and understanding—but we never could be sure who or what might be in back of him at the Kremlin." (Source: Robert E. Sherwood, *Roosevelt and Hopkins: An Intimate History*, NY, Harper and Bros., 1948).

56. Anne Applebaum, *The Iron Curtain: The Crushing of Eastern Europe 1944-1956*, Anchor Books, 2012; Applebaum was able to access both Soviet and Eastern European archives unavailable to historians before 1991.

57. For detailed account of this implosion see the Chapter "The Weakest Link Snaps - 1989" in *Soviet Tragedy: A History of Socialism in Russia*, Random House Inc., The Free Press, 1995, by Martin Malia.

58.George Kennan, the so-called *"Long Telegram,"* Conclusion *(3)*, and *Part 4 #7(a)* sent from Moscow February 22, 1946 to the U.S. Secretary of State by the U.S. statesman.

59. Winston S. Churchill, *The River War: An Historical Account of the Reconquest of the Soudan*, Longmans, Green & Co., 1899, 1902 edition, "The Rebellion of the Mahdi," p. 33.

60. John Adams, letter to Hezekiah Niles, February 13, 1818 paragraph #9

61. George Lichtheim, *The Origins of Socialism*, Frederick A. Praeger, 1969, Part Three, Chapter 9, "The Precursors," pp. 148 and 155.

62. Vladimir Bukovsky, *Judgement in Moscow: Soviet Crimes and Western Complicity*, 1996, 2019, Ninth of November Press, Chapter 3, "Back to the Future," 3.1 "So where did we go wrong?," p. 98.

63. Andre Glucksmann, *The Master Thinkers*, Harper & Row, trans. by Brian Pearce, 1977, Chapter 5 "How I became a Fatality," "A Science of Great Resources," p. 213.

64. Maxim Gorky, who was initially sympathetic and supportive of the Bolsheviks, and later exiled. In *Untimely Thoughts: Essays on Revolution, Culture and the Bolsheviks 1917-1918*, p. 88. Yale University Press. 1995. It should be noted that Gorky was not immune to the corrupting influence of the totalitarian regime that took shape, and thus did not remain a voice of reason and restraint. Despite his criticism of the Bolsheviks during the Revolution, during Stalin's time he helped to justify the cultivation of class hatred, dehumanization, and the extermination of so-called "enemies of the state", as a necessary part of the USSR's ongoing internal "war" against certain of its people.

65. Max Eastman, *Reflections on the Failure of Socialism*, Devin-Adair Company, 1955, Introduction, pp. 17-18; this quote is from his 1940 book entitled *Stalin's Russia, and the Crisis of Socialism*; Eastman was a prominent American Socialist, and editor of *The Masses* until the 1930's when he repudiated socialism in a number of powerful critiques. He had visited the victorious Bolsheviks in Russia, met Lenin, and together with radical John Reed (author of *Ten Days That Shook The World*) prematurely declared the revolution a success.

66. Leszek Kolakowski, *Main Currents of Marxism*, Book Two – The Golden Age, Ch. II, "German Orthodoxy," p. 390.

67. George Lichtheim, *The Origins of Socialism*, Frederick A. Praeger, 1969, Chapter 1. "The Egalitarians," p. 18.

68. Charles Krauthammer, *Things That Matter*, Crown Forums, 2013, Reflections on the Revolution in France, p. 134.

69. De Tocqueville, Alexis, "The Old Regime and the Revolution," 1856, found at pp. 226-227 in *Alexis De Tocqueville On Democracy, Revolution, and Society*, Chapter Six, "The Dynamics of Revolution," edited by John Stone and Stephen Mennell, University of Chicago Press, 1980.

70. Philip Short, *Pol Pot: Anatomy of a Nightmare*, A John Macrae Book, Henry Hold and Company, 2004, This statement by a former Khmer Rouge village chief is found on p. 4 of 539; to get a fuller appreciation of the unrepentant and shameless callousness of Pol Pot's Khmer Rouge atrocities see Chapter 12, "Utopia Disbound," p. 418.

71. J. L. Talmon, *The Origins of Totalitarian Democracy*, 1951, Mercury Books, London, Ch. I, "Natural Order: The Postulate," p.p. 20-21; Talmon notes (p. 269) that "the letter of Salle to Dubois Crance is quoted by Georges Lefebvre in his *Lectures on the French Revolution, 1944-5, La Convention*. Tome I, p. 25, issued by Centre de Documentation Universitaire, Paris.. David Horowitz, *The Black Book of the American Left, Volume 1: My Life and Times*, 2013, 2016, "Goodbye to All That," p. 166.

72. Samuel Huntington presents a full treatment of the nature of modern revolutions in the Chapter "Revolution and Political Order" of his 1968 book *Political Order in Changing Societies,* Yale University Press, 1968, pp. 264-343.

73. Robert M. Gates, *Duty: Memoirs of a Secretary at War* pp. 504-505, Alfred A. Knopf, NY, 2014, 2016, "On the Little Red Flag and the Smile of the Axe," pp. 278-281.

CHAPTER THREE

Socialist Doctrine, Methods, and Consequences
"Hunger performs a progressive function."
—Vladimir Lenin

Socialism's Deadly Recipe

Some have described socialism as idealism run amok. That may be true, but to gain a real understanding one must look beyond the glib cliché. What exactly is socialism and how does it work? These are questions socialists do not answer with clarity. Would that my research had revealed socialism to be simply a matter of good-hearted brotherhood and altruistic service to others. But it is not. Were it so, it would not be a political ideology, not an "ism" people will kill for to impose upon others.

Many today talk of socialism as merely an extensive and generous welfare state funded by "progressive" taxation of the rich, which is also supposed to compensate for "income inequality." But the welfare state is only a part-way approximation. Socialism is much more and different in important ways; it is a mistake to equate them.

To grasp socialism's essence, one must examine its roots and implementation. As far back as 1892, such issues were being raised by French journalists, who then published in *Le Figaro* a list of 600 different definitions they had found for socialism. A British book some years later compiled a list of "only" 263 definitions![1] Such widespread confusion about what socialism really is plays well into the hands of socialists politically. Before the theory of socialism had been "field-tested" on hundreds of millions of wretched victims by real-world criminal regimes during the 20th Century, socialists could seek refuge from the truth and criticism in obfuscation, nebulous platitudes and grandiose promises as to the incredible benefits of totally transforming society from top to bottom and putting "the workers" in charge.

Certain things revealed during the past century have become quite clear, however, about socialism's true nature. As a utopian ideology, socialism certainly condemns the world as it is and insists upon political action to radically change it. Radical change must happen. It is only a matter of the timing and the methods required to effectuate the social, political and economic transformation sought.

Like a messianic religion it has a well-established set of tenets, or precepts, with an existence independent of its flesh and blood adherents. These tenets notwithstanding, before rising to power, and when perceived as a threat to the existing social and political order, socialism becomes an adaptable chameleon-like creed that readily changes "color" (and its labels) according to the culture it is within and tactical necessity, but without ever changing its essence.[2]

After Marx's mid-19th century synthesis of its two hereditary roots, the revolutionary with the theoretical, "socialism" as an ideology became the generic term encompassing "Marxism" and "communism," forming what might be called the Unholy Trinity of "isms." Its central idea can be summed up in a single deceptively simple word: equality, the basis of its claim to moral superiority. But what socialists really mean and intend when they use that word, and how they go about establishing their version of equality is anything but simple.

As a starting point one must first understand the basic tenets of socialist doctrine presented below. It is definitely not the genuine liberal principle embodied in Western constitutions of all citizens being treated equally, each possessing equal rights and an equal say in government, i.e., equality under the law, which means equal freedom for all. There is equality, and then there is socialist equality: a "cookie-cutter" equality imposed by a soulless state on diverse, self-interested, free-willed human beings naturally possessing different likes, dislikes, motivations, interests, abilities, knowledge, thoughts, ideas, and ideals. It is a compulsory equality, a coerced conformity of thought, expression, and action that that can only be achieved by forcefully contravening individual freedom and fundamental human rights and exercising overwhelming political power from the top down to achieve unquestioning subservience. Generally, the deal implicit in socialism is this: "Give all power to the government, give up ownership of your land and property, give up your individual rights, give us custodianship of your children, and we will give you equality and assure your needs will be taken care of." But in the end the state takes everything, and gives nothing to the powerless in return except hardship and repression. Some scholars have argued that this is not what Marx intended in his theoretical writings, but it has nonetheless been the actual result of socialists' all too numerous attempts at applying his theories to reality.

Out of political expediency socialists will change the words and labels they use to describe their "ism" to disguise their real aims. A recent example of this is the disingenuous attempt to twist the meaning of the words: "equity" and "equitable" from fair and impartial treatment for all, into assuring equal outcomes for all. As a result of such language manipulation there are scholars who would insist that modern socialism really has no core set of tenets or principles, only a few attributes, such as collective ownership of the means of production, and "redistribution" of wealth. Nevertheless, with some research into the actual record consisting of the writings, words, and deeds of socialism's proponents from Marx to the present, the specific "tenets," or core concepts, which characterize any fully socialist program become very clear.

The Twelve Tenets of Modern Socialism

Despite obfuscation from twisted words and the strict secrecy under which closed revolutionary regimes have operated, historical records show what the doctrine and attempted implementation of fully-fledged socialism really looks like. Following is a summary of the "12 Basic Tenets of Modern Socialism" distilled from the evidence:[3]

1. The State's demands negate individual rights: The State (central government) can do with you as it pleases, and individualism is outlawed. Essentially, it owns your life. Everyone must talk, act, and even think alike as the State directs, as though each person is nothing but a mere obedient pawn. Basic human rights, such as freedom of speech, assembly, religion, self-determination, self-defense, and right to an impartial trial by an independent judiciary, if acknowledged at all, are subordinate to whatever the State determines. It will determine what your children are taught, what thoughts you may publicly express, and if and how you and your family will be protected from violence and theft. But, as a reward, lifelong economic security is guaranteed in exchange for one's unquestioning obedience to all the State's commands.

2. Everyone is entitled to an equal share of everything that is good: That is the only thing that is fair. Regardless of how hard you work and how productive you are relative to others, you do not deserve to be better off than anyone else. Socialists ironically show contempt for the idea of treating people equally. It is government's job to determine who gets to take how much of what from whom ("distribution"), so that it can make sure that everyone is equal. Some are taken from,

and others given to, based on the category they are placed in, be it economic, racial or some other. Although the talents, capabilities and contributions of human beings are naturally unequal, wealth and all human conditions are to be leveled by the State, through law, and when necessary, by force. This goes beyond just "taking from the rich to give to the poor." It taps into the powerful and destructive impulse of envy, seducing the good-hearted who believe "income equality" is a moral necessity.

3. Labor is the only real source of economic value: The business you thought you created and now own, does not rightfully belong to you. It was created from the labor of the others you employed. Capitalist ("Bourgeois") business owners and successful entrepreneurs are hated parasites living off workers' (the "Proletariat") labor by "keeping them down." Owners produce nothing, while workers produce all, and are therefore rightfully entitled to all the wealth ("profits") gained from production. Compensation paid to a voluntary workforce in wages and benefits, and an owner's work, innovation, investment of savings, and management skills count for nothing. Those who create and own businesses deserve only to be heavily taxed, but once socialism is in full bloom, stripped of ownership, re-educated, imprisoned, or exterminated.

4. The past, present, and course of the future is determined by a constant struggle (until socialism is fully in place) between workers and those exploiting them: Socialists' concept of world history revolves around their belief in inescapable class conflict caused by victimization (the word "exploitation" is often used in their literature) of some by others. For those in capitalism's so-called "working class" betterment can only come at the expense of those of higher economic status who will fight to keep what must be taken from them. There is no "brotherhood of man." To gain the political power to defeat these exploiters, hatred must be

stoked and their blood spilled. This zero-sum falsehood ignores innovation, economic growth, individual initiative, industriousness, and upward mobility in democratic capitalist societies. Workers' are mostly backward, ignorant, or apathetic and don't know what is best for them. But their dissatisfaction with their powerlessness will continue to fester until they have been sufficiently educated in Marxian thought by intellectually superior leaders who show them the way to break their oppressors' chains. Consequently, a workers' revolution, perhaps piecemeal and peaceful, but more likely to be very violent and severely oppressive, will overthrow capitalism with its greedy bourgeoise who control society, and replace them with a socialist dictatorship headed by the revolution's leaders and a collectively owned economy directed by the dictatorship.

5. Your income must be controlled by the State and redistributed for greater equality: Your money is not yours; there is no privately determined income (except in the Black Market); in concept the socialist central government treats all the wealth produced in society as a single pool from which it allocates the amount of it you are allowed to keep for yourself or will otherwise be provided to you in the form of public welfare. Welfare benefits, therefore, are blessings bestowed from the government, not money appropriated from you and other citizens. Such figurative pooling ("socializing") for redistribution from one group to another, with the goal of bringing all to the same level in the name of social justice, is morally rationalized as ongoing reparation owed to the exploited victims of capitalist oppression.

6. Private property is unjust: Property ownership is also a source of unjust inequality that must be taken ("socialized") for redistribution or use by the State. Moreover, material inequality from any cause (business success, being promoted, inheritance, talent, luck, etc.) is unjust. Whatever you have accumulated is

also partly mine. Now everyone "owns" a share of all property, i.e., another form of reparation to victims exploited by the privileged rich. Only your closest personal property is yours alone. Such coerced redistribution ultimately rationalizes theft in all forms: government confiscation of any amount of anything socialist leaders choose to take, looting of businesses by mobs, robbery and even murder, i.e., "You have it; I want it; I am going to take it from you."

7. Everything that is essential to producing and distributing the goods society needs must be controlled by the government: Some socialists have claimed that their demand for collective ownership of all means of producing and distributing wealth is really the central tenet of socialist ideology, or even the more simplistic negation – abolition of the capitalist private profit system.[4] One can understand their lust for simply taking what they did not create and do not own, so that they can assure the "equitable" distribution of all wealth produced. Private investor and family business ownership, along with freely determined market prices, contracts and competition are to be heavily regulated, then outlawed and replaced by State direction and expropriation, and by socialist planning as to who is to produce, and to get, how much of what, and when. Economic competition that rewards merit is unnecessary and wasteful, and leaves some workers (and business owners) better-off relative to others which is unfair. Political competition that might endanger the socialist enterprise also must be outlawed. Businesses most essential to the economy will be first in line for expropriation. Ultimately, the State owns and controls most if not all means of production.

8. Freedom is defined as the individual doing whatever the State (collectively "the people") demands, and the State doing whatever it chooses to individuals: Personal freedom must be rationed to achieve social and economic equality. To fulfill tenets 1-7, all courts of law, legislative bodies, police, military,

news media, literature, education, and cultural institutions must be fully controlled by a single political party which then becomes synonymous with the socialist State as it strips its citizens of all their freedoms, including those involving even the most private aspects of their lives. Competing political organizations and free speech are outlawed to assure permanent socialist control that will force the population into complete submission to "The Will of The People" as revealed through the edicts of party leaders; those who resist must be "re-educated" or "liquidated" (another socialist euphemism for murder). Therefore, despite socialists' use of words such as "Democratic" and "Peoples" to describe their regimes, real democracy does not exist. Similar to fascist dictatorships, voting by citizens to decide between contesting political parties and their values and ideas is rendered meaningless by imprisoning or assassinating would be opponents, by old fashioned rigging of elections, or by phony "voting" for "candidates" all of whom are preselected and controlled by the socialist party.

9. We will create better people: Human nature itself can be reshaped by the human will using political power when applied with sufficient ruthlessness, singleness of purpose, and force. After the existing social order has been destroyed, opponents stifled or eliminated, and consciousness-shaping institutions are under complete control, the socialist State will give birth to a new, perfected human being, the "Socialist Man" who, raised as such from childhood, will dutifully and selflessly only work for and serve the common good, as determined by its leaders. For this to happen, all educational and other cultural institutions must be controlled, and all dissenting voices silenced.

10. The truth is whatever we say it is: There is no objective truth. "Truth" is whatever serves the purpose of the workers' revolution and socialist State, which thereby becomes unchallengeable. Instead, there is utter contempt for the truth.

Words have no fixed meaning. Evil must lie. Therefore, a choreography of lies, sometimes called "organized lying," is integral to the socialist regime.[5] Deceit is not only permissible it is applauded when used to advance socialist ends, such as sowing social discord to gain power, and justify or coverup the Party's criminal actions.

11. Morality becomes whatever we say it is: All the real evil following these tenets creates is ultimately for the greater good, and therefore must be ignored (the end justifies the means until the means become the end). Theft to equalize wealth is applauded. Even political imprisonment, brutal torture, forced labor camps, starvation, and mass murder can be justified. There are no timeless norms that reflect the better angels of our humanity. Instead, all moral precepts arise from and are relative to prevailing economic conditions in society. Good is whatever helps the proletariat in its class struggle. Anything that hampers it is evil. Religion, including the idea of God, is nothing but superstition institutionalized by society's oppressors to control the masses. Therefore, socialists must wage war against it. Socialists' rejection of theistic religion and their belief that they possess the imprimatur of a superhumanly ordained movement of the universe exempt them from the normal laws of morality.[6] In fact, in the counterfeit religion of socialism anything, no matter how horrendous, is permitted if part of class conflict. The workers' revolution socialism calls for is justified in using whatever means are expedient. This invariably leads to turning humans' normal sense of morality upside down.

12. We own the future! Socialists are on the right side of history: The coming of the socialist State is inevitable, and because it is guided by the Will of The People as revealed to socialist leaders inspired by the sacred texts of Marx, Engels, Lenin, Stalin, and Mao it is the infallible source of all truth that matters concerning human affairs. The inevitable progression

into socialism and the perfection of mankind is only questioned or resisted by evil people who must be dealt with severely. To quote the Austrian-born Harvard economist Joseph Schumpeter, "opponents are not merely in error but in sin."[7]

This is not simply a discussion of the history of past socialist regimes, which some might consider of fading relevance to the present. Nor is this characterization of socialism's belief system based merely on an academic analysis of an abstract political theory. Rather, in addition to that which we know from historical examples of socialism, it represents the shared ideology of today's radical left in the West and the socialist regimes in power throughout the world based on their public writings, spoken words and actions.

Are there factions and strains within modern socialism? Certainly, many. I do not wish to imply that it is monolithic. As with any comprehensive political ideology differences about emphasis and assertiveness around particular points are debated. But the commonalities are fundamental, while the differences are largely superficial. The fact is that socialism's many factions occupy the same doctrinal "tent" I described above, or what might also be called the same ideological "space," but for political survival and/or more favorable public perception cleverly adapt themselves and the language they use to varying circumstances without repudiating the underlying doctrine they share.

Therefore, in researching today's avowedly radical left-wing political parties, one does not find all twelve of these tenets specifically spelled out in their overview statements of what they stand for and their aims. Apart from differing doctrinal emphasis, especially pertaining to violent revolution, because they are political activists their leadership is no doubt keenly aware of the likely negative political repercussions among the electorate were they to lay all their cards on the table. However, what is spelled out is awful enough, and with a little bit of drilling down into their literature and actions the tenets do become very clear, including, of course, their adoption of Marx and Engels' thinking concerning the evils of capitalism, the central importance of class struggle, expropriation of property, and the necessity for a workers' revolution (or a relatively peaceful but "radical transformation") to create a society of economic equals.

I should also emphasize that these twelve tenets represent the full expression of socialist ideology. They are interrelated and should be thought of as woven together into a "whole cloth" totalitarian belief system if you will, rather than a menu list of separate items one could select from. Therefore, although some of them may be emphasized more, and others less by various political factions, none can be completely left out in the march toward socialism. They are all necessary ingredients in its "recipe." Nonetheless, in practice they have not all been applied evenly and completely to any real society despite desperate attempts at doing so. The primary reason is that even under severe coercion the reality of human nature and the bewildering complexity of human societies inevitably get in the way of utopian power.

Malia put it this way in giving his account of Stalin's infamous first Five-Year Plan of 1928-1932, referring to its forced collectivization of agriculture which caused a massive famine, killing millions: "Indeed, it is perhaps inherent in the real logic of history that ideologies are almost always debased on contact with political action; the higher the ambition of the ideology, the more drastic the contemplated action, the more likely is the debasement in practice."[8] By "debasement" he was referring to is the immediate unravelling of the Plan, and the incredibly brutal mass death and the scapegoating and murder of whole groups of people that resulted from its utter failure. The Plan, the product of socialist unreality, was presumed perfect, so the socialists' twisted logic concluded that either some people are evil saboteurs, or they simply must be shown the right way with a firm hand. In either case those people, typically numbering in the thousands, if not millions, are the problem and must be dealt with mercilessly.

Because of the stiff resistance often encountered, and the previous failures of socialist regimes, an incremental, one-bite-at-a-time progression toward full implementation of the often-disguised socialists' totalitarian ideal has become the preferred political strategy over trying to advance their agenda simultaneously on all fronts, particularly in relatively prosperous countries. This is only the difference between immediate and ultimate aims. Genuine socialists wish to tear down, not "reform" the system. They view half-way measures as only transient expedients that help in their quest for full political power, at which time they ignore and repudiate the compromises they entered, and any limits to their power. Locked into their ideology, once in power socialists persist like zealous quack doctors who are totally blind to their own incompetence, and to the cost in human misery and social destruction that results from their actions. Such human costs cannot be real in their imaginary utopia, and, therefore, cannot be acknowledged or considered. Instead, once they become publicly known blame must be placed on those who may resist the regime, that is, anyone accused of clinging to the capitalist order that it is destroying (labelled "reactionaries").

These tenets and their consequential human costs are, in effect, symptomatic markers of socialism's progression, like an illness attacking the human body. A very important lesson to be drawn from the history of socialism is that whenever politicians, activists, academic theoreticians, cultural icons, and other elites possessing the utopian mindset push governmental measures that are in the direction of these tenets all should recognize that they are, in fact, pushing society down a road toward the impossible, a fully socialist society, the very definition of "dystopia." This is true whether such advocates themselves truly understand what they are doing. They may be either willing or unwitting accomplices — "useful idiots." By the time they say "Oh my God! What have I done!" it is too late.

A stark illustration of the disasters created by attempts at full uncompromising implementation of socialism is how various socialist dictators applied Tenet No. 7 above with horrific life and death consequences for peasant farmers. Throughout history, because food was often scarce and its supply uncertain, poverty and hunger – sometimes to the point of starvation – were related to one another. It is a cruel paradox that, purportedly to combat a legacy of unequal ownership of productive land and distribution of food, communist regimes in the Soviet Union, China, Cambodia, and North Korea instead caused massive famines that killed millions. This monstrously surreal, ideological warping of the reality of farming and farm communities, as noted before, resulted from putting private agricultural production and distribution under centralized governmental control in "collectives" or otherwise simply confiscating the food produced by farmers by force.

According to a 1946 U.S. government study on The Soviet Union, *Communism in Action*, the Bolsheviks caused massive famines in the Ukraine in 1921, and then again in 1933 and 1934 when their brutal enforcement of Stalin's Five-Year Plan killed approximately 13 million people.[9] Mao's "Great Leap Forward," which collectivized Chinese agriculture, led to the Great Famine of 1958-'62, resulting in an estimated 45 million deaths in what is perhaps the world's worst famine catastrophe of all time. In addition, according to Frank Dikötter's 2010 book *Mao's Great Famine* and "China: A Long March into Night" by Jean-Louis Margolin in the *The Black Book of Communism*,[10] another two to three million more were tortured or beaten to death, or summarily executed as communist cadres took control of food supplies. Mao's regime essentially reduced its people to the status of livestock by controlling their food supplies. After all, to Mao and his followers, common people were nothing more than soil, incapable of independent "correct" thought and action.

Lenin cynically once said, "Hunger performs a progressive function."[11] In addition to motivating revolution by hungry masses, perhaps Lenin meant that manipulating food supplies to starve to death those designated as class enemies, a policy the communists carried out, helps progress toward creation of the socialist State! Though Stalin gets most of the attention today, we should note it was Lenin, not Stalin, who during a terrible food shortage in 1918 emulated Robespierre's Reign of Terror by scapegoating successful farmers, inventing a new social class he branded "kulaks" or "bloodsucking traitors and profiteers," and calling for "death to all of them."[12] Indeed, Lenin demanded that his henchmen spread terror as they confiscated grain from peasant villages and farms. It is now known from examination of Lenin's directives and letters that he was as evil as his protégé, Stalin, having repeatedly demonstrated socialism's unlimited and extreme brutality in practice.

There are always at least a few witnesses to such barbarism who defy the totalitarian regime to tell the truth about it. The so-called Holodomor famine of 1932-33 during which Stalin's evil minions confiscated food supplies and starved to death an estimated 3.5 million Ukrainians, plus more in other Soviet states, is one such case of genocidal socialist policies, but sadly, by no means the only one.[13] Victor Kravchenko, a former Soviet official who "defected" to the United States in 1946 wrote of the nightmarish horrors he encountered during the famine:

> The first consequence of collectivization was death. Although not a word was published about the tragedy, the famine that prevailed in southern Russia and in Central Asia was known to all. We denounced as 'anti-Soviet rumors' events we knew to

be the absolute truth. Although the police took severe measures to keep victims isolated, Dnipropetrovsk was full of peasants starving. Most of them were immobilized for being too weak to beg around the railway stations. The children were skeletons with swollen bellies. In the past, friends and relatives who lived in the countryside sent food packages to their relatives in urban districts. Now it was the other way around. But the ration was so tiny and insecure that few dared send supplies. And the famine coincided with the triumphant end of our first five-year plan after four years, the press became hysterical, boasting of our progress. But not even the propaganda could completely quench the death groans. The cries of 'happy life' seemed to us more pitiful and terrifying than those of the hungry.

Everything depended on the new harvest...An army of more than one hundred thousand men, chosen by the Central Committee of the Party, was sent across the lands to be collected, with the order to ensure the new harvest. I was one of the mobilized.

...the woman began to tell us: 'they must know that half death, slow agony, is worse...I don't know how many people die every day. They are so weak they do not even leave their homes. My car goes around every day and picks up the bodies. We have eaten everything: dogs, cats, mice, birds. Tomorrow, in the light of day you will see the trees barked. He ate that and horse manure too.[14]

Kravchenko then discovered that there were Soviet-controlled storage facilities nearby filled with confiscated grain to be shipped out, hidden out of reach from the starving population!

Immense power can be gained by controlling society's food supplies, provided a person is willing to be ruthless and insensitive to the human suffering and mass death that result. Communists well understood that people can be controlled by restricting their food, just as easily as by using a gun. To paraphrase Stephen Spender in *The God That Failed*, those who are unable to avoid hunger will always be willing to risk loss of freedom for the promise of bread.[15] People who are starving to death will do anything for food; they will unquestioningly obey any demand made by their brutal overseers for even the slightest chance of obtaining mere crumbs of food. Stalin and Mao knew this well, and both believed people are "a problem" easily solved by providing food only to those loyal to the regime and withholding it to punish with starvation those whose fidelity is questionable. Thus, in their brand of utopia, controlling the food supply was a top priority for political control and to kill, not to nourish. For hardened socialists, starving masses of people to death is a means justified by the ends they seek.

The famines in the Soviet Union, China, North Korea and Cambodia were unnatural, ideological famines. Even if as has been suggested, some consequences were unintentional, they were the direct result of forced attempts at supplanting the market by applying the political ideology of socialism to the food supply, with government always dictating prices and quantities of most goods in all locations, as well as controlling the farm work itself. By comparison, a just society provides enough sustenance to those members who are in danger of being destitute, i.e., those truly unable to provide themselves with food and other necessities. Proclamations concerning the rights of human beings have recognized food as the foundation of civilization, and freely sharing food with others, often including strangers, has been a widespread cultural norm even in primitive cultures. For those who are truly poor, with too little food, life-sustaining help in a free nation can come from family members, voluntary organizations within the immediate community (churches and food banks), and from government when necessary. In free, open market societies, farmers are motivated to produce surpluses that are put in trade globally to feed others or stored to prevent shortages. Such abundance stands in stark contrast to the miserable record of socialist regimes in feeding their people.

Moving forward in time, socialists, particularly in the United States, have conjured up a newer version of Marx's class warfare theme under the cloak of humanitarianism. Instead of the simple two-class world of exploiters and workers (Tenet No. 4), they have cleverly migrated Marx's paradigm of an economically "exploited class" to a larger set of victimized "classes" such as those representing race, gender, and sexual orientation. This is essentially a cynical divisive strategy to arouse hatred and passion for group identity based "class struggles," begetting groups whose loyalty is owed to the socialist Left, rather than the nation. As Malia et al. put it: "The paradigm or core concept of Marxism may also be transferred from working class...to any other group that is (or claims to be) deprived, humiliated, offended, exploited, or victimized."[16]

The Left amplifies and exploits the deeply rooted "us versus them" demons latent in diverse communities in order to gain political power, promoting social disunity by placing racial, ethnic, sexual and gender identity ahead of the civic "we." Pronouncing that all such classes of persons are automatically victims with grievances because of their group identity, they incite resentment and promise to redress claims of grievance once in power. Thus, they play off and amplify antipathy and distrust among the different peoples who make up our world and our local communities.

In sum, socialism, with its all-knowing, all-powerful central government and its many labels, masquerades as an idealism put into action but instead has proven to be a highly toxic, hate-driven ideology antithetical to freedom and justice. It mixes predatory envy, deceit, covetousness, and mystical irrationality with a barbarous immorality that includes group-dominated, hate-driven political campaigns, and ultimately, murder of those who might resist. The former American socialist, Max Eastman, quoted Lenin as having told a Russian Youth Conference: "For us morality is subordinated completely to the interests of the class struggle of the proletariat."[17] It is not simply the twisted immorality of "the ends justify the means." Rather, it is the belief that its utopian ends justify any means, including mass murder.

Marx's paradisiacal "Kingdom of Freedom" has never materialized in any socialist state. Quite the opposite. Socialists like to characterize themselves as kind, caring, virtuous people focused on helping others while characterizing their opponents as dangerous fascists, but whether they are self-aware or not, the leaders of the movement are wannabe dictators. They want to command others, not produce anything themselves; as such they are the ultimate social parasites. Like dictators since time immemorial, they desire the power to dictate others' actions to achieve their vision, even if that means destroying some of them in the process. It is they who are dangerous, not the people they enslave and punish. The socialists' dream requires a voracious appetite for power – the power to control others, to take from others and to demand conformance to their will, in order to create their vision of the world and assure their continuing control. In short, socialism is the antithesis of individual freedom. The word "social," the root of "socialist," used in a political context refers to their concern first and foremost with the collective obedience, not the welfare of others.

Use of the word "ought," like the word "should," expresses a prescription for one's own actions or those of others. Rather than being scrupulously concerned with what he or she ought to do or not do individually, the socialist instead focuses on gaining control of governmental power and its potential for use of force to project his or her normative thoughts and feelings via commands for what others "ought to do." As pointed out above, socialist doctrine rejects established moral principles so that anything, no matter how horrific, may be done when it is for the benefit of the "oppressed class."

Socialism is designed to concentrate vast power in the hands of a few who will direct by fiat the lives of citizens from the top down. This drive to control others and shape society from a central source of power is what makes socialism an ideology rather than just an unproven theory, and a grave danger when applied to a genuine society comprised of real human beings.

The concern socialists profess for their fellow man has been shown to be a counterfeit humanism; the philosopher Bertrand Russell's caution about idealists applies: their professed idealism is often a "guise that hides their love of power." In the actual dystopian world of socialism, real flesh and blood people are dealt with as though they are nothing more than a statistic, a mere manipulatable abstraction, or as Charles Krauthammer may have put it, as only means to an end rather than the end itself.

Now having "looked under the hood" of socialism and seen what it's concept of attaining equality through class struggle entails, one might wonder how anyone who is half-way intelligent could believe in such blatantly immoral and dysfunctional rubbish based on outrageous lies. Still a great many people choose to do so as a matter of faith. Likewise, it is tempting to call all socialist doctrine, with its crackpot economics and sinister social theories, stupid and nonsensical. But that is too ready a dismissal of an ideology that spread so quickly and had such terrible impact on hundreds of millions of lives. It is necessary to probe further to understand socialism's spread and collapse, and its potential to undergo a revival in our time.

With good reason, socialists focus on recruiting and indoctrinating youth. As the former communist Whittaker Chambers attested from his own experience, socialists in their youth usually start with a conviction not uncommon among young people, that the world is unjust and must be changed.[18] Socialism presents itself as the perfect vehicle to realize that ambition with a seemingly rational formula. All youth begin life with innocent credulity, but as adults, with age and experience, most people gradually become less susceptible to Pied pipers. Sadly, however, many others, having been taught what to think, not how to think, are unable to escape from the indoctrination of their educational institutions.

Many such institutions in the West have become a means of nurturing ideology and a recruiting ground for the Left. This is a simple matter when students see that if they follow the prescribed path to the far Left, they will be rewarded with the approbation of the institution and many of their peers and lucrative jobs in the public or non-profit sectors, but denied such benefits, and even scorned, ostracized, and attacked as an uncaring fascist pariah if they publicly question the Left's socialist orthodoxy.

The sophistry of radical Left influencers, such as the late Herbert Marcuse, who have taken advantage of the freedoms they so distain to burrow into society's major institutions, has provided the false intellectual justification and strong encouragement for their young disciples to move from earnest conviction to zealous action, often with complete unconditional resolve, freed from any moral strictures.

Marcuse preached that "the capitalist system as a whole is inherently evil, and that therefore freedom and tolerance within the system are likewise evil. Thus, a true, deeper tolerance must involve intolerance towards false ideas and movements...certain things cannot be said, certain ideas cannot be expressed, certain policies cannot be proposed, certain behavior cannot be permitted."[19] So today, after several generations have been influenced by Marcuse's teachings, and that of others like him in the U.S., there exists "Cancel Culture," "Safe Spaces," ANTIFA, and many of the American intelligentsia in media and academia full of self-righteous zeal, censoring, scorning, shouting down and intimidating those who disagree with them. For them morality stems not from any sense of personal responsibility for one's own actions, but only from the righteousness of overturning by whatever means necessary the structural systems of society they believe to be fundamentally unjust. As Michael Horowitz, a one-time leader of the movement, demonstrated Leftists easily become intoxicated by their own virtuosity, and addicted by it as the initial "high" of exercising god-like power over others "for the good of humanity" leads to an irresistible craving for more.

Such people often proclaim that they are acting out of compassion for those in society's lower ranks, but due to lack of honest introspection are unaware that embedded in their compassion is a sense of superiority over those whose interests they purport to champion. They use their positions of presumed authority in academia to viciously attack those who do not kowtow to their vapid moralism, calling them hard-hearted and immoral Cretans, Fascists, racists, or worse. As Allan Bloom pointed out, they hypocritically attempt to channel their irreconcilable inegalitarian impulses into a public egalitarian platform so they can gain highly gratifying political influence, a use of "soft power" that has been cultivated to an art form by the Left's virtue-seeking elites since the 1960's.[20]

Make no mistake, bloodiness and terror have been socialism's markers in history up to the present. But Marcuse and other such academic influencers do not acknowledge the consequential loss of essential freedom and basic rights, and the immorality of the draconian measures socialism requires. Yet the world knows from the painful widespread experience of it that socialism is a disaster; it has never worked in any society anywhere for anyone, young or old, and not for lack of trying, but because it simply cannot be made to work. Despite whatever horrible contortions its commissars may impose on the hapless people they cruelly oppress, socialism still fails. Even the most doctrinaire socialist regimes have often been forced to move away from the demotivating strict equalization of their people or face economic and political crisis (unless heavily subsidized by other socialist regimes). As demonstrated repeatedly and at all levels, being true to socialist principles is an impossibility over the long haul because it is simply contrary to human nature and fundamentally immoral. Attempts to force it to work have been totally discredited everywhere and have buried a hundred million people. Nonetheless, mostly young, true believers of the "progressive" Left, found in every western nation, march on.

In 1878 Frederick Engels wrote *Anti-Duhring*, a critique of Eugen Duhring's *Revolution in Science*, an attempt to create a socialism that would replace Marxism. Anti-During has had great influence on socialist doctrine. A passage in it is cited as the authoritative statement of Marx and Engels' combined thinking about the nature of socialist morality. Marx and Engels would have us embrace the notion that there are no transcendent ethical precepts of good and evil. Instead, they held that moral precepts derive "from the practical relations on which their class position is based – from [prevailing] economic relations in which the classes [bourgeoisie and proletariat] carry on production and exchange."[21]

This belief, namely that man's present desires and antagonisms manifested in class relations determine right from wrong and good from evil, flows throughout all socialist doctrine as a basic premise, and, not surprisingly, opens the door to the atrocious actions of socialism's most earnest adherents. Thus, did the nihilism of socialism's original "sacred scriptures" translate into the absolute evil of its practices in the 20th Century and on to the present day.

A revealing side note about the moral values espoused by Marx and Engels, pillars of socialist wisdom and moral guidance who have enamored Western intelligentsia for so many years: biographical records clearly show that both were fond of using ethnic and racial slurs and stereotyping. Despite Marx's Jewish family background, he wrote a very hateful critique of Judaism. One might postulate that Marx's 1848 essay published in Germany, "On the Jewish Question," linking Judaism with the evils of capitalism, i.e., the exploitation the working class, influenced in some measure the ideology developed by the German National Socialists blaming Jews for the economic problems of Germany; an ideology that resulted in its virulent antisemitism and the Holocaust. The Nazi form of anti-capitalist equality Goebbels and Hitler spoke so enthusiastically about would apply only to Nordic persons, not to Jews. I quote from Marx's essay:

> The god of the Jews has become secularized and has become the god of the world. The bill of exchange is the real god of the Jew. His god is only an illusory bill of exchange.

> The view of nature attained under the dominion of private property and money is a real contempt for and practical debasement of nature; in the Jewish religion nature exists, it is true, but it exists only in imagination.

> The chimerical nationality of the Jew is the nationality of the merchant, of the man of money in general. The groundless law of the Jew is only a religious caricature of groundless morality and right in general, of which the purely formal rites with the world of self-interest surrounds itself.

> Once society has succeeded in abolishing the empirical essence of Judaism – huckstering and its preconditions – the Jew will have become impossible...[22]

The views expressed by Marx and Engels in 1848 regarding what we now call genocide and ethnic cleansing are equally atrocious, and unfortunately were very influential in the first genuinely socialist state, the USSR. They wrote that extermination of numerous ethnic groups scattered throughout

Europe, whom they labeled "counter-revolutionary" should be carried out; i.e., these diverse peoples should be consigned to historical oblivion as soon as possible! In the words of Engels and Marx:

> There is no country in Europe which does not have in some corner or other one of several ruined fragments of peoples, the remnant of a former population that was suppressed and held in bondage by the nation which became the main vehicle of historical development. These relics of a nation mercilessly trampled underfoot in the course of history, as Hegel says, these *residual fragments of peoples* always become fanatical standard-bearers of counter-revolution and remain so until their complete extirpation or loss of their national character, just as their whole existence in general is itself a protest against a great historical revolution.

The essay ends with:

> The next world war will result in the disappearance from the face of the earth not only of reactionary classes and dynasties, but also of entire reactionary peoples. And that, too, is a step forward.[23]

This essay, part of the holy writ of Marxism, was one of Stalin's favorites, giving him ideological carte blanche to order mass deportations into slave labor camps of various ethnic groups within the USSR and then in the countries his Red Army invaded after he and Hitler agreed in 1939 to the secret protocol of the Molotov-Ribbentrop Pact mentioned earlier. Today, this very same Marxian ideological depravity is being replayed by the Chinese Communist Party in its attempts to obliterate the Tibetan and Uyghur ethnic minorities.

True socialists, knowing well their Marxian catechism, play fast and loose with any concept of morality, but ironically, they push their beguiling concept of "social justice" to take the moral high ground in public opinion for political effect. The inherently fuzzy notion of social justice is used by the Left to argue for the application of unbounded governmental power to equalize the living conditions of all members of a society, thereby supposedly assuring all a "fair distribution of property and wealth" that will raise up all who have less. But with the natural inequalities of individuals this means that people must be treated unequally, a contradiction. Can that be just? The basic strategy here is to use existing injustice, poverty and envy as a political lever to divide people into groups or classes (the commonly heard "working class people") that can then be pitted against each other and aroused to violent action. Such has been the standard modus operandi used by ruthless socialist demagogues to incite anger and often violence toward certain "enemies of the people." In addition to political dissenters, these "enemies" may be corporate executives, the rich, members of a prosperous racial group, business owners, a religious group, or any other identifiable segment of society they wish to demonize in order to build political power.

Practical implementation of this strategy, of course, began with Lenin's Bolshevik Communist Party in Russia. One of Lenin's first steps toward implementing "social justice" and establishing socialist "equality" was creation of a vast secret police and informer network to arrest and quickly liquidate anyone suspected of opposing his power. Soon after came the elimination of the kulaks, that relatively prosperous (and productive) class of small farm owners. It must therefore be recognized that the true power of the Bolsheviks' seductive utopian appeal rested not on real justice or moral virtue. Instead, it tapped into humans' basest predatory instincts: "You have it. I want it. I am going to take it from you." Such a starkly immoral thirsting for power, heightened by false ideals, stands in sharp contrast to socialism's deceptively noble-sounding and beguiling mantra of "an equal share for all."

There can be no moral legitimacy in a political movement driven by envy. The moral philosopher Michael Novak has pointed out that "Envy, it turns out, is the most destructive social passion – more so than hatred, which is at least visible and universally recognized as evil. Envy seldom operates under its own name; it chooses a lovelier name to hide behind ["social justice"], and it works like an invisible gas that poison's the relations among people."[24]

Youthful and more mature idealists of this sort may insist their version of social justice is a cause worth going to any lengths to achieve, including even killing others. But in a 1941 essay, the theologian/philosopher Reinhold Niebuhr cautioned that "Idealism is ere but dangerous utopian illusions when not an outgrowth of a healthy awareness that 'all treasures of the spirit are borne in earthen vessels,' and 'no such vessel is ever a perfect vehicle of the treasure which it bears.'"[25]

The facts of history reveal that socialism transforms the social justice-seeking utopian idealism of its naive followers into a primitive impulse to seize power, property, and wealth from others regardless of the moral boundaries they may be crossing. It teaches that the prevailing social order must be destroyed, whether gradually, or better yet, in a sweeping revolutionary stroke, so that it can be rebuilt according to a grand utopian design, to create the perfect system, the perfect order.

As Bertrand Russell made this point in his Nobel Prize acceptance speech: "Much that passes as idealism is disguised hatred or disguised love of power."[26]

Tragically, the most ruthless leaders of today's "freedom fighters" and social justice crusaders inevitably become tomorrow's dictators or commissar-like bureaucrats (provided they themselves survive the inevitable internal purges). Disillusionment of idealist revolutionaries and resistance from previously docile appeasers typically come too late to save their societies. The peaceful, well-intentioned marchers, weakened by the chaos of revolution and purges and desperate for stability of any kind, inevitably fall victim to the soul-crushing barbarity that is socialism, and the egalitarian utopia they desired in which all humans are equalized by design and all souls are purged of love of power, acquisitiveness, and envy, disappears into the vast chasm separating flawed socialist theory from reality.

Gary Kasparov, former World Chess Champion from the USSR, and now chairman of the Human Rights Foundation recently wrote, "Soviet leaders squeezed the soul from their citizens by forcing them to perform in the macabre perversion of human nature that is totalitarian socialism."[27]

A contemporary version of the same social justice ideology is the "war on income inequality," now being used by the progressive Left to propagandize, divide, and politically organize people according to economic strata, so that those in the lower half of the economic spectrum (the "masses" to use a Leninist/ Maoist term) and idealistic young voters can be politically manipulated. Their goal is to seize and concentrate the power of government to appropriate and redistribute income and property to their followers from those targeted as class enemies.

In order to gain support for their political movement Socialism's adherents use messaging that blurs the fundamental meaning of justice, attracting followers among society's disaffected by convincing them that they should hate the "privileged," people who use their undeserved wealth and status to corrupt government, protecting and even further increasing an unfair share of whatever a "zero-sum" world has to offer while keeping everyone else down. The sad irony is this: the more that power is concentrated in government, the more people will seek the favor of those wielding that power, leading to endemic corruption where disillusioned idealists find themselves beholden to modern-day pirates who enrich themselves by controlling government.

Disingenuous Labels and Doublespeak

To escape their moral burden of complicity in the global

disaster of communism and its resulting disrepute, socialists in the political arena today confuse the public by disguising their shared ideology and true agenda with twisted double-speak and misleading labels, calling themselves "Democratic Socialists" or "Social Democrats," "Progressives," or "Liberals." But for the truth, consider the following transcribed account of a 1944 speech by Alexander Trachtenberg in NYC. Trachtenberg was a pro-Bolshevik Russian émigré to the U.S. in 1906 who became a key member of the U.S. Communist Party (its "Cultural Commissar"):

> When we get ready to take the US, we will not take over on the label of Communism. We will not take over with the label of Socialism. These labels are unsettling to the American people and have been spread too much. We will take the US under labels which we have made very lovable. We will take it under Liberalism, under Progressivism, and under Democracy, but take it we will.[28]

Use of a false outward appearance to conceal an evil purpose (the wolf in sheep's clothing) is famously restated by Shakespeare's Lady Macbeth in Act I, Scene V, of the great tragedy: "bear welcome in your eye, Your hand, your tongue. Look like th' innocent flower, But be the serpent under't." Over the ages it has been shown that many people can be fooled by such chicanery.

Let us now start to unravel this obfuscation, this game of masks and labels, which has been played for a very long time to fool those who are too trusting and unable to discern the ugly truth being hidden.

"Democratic Socialists" and "Social Democrats"

True democracy and socialism do not mix. Democracy is not an end in itself, but rather the means to liberty, whereas true socialism inherently requires that individuals' freedom be curtailed and assets be redistributed through governmental control. French political commentator and historian Alexis de Tocqueville made this clear in an 1848 speech on socialism: "Democracy and socialism cannot go together. You cannot have it both ways. Democracy extends the sphere of individual freedom, socialism restricts it...Democracy and socialism have nothing in common but one word 'equality.' But while democracy seeks equality in liberty, socialism seeks equality in restraint and servitude."[29] Surely it is what Lenin had in mind when he noted that "Liberty must be carefully rationed."[30] Perhaps Quang Nguyen, a Vietnamese-American and former refugee said it best in 2010: "Democracy is about freedom, not free stuff."[31]

Examples of socialist political parties misappropriating the word "Democratic" by using it to label what they stand for have abounded for many years. This implies that their ascent into power and once in power, their decision-making, will be subject to democratic processes and thus the will of the people. A great many people are understandably sympathetic to this word label. The point of claiming to be democratic is obfuscation that at once lessens resistance and helps broaden the socialists' appeal to a careless public. In 1900 Russia, the revolutionary Marxist group that the young radical Joseph Stalin joined was known as the Social Democratic Party. The Party was led by the militant revolutionaries Vladimir "Lado" Ketskhoveli and Mikhail Kalinin (a future member of Lenin's politburo). Likewise, according to the German Social Democratic Party (SPD) was formed by the merger of two Marxist-influenced parties in the late 1800's.[32]

So-called "Democratic Socialists" may actually seek to win elections, but don't want the liberty of democracy. Instead, they want to use the collective tyranny of the majority as a club with which to beat down freedom and human rights. The labels "Democratic Socialists," and "Social Democrats" turn democracy on its head; what they really means was well-articulated by Lord Acton in 1878:

The true democratic principle that none shall have power over the people, is taken to mean that none shall be able to restrain or elude its [the state's] power. The true democratic principle, that the people shall not be made to do what it doesn't like, is taken to mean that it [the state] shall never be required to tolerate what it doesn't like. The true democratic principle, that every man's free will shall be as unfettered as possible, is taken to mean that the free will of the collective people shall be fettered in nothing.[33]

While some would believe a "kinder, gentler" Democratic Socialist Utopia is possible, history would warn otherwise. Those who supported the Bolshevik's seizure of power during the Revolution in Russia thought the new government would usher in a new age of equality and social justice following the overthrow of the Czar. Some may have even thought that democratic elections would follow. But many, even fanatical Bolshevik revolutionaries like Leon Trotsky, and large numbers of the intelligentsia later found they were dead wrong; or put another way, both wrong and dead. In truth, many people unhappy with their current government will vote for promises, especially those accustomed to authoritarian rule, who are prone to choose promised security and national pride over the uncertainties of freedom and messiness of democracy. To garner support for the Revolution the Bolsheviks cleverly promised "Peace, Land, and Bread" to a people who were often hungry, and were suffering from recent defeat at the hands of their hated enemy, the Germans, with a loss of over three million Russian dead, not many years after a humiliating defeat by the Japanese in the Far East.

Unable to see and grasp the full implications of his racial determinist ideology, the millions who helped vote Hitler and his National Socialist Party into power in Germany may have expected an era of peace, social tranquility, and just wages. Instead, they got a war that nearly destroyed their nation, and for some, knocks on the door at night, and slave labor and death camps. And for those modern-day radical socialists less inclined toward kindness and gentleness, there is now available an extensive network of revolution-minded Marxist organizations often supported and led by activist college faculty and the students they have indoctrinated.

We therefore are quite right to be concerned with current, elected officials suddenly enthralled by socialist utopian dreams that justify a bigger and ever more domineering government. Socialists have now been elected to the U.S. Congress, and there are 15 national parties calling themselves either "communist," "socialist," "democratic socialist," or "social democratic," and over 20 affiliated state-level parties.

In defense of their political arguments favoring a "social democracy," today's New Left (new as opposed to their discredited communist predecessors) often tout ethnically and culturally homogeneous Scandinavian countries such as Sweden and Denmark as happy examples of a "Third Way" style of socialism. However, these countries have been rapidly drawing-down their "social capital," as a culture of welfare dependency on "free stuff" has increasingly supplanted the trust, personal responsibility and hard work that was their capitalist legacy and that led to their great success in prior years. New business formation and job creation have sputtered with expansion of high tax/high welfare policies. An ever-growing segment of their populations depends on governmental support, and is working less, producing less, and innovating less.

Notwithstanding their creation of large welfare programs, without government takeover of industries through appropriation or more extensive regulatory control, and lacking wage and price controls, these countries have never been, and are not now truly socialist. In fact, some Scandinavian governments have publicly disavowed socialism. To avoid an inevitable fiscal meltdown and a back-door slide into socialism,

188 ■ Some Call it Utopia

they are now beginning to rein in the destructive welfare payments much hyped by Western Leftists.

Great Britain, Germany, France, and some other Western democracies have also at times elected socialists (sometimes, of course, preferring to call themselves "Social Democrats"). These socialists pursued nationalization to institute direct government ownership of important industries (energy, communications, aerospace, and automotive), along with partial wage and price controls and wealth redistribution, causing serious detriment to their countries' economic well-being. As the late British Prime Minister Margaret Thatcher famously said during a 1979 interview: "Socialist governments traditionally do make a financial mess... they always run out of other people's money." Some of these countries are still struggling with the continuing effects of such ruinous policies. In most places, when it failed to produce desired results and instead made their economies moribund, once highly touted socialist central planning schemes were unceremoniously cast aside in favor of a return to private corporations operating in competitive markets. Today, although socialist political parties continue to be represented in their parliaments, none of the Western countries that flirted with socialism are truly socialist to a significant, deleterious degree. Thus far, the electorate has managed to keep socialism's beguiling political appeal in check. These advanced economies remain based on laws and culture that respect the private property rights, private capital, and the primacy of competitive markets that underlie their prosperity.

Attempting to occupy moral high ground in the latter half of the past century, some of the socialist intelligentsia invented even more ludicrous oxymorons: "Libertarian Socialist" and "Humanitarian Socialist."

"Progressives" Without Progress

How is ruining entire economies through increasing state

coercion and by diminishing citizens' freedom meet any rational person's definition of "progress"? The word "progressive" certainly has a far more pleasing ring to it than "socialist." Why cling to a label if it is a political liability? The political label "progressive" and the Progressive movement once stood for advocacy of "good government"; i.e., exposing and rooting out corrupt big city political machines, advocating universal suffrage, improving government efficiency and urban living conditions, support for science, public education and health initiatives, and the famous trust-busting of Theodore Roosevelt. Progressive intervention in the economy was limited to promoting more efficient and honest government and establishing boundary rules that prohibited unfair practices. It was not a grasping political elite seeking power to specify what other people must do, what they can and cannot say, and how they must live their lives.

Will the "progress" of progressivism also ultimately lead to repudiation of religion, control of food supplies, and appropriating the product of others' labor? Do the attacks on Christian beliefs and the growing anti-Semitism, rewriting of history into a false narrative, extreme "green" causes, the banning of certain books and censorship of speakers, and the wealth distribution schemes espoused by today's progressives ring any bells? Should it raise an alarm? Recall again the tactics of socialist revolutionaries. The noble-sounding progressive label has been hijacked by the Left and is now indistinguishable from the early stage of Marxist socialism, which, using Lenin's playbook, is primarily a war to dominate public thought, destroy competing ideas, and ruin those who express them. (See again the Tenets of Socialism) Yes, it is today's "progressives" who believe they know what is best for all and wish to centralize power in a state they themselves control. Like Lenin, they are determined to "drive humanity into happiness."

H. L. Mencken once observed, "The urge to save humanity is almost always a false front for the urge to rule." Indeed,

Progressives may have already gained control of a major political party in the United States, along with many big city and state political machines, most of the national news media, much of the entertainment industry, and many academic institutions. Thus, their political power is now growing within the US Congress. They must be feared, and their gains reversed. Their vision of progress is a forced regression toward an anachronistic, failed, and immoral system that has long been eclipsed by the real progress of free democratic societies.

"Liberals" Without Liberalism

This label certainly falls soft on the ears, since "liberal" is derived from the word "liberty," meaning freedom, and its Latin root "liber" meaning free. The reality behind today's use of the term (particularly in the US) is the opposite.

Like "progressive," the word "liberal" in a political context once had a distinct meaning very different from the label "socialist." Alas, this word has also been misappropriated and twisted into a different meaning by the political Left, giving it an ideological orientation dramatically at odds with the West's hard-won legacy of true liberalism and its foremost concern for preserving freedom and protecting citizens from governmental coercion. The origin of this twisting of language has been traced by the American historians Daniel Yergin and Joseph Stanislaw:

> In the United States, liberalism means the embrace of an activist, interventionist government, expanding its involvement and responsibility in the economy. In the rest of the world liberalism means almost exactly the opposite – what an American liberal would, in fact, describe as conservatism. This kind of liberalism supports a reduced role for the state, the maximization of individual liberty, economic freedom and reliance on the market, and decentralized decision-making. It has its intellectual roots in such thinkers as John Locke, Adam Smith, and John Stuart Mill. It emphasizes the importance of property rights and sees government's role as the facilitation and adjudication of civil society.

During the First World War, some of the leading Progressive writers began to use the word liberalism as a substitute for progressivism, which had become tarnished by its association with Theodore Roosevelt who had run and lost on the Progressive ticket. Traditional liberals were not happy to see their label transformed. In the 1920's, *The New York Times* criticized "the expropriation of the time-honored word 'liberal'" and argued that "the Radical-Red school of thought…hand back the word 'liberal' to its original owners." During the 1930's, Herbert Hoover and Franklin Roosevelt duked it out as to who was the true liberal. Roosevelt won [the election] adopting the word to ward off accusations of being left-wing. He could declare liberalism was 'plain English for a changed concept of the duty of government toward economic life.' And since the New Deal, liberalism in the United States has been identified with an expansion of government's role in the economy.[34]

As I pointed out earlier, for advocates of an ideology language is used for effect to convince and influence actions, not to honestly communicate and inform. One could no doubt create an entire dictionary of the numerous doublespeak distortions of language and labels by the Left. In his book *Reflections on the Failure of Socialism*, the long-time American socialist Max Eastman devoted a full chapter to the "violence to language" and "treachery against civilization" done by the Left in distorting words such as "Freedom," "Equality," "Liberal," and "Progressive," and "Left" versus "Right." Eastman observed that "Marxian revolutionists" first decided to make "class mean party." The term "working class" was detached from actual workers and attached to the Bolsheviks, a party not comprised of workers, but instead "of believers in Marxian theory about what workers were going to do." [35]

A truly liberal society is one based upon freedom tempered by democratically enacted laws, personal and corporate responsibility, tolerance, impartiality, and individual rights, including entitlement of all to equal treatment under the law. In a society that is based upon the moral equality of its members, authority is understood to flow from the bottom up, rather than from the top down. Or, as Larry Siedentop asks in *Inventing the Individual*, "Are humans meant to be governed by Plato's Guardians, or by themselves?"[36]

Unfortunately, as Eastman observed the "Liberal" political label as often used today has become yet another disingenuous debasement of language by socialists. True liberals welcome change, the change which occurs naturally in a free and open society, rather than change commanded by a government. Today's ersatz "liberals" seek instead to concentrate power so its supposedly beneficent "Guardians" can use the State's monopoly on force to bully individuals, control economic activity, limit freedom and suppress dissent by intimidation. This is absolute betrayal of the values of true liberalism.

There are those who claim that modern, "soft" liberalism is morally acceptable because its avowed goal is "only" that of helping those "in need." Calling for more taxes on those possessing more wealth to enable a full "welfare state," these liberals stop short of complete state ownership and control of production and distribution, replacing voluntary exchanges and markets with dictated quotas and prices, total command of what people may and may not do, and the other such repressive, features of fully-fledged 20th century socialist dystopias. However, if the goal is reducing income inequality per se rather than helping those in need of a safety net, their cause is illegitimate. If wealth distribution for its own sake takes root politically as the underlying social welfare goal of government, it follows that other than reaching complete leveling, there is no logical end point where enough is enough in terms of appropriating and transferring wealth.

Today's liberals don't just want to improve the lot of truly poor who might be in serious trouble if not for various kinds of government welfare payments and private charity. Liberal policies would instead use unequal taxation and what are called "transfer payments" to help enrich all those who simply have below average income regardless of the work they do or not do, thereby bringing everyone to the same level. Moreover, if income inequality per se is construed as a social evil rather than the essential motivator of achievement, then an ever-larger portion of incomes will be appropriated and redistributed by government. Those who have managed to prosper beyond the average level will have more and more of their wealth redistributed to those with less than average until the ultimate socialist utopian goal of social leveling is reached.

Ironically, to force such "equality" always requires treating people unequally. Along with such a massive shift of society's wealth to the State where it is pooled for "redistribution" would inevitably come a vast increase in governmental power over the lives of its citizens.

Let us, for the sake of argument, extrapolate from a narrow, single-nation political context. If, as argued by liberals, income equality is truly a matter of morality and justice (some have advocated that equal wealth is a natural "right"), then shouldn't wealth be appropriated from wealthier people in all nations, not just within one's own, and redistributed evenly across the entire globe to level the wellbeing of all earth's inhabitants? Implementation would of course, require not just international taxation but brutal coercion across national boundaries, most likely then leading to war on a global scale, causing countless deaths and leaving most who survive worse, not better off, regardless of who "wins."

Moral and practical consequences aside, the aspiration for such global leveling through ongoing wealth redistribution and the creation of a utopian global government with universal authority appear to be fundamental precepts of contemporary socialist/progressive/liberal ideology. One finds this ideology echoed in international institutions like the United Nations by some so-called less developed nations and by socialist front organizations. Oxfam, for example, claims that inequality is "trapping millions in poverty" and advocates using taxes that soak the rich and increased government control of wages "to ensure a more level playing field." Oxfam is a global non-profit charity, but with an ideological edge, describing itself as "a global organization working to end the injustice of poverty. We help people build better futures for themselves, hold the powerful accountable, and save lives in disasters. Our mission is to tackle the root cause of poverty and create lasting solutions."[37]

However, fairness and justice in a society, and equally important, the motivation that drives human betterment, depend upon freedom tempered by just laws and fair competition. They depend upon unequal but just rewards that reflect the virtuous natural effect of talent, skill, productivity, innovation, risk-taking, and industriousness, not rewards derived from political cronyism, a ready willingness to do whatever the powerful members of the ruling party desire, and payoffs from government corruption, or from familial, heredity, or group-identity favoritism. Such unjustly gained rewards always increase as a Leftist government appropriates more and more of society's wealth and freedom.

The "passion for equality" (Lord Acton used this phrase in his masterful work *Essays on Freedom and Power*) drives the Left's liberalism, destroying both freedom and human motivation for the sake of concentrating power over peoples' lives in the hands of political elites. In their way of thinking no one can earn any more than anyone else, own any more than anyone else, or be better off than anyone else in anything or in any way. But despite all liberal thinking and intellectual rhetoric the facts of human history clearly demonstrate that without human motivation, there is no striving for betterment in society, and soon it begins to decay.

Whether accomplished through unequal taxation

of those having more to benefit those with less, or whether through governmental control of the amount of money people receive for what they accomplish, modern-day liberals would use governmental force directed by an elite few as the leveling agent for achieving uniformity of economic status throughout a society. Consequently, as more and more of the income of people within a society is politically appropriated ("socialized"), and less determined through voluntary exchanges arranged by free individuals participating in open markets, incredible power is concentrated in the hands of those with political authority. This is, of course, just as they intend. Moreover, if much of what you produce in the form of income becomes property of the State to be controlled and used by the politically powerful as they see fit, then does not the government, and by extension the controlling elites, in a very real sense gain ownership of your entire life?

Ruling elites can then also use the government's trough of largess to enrich themselves and "purchase" so to speak, votes giving them a significant measure of political control over the lives of all those who become dependent on the State. In a society with only certain individuals possessing such overwhelming power, what would limit their use of that power? Think of the many ways those with such unchecked political authority would be able to control the lives of any persons or class of persons until their power becomes absolute and overwhelming. As foretold by Lord Acton's famous axiom, where all power flows through the State, the tendency to corruption of the elites controlling the State's functions becomes absolute. Those Liberals who are truly compassionate and well-meaning may not have such dire consequences in mind, but the monsters of history prove otherwise.

Such nice-sounding labels as Democratic Socialist, Social Democrat, Progressive or Liberal, make the truth about what these and other identifications stand for conveniently difficult to pin down. Different groups of scholars, based on their own political biases, have created radically different definitions for each of these monikers of socialism. Some definitions simply imply forms of socialism that follow an electoral and gradual evolutionary path to the socialist utopia rather than a revolutionary one. These may be presented to the public as a "reformist" approach. The definitional confusion provides advocates an escape from accountability for socialism's enormous sins of the past and present. The path from any "soft" to "hard" socialist State may be insidious and incremental rather than a dramatic and violent revolution, but despite the Left's attempts at misdirection, with the same ultimate aims the path must lead to the same result; namely, an undemocratic and coercive Socialist dystopia. Alexandr Solzhenitsyn warned that rosy, noble sounding words are designed to conceal socialism's horrific moral contradictions.[38] Once the proverbial camel is inside the tent, it refuses to leave and destroys everything, including the tent itself.

Boundless Arrogance

The arrogance of socialists can well be characterized as follows: certain of us know how people should live and have the right to make them adhere to our vision. A grotesque irony of socialism in practice is that when its leaders accumulate enough power, they abandon all principles of social equality where they themselves are concerned. Remember that Mao had said: "We Communists are like seeds and the people are like the soil."[39] Such incredible arrogance! Such pretension!

In the 1920's, Lenin invented a new source of terror, a version of slavery named the "Gulag," a vast system of prison labor death camps (replicated later by Mao's "lao-gai" labor camps), eventually numbering in the hundreds, into which 18-20 million were ultimately consigned by him and Stalin to a horrible fate. The one thing we can say with certainty about socialism with its history of totalitarian barbarism, is that it is not an ideology based on compassion for people and social issues, despite its proponents' honeyed words! Instead, masses of people who "get in the way" are a problem to be "managed" through use of imprisonment, ghoulish torture, "re-education," bullets, and starvation. For those subject to the rule of Lenin, Stalin, Mao, the Kims, Castro, Pol Pot, and now Venezuela's Maduro, who have lived in fear of their government, the question they silently ask is, "If this is the socialist paradise on Earth they promised, what then is hell?"

In 1945, British philosopher Bertrand Russell, who by then had lost his youthful enthusiasm for Russia's bloody "experiment" in socialism, wrote "Marx's Socialism is a doctrine of a dictatorship of the Master Class instead of Master Race, with his final stage of development, complete political and economic harmony, like the Second Coming; in the meantime, there is war and dictatorship, and insistence on ideological orthodoxy."[40]

One hundred years before Marx and Engels, Adam Smith wrote of the paradox of bitter social strife caused by individuals enamored by the theoretical beauty of their utopian plans:

> The man of system (utopian) . . . is apt to be very wise in his own conceit; and is often so enamored with the supposed beauty of his own ideal plan of government, that he cannot suffer the smallest deviation from any part of it. He goes on to establish it completely and in all its parts, without any regard either to the great interests, or to the strong prejudices which may oppose it. He seems to imagine that he can arrange the different members of a great society with as much ease as the hand arranges the different pieces upon a chess-board. He does not consider that the pieces upon the chess-board have no other principle of motion besides that which the hand impresses upon them; but that, in the great chess-board of human society, every single piece has a principle of motion of its own, altogether different from that which the legislature might choose to impress upon it. If those two principles coincide and act in the same direction, the game of human society will go on easily and harmoni-

ously, and is very likely to be happy and successful. If they are opposite or different, the game will go on miserably, and the society must be at all times in the highest degree of disorder.[41]

Marx and Engels could barely disguise their condescension and scorn for those of the true proletariat they encountered. The myth of the "dictatorship of the proletariat" is soon transformed in any socialist society into the reality of a ruling oligarchy that has accumulated power with special rights and privileges. The new socialist elite live and act like a despotic royalty and are led by individuals who assume cult-like deity status. In many cases, they claim hereditary dynastic privileges for their family and offspring, such as the Castro family in Cuba and Kim dynasty in North Korea. Mao and his inner circle had nothing but distain for the China's peasantry they manipulated en mass almost as one would livestock. Rather, they were members of the prosperous middle and upper classes and regarded the peasant masses as merely useful in helping them gain power. In *The Age of Napoleon*, the Durants pointed out that only one of the twelve-member "Committee on Public Safety" that carried out the French Reign of Terror in 1793 had engaged in any manual labor, and ironically observed, "A proletarian dictatorship is never proletarian."[42] Despite all pious proclamations about oppression of "the workers," before seizing power few if any socialist dictators ever worked in a factory or field. Very soon after taking power the "Great Helmsman" Mao and his insider group became the founding members of what is referred to today as the CCP's "Red Royalty" enjoying almost unlimited perquisites.

Unwilling to "get their hands dirty" (at least in the conventional sense), how then do these arrogant socialists convince the proletarian masses to accept their vision of utopia? Will setting class against class, for example, ultimately contribute to their welfare? Not exactly, as it turns out. The answer to "how," of course, is raw power: they initially bribe "the masses" (working class) with money from the public treasury (welfare entitlements) until that runs out, and property seized from others,[43] then soon enough turning to intimidation and the use of force to keep everyone in line. They pave the way for their power grab through gradually colonizing and then, once a tipping point is reached, controlling the "commanding heights" of culture, education, and mass media through which they dissemble, propagandize, indoctrinate, and intimidate the population until it becomes malleable. We have seen how during the 20th Century, communist/socialist revolutionaries crusading under the populist banner of "equality for all" caused an almost unimaginably vast amount of human suffering, enslavement, and death. Whenever and wherever their ideology began to take root ruthless tyrants accreted government power to themselves through systematic imprisonment, torture, and outright murder of thousands upon thousands, and in some places millions of those who might stand in their way. Contrary to Marxism, once political power had been achieved, "class warfare" simply became the Socialist State eliminating many of its own citizens, both selected groups and individuals. The violence in these police states was so irresistible and on such a colossal scale as to evoke terror even in those at a distance who were aware of the horror but not yet subject to it, thus weakening any incipient resistance to the socialist utopian paradise. Much as in the days of Hitler's Gestapo and Beria's NKVD, it became widely understood that a knock on the door in the middle of the night meant the end of any utopian dream for you, comrade! You could expect to be hauled off by extrajudicial secret police to a prison for torture, execution, or exile to a remote slave labor camp where you were likely to die or spend years in abject privation even if you survived.

Throughout such a hellish society, family members, under duress, were encouraged to spy upon and turn in each other to authorities in the hope of avoiding a similar fate. And what were the horrendous crimes of these enemies of the state? It was having the temerity to speak out or otherwise resist the diktats of the totalitarian regime. It bears repeating that Lenin was the one who established the Soviet Gulag system, which Stalin later expanded., Forced labor camps kept "troublemakers" out of circulation, and became a key factor in cementing socialism's absolute power over its citizens. As demonstrated by France's Reign of Terror, not a drop of liberty drips from the blade of a guillotine, only an ocean of blood.

The Immense Tragedy Unfolds

"If only one man dies... that is a tragedy. If millions die, that's only statistics."
—Joseph Stalin, Premier of the Soviet Union

Despite promises to the contrary, mankind has seen over and over that an ideology built around the seemingly righteous notion of universal equality, not of rights under the law, begets an earthly hell of coerced conformity, brutality, and terror. This, in fact, is the socialist State, the end game of human utopian delusions. Emulating and far exceeding the Jacobins' murderous order in the 18th Century for the people of the Vendee, Lenin, Stalin, Mao, Castro, Kim Il-sung, Pol Pot, and Eastern European and African despots of the 20th Century used absolute power for the systematic persecution and extermination (in their words "liquidation") of vast numbers of unarmed innocent people.

But let us look past 100 million dead--if that were even possible. What of those left alive? The   demons of socialism earned the label "totalitarian" from ceaseless efforts to use governmental force to control all the fundamental aspects of human life. Their instrument of control was fear, their subjects' fear of the absolute power they wielded. Totalitarianism extended not just into government seizure of property owned by individuals and control over the ability of merchants to produce and trade goods in markets. It also reached into the expression and exchange of ideas, into forced indoctrination, thought control, severe restriction of movement, and command of food supplies. It treated human beings as livestock in order to furnish slave labor, controlled reproduction, and sanctioned the bestial practice of systematic "organ harvesting" from those institutionalized and enemies of the State. (See *The Slaughter* by Gutmann.[44]) Imagine if you will a world in which the nation's gene pool becomes a resource that is controlled and, through selective human breeding, is manipulated by a godless Socialist State in order to engineer "superior" human beings by culling-out "inferior" genes (a practice like the Nazi eugenics policy of sterilizing "undesirables" and allowing only the "racially pure" to marry).

When the State owns your life, it owns all life, and no life has any value other than for service to the State. Accordingly, anyone's life may be manipulated, used or extinguished at any time at the whim of ruling elites and their henchmen. Lenin and Stalin's secret police and gulag prison system, Mao's Cultural Revolution, Pol Pot's Killing Fields, Castro's goon squads and prisons, and the Kims' system of North Korean forced labor death camps share a common socialist utopian origin. In the minds of such monsters and their ideological adherents, any means of achieving their illusionary utopia, or simply staying in power, are justified.

Today's Western socialists and communist sympathizers in Europe, the U.S., and Latin America try to pretend this vast holocaust of the 20th Century really did not happen. Like Holocaust deniers, they misrepresent and ignore history, or they persist in the "Big Lie" that the vast slaughters that occurred were not caused by the nature of utopian socialist ideology itself. The horror was instead a consequence of (a) the fierce post-revolution resistance of the privileged elites and the external forces that supported them, or (b) the ideology not being fully and faithfully followed, or (c) simply poor leadership. Indeed, despite leaving a massive trail of human sacrifices to the modern Molech, revisionist socialist politicians still ridiculously contend that they are "on the right side of history." In rebuttal, Maila asserts in *Soviet Tragedy*, "There is no such thing as socialism. Real socialism has never existed anywhere because it cannot exist; with its internal contradictions, it is an impossible but very deadly utopian fantasy. How can anything good ever come from a system whose foundation rests on envy and hatred of others?"[45]

How bad can socialism be? Numerous personal accounts of victims and escapees leave no room for even the slightest doubt about the realities of living under socialism.[46] But Svetlana Alexievich answers in a slightly different way. Incorporating numerous eye-witness accounts gathered of socialism's horrors from both survivors and perpetrators alike into her book, *Secondhand Time*, she wrote: "People who've come out of socialism are both like and unlike the rest of humanity – we have our own lexicon, our own conceptions of good and evil, our heroes, our martyrs. We have a special relationship with death."[47] One of her interviewees, a man who worked at a Soviet execution factory, said: "We were always covered in blood, we'd wipe our hands in our hair... We'd wash ourselves with cologne from the waist up...By the end of my shift my arm would be hanging down like a whip... It's been so many years, but I still can't forget it..."[48]

Notes

1. F. J. C. Hearnshaw, *A Survey of Socialism: Analytical, Historical, and Critical*, Macmillan and Co. Ltd., 1928, 1929 Edition, Chapter I, "What is Socialism? - Definitions of Socialism," pp. 27-28; In 1892 French journalists published in Le Figaro a list of 600 different definitions they had found for Socialism. A British book some years later compiled a list of "only" 263.

2. Ibid. On page 25 Hearnshaw uses the phrase "Chameleon-like" to describe Socialism.

3. Ibid. This list of twelve is considerably expanded and modified from a list of six principles found in Hearnshaw Chapter II: "The Six Essentials of Socialism," p. 34.

4. An example is G. R. S. Taylor in his *Leaders of Socialism*, p. 11, The New Age Press, London, 1908; Echoing Gracchus Babeuf's Conspiracy of Equals manifesto from the French Revolution, Taylor stated that "The main theory of socialism is that private ownership of the instruments of production, distribution, and exchange is the radical evil of the present social structure; and there will be no radical improvement until the ownership by individuals is supplanted by the united ownership of the whole collective community...public ownership must be extended to factories... the land... to avoid a loophole that would spoil the whole scheme by giving the capitalist a way to escape...All else is mere tinkering which leaves the cause of the evil untouched." Discussion of the definition of socialism as "anticapitalism" is found in *The Two Souls of Socialism* by Hal Draper, p.3, a pamphlet published by the Independent Socialist Committee, 1966

5. George Orwell, *Orwell and Politics*, Penguin Books, London 2001, quoted by Eric Litwak on p.44 in "Epistemic Arguments Against Dictatorship" in the journal Human Affairs 21, 44-52, 2011, published by Institute for Research in Social Communication, Slovak Academy of Sciences

6. Max Eastman, *Reflections on the Failures of Socialism*. Chapter 7, "The Religion of Immoralism," p. 84, the Devin Adair Company, 1955.

7. Joseph A. Schumpeter, *Capitalism, Socialism, and Democracy*, 1942, 2008 Harper 3rd Edition, Chapter 1 "Marx the Prophet," p. 5 footnote 1.

8. Martin Malia, *The Soviet Tragedy: A History of Socialism in Russia 1917-1991*, The Free Press, 1994, Chapter 6 "And They Built Socialism, The Ultimate Class Struggle," pp. 190-196 in e-version.

9. A 1946 U.S. government study of the Soviet Union, *Communism in Action, Chart of Major Events*, Legislative Reference Services of the Library of Congress, pp. 140.

10. Frank Dikötter's 2010 book *Mao's Great Famine* and "China: A Long March into Night," by Jean-Louis Margolin in the *The Black Book of Communism*, Harvard Press, 1999, pp. 463-464; the estimate of 38 million deaths is found on pp. 430 of *Mao: The Unknown Story*, by Jung Chang and Jon Halliday, Anchor Books, Random House, 2005.

11. Lenin's cynical statement "hunger performs a progressive function" can be traced to *Marxism-Leninism and Religion* in B. R. Bociurkiw et al. (eds) *Religion and Atheism in the USSR and Eastern Europe* (London 1975); and it is found in

Chapter Two, "The First Despotic Utopias" in Paul Johnson's *Modern Times*, Harper Collins, 1991, pp. 50.

12. Victor Sebestyen, *Lenin: The Man, the Dictator, and the Master of Terror*, Panther Books, 2017, Chapter 42, "The Battle for Grain," pp. 392-397. Sebestyen quotes Maximilien Robespierre in 1792: "If the rich farmers persist in sucking the people's blood, we will turn them over to the people themselves. If we find too many obstacles in dealing out justice to these traitors, the conspirators, the profiteers, then we will let the people deal with them." It was Lenin, not Stalin, who during a terrible food shortage in 1918, emulated Robespierre by scapegoating successful farmers, inventing a new "class" he branded "kulaks" ("bloodsucking leeches, traitors and profiteers"), and calling for "death to all of them." In 1918 Lenin cabled Stalin, who was responsible for securing food supplies near Tsaritsyn (later renamed Stalingrad) to be "merciless," a directive Stain had carried out faithfully! Under Lenin's orders the "kulaks" were murdered wholesale for being part of a capitalist class. Those who weren't shot or hung on the spot to terrorize others were arrested and sent to Siberia as Stalin carried out Lenin's policy of kulak liquidation on into the 1930's.

13. The origin of Soviet collectivization and the Holodomor famines was ideological, a product of central planning and totalitarian control, not a result of natural resources such as soil, or drought. Read that history (Wikipedia covers it fairly well). Ukraine was always a bread basket with good soils, but Stalin's socialist policy imposed on its people by force turned it and the surrounding region into a death trap in which an estimated 3 -7 million (perhaps even more) perished from 1932-33. This was an atrocity, not a natural disaster. Most of the co-opted Western press ("useful idiots") including Walter Duranty and the New York Times, were complicit in hiding it from the rest of the world.

14. Victor Kravchenko, *I Chose Freedom: The Personal and Political Life of a Soviet Official*, Charles Scribner & Sons, 1946, pp. 229-233 of Kindle version.

15. Paraphrase of the famous English poet, novelist, essayist, and repentant socialist Stephen Spender in *The God That Failed*, Harper Colophon Books, 1963, a collection of biographical essays by famous authors disillusioned with communism who could write with authority about it from first-hand experience. p. 273. Spender's works were often inspired by social protest and class struggle. He was a socialist for much of his life, communist for a short while and spent time in Spain along with many other Left-wing anti-fascist intellectuals during the civil war there.

16. Martin Malia, *Soviet Tragedy: A History of Socialism in Russia*, The Free Press, 1994, Part I, "The Origins," Chapter 1, "Why Socialism? Marx and Class Struggle," p. 40 and Part IV, "The End," Chapter 13, "The Perverse Logic of Utopia," "Socialism After Sovietism," p. 517 of 576 in e-version.

17. Max Eastman, former socialist and friend of Lenin *Reflections on the Failure of Socialism*, The Devin-Adair Company, 1955, "The Religion of Immoralism," pp. 87-88.

18. Former socialist Whittaker Chambers' famous 1952 book *Witness*, "Forward in the Form of a Letter to my Children," p. xxxviii, Published by First Regnery History, Washington, DC., 2014.

19. Leszek Kolakowski, *Main Currents of Marxism*, W.W. Norton & Company, 1998, Book Three: *The Breakdown*, Chapter XI "Herbert Marcuse: Marxism as a Totalitarian Utopia of the New Left," p. 1117.

20. Allan Bloom, *The Closing of the American Mind*, Part III, Ch. "The Sixties," pp. 330-331, Simon & Schuster Inc., 1987

21. Friedrich Engels' 1878 *Anti-Duhring* is considered the authoritative statement of Marx and Engels' oxymoronic thinking specifically about the nature of "socialist morality." Engels writes "We forever reject every attempt to impose on us any moral dogma whatsoever as an eternal, ultimate and forever immutable ethical law on the pretext that the moral world, too, has its permanent principles which stand above history and the differences between nations. We maintain on the contrary that all moral theories have been hitherto the product, in the last analysis, of the economic conditions of society obtaining at that time. And as society has hitherto moved in class antagonisms, morality has always been class morality; it has either justified the domination and interests of the ruling class, or, ever since the oppressed class became powerful enough, it has represented its indignation against this domination and the future interests of the oppressed." Refer to p. 726 in "On Morality" in the The Marx-Engels Reader, 2nd Edition, W.W. Norton & Company, edited by Robert C. Tucker, 1972, 1978. For Marx's and Lenin's restatements of this principle see Max Eastman *Reflections on the Failures of Socialism*. Chapter 7, "The Religion of Immoralism," pp. 87-88.

22. Karl Marx essay "On the Jewish Question" written in the autumn of 1843; first published in the Deutsch-Franzosische Jahrbucher, 1844; found at p. 172 and 174 in *Karl Marx Frederick Engels Collected Works, Vol. 3 Marx and Engels 1843 to 1844*, in Marxist Internet Archive (mecwsh-3_1).

23, Frederick Engels and Karl Marx (editor) essay entitled *"The Magyar Struggle"* in Neue Rheinische Zeitung No. 194, written January 8, 1849, published January 13, 1849, found at p. 227 of Vol. 8 of *Marx and Engels Collected Works*. The passages quoted here are at p. 234 and 238 respectively.

24. Michael Novak, "Democracy, Capitalism and Morality," article in *The Wall Street Journal*, February 17, 2017.

206 ■ Some Call it Utopia

25.. Theologian/philosopher Reinhold Niebuhr essay titled *New Allies, Old Issues*, July 19, 1941; in his early years Niebuhr was sympathetic with socialism, but later saw its weaknesses and consequences, and as a result turned toward defense of common sense, liberty and democracy, and against Marxism in his later years.

26. Bertrand Russell's Nobel Prize acceptance speech *The Four Desires Driving All Human Behavior*, December 11, 1950

27. Gary Kasparov quoted in *The Washington Post*, March 15, 2016, and in his article *The U.S.S.R. Fell and the World Fell Asleep*, in the December 17-18, 2016 Wall Street Journal

28. A 1944 speech by Alexander Trachtenberg in NYC. Trachtenberg was a pro-Bolshevik Russian émigré to the U.S. in 1906, who became a key member of the U.S. Communist Party (its "cultural commissar"). The quote is taken from a transcript by this author of recorded remarks by former NYC Communist Bella Dodd in a 1953 speech in Utica, N.Y. Dodd was describing for her audience the 1944 Trachtenberg event she attended in NYC. Dodd, like Max Eastman, had been a high-level functionary in the U.S. Communist Party from its very early days until the 1950's, who turned against communism.

29. By the French historian Alexis de Tocqueville in an 1848 speech on Socialism quoted by Hayek in *The Road to Serfdom*, University of Chicago Press, 1994, pp. 29; Hayek's footnote refers to the *Complete Works of Alexis de Tocqueville*; a nearly identical translation of this quote was used by John Rae in *Contemporary Socialism*, p. 20, Charles Scribner's Sons, 1891; Tocqueville's entire September 12, 1848 speech to France's Constituent Assembly advocating the rejection of socialism in the guise of democracy, translated into English, can be found at www.oll.libertyfund.org, with attribution to *New Individualist Review*, Chapter: "Tocqueville on Socialism," edited by Ralph Raico, translated by Associate Editor Ronald Hamowy, Liberty Fund, Indianapolis, 1981.

30. Quote from *Soviet Communism: A New Civilization?*, Volume 2, Charles Scribner's Sons, a widely criticized pro-Stalinist book by Sidney and Beatrice Webb, published in 1936 while the massive purges of Stalin's Great Terror were underway. According to the Webbs in Chapter XII "The Good Life," p. 1036; Vladimir Lenin "is said to have observed in his epigrammatic way: 'It is true that liberty is precious – so precious that it must be rationed.'"; in a footnote the Webb's attempt to draw a parallel between Lenin's reference to rationing of liberty to Britain's use of sugar ration cards in WWI; However, it is quite a stretch to compare government rationing of scarce essential commodities during a wartime emergency that assures everyone gets an equal share, to the socialist idea of "rationing" liberty. We can never know for certain the full intent of this quote, but perhaps the idea is that under socialism it is the government's

intent to make liberty scarce, so that it can "ration" it, reflecting its fulsome control of its subjects.

31. From a speech by Quang Nguyen, a Vietnamese-American, survivor of the Tet Offensive as a six-year old, and former refugee, given in July 2010 at the Prescott Valley Freedom Rally.

32. Joshua Muravchik, *Heaven on Earth: The Rise, Fall, and Afterlife of Socialism,* Encounter Books, 2002, 2017 edition, Chapter "What is to be Done?: Bernstein Develops Doubts," p. 98; Karl Kautsky, a committed orthodox Marxist, was the leading theoretician of the Social Democratic Party of Germany (SPD). He was a close friend of Engels, and was therefore recognized in Europe as an authority on Marxism. From 1883-1917 he was the editor of the Die Neue Zeit, the chief Marxist forum in Europe, and wrote numerous books about it. Germany's two major socialist groups merged in 1875 at the Gotha conference to form the SPD. Another committed Marxist friendly with both Marx and Engels, Eduard Bernstein, was also involved in the merger, and became inseparable with Kautsky. Essentially both were disciples of Marx and Engels with tremendous influence on the SPD and propagation of Marxism.

33. Lord Acton, *Essays on Freedom and Power,* published 1949, Chapter V, "Sir Erskine May's Democracy in Europe," pp. 158-159; Acton's essay first appeared in the January 1878 *Quarterly Review,* CXLV, No. 289, 112-42

34. Daniel Yergin and Joseph Stanislaw, *The Commanding Heights: The Battle between Government and the Marketplace that is Remaking the World,* by Daniel Yergin and Joseph Stanislaw, Simon & Schuster, 1998. To learn exactly how the word *"liberalism"* was hijacked 100 years ago by American progressives hiding from their tarnished label see the extensive and very informative footnote on p. 15. Since the election of FDR being a Liberal has meant "one who believes in utilizing the full force of government for the advancement of social, political, and economic justice at the municipal, state, national, and international levels." (quote of Joseph Clark, mayor of Philadelphia in 1953, taken from *Reflections on the Failure of Socialism,* pp. 75). By "justice" they mean equalization of society by any means necessary. Equalization is not equal rights or equal treatment by government. Equalization, in fact, requires unequal treatment; i.e., discrimination based on observable differences among people.

35. Max Eastman in *Reflections on the Failure of Socialism,* Chapter Six, "What to Call Yourself," Devin-Adair Company, 1955, pp. 68-88, particularly 75-78 for his discussion of the distortion of "liberal" and "progressive" labels by the Left. Eastman, a former radical socialist, explains the violence consciously done to language by the Left. The first example given is Marxists equating "working class" with "party," as though their political party, led by true believers in Marx's creed, legitimately represents workers and the lower classes, and not

simply the lust for power of the Leftist elites who control it. Similarly, we had nations supposedly "liberated" by murderous socialist dictators. He goes on to discuss the perversion of the labels "Left" and "Right" with the Left originally representing freedom, and the right, zealous allegiance to a powerful central state, now reversed in reality, but not in public use. The Left long ago abandoned the ideal of freedom in pursuit of an overgrown state as the solution to all social ills through attempts to force greater material equality instead of equal citizenship. In so doing, they also began to confuse the principle of egalitarianism (moral and political equality of human rights) with material equality, which can only be obtained by forcefully contravening the natural inequalities of human beings, abusing what should be egalitarian institutions, resulting in unequal treatment and diminished freedom that destroys the civil equality guaranteed by democratic constitutions.

36. Larry Siedentop, *Inventing the Individual: The Origins of Western Liberalism*, Penguin Books, 2014, p. 236.

37. Found at Oxfam America's website: www.give.oxfamamerica.org.

38. Alexandr Solzhenitsyn, "Foreword" to Igor Shafarevich *The Socialist Phenomenon*, 1975, Harper and Row, 1980, pp. vii an viii.

39. Mao Zedong; taken from his famous "*little red book,*" *Quotations From Chairman Mao Tse-Tung*, p. 299; Mao wrote condescendingly of "the masses" who must be led into his socialist promised land by the members of the Communist Party: "We communists are like seeds and the people are like soil. Wherever we go, we must unite with the people, take root and blossom among them." This quote was extracted from Mao' "On the Chungking Negotiations" (October 17, 1945), *Selected Works, Vol. IV*, p. 58. Mao's phrasing sounds almost poetic until you realize its true meaning, i.e., that the unelected Communist Party representing less than seven percent of Chinese populace, once the Party "takes root" (like a noxious weed!) will rule the lives of the other ninety-three percent who will never have any say whatsoever! Consider also how the Party took root, that is, there were no elections of communists competing with non-communists; its "political power grew out of the barrel of a gun" to use one of Mao's famous phrases.

40. Bertrand Russell, the Nobel prize-winning British philosopher, *A History of Western Philosophy*, Simon and Schuster, 1945, 1966 edition, p. 790, "Marx's Socialism is a doctrine of a dictatorship of the Master Class instead of Master Race, with his final stage of development, complete political and economic harmony, like the Second Coming; in the meantime, there is war and dictatorship, and insistence on ideological orthodoxy." Russell's work also contains very interesting critiques of Plato's Republic, and Rousseau's social philosophy.

41. Adam Smith, *Theory of Moral Sentiments*, 1759, Part VI, Section II, "Of the Character of the Individual, so far as it can affect the Happiness of other People," para. 17.

42. Will and Ariel Durant, *The Age of Napoleon*, 1975, "The Great Committee," p. 59.

43. The attack on property ownership dates back to the French revolution. Francois Noel Babeuf (aka Caius Gracchus), *Manifesto of Equals, Republic of Equals: Analysis of the Doctrine of Babeuf* (1796) Article VI: "Explanation And Proofs," at p. 255 in *French Utopias: An Anthology of Ideal Societies*, Edited by Frank and Fritzie Manuel, The Free Press, 1966; the full quote is "Miseries and slavery are consequences of inequality, which is itself the result of property. Property is, therefore, the greatest scourge of society; it is a veritable public crime."

44. Ethan Gutmann, *The Slaughter: Mass Killings, Organ Harvesting, and China's Secret Solution to Its Dissident Problem*, Prometheus Books, 2014.

45. Martin Malia, *The Soviet Tragedy: A History of Socialism in Russia, 1917-1991*, The Free Press, 1994, Chapter "The Party Strikes Back," p. 225, "There is no such thing as Socialism...Its failure is not from having been tried in the wrong place...but from the socialist idea per se...an effort to suppress the real world...something that cannot succeed in the long run."

46. Aleksandr Solzhenitsyn's acclaimed *Gulag Archipelago* (written 1958-68) published 1973, Harper Perennial, 2020 edition, is the best known, but several others provide equally gut-wrenching, more recent, personal accounts of socialist totalitarian rule under Pol Pot in Cambodia (and the dynastic Kim regime that has ruled North Korea for almost 70 years; these include: *Stay Alive My Son*, by Pin Yathay, *Alive in the Killing Fields: Surviving the Khmer Rouge Genocide*, by Nawuth Keat, *and The Girl with Seven Names: Escape from North Korea*, by Hyeonseo Lee. Still more chilling details are presented by Courtois, et al in *The Black Book of Communism*, and Jung Chang and Jon Halliday's *Mao The Unknown Story*.

47. Svetlana Alexievich, winner of the Nobel Prize in Literature, Random House Publishing Group, *Secondhand Time: The Last of the Soviets, An Oral History*, 2013, trans. 2016, "Remarks from an Accomplice," p. 3.

48. Ibid., "On the Little Red Flag and the Smile of the Axe," pp. 278-281.

CHAPTER FOUR
Three Faces of Evil

"The only difference between Socialism and Communism
is an AK-47 pointed at your head."
—Quang Nguyen, refugee from Vietnam

The Unholy Trinity: Socialism, Marxism, and Communism

Why is understanding the ideological lexicon so important? As I and others have noted, political labels and terms can be used to deceive rather than inform, much like the con artist lying to achieve schemes that truth would undo.

Solzhenitsyn maintained that "The language of the lie"[1] is what held the Soviet Socialist regime together. How is it that lies may take hold and begin to rule a nation? Perhaps, to paraphrase H. L. Mencken, it is often easier in the short run anyway to "seek refuge in delusion's warm embrace" than to face uncomfortable facts.[2]

To defend our rights and freedom we must clear away the Left's obfuscation and look reality straight in the face to see the truth. We must refuse to accept the lie, the New Left's bold revisionist lie that the ideological structure of socialism is fundamentally different from Marxism and communism and occupies some kind of moral "high ground." They are three in one, an ideological trinity of "isms" that comprise the philosophical foundation of what is commonly referred to as the political "Left."

210

You have likely noticed my use of socialism and communism interchangeably. There is ample reason for this. Putting modern popular labels aside, let us now focus on the critical underlying utopian "isms": socialism, Marxism and communism, especially the way they have been used in speech and in writings by the very persons who originated, defined and made famous--or infamous--the terms, as well as by those who have carefully documented its history. For the sake of historical convenience, we should begin with that "world's guiding light" of the Leftist thinking for the past 172 years: Karl Marx.

Though he would have vehemently denied it, Karl Marx was arguably the history's most famous purveyor of utopian political ideology. I have already touched briefly on how Marx and his close associate Friedrich Engels sought to differentiate his ideology from that of other utopian thinkers by their pseudoscientific predictions and expectation of a violent proletariat revolution, a revolution caused by "inevitable" class warfare that would precipitate establishment of a socialist society everywhere the Industrial Revolution had taken hold. In this regard, Marx and Engels rejected the idea that his *Communist Manifesto* was utopian. Pretentiously presenting themselves as "scientific" socialists to gain the approbation and legitimacy they longed for, they scoffed at those he labelled "Utopian Socialists" for shrinking from his prophesied violent revolution of the proletariat and class warfare. Yet the ultimate utopian ends of both socialism and communism as described by Marx and Engels are the same: assurance of full, unqualified social and economic equality, a perfect world without envy or greed.

As Marx and Engels were fully aware, achieving this end would, however, require that certain distasteful measures be taken: suppression of liberty, elimination of all political opponents, confiscation of property, abolishment of property rights, and the control of cultural institutions, news media and industrial production by a central authority; all necessary means to the end. Equal distribution of wealth would, in the last stage, lead to a "classless society" in which the state and corresponding governmental authority entirely wither away because they are no longer necessary. One can't help but think of the current Black Lives Matter mantra "defund the police!" The reality, Karl Popper points out in *The Open Society and Its Enemies*, is quite the opposite. Leaders who survive the struggle for dominance instead form a new ruling class, maintaining their control by ruthlessly exercising the same absolute authority they used during the revolution.[3]

Though masquerading as objective science—a pretentious hoax—Marx's violent creed of continuous social conflict and hatred, bogus economics, and false prophecies has nothing at all to do with true science. It is purely a matter of faith. Calling his prophetic theories "scientific" was merely a ploy to gain respectability among the intelligentsia whose acceptance he craved. Popper correctly notes that both the so-called Social Democrats, who were the object of Marx's scorn in the *Manifesto*, and the communists were socialist, the difference being the latter "possessed a blind faith" that their "Russian experiment" would finally result in the fully Socialist Utopia promised by Marx. Both also shared the belief that their movement must be international.

Marx's efforts to connect his social theories with science may be entirely discredited, but according to George Lichtheim, what Marx and Engels accomplished together was much more significant. They were able to synthesize the two historical threads of socialism, *theoretical and revolutionary*, into a single doctrine.[4] This accomplishment should not be under appreciated. The British historian F. J. C. Hearnshaw in *Survey of Socialism* characterized Marx's synthesis metaphorically as "bringing together and intermingling... streams of influence into one single raging and destructive torrent."[5] Likewise, in the concluding chapters of his definitive 1969 work, *The Origins of Socialism,* Lichtheim described Marx as "Socialism's great-est thinker" because the foundational structure of communism was the "Marxian Synthesis" that fused socialism's two strains, political theory and revolutionary activism. This, according to Lichtheim was the "great achievement" that secured his place in history. And as further acknowledgement of Marx essential for-mative role: "The historian of socialism who has taken the mea-sure of Marx need not trouble himself unduly over his rivals."[6] The famous British philosopher and self-proclaimed socialist, Bertrand Russell, wrote in his 1918 *Proposed Roads to Freedom: Anarchism, Socialism, and Syndicalism* that "...the socialists who preceded Marx tended to indulge in utopian dreams and failed to found any strong and stable political party...To Marx, in collaboration with Engels, is due both the formation of a coher-ent body of socialist doctrine, sufficiently true or plausible to dominate the minds of vast numbers of men, and the formation of the International Socialist movement."[7] Another example of the authority of Marx's doctrine in shaping the modern social-ist movement is this characterization of the "great" man: "One writes down the name of the greatest figure in Socialist history with a sense of very real reverence, for, criticize him as you will, or as you can, when all is said he yet remains the leader of lead-ers. Whether you think of him as scientific economist or as prac-tical politician Karl Marx stands first and alone, a colossus of thought and action." In the words of yet another scholar: "Karl Marx is the greatest name on the roll of socialism...his theories have been the intellectual backbone of the movement."[8]

Such noted Marxist theoretician-activists as Karl Kautsky and the Bolshevik Nicholai Bukharin credited Marx (aided by Engels) with having fused the trade union movement and so-cialist theory together to create a truly proletarian socialism guided by a single overarching formula (Marx's) aimed at po-litically defeating capitalism and taking ownership of the means of production. According to Kautsky in 1932:

Marx realized, and in this he proved superior to other Socialists of his day, that the liberation of the working class could be
achieved only by the working class itself...Marx expected it to
come as a result of revolution, the advent of which he correctly
foresaw. He had studied the French Revolution...he was influenced by their [the Blanquists'] Jacobin traditions...Marx and
Engels sought to bring about the union of all elements participating in the class struggle for liberation of the working class
into a strong mass party. Before their arrival upon the scene,
each of the various socialist leaders and thinkers had put forward their own distinct method for the solution of the social
question and opposed all other socialists who would not follow their methods...Marx and Engels understood well how to
bring about a firm union between the world of socialist ideas
and the labor movement.[9]

The Bolsheviks' Marxist theoretician Bukharin wrote in 1918:

The dictatorship of the working class means the governing
power of the working class, which is to stifle the bourgeoise
and the landowners. Such a government of the workers can
only arise out of a *Socialist revolution of the working class*, which
destroys the bourgeois State and bourgeois power, and builds
up a new State on its ruins...[10] [emphasis added]

In creating that fusion, Marx's 1848 *Communist Manifesto*
became the ideological spark that lit the fire of the socialism we
are living with today. Indeed, Marx and Engels made very clear
their intent to refashion the sterile theories and romantic idealism of the bourgeois socialists who had preceded them into a
revolutionary political movement that would take advantage of
the widespread problems and discontent associated with capitalism during what historians commonly refer to as the age of
the Industrial Revolution. Their presumption was that enlightenment of the working-class, who were (in theory) being subjected to ever worsening conditions, to the cause of their plight
and path to their salvation, would lead the workers to revolu-

tion. The Marxists intelligentsia would primarily be educators showing the way, but the revolution would be proletarian.

Marx has easily and well earned his reputation among socialists and historians as the father of modern socialism, even though some socialists today might want to downplay or deny altogether his dominant influence, and even hesitate to mention his name in their public statements. When one looks at Marx's pivotal role in shaping socialism's doctrines and transforming it into an activist political movement, I think it is quite reasonable to describe the socialism of today as simply *Marxism in action*. True to Marx, socialism's bias for real world action – the zeal for undertaking grandiose human social and economic experiments based on an abstract theory that is now belied by dreadful real-world experience, has often overridden any concern for the unintended consequences that might ensue. For its adherents, Marxism is not a sterile political theory, it is an animating spirit, an instrument, and a working weapon to be aggressively used against non-socialists to undermine them and the institutions they support.

Revolutionaries such as Bukharin, a close associate of Lenin, Trotsky and Stalin, who came to have reservations about the methods used to "build a socialist society," and counseled restraint as events unfolded, were often purged by their more zealous comrades. It is in the nature of socialist movements that sooner or later such disenchanted revolutionaries who voice dissent against the extreme measures being taken in the name of social justice, lose the power struggle and end up in an unmarked grave somewhere with a bullet in the head. Dissent can never be tolerated in a one-party system.

Marx mocked contemporary "Utopian Socialists" for their sentimental humanitarianism and cowardly avoidance of the violence he believed both inevitable and desirable. Instead, Marx drew inspiration from the undercurrent of revolutionary violence, always latent within socialism, that traces back to the legacy of the Jacobins and Babeuf and Buonarroti. In the *Communist Manifesto* he writes of the Utopian Socialists:

> They reject all political, and especially revolutionary, action;
> they wish to attain their ends by peaceful means, and endeavor
> by small experiments necessarily doomed to failure, and by
> force of example, to pave the way for a new social Gospel...
> They still dream of experimental realization of their social Uto-
> pias...and to realize all these castles in the air they are com-
> pelled to appeal to the feelings and purses of the bourgeois...
> and [cling to] their fanatical and superstitious belief in the mi-
> raculous effects of their social science.[11]

He further wrote of socialism following from the forceful overthrow of capitalism, as the "first stage of communism."
But he also claimed that communism could not be described in
any concrete way because it "is not a state of affairs which is to
be established, rather it is the real movement which abolishes
the present state of things."[12] In Marx's vision, socialism would
raise the quality of life for everyone by "eliminating want" (an
ambiguous catch-all utopian syntax embraced by many socialist
writers) and assuring equal distribution of products by the state
without the waste supposedly caused by competition among
industrial enterprises, and magically, without division of labor.
Thus, would arise a society of equalized saints in which, to
quote Hearnshaw, "All shall work together in brotherly love for
the common good, and there shall be enough for all."[13] Eventually Marx's imaginary world would enter a final stage that is
stateless, property-less, and classless. Unfortunately, the noble
spirit of brotherhood that was the touchstone of the early utopian idealists Marx mocked was soon tossed out the window
in Marx's world of oppression, violent class conflict, envy, and
retribution.

Because of Marx's explosive views, his no less inflammatory expressions, and the political consequences of his actions,
it is crystal clear that the Manifesto he and Engels wrote in the

mid-1800's was the spark that ignited the latent fire of socialism whose ashes are still smoldering in many countries, ablaze
in some others, and still spreading. They armed the movement
with a simple and seemingly plausible theoretical basis and a
clear call to action that would propel it into the next century,
when it would cause political conflagrations across the globe
under three interchangeable names: socialism, Marxism and
communism, the Unholy Trinity.

A critical point is often missed by those who equate socialism with concern for the poor. Marx taught and those who
followed him believed that "The proletariat's struggle is *not the
result of poverty but of class antagonism*, and *the condition of socialist victory* is not the absolute impoverishment of the working
class, but *the sharpening of class antagonism*, which is not the same
thing."[14] [italicized emphasis added] This helps to explain why
fomenting class antagonisms as the avenue to taking political
power, rather than raising up the poor, has been the true priority
of socialist movements everywhere. In this, the poor are useful to
the cause as a propaganda weapon to be politically manipulated.
Helping people to lift themselves out of poverty is not the socialists' true aim at all. Instead, it is fostering social division and
antipathy. It may come as a shock to those who see socialism as
a source of virtue, but in fact, reducing poverty before they gain
political power necessarily weakens the movement! This explains
why the Left loudly supports welfare programs that expand governmental powers but fail to address root causes of poverty; thus
preserving an underclass whose votes can still be manipulated
by demagogues.

There are many today, claiming to be well informed, who
question whether socialism and communism are fundamentally
different and are quite willing to insist they are. But, history has
proved that to be counterfactual. Solzhenitsyn and innumerable other witnesses have testified that this differentiation is a

lie, and those who have been compelled to live with such a lie like he was do indeed know better.

It has been said that "Communism is the bastard offspring of Socialism," and "Socialists are the cultivated parents of barbarous offspring."[15] Also "The only difference between a communist and a socialist is that the communist is simply a socialist with the courage of his convictions," "The only difference between socialism and communism is an AK-47 pointed at your head,"[16] or "A communist is a socialist in a hurry." Then there is the more meaningful: "Socialism is the tadpole and communism the frog;" more meaningful because communism can be considered the mature, fully-fledged (and fully metastasized) version of socialism. Until that point is reached, socialism is only a work in progress aiming to (supposedly) transform society slowly and harmlessly through democratic legislative means, Communists supposedly go further in calling for Marx's prophesized revolution to create the socialist society (often referring to "building socialism"). However, in truth there is no fundamental difference to be found in socialist and communist aims, and any perceived sequence in terms of socialism preceding communism cannot be clearly demonstrated. Marxist/communist organizations undertook revolutions to install dictatorial socialist (their word) regimes.

During his famous 1983 Templeton Address "Men Have Forgotten God," Alexandr Solzhenitsyn said "Communism is breathing down the neck of all forms of socialism, which are unstable," and in which "everyone other than the authorities does indeed attain 'equality' – the equality of destitute slaves;" or what I refer to as "abject equality."

In 1937 Kautsky, horrified by the realities of the Russian example of Marxian socialism, attempted to redeem himself with a full-throated critique of Lenin's dictatorship of the proletariat,[17] and with a futile effort to separate communism from socialism, despite their unitary history and common father, Marx.

By that time, sadly, it was too little, and much too late to help the Russian and Chinese people. Kautsky had remained figuratively blind in one eye and with clouded vision in the other as he tried desperately to refashion Marxian beliefs into being something benign. The aging Marxist theoretician, once called "the pope of Marxism" by Lenin, had long since irrevocably defined his place in socialism's Pantheon and history of the worldwide movement he helped to create by his fervent advocacy of Marx's revolutionary doctrine[18] as it took shape prior to WWI in a concrete political movement in Germany and the Second (Socialist) International. In 1896, at the London Congress of the Second International socialists from around the world had, in fact, debated and expressly rejected a gradualist, reformist path to socialism and democratic cooperation with non-socialists, and instead "reaffirmed the Marxist doctrine of class struggle and the inevitability of revolution."[19] Although toward the end of his life Kautsky protested against the monster he helped to create, in 1938, he, like Doctor Morbius in the movie *Forbidden Planet*, died without redemption, his beloved socialist ideology having crystallized around Marxist doctrine forty years earlier and become a highly destructive and deadly anti-democratic crusade that had quickly spread around the globe as a result of his efforts, and those of other disciples of Marx and Engels.

Socialism and communism each demand that property and wealth is owned or otherwise controlled by the State in a collective pool, so that it can make all members of society equal in income, property, and status. Fully-fledged socialist and communist societies always attack ownership of businesses and other private property while dismantling rewards for harder work, initiative, or greater talent and productivity. (A Russian joke goes: "We pretend to work and they pretend to pay us."). Under either, no one is free to start their own enterprise or work where they choose doing the work they choose to do. There is no motivation save fear of punishment or want of food that is withheld. People have few choices. They must accept what State overlords decide and dole out regarding shelter, food, health care, employment, etc. In such a socialist/communist economy, governmental authorities make the planning, investment, production and distribution decisions, and allocate by diktat all land, labor, wealth, housing and other goods. This is often referred to as a "command economy," as in "you are commanded to..." and backed-up by force and fear. (Force and fear happen to be specialties of such overlords and "guardians" of the "revealed will of the people.")

Perhaps the best way to understand the intimate connection between socialism and communism is to hear directly from the infamous dictators of the 20th Century themselves. It is they, following Marx and Engels, who provide the definitive relationship. To begin with, Marx's most steadfast devotee, Vladimir Lenin wrote in *The State and Revolution*: "The goal of socialism is communism," and "Socialism is the first phase of communism," making clear that "under socialism all will govern in turn and will soon become accustomed to no one governing."

It is a theme he returns to often. In his little-known pamphlet *The Task of the Proletariat in our Revolution* he wrote: "From capitalism mankind can pass directly only to socialism...Our Party looks further ahead: socialism must inevitably evolve gradually into communism, upon which is inscribed the motto 'From each according to his ability, to each according to his need'."[20] In other words, communism is the desired end state while socialism is its necessary predicate.

Lenin makes clear his belief, quoting Marx, that during the transition between a capitalist society and communism a revolutionary dictatorship must rule. In another pamphlet, *Socialism and War* (1915) Lenin declared: "Outside of socialism there is no deliverance of humanity from wars, from hunger, from the destruction of still more millions and millions of human beings." This must be one of the most tragically ironic statements of all time because, of course, it was Lenin and his followers who caused the destruction of millions and millions of human beings. In the same pamphlet Lenin writes of "Marxists wanting to create socialism" and of "Marxism educating the vanguard of the proletariat which is capable of assuming power and of *leading the whole people* [emphasis in original] to socialism..." Further, using Marx's and Engels' work as his guide, Lenin writes "What is generally called socialism was termed by Marx the 'first' and lower phase of communist society; collective ownership of all means of production, but with lingering inequality in the distribution of wealth resulting from the uncured inequality of individual human beings."[21]

His plan was to create the conditions under which he could cure this "uncured inequality" of individual humans, whatever that might take. It sounds like he was on a voyage headed to Cabet's 1839 utopian beehive vision of the living dead, *Icaria*, or perhaps time warped forward into Orwell's *1984*.

So, was Lenin a communist, a socialist, or a Marxist? All three, sharing a doctrinal unity, the terms interchangeable if not synonymous. The title "socialist" perhaps stands as the most generic since it has the longest and broadest history of usage, and since it was considered by Marx the *initial phase* of communism.

Now let us hear what Lenin's successor, Josef Stalin has to say on the subject. In his *The History of the Communist Party of the Soviet Union*, considered the "Catechism of Communism," and widely read worldwide, he referred to "The October Socialist Revolution of 1917-18," and "the Bolshevik Party in the struggle to complete the building of the Socialist Society," and "Lenin's plan for the building of a Marxist Party"[22] The arch-communist Stalin had this specifically to say about socialism during the pivotal period of 1923-24:

...What was to be the destiny of socialism in the Soviet Union? In what direction was economic development in the Soviet Union to be carried on, in the direction of socialism, or in some other direction? Should we and could we build a socialist economic system; or were we fated but to manure the soil for another economic system, the capitalist economic system? Was it possible at all to build a socialist economic system in the U.S.S.R.[23]

A year earlier Stalin had written that the final "victory of socialism" in the USSR required Lenin's affirmative answer to this question:

"Can the working class in alliance with our peasantry, smash the bourgeoisie of our country, deprive it of the land, factories, mines, etc., and by its own efforts build a new, classless society, complete socialist society?"[24]

It must be obvious to any student of Russian history that Lenin and Stalin, two of history's most well-known and ardent communists, well understood the meaning intended by the label socialism. So, we ask again. Were Lenin and Stalin communists, Marxists, socialists, or all three? Frankly it hardly makes a difference to their millions of victims.

For further evidence of the unity of socialism, Marxism, and communism, let us turn to fellow traveler Mao, who is sometimes described as a "Marxist-Leninist." Note how, based on many quotations from his infamous little red book *Quotations From Chairman Mao Tse Tung*, Communist China could just as easily be called Socialist China. Mao clearly states that while the Communist Party is the means, socialism is the desired result. Consider these quotations:

Without this core [the Communist Party] the cause of socialism cannot be victorious.

It will take a fairly long period of time to decide the issue of the ideological struggle between socialism and capitalism...the socialist system has been established in our country. We have won the decisive victory in transforming the ownership of the means of production.

Revisionists…oppose or try to weaken socialist transformation and socialist construction. After the basic victory of the socialist revolution in our country.

The socialist system will eventually replace the capitalist system; this is an objective law independent of man's will…the Chinese revolutionary movement led by the Communist Party embraces two stages, i.e., the democratic and socialist revolutions, which are two essentially different revolutionary processes, and the second process can be carried through only after the first has been completed. The democratic revolution is the necessary preparation for the socialist revolution, and the socialist revolution is the inevitable sequel to the democratic revolution. The ultimate aim for which all communists strive is to bring about a socialist and communist society.

We must have faith, first, that the peasant masses are ready to advance step by step along the road of socialism under the leadership of the Party.[25]

The talk of a "democratic revolution" was nothing but a ploy. Mao never had any intention of establishing a democracy that might one day challenge the CCPs authority. Mao's "ultimate aim" of "a socialist and communist society" led to the slaughter tens of millions of innocent people in the effort to achieve it. And then there is Fidel Castro, who described himself as "socialist, Marxist, Leninist." Speaking to a French journalist in 1962 he said:

The fundamental influence in a socialist revolution is…that of the founders of Marxism: Marx, Engels, and Lenin…Today many reactionaries seek to invoke the thought of the (French) revolutionaries of two centuries ago, while at the same time representing the same interests of those reactionaries who persecuted those ideas two centuries ago. During their time all those thinkers were persecuted by the ruling classes by the reactionary classes, with the same hatred and the same determination as the reactionaries of the world persecute socialist ideas today.[26]

It is equally obvious that Nikita Khrushchev, Stalin's successor, one of the original Bolsheviks, and a lifelong member of the Soviet Union's Communist Party, understood that the labels socialism, Marxism, Leninism, and communism all essentially represent a single ideology. In his memoirs he described Fidel Castro's role in the Cuban Missile Crisis:

> If, for example, Cuba were to be wiped out as a socialist country, but the Soviet Union still remained, the people of Cuba would, after some time, regain their strength and again become free and socialist. But we must also contribute to the further development and strengthening of socialist construction in Cuba[27]...so that it could remain as the standard-bearer for the socialist countries on the American continent and carry on with its development under the banner of Marxism-Leninism[28]... Castro insisted that our action [withdrawal of the Soviet missiles from Cuba]...would bring harm to the entire socialist camp[29]...A high standard of living had to be achieved in order to make the new socialist system attractive for the inhabitants of Latin America...the most powerful magnet drawing people toward socialism and the socialist system.[30]

Referring to the Soviet Union, Khrushchev goes on,

> we are a socialist country...We stand firmly on Leninist positions[31]...the aim I pursued was to destroy capitalism and build a new social system based on the ideas developed by Marx, Engels and Lenin...Two primary forces exist in the world today – capitalism and socialism. During the first years after the October revolution, we were the only socialist country, an island of socialism surrounded by a sea of capitalism. But today [approximately 1970] the economies of the socialist countries produce approximately 35 percent of world production.[32]

In Czechoslovakia, a Soviet-bloc nation, he sees in socialism a singularity of purpose and ideology with communism:

> the people of Czechoslovakia will walk in step with the other peoples of the socialist countries, above all with the Soviet people. Our people and our party are the sincere friends of the Com-

munist Party of Czechoslovakia and of the Czechoslovak people. We have one goal in common: fraternal cooperation of all people who are fighting for socialism, fighting for communism.[33]

Pol Pot was architect of the Cambodian Killing Fields. While studying in Paris, this mass murderer was profoundly influenced by The French Revolution, Robespierre (his hero) and the Paris socialist Commune of 1871. The principles the budding communist drew from this history were the need for his own uncompromising and absolute faith in the revolution, without hesitation and second thoughts, and its egalitarian attack on property ownership. He made plans for as he put it "carrying on the socialist revolution," and "building socialism through the Kampuchea Communist Party," which he "based upon Marxism-Leninism." He constantly referred to "the construction of socialism in Kampuchea (Cambodia)."[34]

It is difficult to understand how anyone who has studied the history, much less paid any heed to the statements of those who ruled states commonly referred to as communist can legitimately claim that there is a meaningful distinction between communism and socialism. Mostly they referred to a revolutionary communist party creating a socialist society to fulfill Marx's prophecy, that would be exclusively ruled by the party. Communism and socialism are nothing but two sides of the very same creed, and together with Marxism, they constitute the Unholy Trinity of Evil.

Alluding to the dual-faced Roman deity, Janus, one might conjure a mental image of this Trinity as a three-faced Janus with, contrary to the deity, each face wearing an identical friendly-looking mask. Unmasking the three faces then reveals a stern Marxist Janus preaching the advancement of mankind by overthrowing capitalism, which makes the socialist face grin from the overwhelming power over others Janus stands to gain, while the communist face maintains an impassive expression as Janus considers the vexing question of how it will destroy so many "enemies of the state."

The essential truth behind this image is that Janus is a single creature, a monster masked to appear virtuous, but with all three of its faces controlled by a single sociopathic utopian ideology manifesting unlimited intellectual arrogance, an insatiable lust for power, and a complete callousness in treatment of people. We dare not ignore this monster in our midst, because although as an ideology it is metaphysical, the creature demands that its human followers obediently feed it the actual flesh and blood of those that stand in its way of forcing the total devotion by all elements of society to it. It is "in death" that "the metaphysical [ideology] becomes real."[35] It is through ordering the death of human beings that the ideological monster seeks to grow and multiply itself.

Many of those who call themselves socialists today will profess that their ideology is merely evolutionary in the direction away from capitalism and toward their utopia of equality. They claim they will achieve their ends not by Marx's violent revolution and a Lenin-style dictatorship, but more gradually through the democratic ballot box. In this concept, the sheer force of numbers will gain for them the power they need to abolish the capitalist system and create the socialist state. The dominant majority who will have become takers will decide like Mancur Olsen's "stationary bandits"[36] how much they will take from the wealthier minority; theft they may attempt to legalize through confiscatory taxation or expropriation, while criminalizing resistance and using police power to force compliance.

But, despite historical evidence, today's socialists will claim their aim is democracy, not dictatorship, freedom, not servitude to an all-powerful state. They claim they are pacifistic, not militant, they are evolutionary, not revolutionary, reformist, not destructive, that they are good-hearted with concern for the downtrodden while their opponents are hard-hearted evil fascists lacking a social conscience.

They will say that while militant communism exterminates its opponents, modern socialism, being peace-minded, simply desires to enlighten those who have doubts--by educational propaganda and proper training--until governmental, educational and key cultural institutions have been sufficiently infused with socialist dogma.

The honeyed words and promises issuing from the socialist intelligentsia of today are disingenuous and devious. They are a con meant to mislead. Meanwhile, provocateurs of the Left look for opportunities to promote racial rioting and looting to undermine civil society. Make no mistake, their immediate aim is to increase their power by sowing social discord by setting "victim" groups against "the privileged establishment," and to use the resulting divisions in society to take control of the machinery of government – legislative, administrative, judicial, civil service, military and police. Their overall goal is for the state to acquire and concentrate all the power widely dispersed within a democratic society so that it can take full control of people's lives.

To pursue its immediate goals in the Western democracies the Left does not require a unified, revolutionary umbrella organization. Instead, its committed ideologues operate within broad-based networks of not-for-profit organizations, groups, and individuals, often funded by extremely wealthy people with an ambitious Left-wing agenda falsely characterized as advocacy of democratic rights and processes, and anti-fascist, and/or pro social, criminal, and racial justice initiatives. Such networks link together individuals and groups who occupy positions of great influence in news media, publishing, entertainment, academia, and government. This then enables the application of ever-greater political and cultural pressure directed by these elites from such "commanding heights." Once their

favored candidates succeed in gaining political office they will
have the irresistible force of the State behind them, through
which they can employ legislative statutes, executive orders,
judicial decrees, and directives threatening arrest of the opposition which they have criminalized,

Through such means they will gradually "right all
wrongs" by destroying capitalism, redistributing wealth and
equalizing property ownership. At the same time, they will seek
to silence all opposition with vicious attacks that destroy careers, and when necessary, by stealing elections to give themselves permanent controlling power. Given the chance, the socialist, like the idiot sawing off the tree branch he is perched on,
will destroy not only the freedom our collective future depends
upon, but also the very system that provides the sustenance
upon which he/she and everyone else depends.

It is worthwhile at this point to pause and highlight a truth
perhaps not well appreciated by some in a democratic society.
Socialist and communist "parties" are not authentic political
parties at all in a normal democratic sense. Unlike the democratic structure in which political parties are differentiated from
government and regularly compete in open elections, once in
power the socialist/communist Party seeks to destroy other parties and thereby install itself as the single and absolute controlling function of a one-party State. In addition to being true
in the case of the now-defunct Soviet Union, one need only
look at a few other current examples such as China, North Korea, Cuba, Venezuela, and Nicaragua to see that this is so. The
Party's aim is to drive all other parties that represent differing viewpoints out of existence and thereby become the government itself. Of course, as previously noted, socialist parties
may not label themselves "communist" or "socialist" so that
their full agenda remains hazy to voters they can then sucker
in. However, once securely in power, instead of competing political parties having to prove themselves for public support

and trust in free elections, the government is transformed into a symbiotic duality combining the Party and State. From this union arises a new vampire-like government, an indestructible monster organized around socialist doctrine rooted in the blood of the French Revolution and the pen of Karl Marx. Differing political ideas, much less any competing political parties, are unacceptable. Indeed, the Socialist god is a very jealous god that severely punishes any who dare to deviate from the path that leads to an earthly, utopian paradise.

Of course, it is completely expected that the label "communism" has fallen into general political disrepute since the atrocities, totalitarianism, and economic dysfunction of the regimes of communist leaders became more widely known in the outside world. Socialists who crave respectability have adopted new kinds of labels discussed and even invented others that fewer prospective recruits and potential opponents associate with the historical record (assuming they know history at all). But "intellectuals" of today who attempt to characterize socialism as noble, humane, compassionate, equitable, and concerned with the betterment of society are only spinning a lie, an old brazen fabrication, the opposite of socialism's true nature exposed in practice. As a new twist, some academics excuse communism as an aberration from real socialism, the "black sheep" of socialism's honorable family.

A shared history of mendacious doctrine, bloody revolutions, and widespread atrocities must not be openly discussed, much less taught to younger generations. They play a semantic shell game to hide the historical record, calling such regimes "bureaucratic collectivism" or "state capitalism" and denying that they ever were or now are Marxist and socialist. But such a slight-of-hand con quickly falls apart when one looks more closely and compares the tenets of this "New Left" with the practices and voluminous writings of these regimes.

Looking under the shell we see the same discredited Marxian fixations, such as: 1) economic leveling – redistributing wealth by confiscating ("reassigning") profits, 2) doing away with free markets 3) attaining cultural predominance (by controlling society's "commanding heights" of academia, news media, literature, and entertainment) in order to squash dissent, and 4) creating an international utopian order that will once and for all give everyone in the world an equal share of everything ("global justice") by redistributing wealth from richer societies.[37]

This lying and deceit began in earnest in the late 1950's with the Left's efforts to distance itself from its past when the horrors of Stalin's rule were revealed to the world, soon after he was posthumously denounced (the so-called "Secret Speech")[38] by his successor, Nikita Khrushchev. As Leftists have taken control of the commanding heights of culture in the West, they have continued to suppress awareness of the equally catastrophic horrors of "building socialism" in Asian, African, and Latin American societies that have been revealed since. It's the con game I described earlier in which the aging chameleon-like gurus of New Left socialism in the capitalist and highly prosperous West invent labels to disguise their true ideological roots. As a result, the Left has been little challenged as to its cleansed version of socialism's history, and it's immoral, some would say criminal, ideological roots, having become ever more adept at playing this game of deceit. In fact, sixty years later they are close to winning it.

It is shameful that by something as simple as adopting deceptive labels for socialism and its essential elements these intelligentsia have for decades escaped accountability for their past support of murderous regimes that were the enemies of freedom, human rights, and democracy. Having infiltrated all the West's major consciousness-shaping institutions they have faced little difficulty in promoting a morally indefensible utopian ideology, the essence of which has changed hardly at all from its Marxian origins.

But at a superficial level they have been adaptable. Because the foundational liberal principle of "equal" treatment under the law does not automatically produce equal outcomes, the New Left has begun to promote the elastic term "equity," shrewdly but disingenuously conflating it with equality in order to reconstitute the law with this entirely different social and economic principle, one that they interpret to require unequal treatment of people to achieve restitution for claims of past injustice.

With less emphasis on politically organizing around purely economic classes, and with their new mantra of "equity" they have been applying Marx's paradigm of oppressors and oppressed to fracture diverse societies along racial and other lines, gaining political power by promoting grievances, and sowing resentment, envy, and hatred. They employ a strategy of "visionary" gradualism which uses intolerant censorship and "cancel culture" intimidation rather than outright revolution as the avenues to accumulating the power they need to "push humanity into happiness." In recent years this strategy has led to insinuating into, and then radicalizing major political parties, rather than pursuing electoral politics through separate, honestly named socialist parties. Thus hidden, with the aid of semantic camouflage, and an aura of respectability gained from mainstream party membership, the ideology is less vulnerable to criticism and can metastasize within the body politic.

China's Communist Party might still raise the red banner, shout their slogans, and publish the unquestioned wisdom contained in the "thoughts of our great leader" Mao (or now Xi Jinping), and the writings of Karl Marx, but in the West, communism is now only spoken of among political comrades and brain-dead true believers in hushed tones, or carefully hidden beneath much more politically appealing labels.

In sum, the writings of Marx, Lenin, Stalin, and Mao, in the literature published by socialist/ communist regimes, written by their "theoreticians," and as acknowledged in the past by Western intelligentsia, the terms "socialism," "Marxism," and "communism" are like strands of a rope closely interwoven in their prescribed dogma, sharing a common origin, and are very often used interchangeably. They describe a political ideology in which government (the State) expropriates private property, controls (commands) the basic means of economic production, determines the distribution of wealth, goods and wages, and directs the application of all of society's financial capital to achieve centrally planned targets or geopolitical goals. In this common ideology, dissent is outlawed or punished by dissenters being demoted or fired from their job, and those who continue to resist being subject first to intimidation, then deprivation, imprisonment, or even death. The ultimate utopian aim of this ideology is unconditional material equality despite the manifold natural differences among individual people. What is inside a person, and what they can, and want to do with it matters not. Individual merit becomes irrelevant. No one can outrank another in any aspect of life except through loyalty to the Party, the sole avenue to power, prestige, and better treatment.

To achieve complete social and economic equalization, the Party-run State must control its people, their occupations, the money they earn, all products of their labor, their speech, and their actions through indoctrination and when necessary, brute force. Socialism, communism, or Marxism? Choose your poison! The essence of socialism has not changed, only its semantics.

The Incredible Success and Transformation of Democratic Capitalism

In order to mobilize support for their ideology and agenda, Leaders of socialist movements and progressive politicians in the West proclaim it a principal duty of government to achieve social justice by waging war on income inequality. This policy appeals to many who see a "zero-sum" world and consequently believe the only way they can raise themselves up is to tear others down. However appealing it may be to the grievance community, such a policy ignores the obvious truth that when parties engage in voluntary exchanges, *both* believe they will be made better off, otherwise they would not freely do it! As Mises wrote in *Human Action*, the idea that one man's boon is necessarily the other man's damage only applies in robbery and war,[39] and I believe everyone would agree that war and robbery are fundamentally different from voluntary exchanges.

Perhaps Marx's failure to understand these basics influenced his philosophy of plundering the bourgeoisie to create his utopia. Despite superficial intellectualism and the pretext of science he draped over his theories, Marx seems to have been trapped in a "clean and well-lit prison of one idea" to quote G. K. Chesterton. Once in power, his socialists truly become Olsen's "stationary bandits" with a license to steal not just others' wealth, but also the product of their labor and their freedom. The very idea that people are willing to voluntarily part with the products of their talents and labor without compensation, as well as with their freedom, exists only in the dream state of the most deluded socialists.

Rather than focusing on the poor becoming more prosperous, the Left's demagogic slogans propagate the falsehood that the greater rewards gained by some members of society are not from variations in knowledge, skill, industriousness, and productivity. They are instead the undeserved and illegitimate result of unearned inheritance, virtual enslavement of workers, or corrupt manipulation of politics and markets by a privileged few. In other words, they result from the wickedness of "unbridled capitalism," a system which socialists claim cannot function except for the exploitation of the many by a powerful few, and which they seek to destroy.

But let us step back and take a closer look at capitalism from that viewpoint. The term "Capitalism," was initially used in its modern sense by the French socialists Louis Blanc and Pierre Proudhon (who called himself an anarchist). Theirs was a mid-1800's world dominated by exploding use of natural resources, particularly coal. Labor was becoming industrialized and tied to machines for the production and transport of goods using new technologies such as coal-powered steam. This new era touched civil societies profoundly. In some cases, these technologies caused severe and unhealthy environmental damage (what economists call "externalities") until the advent of comprehensive antipollution regulation many decades later. Working and living conditions were often very bad and unacceptable by today's standards. They furnished the basis for Marx's oversimplified version of a binary society[40] consisting of capitalist business owners (the bourgeoisie) and exploited workers (the proletariat). The bourgeoisie could then be conveniently demonized by Marx's followers as "lazy, bloodthirsty, parasites without the slightest right to live." Having no real insight into the working of markets and democracy, to Marx class warfare seemed a justifiable inevitability.

It is true, as dramatized by Emile Zola's fictional work *Germinal*, that by today's standards life was extremely harsh for workers in the factories and mines of the Industrial Revolution. They were often exploited and faced with the choice of either performing their jobs under dreadful working conditions or leaving to face an uncertain fate elsewhere. Marxists called them "wage slaves." Oppressive conditions during the Industrial Revolution certainly helped give rise to widespread unrest and may have seemed an immutable by-product of capitalism. For example, in Russia's Czarist regime, as pointed out by Stephen Kotkin in *Stalin: Paradoxes of Power*, miserable conditions such as those in the Chiatura manganese mines and giant Baku oil fields were fertile ground for the various forms of mayhem Stalin helped organize during and after the failed 1905 Russian Revolution[41] and helped set the stage for the later, successful 1917 Revolution. (Russia's agrarian legacy of land ownership concentrated in the hands of its aristocracy also played into the hands of the revolutionaries.)

One could say that despite all his talk of the evils of capitalism and the inevitable progression toward socialism, Marx's socialist model was, already at the time it was conceived, really a historically obsolete "flat earth" view of reality and possibilities for the future. Of course, the world today is not the same as it was in the days of the Industrial Revolution. It never truly was as Marx portrayed it, and one might add, neither is capitalism. In *Post-Capitalist Society*, Peter Drucker saw "capitalism" as a term ill-fitted to ever-evolving market economies dominated by knowledge, including intellectual property, and innovation, supported by countless informational feedback loops.[42] As a single word, capitalism cannot fully describe the waves of financial resources naturally flowing toward better ideas for meeting peoples' needs and wants as exhibited by the choices they make in the open markets. It cannot fully capture the spirit of free choices expressed at ballot boxes in democratic countries, nor the natural flow of production away from outmoded ideas and technologies and toward better ones. Simply put, far more than any socialist system, capitalism's inherent dynamism encourages better ideas that will benefit society, and makes their rapid implementation possible by allowing individuals and corporations to make their own risk-reward decisions based on expectations of how the public will respond to their offerings. Moreover, capitalism itself has benefited from a flood of "better ideas." Since the Industrial Revolution, for example, democratic capitalist societies have witnessed:

- The rise of the modern corporation, a voluntary association of free individuals committed to a common goal of producing competitive goods and services the public can choose or not choose in free and open markets. Through the trading of their stock in open markets, modern corporations are now owned by many millions of people from diverse social backgrounds, compared to Marx's Industrial Age world in which enterprises were frequently owned by a few extremely rich "Robber Barons." Utilizing the capital of its shareholders and that which they borrow, corporations continually look for more efficient ways to produce and offer better products and services. If the modern corporation loses touch with what the people want and are able to afford, it dies;

- Mass consumption that went hand in hand with mass production in factories. As Mises pointed out in a chapter of *Human Action* titled "Work and Wage," armies of workers became armies of consumers with a vastly improved quality of life. Industries in an open market economy exist to serve the wants of Marx's masses, not the richest few;[43] Ironically, Marx despised the division of labor that makes such greater productivity and general prosperity possible.

- Privately established non-profit corporations and charities independent of government, often with vast endowments of wealth dedicated to improving social conditions;

- Labor laws and legally sanctioned labor unions with elected leaders and the power to bargain effectively for better working conditions and higher wages;

- Guaranteed political equality for all citizens, including universal suffrage;

- Universal availability of free primary and secondary education;

- Comprehensive government regulation to police against abusive business practices;
- Numerous government programs using some of the abundant wealth produced to ameliorate poverty and unemployment and to provide care for the aged and infirm;
- The invention of modern agricultural methods, technologies, and markets, which wherever adopted, vastly increased the quantity, variety and dependability of food supplies, while lowering the cost, and thus erased the threat of famines in those places;
- A system of democratically enacted laws with courts independent from the governing authority and privileged owners of property;
- Mass-produced home labor saving technologies, and birth control, which, with universal education and cheaper transportation liberated women from male domination and all-consuming household tasks, to the benefit of the whole of society; and
- Creation and rapid diffusion of innovations spurred by better ideas and competition which have dramatically decreased the amount of material inputs, land, energy, and physical labor needed to produce and transport virtually everything, and in turn, multiplied abundance far beyond even the wildest dreams of anyone in Marx's day, increased the efficiency and affordability of almost everything, and importantly created the surpluses that enable them to take care of their citizens in need. More than a little nostalgic anti-technology Ludditeism[44] is manifested in Marx's fixation with the transformative impact of technological innovations on the social order, which are rapidly adopted because of the massive overall societal benefits they produce.

Marx and his followers, forever locked into the world of

the Industrial Revolution, based their prophecies on an unreal, simplistic world of frozen technologies and thus were unable to foresee the ongoing transformation of human productivity and progress brought about by the spread of the liberal values imbedded in capitalism. The diffusion of such values and resulting institutions has raised billions of people out of poverty and hunger by fostering the genesis and ascension of better ideas.[45] As Joseph Schumpeter argues in *Capitalism, Socialism and Democracy*, Marx's socialist theories failed to account for: a) the economic mobility of people based on their own talents and industriousness, and b) the process of constant competitive technological innovation in open democratic capitalist societies. These key factors soon invalidated Marx's implicit assumption that certain technical means of production (which Marx argued were the primary determinant of social and economic organization) would remain static indefinitely.[46]

For the utopian vision of Marx, Proudhon, Babeuf, and others to take hold, strategies would have to be implemented to destroy the "evils" of free-market, democratic capitalism, especially private property. For them, accumulation of property was theft pure and simple. Marx never comprehended, much less acknowledged, that by eliminating property and open markets, his system would at once be destroying both freedom and the very engine of prosperity he promised. The spread of democratic capitalism has resulted not in oppression of a voluntary workforce, but instead democratized that workforce's access to abundant life-improving products and to luxuries previously available only to the wealthiest.

Despite the violence and sustained terror caused by socialist regimes throughout the twentieth century, a technical, social and economic revolution of increased prosperity swept across parts of the globe. This was a revolution of freedom and creativity, and not the upheaval envisioned by the Marxist intelligentsia and their corrupted enforcers. Private ownership of property and small businesses expanded beyond the grasp of the nobility, domineering governments, and the wealthy elites. Not only did Marx's prediction of increasing misery, degradation and pauperization of the proletariat fail to occur in democratic capitalist societies, it instead occurred --along with mass murder and famines-- in those hapless places where socialist doctrine was politically imposed by his adherents.

Capitalism has been both dramatically transformative and auto-adaptive, responding to feedback from voters at the ballot box and from billions and billions of voluntary daily exchanges between buyers and sellers. While it cannot be denied that it has produced extremely wealthy individuals, in so doing it has without question also generated incredibly vast wealth that has enriched the lives of the ordinary citizens in such societies, far beyond anything Marx and Engels could have imagined, and continues to do so. Goods and services offered, be they material or political, must continually adapt to better reflect the desires of the individuals who make up society or give way to those goods and services that do.

In open societies, democratic capitalism has been significantly transformed in countless ways from Marx's day and his overly simplistic model of the bourgeoisie and the proletariat. This transformation came about as a consequence of the political freedom in democratic societies both to imagine and incent continuous improvements. It did not come from the dictates of socialism or Marxism. Through trade and diffusion of its innovations around the globe, capitalism has benefited human beings everywhere, even those in socialist countries, and not just those fortunate enough to be citizens of democratic capitalist countries!

Marx failed to understand how open markets, individual rights, and political freedom all go together and promote well-being in all segments of society, not just the wealthiest. Markets in which people freely trade for mutual benefit are both necessary for freedom and a natural result of it. Indeed, one could argue that spontaneous trade and with it, the creation of markets, is one of humankind's greatest achievements, comparable to spoken language and the adoption of behavioral norms, including the conception of law and personal virtue, writing, agriculture, mathematics, and science. Democracy now belongs on that list as well. Some archaeologists even correlate the emergence of written language and mathematics thousands of years ago with the need of early merchants for reliable records of goods traded.

Perhaps equally important, as Lord Acton's observed, is that democratic capitalism does not merely enable people to pursue their own prosperity and well-being, but also, through its diffusion of power and rule of law, limits the harm that can be done when people are at their worst. It does not depend on creating a better human nature, nor on the rise of wise and good "guardians possessing overwhelming power."

To illustrate its differences between capitalism and the other "ism's," I refer back to a piece some years ago by the columnist Ann Landers. An English teacher whose students were reading George Orwell's *1984* wrote to her.

> I am an inner city English teacher, and my students are reading George Orwell's "1984." I am having a difficult time explaining communism, socialism and fascism to my students without giving a full-blown, time-consuming history lesson. I recall you printed a humorous column some time ago explaining these concepts using cows as examples. Will you please print it again for my students? I'm sure it will kick-start a lively class discussion. I'd appreciate your help. — A Teacher in Mississippi

> Dear Mississippi Teacher:
> Thank you for asking. It's an "oldie," but a "goldie." Here it is:

> Socialism: You have two cows. Give one cow to your neighbor.
> Communism: You have two cows. Give both cows to the government, and they may give you some of the milk. Fascism:

You have two cows. You give all of the milk to the government, and the government sells it. Nazism: You have two cows. The government shoots you and takes both cows. Anarchism: You have two cows. Keep both of the cows, shoot the government agent and steal another cow. Capitalism: You have two cows. Sell one cow and buy a bull. Surrealism: You have two giraffes. The government makes you take harmonica lessons.

Certain progressives and self-proclaimed socialists continue to condemn capitalism, both lionizing and idolizing Karl Marx as the great social economist who inspired their vision of what is needed to create an ideal society. However, a forty five-year Cold War, including bloody conflicts in Korea, Southeast Asia, and elsewhere, was fought to contain Marx's virulent ideology until the tipping point of economic and social dysfunction brought about meaningful change. Millions upon millions perished in rivers of blood as a result of Karl Marx's followers. Is the hard-won victory of the Cold War, which vanquished the expansive socialism of the Soviet empire, going to be frittered-away by a frivolous, ignorant and unsuspecting generation in the West? That is why telling the truth about capitalism, as well as the nature of the socialism's unholy trinity is so important.

Notes

1. A. Solzhenitsyn, 1974 essay, *Live Not By Lies*.

2. An insight about human nature, the quote is attributed to H. L. Mencken "Cold, uncomfortable facts lead the weak to seek refuge in delusion's warm embrace." Mencken was a famous journalist of the 1920's -1930's.

3. Karl Popper, *The Open Society and Its Enemies, Marx's Prophecy*, Chapter 18 "The Coming of Socialism," II. and IV., pp. 828 and 840 of 1930 in e-version, Princeton University Press, 1945.

4. George Lichtheim, *The Origins of Socialism*, "The Marxian Synthesis," Frederick A. Praeger, 1969, p. 185; What Marx actually accomplished, instead of precipitating a proletarian revolution in industrialized Europe, was to synthesize the two historical strands of Socialism, theoretical and revolutionary,

242 ■ Some Call it Utopia

into a single doctrine, his greatest achievement, what Lichtheim called "the Marxian Synthesis," which signaled the birth of modern socialism and helped fuel revolutions in Russia, Asia and elsewhere. For all of Marx's railing against capitalist oppression of industrial workers, the revolutions carried out under his name actually had very little to do with any spontaneous uprising by the urban proletariat, and much more to do with getting rid of emperors, and land reform historically popular with rural peasants. The rural peasantry was however cheated by socialists' doctrinaire insistence on the disastrous collectivizing of agriculture rather than distributing ownership.

5. F. J. C. Hearnshaw, *Survey of Socialism: Analytical, Historical, and Critical,* Macmillan and Co. Ltd., 1928, 1929 edition, Chapter VII, "Marxian Socialism," pp. 185 and 207-208.

6. George Lichtheim, *The Origins of Socialism,* Frederick A. Praeger, 1969, p. 185; In the concluding chapters of this definitive work the famed author and early Marxist admiringly described Marx as "socialism's greatest thinker," and the structure of communism conceived by Marx and Engels as the "Marxian Synthesis" that fused socialism's two historical strains, political theory and revolutionary activism, and thus was their "great achievement."

7. Bertrand Russell, *Proposed Roads to Freedom: Anarchism, Socialism, and Syndicalism,* George Allen & Unwin, 1918, p. 17.

8. This quote is from G. R. S. Taylor, *Leaders of Socialism,* Ch. VII "Karl Marx," p. 57, New Age Press, 1908; In his treatise, *Socialism: A Critical Analysis,* Oscar D. Skelton wrote: "Karl Marx is the greatest name in the roll of socialism." (p.13); Skelton quotes from the American economist and sociologist, and critic of capitalism, Thorstein Veblen: "The socialism that inspires hopes and fears today is of the school of Marx. No one is seriously apprehensive of any other so-called socialistic movement…The socialists of all countries gravitate toward the theoretical position of avowed Marxism. In proportion as the movement in any given community grows in mass, maturity, and conscious purpose, it unavoidably takes on a more consistently Marxian complexion." (p. 13, FN No. 1 attributed to T. Veblen), University of Chicago, published by The Riverside Press, Cambridge, Mass., 1911. In well over 100 years there has never been any serious debate about Marx's central role in formulating and advancing modern socialism.

9. Karl J. Kautsky, *Social Democracy versus Communism,* Rand School Press, 1946, Part 1 "The Origin of Socialism," and Part 2 "Marxism and the Dictatorship of the Proletariat," pub. by Rand School Press, source: Marxist Internet Archive. transl. David Shub and Joseph Shaplen; Kautsky (b. 1854, d. 1938) was a Czech-Austrian Marxist theoretician, and one of those who led the socialist Second International (later to become the Comintern under Soviet

control) from 1889 to 1916. A close associate of Friedrich Engels, founder of the German socialist journal "The New Times," leader of the Social Democratic Party of Germany, and a prolific author, Kautsky was considered the leading authority of Marxism prior to the Bolshevik's successful revolution in Russia. He was highly critical of the Bolshevik dictatorship, which he considered a deviation from true Marxism. Based on its manifest economic failures, late in life Kautsky became a harsh critic of Lenin and Stalin, saying "State slavery does not become socialism merely because the slave-drivers call themselves communists."

10. Nicholai Bukharin (b. 1888, d. 1938 – executed in Stalin's Great Purge) was also a noted Marxist theoretician and revolutionary, and one of the top leaders of Lenin's Bolsheviks. A close associate of Lenin, Trotsky and Stalin, he was described by Lenin as "a major theorist of the Party." His ideas in economics are said to have had great influence on Deng Xiaoping's CCP policies toward market socialism. Like Kautsky, Bukharin was also a prolific author as well as a political activist. In Chapter V of his *Programme of the World Revolution* (1918), pub. by S L Press, source: Marxist Internet Archive, he wrote about: "a Socialist revolution of the working class, which destroys the bourgeois State and bourgeois power, and builds up a new State on its ruins..."

11. Karl Marx, *The Communist Manifesto* (a.k.a. *Manifesto of the Communist Party*), 1848, Part III "Critical Utopian Socialism and Communism," pp. 497-99 in The Marx Engels Reader, Second ed. Edited by Robert C. Tucker, 1978-1972, W. W. Norton & Company, Inc.

12. Karl Marx, *Karl Marx and Frederick Engels Collected Works 1845-1847*, Vol. 5, 1. "Feuerbach. Opposition to the Materialistic and Idealistic Outlooks," p. 49, Lawrence & Wishart Electric Books, 2010, trans. W. Lough.

13. F. J. C. Hearnshaw, *A Survey of Socialism: Analytical, Historical, and Critical*, Macmillan and Co. Ltd., 1928, Chapter II "The Six Essentials of Socialism, #6 Eradication of Competition," p. 67.

14. Leszek Kolakowski, *Main Currents of Marxism, The Golden Age*, Ch. II "German Orthodoxy: Karl Kautsky," p. 389, Transl. by P. S. Falla, 2005 W.W. Norton & Company, 1978 Oxford University Press.

15. F. A. Hayek, *Road to Serfdom*, University of Chicago Press, 1944, p. 84.

16. From a speech by Quang Nguyen, a Vietnamese-American refugee who fled his native country as a teenager after it fell to Ho Chi Minh's communists, given in July 2010 at the Prescott Valley Freedom Rally. He survived the bloody Tet Offensive as a six-year old.

17. K. Kautsky, *Social Democracy vs. Communism*, written in 1937, published by Rand School Press.

18. K. Kautsky, *The Class Struggle*, "The Erfurt Program," 1892, Charles H. Kerr & Co., 1910; for several decades this work, translated it into 16 languages, defined the tenets of Marx's socialism for millions in the movement worldwide. In this work Kautsky the Marxist exemplfies the F. A. Voigt critique of Marx (*Unto Caesar* p. 45) by inventing a *past* that never was (bogus history of economic development), a *present* of "wage slaves" that is not (not then in 1892, nor now), and a *future* that can never be - a socialist propertyless utopia totally free from envy and ambition, in which the "workers" are in charge of all production and distribution to assure justice and equality.

19. Encyclopedia Britannica, "Second International," p.1, on-line version, July, 12, 2022.

20. V. I. Lenin's major work, *The State and Revolution*, 1917, 4. "The Higher Phase of Communist Society," pp. 344-346, and 2. "The Transition From Capitalism to Communism," p. 335 of *Essential Works of Lenin*, Edited by Henry M. Christman, Dover Edition, 1987; and V. I. Lenin *Collected Works – Volume 24*, Progress Publishers, pamphlet *The Task of the Proletariat in Our Revolution*, 1917, p. 90 of 636..

21. V. I. Lenin, *V. I. Lenin Collected Works*, Vol. 24, April-June 1917, "Blancism," p. 37; originally published in Pravda No. 27, April 8, 1917; translated by Bernard Isaacs.

22. Josef Stalin's famous *The History of the Communist Party of the Soviet Union*; edited by the Central Committee, International Publishers, 1939, became known worldwide as the "catechism of communism," its official doctrine, and was very widely distributed and read. These quotes are found at Chapter Seven, p. 189, Chapter Two, p. 30, and Chapter 12, p. 330.

23. J. Stalin, *The Results of the Work of the Fourteenth Conference of the R.C. P. (B.)* published in May 1925.

24. J. Stalin, chapter entitled "The Question of the Victory of Socialism in One Country," pp. 188-189 in *Problems of Leninism*, English translation 1954; the quote was originally in a response Stalin wrote in February 1938 to a question he received from Ivan Philipovich Ivanov of the Young Communist League; This document can be found at Red Star Press (1978) Works, Vol. 14 on the Marxist Internet Archive.

25. Mao Zedong, this quote is found in the chapter entitled "Socialism and Communism" in *Quotations From Chairman Mao Tse Tung* (aka "Zedong"), his famous "Little Red Book" published from 1964-1976, pp. 47, 49, and 57.

26. Fidel Castro, interview by the French journalist Andre Camp in October 1962 not long after Castro had become Cuban Premier.

27. Nikita Khrushchev, leader of the Soviet Union from 1953-1964, *Memoirs of Nikita Khrushchev*, Volume 3 *Statesman [1953-1964]*, Edited by Sergei Khrushchev, translated by George Shriver, 1999, 2007, The Pennsylvania State University Press, p.327.

28. Ibid, p. 331.

29. Ibid, p. 343.

30. Ibid, p. 354.

31. Ibid, p. 345.

32. Ibid, pp. 354-356.

33. Ibid, p. 695.

34. Philip Short, *Pol Pot: Anatomy of a Nightmare*, A John Macrae Book, Henry Holt and Co., 2004, pp. 66, 68, and 72-74, and a September 27, 1978 speech by Pol Pot *"to the Central Committee of the Communist Party of Kampuchea In Order to Defend Democratic Kampuchea Carry on Socialist Revolution and Build Up Socialism."*

35. This quote is taken from p. 182 of Arthur Koestler's famous 1941 novel about socialism and Stalin's Great Terror, *Darkness at Noon*, Signet Book, Macmillan Company.

36. Mancur Olsen, *"Dictatorship, Democracy and Development,"* American Political Science Review, Vol. 87, No. 3 September 1993, p. 568.

37. A good example of "New Left's" attempts at escaping from its complicity in the catastrophe of Twentieth Century socialism through redemptive redefinition of its ideology's semantics is found in Michael Harrington's 1989 book *Socialism: Past and Future*, Arcade Publishing. Harrington was a leading American socialist theoretician during the 1960's – 1980's who advocated that the Left pursue its "change the system" Marxist agenda in a gradual non-revolutionary manner through the Democratic Party. Like Marx he blamed "amoral Western capitalism" for the world's ills (p.62), while trying to exculpate socialists from guilt for the bloody socialist debacle by incredibly claiming that communist societies are "authoritarian collectivist, and antisocialist," not socialist (pp. 60-61). While being wary of authoritarian communism, Harrington was nonetheless an admirer of the Socialist Party of America's radical Eugene Debs, the self-proclaimed American Bolshevik. Debs declared in his February 1919 article titled "The Day of the People" published in *The Class Struggle* "From the crown of my head to the soles of my feet, I am a Bolshevik, and proud of it."). It is worth noting that Debs had also at one time been a member of the Democratic Party and Social Democratic Party of America. A very illuminating account of the founding and rapid rise of the "New Left" in America during the

early 1960's, and insights as to its true ideology are found in David Horowitz's very well-written autobiographical *Radical Son: Generational Odyssey* (2020, Bombardier) particularly in the Chapter "Berkeley," pp. 114-125. His account in *Radical Son* is that of a founding member of the New Left, not of an observer or latecomer.

38. A copy of Krushchev's "Secret Speech" can be found in declassified FBI files; It is titled *Speech of First Party Secretary N. S. Krushchev at Session of the XXth Party Congress of the Communit Party of the Soviet Union February 5, 1956*; one source is governmentattic.org which refers to FBI File No. 62-HQ-104045; the speech is contained on pdf pages 35-72 of the file; this is a very significant historical document which marked the beginning of de-Stalinization of the Soviet Union, and perhaps the end of Russia's grandiose experiment in socialism as well.

39. Ludwig von Mises, *Human Action: A Treatise on Economics*, 1949, Chapter XXIV "Harmony and Conflict of Interests," "The Ultimate Source of Profit and Loss on the Market," p. 662. This is one of several places in *Human Action* where Mises explains why the widely believed "Montaigne dogma" that the gain of one man is the damage of another, is fallacious; that is, "There are in the market economy no conflicts between the interests of the buyers and sellers." (i.e., obviously, a freely undertaken transaction is in the interests of both, otherwise they would not do it.).

40. Joseph A. Schumpeter, *Capitalism, Socialism and Democracy*, 1950, Harper Perennial 2008 edition, Part I "The Marxist Doctrine," II "Marx the Sociologist," p.15.

41. Stephen Kotkin, chapter entitled "Tsarism's Most Dangerous Enemy" in *Stalin: Paradoxes of Power*, Penguin Press, 2014, p. 76.

42. Peter Drucker, *Post-Capitalist Society*, Harper Collins, 1993, "Introduction: The Transformation, The Shift to the Knowledge Society," pp. 6-9 1993, One among the many insights presented by Drucker is that "Capitalism" is perhaps a term ill-fitted to ever-evolving market economies dominated by knowledge, innovation (better ideas, some of which become "intellectual property"), countless informational feedback loops, and financial resources naturally flowing toward better ideas for meeting peoples' needs and wants as exhibited by the choices they make in the open markets and at ballot boxes of democratic countries, and away from outmoded ideas and technologies.

43. Ludwig von Mises, *Human Action*, Chapter "Work and Wages," Ludwig von Mises Institute, p. 587.

44. The Luddites were bands of English handicraftsmen who rioted in 1811-16 to destroy the textile machinery that was displacing them and had made clothing far more affordable.

45. This is one of the primary points made by Deirdre McCloskey in *Bourgeois Equality: How Ideas, Not Capital or Institutions, Enriched the World*, University of Chicago Press, 2016.

46. Joseph Schumpeter, *Capitalism, Socialism and Democracy, Third Edition*, Harper Perennial, 1950, Chapter "Marx the Prophet," pp. 12-13, 18-19, and Chapter "Marx the Sociologist," pp. 31-37 in which Schumpeter writes "As a matter of fact, capitalist economy is not and cannot be stationary. It is incessantly being revolutionized *from within* by new enterprise, i.e., by the intrusion of new commodities or new methods of production or new commercial opportunities into the industrial structure as it exists at any moment."

CHAPTER FIVE

The Socialist Welfare State

"Remember governments create nothing and have nothing to give but that which they have first taken away."
—Sir Winston Churchill, Prime Minister of Great Britain

One cannot begin a discussion of social welfare based on socialist thought without first considering Marx's well-known slogan: "From each according to his ability, to each according to his needs."[1] In the 1890's the Italian anarcho-communist Errico Malatesta elaborated:

> ...Instead of running the risk of making a confusion in trying to distinguish what you and I each do, let us all work and put everything in common. In this way each will give to society all that his strength permits until enough is produced for every one; and each will take all that he needs, limiting his needs only in those things of which there is not yet plenty for everyone.[2]

Rather than seeking to maximize one's personal welfare, we can all be encouraged to work for the common welfare, and those who are unwilling are either antisocial or insane. This captures the misapprehension at the core of socialism. Marx, apparently clueless about incentives and human motivation related to the well-being of one's self and family, somehow convinced himself that "each person would be motivated to work for the good of society because [under socialism] work would have become a pleasurable and creative activity."[3] Accordingly, no one should want or try to work less or want or try to take more than anyone else. However, this basic premise of socialism is at odds with natural human interests and with the creativity and innate striving to improve one's lot according to one's own skills and industriousness. This also includes the tendency to take that which is freely available, rather than working to produce it for oneself.

As Hayek explains in *The Road to Serfdom*: "To undertake the direction of the economic life of people with widely divergent ideals and values is to assume responsibilities which commit one to the use of force."[4]

Under socialism, equality is distorted into a punishable demand for complete uniformity and conformity, because the differences among people inevitably undermine its false premise. A former Soviet official during the Stalin era who had been purged and sent by the NKVD (Soviet secret police) to the gulags commiserated: "My generation of Communists everywhere accepted the Stalinist form of leadership. We acquiesced in the crimes...How was all this possible?...We saw these Stalinist crimes as the opposite of what they were, as important contributions to the victory of socialism. We thought everything that promoted the power politics of the Communist Party in the Soviet Union and in the World was good for socialism."[5]

He wasn't alone. Hannah Arendt noted in *Origins of Totalitarianism* that a Nazi or Bolshevik is unlikely "to waiver when the monster begins to devour its own children, and not even when he becomes a victim of persecution himself, if he is framed and condemned, if he is purged from the Party and sent to a forced-labor or concentration camp. On the contrary, to the wonder of the whole civilized world, he may even be willing to help in his own prosecution and frame his own death sentence..."[6]

It is a paradox of moral blindness that whole organizations will participate in every manner of atrocity for the goal of creating the "perfect welfare state." This illusion of humanitarian good is what makes socialism especially dangerous when adherents zealously embrace it like a religion they will kill for. Some have interpreted or tried to rationalize the behavior of such utopians as "collective madness." Others say it is the irrationality of seemingly sensible people when fear of authority is conjoined with ideological indoctrination. In either case, the darker side of humanity is inevitably summoned and overwhelms compassion and reason. In the upside-down world of the USSR, any dissent of communist orthodoxy was treated as a mental illness, often leading to confinement and treatment with drugs.

Socialism and the Liberal Welfare State

For political effect, some among the Left advocate an expanded government duty that goes far beyond meeting basic needs, implying that government must be responsible for making people happy, i.e. achieving their aspirations. In the US, for example, it attempts to ensure that "the American Dream" comes true for everyone, regardless of their individual contribution to that end or their misfortune. Contrast that with psychologist Abraham Maslow's well-known "Hierarchy of Needs,"[7] which begins with satisfying more basic needs such as shelter, sustenance, and social interaction, but climbs pyramid-like to more aspirational human desires for love, belonging, esteem, and self-actualization, which requires individual freedom.

Some people may be happy if they have enough to eat and a place to stay out of the rain. But real human fulfillment depends upon far more than that. It also depends on one's own attitude, expectation of a better tomorrow, and constructive behaviors and responses with respect to others. Government intervention, no matter how well-intended, that bestows unearned "free stuff" on certain of its citizens in the name of equalizing social conditions can never truly satisfy a people's aspirations. Lenin's Bolsheviks claimed they would "chase humanity into happiness," but they would have to use an "iron fist" to do so. To them, sufficient totalitarian power would make anything possible, including the reengineering of human nature itself. Only socialists and other delusional fools want to believe that people's fulfillment can be engineered through government social programs at the cost of people losing control over their lives to political authorities.

While organizing the overthrow of existing governments and establishment of welfare states, utopian revolutionaries begin with a guarantee of free government services but conclude with unbridled property and wealth confiscation, usually including all food that is produced. This requires the merciless exercise of absolute power. Lenin is reported to have said: "We will ask a man [any man] Are you for us or against us? If he says against us, we will stand him up against a wall." [8]

In creating a social welfare system, we must ask what will limit governmental power and the exercise of it in such a system. Under no circumstances should any person be allowed to possess the power to dictate the terms of another person's existence. No one, not even the best-meaning socialist, can be given such a right or possess such power. If there is one thing we can say with certainty about socialism, considering its history of totalitarian barbarism, it is that this ideology in practice is not based on brotherhood and compassion for people and their social welfare, despite its proponents' clichéd declarations. Instead, people are a problem to be "managed" through constant monitoring of their actions and intimidation, and if necessary, through use of imprisonment, torture, "re-education," bullets, and starvation.

Utopianism therefore is not really about the common welfare. It is not about human diversity, or "big tent" inclusivity, or accommodating the differing desires of persons within a free society. It is about the government ensuring conformance to an ordered society with citizens much resembling puppets. But if the masses are indeed puppets, who then are those who proclaim themselves to be superior—Grand Puppeteers—and would crown themselves self-anointed leaders holding the one true answer and absolute authority to create Heaven on Earth? We must be very suspicious of self-righteous people seeking to control all the levers of state power, ostensibly to "do good," and we must uncover their real motives. What if instead of Plato's benign "philosopher king," they become evil despots seizing power through terror and political murder? What if citizens are encouraged to rage against and kill each other in the name of a seemingly righteous cause? What if the result is truly Hell on Earth? True social welfare depends on free, democratically equal people making wise decisions together, not on the false promises of arrogant and charismatic utopian ideologues.

Welfare Without Socialism, "Third Way" Socialism, and Democracy

Socialism is not simply, as many believe, "taking from the rich to give to the poor." In fact, it is wrong to use the term "socialism" to describe the morally justifiable programs of democratically established welfare systems. We are not talking about Robin Hood bandits that spring out of a forest and collect people's money at gunpoint (or arrow-point) for redistribution as they see fit. We're talking about a democracy that uses effective needs-based wealth transfers to ameliorate real poverty, and to provide for the unemployed, infirm, and aged. It is not socialism when a democratic people, acting together, freely decide to appropriate wealth from those who can afford it to support the real needs of those fellow citizens who are truly poor and unable to support themselves, but are endeavoring to do so to the best of their ability. It is not socialism when a free people vote to provide the needy with the physiological requirements of food, shelter, clothing, basic health care, etc., or to provide the funding required to cover the cost of government functions benefiting society at large, such as security and education.

In a free and democratic environment, societies can supply comprehensive needs-based benefits without endangering the fundamental rights of their members. This is provided the benefits do not discriminate based upon immutable character- istics like skin color, national origin, gender, or religious beliefs, and provided the benefits are directed toward those who are truly unable to meet their own needs. Even those societies with high "progressive" taxes imposed on their wealthier citizens, such as many European countries, are not truly socialist unless and until they cross the line from addressing actual needs into redistributive confiscation. I am referring specifically to dispro- portionately taxing those with more for the single-minded goal of creating an equal distribution of wealth, and to give govern- ment complete command of key parts of the economy. In fact, it is the admitted goal of self-described "Evolutionary Socialists" to ratchet progressive taxation over time to such extent that it negates the individual benefits derived from talent, hard-won skills, industriousness, and prudent behavior.

Confiscatory redistribution occurs when governments es- sentially legislate an equally bright place in the sun for those who are unsuccessful or less successful by commandeering the fruits of those more successful. Socialists even try to ignore the inevitable economic impact of ever more generous welfare "en- titlements" coupled with demographics; by this I mean the cer- tain decrease in the wealth-producing segment of society ver- sus the certain growth in the welfare-consuming segment. The socialist State must then assume impossible welfare burdens funded with borrowed money, and unless reformed, these bur- dens next lead to financial collapse and finally to social disin- tegration. As the hold of socialism is gradually tightened and chokes off freedom, a nation's economic vitality is undermined until the most productive members of society disinvest and flee, or simply become demotivated and produce less. For the many who then look to the state to guarantee their income, it leads to further erosion of their motivation to work and produce, resulting in an increasing portion of the population essentially living off a diminishing portion who continue to produce. Perhaps socialist crusaders secretly believe that the resulting social disgruntlement and disintegration helps their cause. Perhaps social disintegration creates an opportunity for them and their media stooges to convince a desperate public to abandon democracy and open markets altogether in trade for a promise of lifelong government welfare and cocoon of economic security.

History shows that after socialist revolutionaries consolidated their power, the creation of a welfare state as people understand that term today vanished. It is an odd version of social welfare that accommodates a network of internment camps and prisons to hold political prisoners. It is a strange system of welfare that prescribes forced relocation, blood and carnage for millions of a nation's citizenry who are considered "reactionaries" and "enemies of the people!" While, the realization of a free society supplying comprehensive welfare benefits without endangering individual rights is indeed possible, there are many within Western democracies today who want to go much further, to create a welfare state whose primary goal is not to provide a legitimate safety net for the needy, but rather to eliminate income inequality or a so-called "wealth gap." Sadly, the effort to achieve these "nobler goals" has again and again led to arrogant tyrants forcing their dystopian vision down the throats of their people.

Though they have never crossed the tipping point into socialism, Sweden, Denmark, and other ethnically and culturally homogeneous Scandinavian countries have often been touted by the Left as examples of a fantastically successful brand of socialism lite - the "you can have it all," "Third-Way," the supposedly optimum balance between Marx's socialism and democratic capitalism; It promises to provide strong, economic growth on the one hand, and on the other, fair taxes on the "truly rich" to fund expanded government-provided social welfare benefits that do more to equalize income. However, after roughly 30-40 years, reality has finally begun to overtake such delusion. It turns out that the "Third-Way" has drawn down those nations' pre-existing resources of social capital and market-based success, in the process eroding their previously strong cultural norms of trust, personal and fiscal responsibility, and hard work. It is perhaps telling that Sweden's Social Democratic Labour Party's founding document announced its intention to "struggle towards Democratic Socialism" based on "from each according to his ability, to each according to his need." This is not some kinder ideology concerned with brotherhood, but a slogan parroted from Karl Marx and Lenin and entails eventual control of all means of production to create a Swedish utopia of equality. As economist Phillip Bryson states in *Socialism*, the "Objective and ideal of the modern socialist welfare state is the complete elimination of an obligation or necessity for anyone in society to be constrained to hold a job;"[9] Socialist policy would thus beget legions of non-working and never-working "workers" who, in an inconceivably ironic twist, would become the "idle, blood-sucking parasites" Marx claimed of the bourgeoisie. Instead of being free, those who depend on the State for their daily bread are more in the position of paternalistically cared-for, easily controlled slaves, who, can be depended upon to vote for those who feed them. Again, as the case in point, expanding "Third Way" welfare states in Scandinavia consumed a growing share of their economies' wealth and employment, and their private sectors' share has shrunken. Job creation, GDP, and new business formation have languished with the introduction and expansion of high tax welfare intensive socio-economic policies, and with the dependency of a growing segment of society on government support.[10] Peoples who had long been at the top of the world's economic pyramid before their Leftward tilt were on average now working less, and, of course, also producing less, setting the stage for long-term national decline.

In short, Nordic nations were on the path to the socialist "butchers' economy" presciently described years earlier by Victor Hugo in the novel *Les Miserables*, where a command economy necessarily kills the very wealth it wants to distribute by destroying emulation, entrepreneurial spirit, and a culture of hard work.[11] Rather than miraculously providing the proverbial "free lunch" for all, the Scandinavian welfare model has predictably planted the seed of an ethically bankrupt subculture of dependency. Parasitic freeloading off society's producers whose high taxes "redistribute" their income has stifled savings and discouraged investment.

More recently, as the danger of the downward economic spiral in European countries due to welfare expenditures became apparent, reforms began to be considered that would reverse some of the ill-considered economic policies and negative behavioral consequences. Here is a clear lesson from Europe's experience with welfare programs: no matter how much may be expropriated from the wealthy, socialism cannot create a free lunch for all, miraculously multiplying fishes and loaves of bread until desires are fully satisfied. The desires of man are essentially limitless. Yet something cannot be created from nothing. It's an iron law. People must work, and the economic system has to attract investment and create jobs that utilize their individual talents and abilities to produce what people want and need. On a purely material level not even relatively modest welfare support for those who are nonproductive can be funded by a socialist economy obsessed with distribution, the very nature of which precludes the motivation, rewards and types of organizations that drive innovation, productivity and growth. Welfare programs require a surplus of wealth that will simply not exist. People must produce and accumulate savings while they are productive. Only then will the productive segment of society generate wealth which government can acquire through taxes and dedicate to caring for those who are temporarily unemployed, sick, too old and frail, children, those who are incarcerated, and others in need, and still be able to save and invest adequately in the future for themselves, their families, and broader society.

While the so-called welfare state has an easily opened front door, it too often also has a disguised back door into socialism. Certainly not all those who identify as progressives or liberals, or who wish to see more needs-based welfare benefits, are sympathetic to fully-fledged socialism. The clear fork in the ideological road separating those who are closet socialists from liberals legitimately focused on helping the poor and the helpless is evidenced in those conflating political equality – equality based on equal freedom, nondiscrimination, a right to equal respect and treatment under the law, and an equal say in government – with economic equality. The latter mandates "equalizing," or governmental appropriation of wealth and economic resources, to force an equal share of wealth for all. Where does this socialist fixation on mandating equality of wealth as the bedrock of "welfare" come from? Compassion? Ethics? Tocqueville suggests that for socialists the thought of equality begins with envy, meaning no one should be better off than I am and no one should have more than I have. If my neighbor has two cars, I want two cars; if she wears silk dresses, I should have silk dresses; if they have a 3,000-square foot house, I should have a house at least that large. I am naturally entitled to equivalent things because we are all "equal." However, Deirdre McCloskey quotes an old Spanish proverb that says "Widespread evil is a comfort to fools, making them feel that they are all equal, and have no one to envy," and also points out that the politics of "insatiable envy" drive society into a vicious plunging spiral rather than the upward spiral created by envy's industrious and virtuous opposite, namely motivation, which is the most essential ingredient of human betterment, if not human survival itself. [12]

Perhaps the most important argument concerning the dangers of an ever-expanding welfare state is that raised by Frederick Hayek: "The reason the welfare state can easily evolve into full socialism is that "correcting" the distribution of incomes to make it more "just" is *distributive justice*, which in practice is obstructed by the rule of law requiring *equal treatment*. When the rule of law is recognized as an obstruction to those with redistributive aims, they will naturally seek to circumvent it, disregard it, and finally abandon it altogether by replacing it with a command economy."[italicized emphasis added] [13] Hayek goes on to write that the chief danger is that if an idea such as redistribution of income is accepted as a legitimate aim of government, the fact that such an aim is inimical to freedom will not stand in the way of exhausting all means to achieve it. As more such redistribution schemes are added as mandates, they subtract from freedom and true justice until coercion is all that is left. You cannot have it both ways. You cannot have both equal treatment of all and equal outcomes for all. Lenin at least was honest enough to admit that fact in his writings.

Unfortunately, within Western democracies, there is a growing push to create welfare states whose primary goal is to "fight income inequality" rather than providing a legitimate safety net for the needy. This has lately become the new ethically twisted, ideological con of 21st Century socialism. This is the new rebranding that supplants the old Marxian call for "Workers of the world to throw off their chains and unite in revolution to overthrow the bourgeoisie!" It attempts to disguise the socialist aims hidden behind labels like "Liberal" and "Progressive." By differently framing their old demand for revolution with new demands for income equality as a matter of social justice, the modern socialists of today are seeking to claim the moral high ground that socialism forfeited due to its grotesque immorality in the past century.

Marx's clarion call to battle sounds quaint, odd, and irrelevant today. Although it and Marx's underlying doctrine have never been repudiated by socialism's followers, its allusion to violent conflict has now become counterproductive to their cause. Such a revolutionary slogan inspired by the Industrial Revolution of the mid-1800's has no appeal to workers in modern societies that have become incredibly prosperous owing to increased freedom, freedom that has allowed opportunity to compete for greater rewards and freedom that led to a revolution in innovation, productivity, and economic opportunity based upon true liberal values. In terms of real societal welfare, when all forms of wealth transfers and differential tax burdens are included those in the bottom quartile of overall income in Western democracies have risen to an income level far above that of any pre-1950 middle class—the exact opposite of Marx's dire social predictions. This "freedom revolution" also led to much greater social mobility, where those who are industrious and talented can reach ever higher levels of prosperity, many joining a new, wealthier middle class or even becoming rich.

We should all be disturbed, however, that in our increasingly knowledge-based, highly prosperous societies where Marx's call to social revolution should have no appeal whatsoever, liberals are succeeding in using the phony cause of income inequality to tap into envy, creating antagonisms that polarize society and allow socialism's ugly nose under democracy's tent. Vast, historically unprecedented economic improvement notwithstanding, the progressive Left is nonetheless trying to convince those who, in a relative sense are in lower economic strata that they have no real chance for betterment on their own; they are doomed to failure because "The Man is keeping them down." This is a demoralizing and immoral deceit. It robs the very people the Left loudly proclaims it is trying to help of dignity, respect and hope – hope that nourishes human development. If one is continually told that those wealthier have stacked the deck, why even try to become better educated, learn valuable skills, or seek opportunities for upward mobility? This duplicity is a part of the propagandized economic delirium that characterizes all socialist movements.

Even if it were possible to accomplish through non-violent means, "socializing" all income to levelize wealth and essentially making all individuals' income property controlled by the State would result in an unjust system of twisted ethics and dysfunction. To paraphrase Hayek, it would be a system in which it is not a majority of givers who decide how much to give but a majority of takers who decide how much to take.[14] Since the paradox is true, that to create wealth equalization government must treat its citizens unequally, the process necessarily undermines the motivation and self-respect of the recipients. Government's distribution of unearned wealth to them is essentially purchasing their loyalty; in effect, it is bribery. One must also logically reach the same conclusion as did the journalist Louis Fischer who spent many years in the hope a humanitarian form of the socialist ideal could arise. In *The God That Failed*, he wrote that if the means used by government are immoral, then of necessity government must foster immoral people to be its leaders and to carry out its dictates. Knowing well what it takes to turn socialist theory into a promised reality – a train full of goodness that never arrives, he concluded that "a system founded on the principle of 'the end justifies the means' could never create a better world or better human being." Fischer recognized that "Immoral means produce immoral ends – and immoral persons" under any system. [15]

Fisher was by no means the first to recognize the moral absurdity of socialism's concept of equality. Famed American sociologist W. G. Sumner in his 1877 classic *What the Social Classes Owe To Each Other* observed from another but equally valid vantage point that in a system of forced wealth equality:

Poverty is the best policy. If you get wealth, you will have to support other people; if you do not get wealth, it will be the duty of other people to support you...such schemes for producing equality [are] based on...the right to claim and duty to give one man's effort for another man's satisfaction. He whose labor and self-denial may be diverted from his maintenance to that of some other man...approaches the position of a slave. [16]

Your Labor, Whose Fruits?

Standing in direct opposition to communism's most essential welfare tenet, "from each according to his abilities, to each according to his needs," is a most fundamental human right: the fruits of a person's labor belongs to that person alone. According to Deirdre McCloskey, both Adam Smith and Locke before him viewed ownership of one's labor as the "most sacred and inviolable right of property because it is the original foundation of all other property."[17] This is one of the reasons why slavery is so abhorrent. No one today would consider slavery a consequence of social welfare, but regardless of the purpose, taking the product of a person's labor without their consent constitutes stealing and places those whose labor has been appropriated in a position of servitude unless they can somehow escape without losing what they have. Hence, the prohibitions placed on movement and emigration by certain socialist states, as epitomized by the infamous Berlin Wall erected by the Soviets in 1961 to halt the flow of people from the German Democratic Republic (GDR). Thousands had been escaping the GDR, which described itself as a "socialist workers' and peasants' state," to seek new lives in the free sector of Berlin. By the time the Berlin Wall was torn down in 1989, hundreds had been arrested or shot trying to escape. In those few places where people are permitted to escape socialism, many thousands often "vote with their feet," fleeing to more prosperous democratic capitalist states and sadly leaving their less productive and less fortunate countrymen behind. It was Cuba's great freedom-loving patriot Jose Marti who wrote: "Man loves liberty, even if he does not know that he loves it. He is driven by it and flees from where it does not exist."[18]

In democratic countries in which the elected representatives of the people freely vote to fund welfare programs and other public programs, the people's consent to giving up a portion of the product of their labor via taxes must be assumed. That is in stark contrast to socialist states in which the entirety of that product is appropriated and controlled by a state in which the only people with a say are the Party's ruling elites who produce nothing, only command others and enjoy special perquisites.

Put simply, we each rightfully own the product of our work unless we willingly contract it to others. Every human who reaches the age of reason possesses the natural right to manage or dispose of their own labor as they see fit, beyond what they morally owe to their family. Without this right people become virtual slaves to a governmental system that determines how much they are allowed to keep. Welfare recipients do not as a natural right have any call on their fellow human beings' labor to provide for their own needs if they behave irresponsibly, indolently, or criminally. No system mandating social cooperation to produce what people want and need can function in the long term when it also rewards laziness and irresponsibility.

An inevitable side effect of socializing wealth is to make those who are responsible, prudent, and hard-working the slaves of those who are not!

Complete economic leveling can never be accomplished voluntarily. It requires coercion and destruction of liberty using irresistible governmental power. On the road to the socialist utopian fantasy, one cannot earn more from one's extra effort, innovation, productivity, initiative, or risk-taking. Such positive rewards become non-existent, and the bases of human striving, competition, and motivation are repudiated. In such a "paradise" of economic equalization, drivers of growing prosperity and upward mobility do not exist, resulting in economic stagnation and decline. As envisioned in Etienne Cabet's dystopian *Voyage to Icaria*, equality of individuals' rights is twisted into an imposed hellish soul-crushing beehive uniformity in all aspects of life and secured with severe punishment of deviations. [19]

Some of today's self-proclaimed liberals, led by those who have gained considerable control of the media, entertainment, educational institutions, and much of the 'non-profit" (NGO) sector, tilt further toward messianic socialism. Rather than making arguments based on Reason and promoting tolerant pluralism and the shared values that bind society together, they engage in classic Marxist/Leninist tactics used to fracture society into irreconcilable camps, tactics that include harnessing envy to foment class and ethnic hatreds, stifling freedom, engaging in character assassination, bullying, shouting down, censoring speech, trafficking in clever lies, creating agitation-propaganda incidents for use by their media stooges, demonizing any political opponents as racist and xenophobic "fascist oppressors," and attempting to de-legitimize unifying patriotic symbols and practices, calling them "symbols of class oppression." Recall that Karl Marx's communist mantra "workers of the world unite!" demands greater loyalty to the Marxist creed than to one's own nation.[20]

To live-out Marx's theory of social conflict arising between different groups or classes within society, but without incurring any personal risk to themselves, liberals continually sow the seeds of discord and besmirch all things that strengthen social unity. Should any object to their efforts, the Left then uses the very hatred they themselves have aroused to target, discredit, and if possible, destroy the reputation of any individual or organization that might dare to oppose them, which also discourages others from coming to their defense. This is straight from Lenin's playbook, who gave the following directions to his followers: "We can and must write in a language which sows

264 ■ Some Call it Utopia

among the masses hate, scorn and the like toward those who disagree with us."[21]

Liberals who become radicalized also often similarly debase themselves and the institutions they are a part of by speaking and writing in the language of violence similar to Lenin and the other ideological progeny of Marx. They often shout obscenities, they attack and bully others in social media, and they paint obscenities on the walls of homes and businesses and on public structures. They highlight and encourage grievances that attract adherents and followers, and then characterize them as "victims" of oppression. They say they want more diversity, but then pursue the diabolical agenda of stoking ethnic and racial resentment to gain political advantage from the divisions that result. Their language of violence leads to riots by street mobs, attacks on officials, vandalism, looting, arson, desecration of honorific and patriotic symbols and monuments, and too often, bloodshed. They shout, "No justice, No Peace!" These are hallmarks of socialist agitation, harmful, not helpful to social welfare.

One must conclude that, rather than working to serve the welfare of society in a spirit of brotherhood, such liberals instead take up what they see as the unfinished business of a long-suppressed Marxian class war between those they paint as powerful "haves" and those they portray as powerless and oppressed "have-nots." Note, however, that while those who espouse the liberal/progressive flavor of socialism may not hesitate to employ personal intimidation to create fear, they are loath to risk their own lives by personally pursuing open rebellion and the violent class warfare predicted by Marx. They are quick to distance themselves from the ghastly history of their socialist creed that cost the lives of many millions, preferring to ignore any possible connection they may have with it through duplicity, intentional ignorance, or cognitive bias. They hum the empty, irrelevant phrases of the socialist anthem, The Internationale while hiding behind a cloak of false humanitarianism, and they feel good about themselves as "moral" people enjoying the excitement of being part of something bigger than themselves, part of a movement, part of a cause!

Such arrogant, true believers eagerly become, to quote Joseph Epstein, "Virtucrats: people convinced their political views are not merely correct, but deeply, morally righteous in the bargain; people whose politics lend them the fine sense of elation that only false virtue makes possible."[22]

These charlatans' false virtue and false promises are the flimsy cover Leftists of various stripes cling to, not wanting to be confronted by difficult questions concerning socialism's abominable trail of death, economic dysfunction, internal contradictions, and gross injustice.

To illustrate the contradictions and consequences of virtue-seeking through edicts, one need look no further than the self-righteous Maximilien Robespierre, a Jacobin and a leader of France's revolutionary "Committee of Public Safety" largely responsible for France's infamous "Reign of Terror." With near boundless arrogance the "incorruptible" Robespierre, who was responsible for the guillotining of thousands, pronounced that:

> Since virtue and equality are the soul of the republic, and that your aim is to found, to consolidate the republic, it follows, that the first rule of your political conduct should be, to let all measures tend to maintain equality and encourage virtue…Again it may be said, that to love justice and equality the people need no great effort of virtue; it is sufficient that they love themselves…If virtue be the spring of a popular government in time of peace, the spring of that government during a revolution is virtue combined with terror: virtue, without which terror is destructive; terror, without which virtue is impotent. Terror is only justice prompt, severe and inflexible; it is then an emanation of virtue…[23]

Such contradictions were all too familiar to Solzhenitsyn:

> World socialism as a whole, and all the figures associated with it, are shrouded in legend; its contradictions are forgotten or concealed; it does not respond to arguments but continually ignores

them--all this stems from the mist of irrationality that surrounds socialism...The doctrines of socialism seethe with contradictions, its theories are at constant odds with its practice, yet due to a powerful instinct...these contradictions do not in the least hinder the unending propaganda of socialism. Indeed, no precise, distinct socialism even exists; instead there is only a vague, rosy notion of something noble and good, of equality, communal ownership, and justice: the advent of these things will bring instant euphoria and a social order beyond reproach.[24]

In truth, no moral virtue is conferred from making pious pronouncements about what others ought to do to promote social welfare, much less from any politically coerced redistribution of wealth that substitutes for the common welfare created by voluntary sharing and genuine fellowship. Nor can there be a scintilla of virtue in actions motivated by the vice of envy. As Peter Drucker put it in referring to "the first prophet of this secular religion" Jean-Jacques Rousseau, seeking "salvation through society to atone for the 'sin' of being more prosperous than some others is a self-flattering moral dead end."[25] The disenchanted former socialist Louis Fischer wrote in his autobiographical account *The God That Failed,* "A cause is more compelling than all but the most shocking facts about it."[26] Adherents to the cause of salvation through society are insensible to the pull of socialist pseudo-religious hucksterism that left unopposed sucks everyone it touches down a dark dystopian drainpipe. In the end, attempting to socialize responsibility for everyone's wellbeing is a fool's bargain that would sacrifice the true liberal foundation of humane government and the exponential increase in human prosperity over the past 200 years.

Notes

1. Marx's famous quote popularized Part I of his 1875 Critique of the Gotha Program (see p. 531 of *The Marx and Engles Reader, Second Edition,* W.W. Norton & Company, Edited by Robert C. Tucker, 1978). The full quote is: "In a higher phase of communist society, after the enslaving subordination of the individual

to the division of labor, and therewith also the antithesis between mental and physical labor, has vanished; after labor has become not only a means of life but life's prime want; after the productive forces have also increased with the all-around development of the individual, and all the springs of cooperative wealth flow more abundantly – only then can the narrow horizon of bourgeois right be crossed in its entirety and society inscribe on its banner: From each according to his ability. To each according to his needs." (emphasis added).

2. This is an example of Marx's wide influence, penned in the late 1890's by the Italian anarcho-communist Errico Malatesta Malatesta. Malatesta was a devotee of the short-lived Socialist revolution of the Paris Commune of 1871, and advocate of social revolution in his native Italy. After being exiled he met Peter Kropotkin and other Socialists in Geneva. After sneaking back into Italy he founded the anarchist paper *La Questione Sociale*.

3. Karl Marx, paraphrased from Part I of his 1875 Critique of the Gotha Program (see p. 531 of *The Marx and Engles Reader*, Second Edition, W.W. Norton & Company, Edited by Robert C. Tucker, 1978).

4. F. A. Hayek, *The Road to Serfdom*, University of Chicago Press, 1944, p. 157.

5. Courtois et al, *The Black Book of Communism: Crimes, Terror, Repression*, Stephane Courtois Introduction: "The Crimes of Communism," pp. 11-12, Harvard University Press, 1999; Quote of a former Soviet Comintern member, Joseph Berger, from a letter received from a gulag deportee who had been purged during the Stalin era. It is footnote (13), as follows:

> Joseph Berger *Shipwreck of a Generation: The Memoirs of Joseph Berger* (London: Harvill Press, 1971), p. 247. The full quote is: "My generation of Communists everywhere accepted the Stalinist form of leadership. We acquiesced in the crimes. That is true not only of Soviet Communists, but of Communists all over the world. We, especially the active and leading members of the Party, carry a stain on our consciences individually and collectively. The only way we can erase it is to make sure that nothing of the sort ever happens again. How was all this possible? Did we all go crazy, or have we now become traitors to Communism? The truth is that all of us, including the leaders directly under Stalin, saw these crimes as the opposite of what they were. We believed that they were important contributions to the victory of socialism. We thought everything that promoted the power politics of the Communist Party in the Soviet Union and in the world was good for socialism. We never suspected that conflict between Communist politics and Communist ethics was possible."

268 ■ Some Call it Utopia

6. Hannah Arendt, *Origins of Totalitarianism*, Meridian Books: The World Publishing Co., 1951, 1958 edition, Chapter Ten: "A Classless Society," p. 307.

7. "Maslow's Hierarchy of Needs" is a theory in psychology proposed by Abraham H. Maslow in his paper titled "A Theory of Human Motivation" in *Psychological Review* 50 (4): 370-396 in 1943, and in his book *Motivation and Personality*, in 1954. It is depicted as a layered pyramid with Physiological needs (air, water, food, shelter) at the base, followed by the next layer, Safety, then by Love and Belonging, and by Esteem, and finally Self-actualization at the very top. The more basic needs must first be met in ascending order before humans desire and focus attention on the next, higher level need.

8. This quote is unverified, but consistent with the brutal orders Lenin issued. For example, similar language is found in a V. I. Lenin directive dated February 21, 1918, "The Socialist Fatherland is in Danger!" first published in *Pravda* No. 32, which directs that "battalions are to be formed that include all able-bodied members of the bourgeois class, men and women, under the supervision of the Red Guard; those who resist are to be shot." This directive is found at the Marxist Internet Archive at www.marxists.org/archive/lenin/works/1918/feb/21b.htm.

9. Phillip Bryson, *Socialism: Origins, Expansion, Decline, and the Attempted Revival in the United States*, Xlibris, 2015, Chapter 15, "Socialism in Democratic Western Europe," p. 541.

10. Nima Sanandaji of the Institute of Economic Affairs, "Scandinavian Unexceptionalism: Culture, Markets and the Failure of Third-Way Socialism," 2015

11. Victor Hugo, *Les Miserables*, chapter "Cracks Under The Foundation," pp. 505-506, Barnes & Noble Classics, NY, edited and abridged; *Les Miserables* was published in 1862 only 14 years after Marx and Engels had published the Communist Manifesto; the full quote is: "By good distribution, we must understand not equal distribution, but equitable distribution. The highest equality is equity." (The word "equity" means fairness, justice, and impartiality.) "Communism and agrarian law think they have solved the second problem (distribution). They are mistaken. Their distribution kills production. Equal division abolishes emulation. And consequently labour. It is a distribution made by the butcher, who kills what he divides. It is therefore impossible to stop at these professed solutions. To kill wealth is not to distribute it." A "butcher's economy" is thus a command economy that necessarily kills the creation of the very wealth it wants to distribute, by destroying emulation, entrepreneurial spirit, and culture of hard work.

12. Deirdre McCloskey, *Bourgeois Equality: How Ideas, Not Capital or Institutions, Enriched the World*, The University of Chicago Press, 2016. McCloskey

is distinguished professor of economics, history, English, and communications at the University of Illinois. Her thought, paraphrased, is that socialism creates a vicious downward spiral driven by "insatiable envy" rather than a virtuous upward spiral driven by envy's industrious and virtuous opposite, motivation, which is the essential driver of humanity's betterment; it is found in pp. 1621, 2089, and 12358 of 18935 in e-version.

13. Frederick Hayek, *The Constitution of Liberty*, The University of Chicago Press, 1960, Part II, "Freedom and the Law," Chapter 15 "Economic Policy and the Rule of Law," pp. 341 and 376.

14. Frederick Hayek, *The Constitution of Liberty*, The University of Chicago Press, 1960, Part III, "Freedom in the Welfare State," Chapter 19 "Social Security," pp. 409-410.

15. Louis Fischer, *The God That Failed*, 1949, Harper & Row, 1963, edited by Richard Crossman, p. 225, this quote is found in Louis Fischer's biographical essay from his experience as a former communist sympathizer in the book's Part II Worshipers From Afar; this book is a collection of such testimonial essays by disenchanted writers who had previously championed the Bolsheviks and the worldwide communist movement as the means to a new and better form of civilization, but had awakened to its dire consequences.

16. W. G. Sumner, American sociologist and Yale professor, What the Social Classes Owe To Each Other, Caxton Printers Ltd., 1877, pp. 22-26 in Chapter I, "On A New Philosophy that Poverty is the Best Policy;" Sumner's book is an early classic of the social sciences, full of astute observations about human nature and social order.

17. Deirdre N. McCloskey, *Bourgeois Equality: How Ideas, Not Capital or Institutions, Enriched the World*, The University of Chicago Press, 2016, at location 3932 of 18935 in the e-version she paraphrases Adam Smith; The original passage is in Adam Smith *An Inquiry into the Nature and Causes of the Wealth of Nations*, 1776, Part One, Wages and Profit, X, p. 225 of Penguin English Library version, 1974; it reads as follows: "The property which every man has in his own labour, as it is the original foundation of all other property, so it is the most sacred and inviolable...To hinder him from employing [his natural talents] in what manner he thinks proper without injury to his neighbor is a plain violation of this most sacred property."

18. Jose Marti, *Jose Marti: Thoughts*, Edited by Carlos Ripoll, published by Endowment for Cuban American Studies, 1994.

19. Etienne Cabet, *Voyage to Icaria*, 1840, in Berneri *Journey Through Utopia*, Beacon Press, 1951, pp. 224-232; Cabet was influenced by the early French socialist Fourier, and organized model Icarian-style communities in Texas and

Illinois in North America in 1848 that were a failed experiment in authoritarian socialism; as described in Cabet's book, Icaria called for Hellish soul-crushing uniformity in all aspects of life, with severe punishment of deviations. Books were burned at its establishment. Rigid censorship controls all art. etc., etc.; to quote from Cabet's Voyage "The unanimous will of the people is always to create political and social equality, the equality of happiness and rights, universal and absolute equality: education, food, clothing, houses and furniture, work and pleasure...our communes, our towns, our villages, our farms, and our houses are, as far as possible, similar. Everywhere, in a word, you will find equality and happiness. Take food. Everything concerning food has been regulated by the law. As with food, so it is with the law which regulates everything connected with clothes. And so on..."

20. Ending statement of the Manifesto of the Communist Party, more commonly referred to as *The Communist Manifesto*, 1848; written by Karl Marx and Frederick Engels, the Manifesto is based upon the doctrine of class struggle between the oppressed (proletariat workers) and oppressors (bourgeoisie); it is the most widely read and influential document of modern socialism, and without a doubt the indispensable catechism for all who consider themselves socialists. The Communist League was formed in Paris in 1836 by German radical workers living there who had been calling their hitherto secret organization the "League of the Just."

21. Max Eastman, *Reflections on the Failure of Socialism*, Devin-Adair Company, 1955, pp. 87, Eastman wrote that Lenin gave this direction to his followers: "We can and must write in a language which sows among the masses hate, scorn and the like, toward those who disagree with us." Eastman was a leading U.S. socialist who knew Lenin and studied at the feet of the master in Russia shortly after the Bolsheviks came to power. He later in life became a staunch anti-communist, repudiating and refuting socialism/communism in a number of written works.

22. Joseph Epstein quoted in the November 4, 2014 *Wall Street Journal* "My single contribution to the English language is the word "virtucrat." I invented it to describe those who derive their grand sense of themselves from the virtuousness of their opinions, and of no opinions more than their political opinions. These opinions fortify virtucrats morally, assuring them of their essential goodness...Their politics endow them with their virtue, and make them better than you or me and anyone else whose political opinions differ from theirs." Such arrogant virtucrats are "those who are convinced their political views are not merely correct, but deeply, morally righteous in the bargain; those whose politics lend them the fine sense of elation that only false virtue makes possible."

23. Maximilien Robespierre, "Report on the Principles of Political Morality Which Are to Form the Basis of the Administration of the Interior Concerns of the Republic" (Philadelphia 1794) source: Paul Halsall, *Modern History Sourcebook*, August 1997.

24. Alexandr Solzhenitsyn, Foreword to fellow dissident Igor Shafarevich's 1975 book *The Socialist Phenomenon*, Harper & Row, 1980.

25. Peter Drucker, *Post-Capitalist Society*, Harper Collins Publishers, 1993, Introduction, p. 7; The secular religion created by Jean-Jacques Rousseau of "seeking salvation through society to atone for the 'sin' of being more prosperous than some others, or simply out of righteousness is a self-flattering moral dead end." Drucker concludes that "the collapse of Marxism as a creed signifies the end of belief in salvation by society." The growing popularity of socialism in the West seems to belie Drucker's optimism. As he himself put it, "pesky human nature keeps sneaking in through the back door after being tossed out the front [by socialists] with a pitchfork" in their failed attempts at creating the "New Man."

26. Louis Fischer, "Worshipers from Afar" in *The God That Failed*, 1949, Harper & Row, 1963 edition, edited by Richard Crossman, p. 203, see all of pp. 196-228; Fischer, autobiographical essay from his experience as a former communist sympathizer, wrote "One's alignment with a cause is more compelling than all but the most shocking facts about it. Just as religious conviction is impervious to logical argument and, indeed, does not result from logical processes, just as nationalist devotion or personal affection defies a mountain of evidence..."

CHAPTER SIX
Socialism, Human Nature, and Spirituality

"Once abolish the God, and the government becomes the God."
—G.K. Chesterton, English writer, philosopher, and lay theologian

Much about people's political sympathies can be traced to their view of human nature. Once such beliefs have taken root, they may be very strongly held, even when not well-informed. Differences in such beliefs can, therefore, be the underlying origin of political conflict. Hence, it is unsurprising that political ideologies are laden with assumptions, implicit and explicit, concerning how malleable we are in response to the influences of our social environment. Moreover, it is characteristic of ideologies that they are premised upon certain theoretical beliefs about human nature, which their proponents present as indisputable facts. The idea that mankind can be fundamentally changed for the better according to their prescriptions, is a necessary part of the Socialist appeal.

Problematic Suppositions

I have argued that the root cause of socialism's divergence from reality and consequential failure to live up to its promises can be traced to its fanciful premises on human nature. One of its fundamental suppositions that "Man is naturally good, and only through society is he made bad,"—what I have termed the

"Rousseauian delusion." Marx shared a similar view, maintaining that "Man is the sum total of his social relations."[1] Sometimes called the denial of "Original Sin" residing within humanity's nature, this misconception is shared by many. It may be thought of as a belief in the complete malleability of human nature unconstrained by heritable traits. Socialists would call their belief in the overwhelming power of a properly guided social environment to shape behaviors and eliminate frailties, hopeful and positive toward human progress. Indeed, this supposition has very profound implications for the foundations of socialism and of government in any form.

A corollary of the first assertion, is that "Man's" fundamental nature can be changed through an act of human resolve; he wills himself into a "perfected" superior creature, what socialists envision as the new "Socialist Man." It is what Marx called "the reshaping of men by men," much as humans are able to purposefully reshape certain physical elements of Nature around them.[2] The work of God, the Creator, the evolution of human beings, and even Nature itself either have no role or can be overridden by deliberate human design. Both these key suppositions rely on the belief refuted most ably by scientist Steven Pinker that human beings are a "blank slate" from birth; humans are totally shaped by society, and therefore the evolved attributes and instincts of the human species have little or nothing to do with our norms, proclivities, abilities, decisions, and behaviors, for better or worse.[3] According to this line of thinking, conditioning by social environments make humans feel envy, be acquisitive and competitive, and likewise to express hatred and aggression.

These impulses are assumed to be unnatural, even though they are known to exist in every human society, whether primitive or advanced. Hence, if an individual does bad things, that person's social imprint from collective society is fully to blame. Everyone is presumed to share responsibility for crimes and other socially destructive behaviors and for finding the remedy, while being sympathetic for criminals who are the "victims of society." Individual choices, proclivities, and willed behavior are given little or no weight in this theory, sometimes also called "social determinism." Imprisonment is only a practical necessity for public safety, not a moral judgement made by society to condemn a criminal's actions. This train of thought, which in some places today drives policies on crime, exemplifies the proverbial "slippery slope." After all, who wouldn't want to be able to blame others, society in general, or a certain group within society, rather than accept personal responsibility for their own shortcomings, mistakes, and misdeeds?

To be clear, no one would deny that a person's attitudes, skills, behaviors, and opportunities are profoundly influenced by family members, peers, teachers, and mentors throughout life, by one's experiences, and from literature and other sources within their cultural milieu. These influences can be very helpful or harmful, but contrary to the presuppositions of Rousseau and Marx, cannot alter that which is heritable and an innate part of our evolved human nature. Nor do such influences entirely negate free will. Humans are far from mere automatons lacking self-consciousness, instincts, moral agency, and a will, who can be programmed from birth to eradicate their tendency to sin, and thus assure they always act with saintly virtue - however "sin" and "virtue" might be defined by their utopian master programmers.

Picture, if you will, a three-legged stool of socialism, sure to collapse if any of the three "legs," it's essential suppositions, fall away. These intellectual "legs" guide the rhetoric and fantasy scribblings of socialist thinkers. They surmise that while society is collectively responsible for the evil deeds of individuals, somehow certain exceptional individuals possessing great determination, purity of spirit, and extraordinary insight are nonetheless justified in using political power to reshape not only society but human nature itself, permanently curing all of society's ills. Once reactionary elements are cleansed away, and a fully socialist system established, a very powerful guiding hand will enable the collective "we" of socialist society to make things right and just in every individual's life. The superior model of "Man" will be created and become universal. Consequently, in generations hence there will no longer be any need for authority and coercion, and everyone will then bask in the sunlight of perfection as is their right, having all become completely equal, highly advanced human beings. These beliefs concerning the nature of humanity, when amplified by arrogance, motivated by misguided idealism, and subject to an evil will to power, explain much of the socialist utopian impetus.

In recognition of innate human frailties, it is often said that "we are all sinners." Ample proof provided by the research of neuroscience, psychology, and anthropology, demonstrates that the first two key assumptions just mentioned above are nothing but the wishful delusions of socialists and their sympathizers who are unwilling to acknowledge that our human nature contains the seeds of both goodness and evil, virtue and vice. Humans simply possess both tendencies by nature. However, as weak and imperfect as humanity tends to be, it turns out we are also endowed with reason and self-consciousness which enable us to reflect on our own personal responsibility, make our own choices, and willfully control our base impulses, as well as to exhibit compassion and aspire to virtue. Humans have created rational laws and institutions to control such negative impulses and accentuate the positive. Socialists prefer to believe that human nature itself, the core of our being, can be molded to eliminate our negative impulses and frailties, if only wise people are given full control of everyone's lives. These two false "legs" supporting socialism's metaphorical "stool," have led the socialist intelligentsia to adopt doctrines equally incongruent with reality, which only leads them down a blind alley.

But there is a third essential leg supporting the ideology of socialism: the dark and divisive theory of "social justice." That is, certain classes of people aren't getting what they justly deserve—a "fair," more equal share of whatever society produces—because of systematic and malevolent exploitation of them by a more privileged class of people with "opposing" economic interests. Accusations of racial privilege, discrimination and oppression makes this theory even more explosive. Those who are part of an exploited class have an unconditional right to that equal share and are justified in taking it by any means, achieving both "social justice" and the security of "freedom from want," eliminating the two hypothetical root causes of antisocial behaviors.

Socialism's grandiose ethical claim is wrapped up in this resentful, envious, and sometimes racial concept of justice. It is this accusation of social injustice based upon unequal material results and a promise to create a leveled society that allow socialism as a theory to become rooted in the human consciousness and as an ideology firmly planted in hearts and minds. The link of social justice to material equality has proven to be a beguiling claim, notwithstanding that making material outcomes equal for all inescapably requires destroying freedom with compulsion, and treating people unequally, with disregard for merit, a moral contradiction with terrible social and economic consequences.

When scientists have probed and questioned what is known about humans as social beings, this third premise, socialism's remaining leg, has been proven to be every bit as hollow as the other two, readily collapsing under the weight of common sense and logic and confirmed by observation.

Indeed, as all three legs crumble under even cursory scrutiny, we find that the truth about socialism today is no different from the description former socialist Max Eastman gave 65 years ago: "[socialism is] a dangerous fairy tale... one that beguiles a large group of liberal-minded reformers creeping into power" in order to "bend democratic states to their will and take charge of the economy."[4] For those socialists whose true heartfelt intentions are untainted by the dark side of their human nature, and are not "wannabe dictators," socialism is, again, simply a case of "idealism run amok," endangering individuals, families, communities, and whole nations. From observing socialism's track record, it is apparent that strong-willed good intentions of moral crusaders that are not also shaped by Niebuhr's common-sense realism concerning human nature are a grave danger to others.

In the end the human spirit is the final arbiter standing in judgement of socialism. The spiritual void socialism calls for cannot be satisfactorily filled by morally vapid materialist scripture and supreme leaders posing as human gods ruling over an omnipotent secular state. Its rejection of ancient religious wisdom and universal norms in favor of expediency and its embrace of the concept of collective and heritable guilt places socialism on a fatally infirm moral foundation that itself collapses beneath the weight of its undeniably vast crimes against humanity. Socialism's stool, already with its legs collapsing, is left with only spiritual quicksand to support it. Let us now look more closely at how socialism's most fundamental error, a denial of human nature, causes its collapse.

Our Natural Sense of Justice Differs from Socialism

What could possibly be confusing about our feelings of justice and injustice? Alexandr Solzhenitsyn said it well in his novel *In The Inner Circle*, "We were born with a sense of justice in our souls, and do not want to live without it."[5] The innate craving for freedom and justice are like precious air filling our lungs in every breath we take, without which we perish. Likewise, human desire to receive justice from others is as strong as the natural desire for the freedom to act according to our own will.

Our natural sense of justice deepens when we understand the difference between fair treatment, receiving one's desires, and receiving as much as those around us. Being treated fairly does not necessarily mean always getting what we may want or getting as much of something as anyone else. This applies to almost everything, be it possessions, money, love, parental attention, or services from others. As infants quickly learn and internalize, their willed behavior evokes both positive and negative responses from those around them. Throughout our lives, we are rewarded and punished by those affected by our actions. That is part of the process of socialization through which humans learn to live in relative harmony. Children often desire something possessed by another child and will attempt to take it unless stopped by that child or by an adult.

Although voluntary sharing without a corresponding demand for reciprocation or reward is a virtuous act, we are not entitled to the property of any other person. Unless we become thieves, we very early in our lives come to understand that justice is not appropriating that which we may desire from others. Justice lies in getting that which we have earned through our own decisions and actions and by doing things others value and appreciate, contributing to the well-being of our family and society.

Cornerstones of freedom therefore include the ability to act according to our own will so long as we do not interfere with the rights of others, acceptance that being treated fairly does not always mean getting what we might want, and the understanding that consequences result from our actions. For a society to function freely and peaceably, every person must buy into the basic ethical premise that no one has an automatic entitlement to the property or wealth of someone else. The concept of personal property, whether obtained by one's industry, trade, or inheritance, is an element of our essential humanness that is universal across cultures.

The tenets of socialism are quite contrary to this. Socialism, no matter how dressed-up, rejects these principles of a free society along with its legal and moral basis. Somewhere in the socialist theoreticians' intellectual quest for utopia ideals morph into ideology and justice is tossed aside. Instead, to gain political power socialism gives license to the destructive human impulse of envy, and by replacing individual responsibility with collective responsibility, supports claims on others' property and wealth in the name of social justice and equality. In the end, despite its demand to make all equal, socialism asserts the right of a self-chosen few to control the lives of many non-consenting fellow citizens.

Collectivizing moral responsibility is a cornerstone of socialism's concept of "social" justice. However, as Hayek points out, our natural sense of justice is that "only those persons responsible for a particular outcome should be held to account." The Left's social justice, on the other hand, "holds that the whole group of which the victim is a member should be recompensed, while the group to which the perpetrator belongs should all be equally penalized."[6] Determining rewards and punishments on the collective basis of group identity is a primitive and dangerous concept. It is hard to overstate the level of evil prompted by this concept, particularly when it is part of "race theory" that gives rise to Racial Socialism, a type of ideology antithetical to colorblind reason and justice. This is important because neutral reason and justice are essential cornerstones of any peaceful, successful civil society co-habited by diverse groups. As I pointed out, the consequences of allowing race theories that call for collectivist social justice based on group membership can be quite horrible, as the world has seen from the many episodes of ethnic cleansing and genocide as well as the chronic ethnic strife in multiracial societies.

"Fairness" is Being Treated the Same, Not Getting the Same

A society in which people are treated in a fair manner is often described as "egalitarian." A society is egalitarian if everyone has equal rights and an equal say in government through universal suffrage, and none are discriminated against because of their group identity. However, egalitarian societies do not guarantee that each individual gets the same share of the available material rewards irrespective of what they produce. Similarly, the idea of fairness is often conflated by the Left's propaganda into government assuring an equalized distribution of material rewards, such as income, property and goods.

With semantic gimmickry, Leftist politicians and academics stretch and twist the *Oxford Dictionary's* meaning of "equitable" from fair and impartial treatment into guaranteeing an equal distribution of benefits and rewards, that is, an equal economic outcome. But equalization enforced by government decree is not the same as treating the members of society fairly. Forced equalization, a fundamental tenet of socialism, is indeed unfair to those members of society who with motivation, mastered skills, creativity, and industriousness create more value for society through their work than another. Indeed, with everyone entitled to an equal share of everything, the socialist idea of equality contravenes the very idea of individuals being fairly rewarded for exemplary effort, work, and achievement. Likewise, it is patently unfair to ignore an individual's investment of time and effort, deferral of gratification required to master valuable and productive skills, and personal entrepreneurship in order to create something new or better.

In truly egalitarian societies, there is no special privilege conferred upon nor prejudice applied to individuals based upon their group identity (class, gender, ethnicity, religion, or kinship). Rather, the idea of merit is the true lode star of our innate sense of fairness. I am referring in this context to the accomplishments of an individual who has been provided the same dignity and respect as any other member of the community, the same opportunity, and rewards measured according to behavior and achievement (to include special reward for outstanding achievement). Our sense of fairness tells us that everyone being given the same rewards regardless of merit, regardless of what we do, regardless of skills, inclination to work, and contribution to society (or harm), is manifestly unfair and offensive. While some people can be especially deserving, others may be less deserving, and indeed some, such as those who simply refuse to work or engage in destructive and criminal activity, may be altogether undeserving, or deserving of punishment.

Reason concludes that both justice and fairness require unequal outcomes for individuals. In fact, unequal outcomes drive human progress by rewarding and thus motivating success and productivity. The history of the 20th Century teaches us that governments that equate fairness (or again, "social justice") with an equal rather than equitable distribution soon become dysfunctional and start to regress. Distribution of all good things based on group identity, ostensibly to create a "classless society," or on one's unquestioned loyalty to those in authority, renders pursuit of individual achievement pointless. The consequential destruction of essential human motivation means these systems will ultimately fail.

Ameliorating Poverty is Fundamentally Different than Equalizing Wealth

According to Marx, the poverty of some is a result from the wealth of others (as the rich get richer, the poor must get poorer), rather than from the differences in what people are willing and able to do themselves, tempered by the vagaries of fortune. More importantly, Marx seems to have regarded the technological basis of society and its man-machine system of production he was reacting to as essentially having reached a stasis in his time. He apparently could neither imagine nor foresee the dramatic social and economic changes that would result from continuing innovation in open markets, not only in the means of production, but also in the creation of entirely new and better products to meet human needs and wants. Instead, he predicted worsening immiseration of the industrial working class. This is at least partly a reflection of Malthusian thinking applied to an increasingly industrialized world; a relic of feudal era struggles with feeding a growing population from a fixed amount of land using rudimentary tools, which becomes less and less relevant as societies modernize. To wit, by assuming the size of the imaginary pie to be fixed, if someone more powerful can grab a larger piece, others must be left with less and be worse off. Since Marx's time it has become abundantly clear from long-term per-capita economic growth that such "zero-sum" thinking is a fallacious, static concept of economics. This is a fallacy fixated only on distribution. Global per-capita production and income have increased exponentially since Marx, while the percentage of people living in poverty has dropped nearly ten-fold from 84 percent to under nine percent. All this while, the amount of labor required for production has declined, and life expectancy has dramatically increased.[7] Some people gaining more than others as the total amount of wealth increases does not mean the others are not much better off as well. Envy can blind people to this reality.

Poverty, the condition of serious economic deprivation, is not the same as some simply having less money than some others. In all societies one will find a continuum of some with relatively more and others with relatively less, even when those with less are actually far more prosperous than ever before. Furthermore, the line between poorer and richer is continually shifting, and so the members of both groups are continually shifting, most typically over the course of an individual's work life. As Deirdre McCloskey points out, "solving absolute poverty came [about] in fact from the Great Enrichment [resulting from freedom and markets, [while] attempting to solve a logically insoluble relative 'poverty' resulted in slowing growth and the encouragement of insatiable envy." She elaborates that "Slow growth yields envy…and envy yields populism, which in turn yields slow growth," thus a vicious downward spiral.[8]

Having enough to live a dignified life without becoming destitute and having met the threshold giving one a chance to improve one's status are entirely different from being entitled to someone else's money and property for the sake of increased financial equality. For Hayek this means that the security of a minimum income is also fundamentally different from the security provided by a particular income.[9] A sufficient income is one necessary for sustenance and a chance to become financially better off through one's own industry. A particular income is one prescribed by outside interests for the purpose of promoting social justice, income equality, and "happiness" in general. In the name of social justice, real poverty is often confused with economic inequality by fuzzy-thinking or obfuscating demagogues. Wants that are simply desires are equated with true needs, and both are bundled together under the rubric of "rights" and "entitlements." However, the condition of poverty is by definition "not having enough of that which is needed to sustain oneself and one's dependents," not simply having less than others may have. Thus, one's relative wealth is not the criterion for poverty, even though it may be a source of envy and thus leverage for left-wing political opportunists.

It is the poverty of those lacking what they truly need – and who are not indolent or otherwise self-destructive – that must trigger a social response. Moreover, poverty cannot be considered an ever-expanding concept that includes goods and services people may simply want layered on top of those they truly need. Otherwise, the words want, need, and poverty lose real meaning. "Want" is a broader term than "need" because it includes all that we desire. The elastic ambiguity of this lexicon well suits the Left's envy politics with its political advocacy of ever-expanding entitlements to achieve distributive equality. Their cheerleaders may keep chanting "justice" and "fairness" into megaphones, but the sound that comes out the other end is always "No one should have any more than I have!"

Socialist ideology nonetheless openly and unabashedly mingles wants and needs without differentiation and turns this mishmash into an ever-expanding number of entitlements and welfare programs. This then cynically vindicates a claim on the labor of the other members of society to assure personal wants and needs are met, and to create a grievance if they are not. Indeed, the essentially unlimited nature of human wants makes the oft-stated socialist demand of "freedom from want" an absurd impossibility when taken literally. It follows from such a twisted notion of entitlement that simply by virtue of my being born into the world, I have the right throughout life to demand that others provide for my needs, and that a growing list of my wants and wishes must also be included in the benefits to be provided. Promoting and manipulating phony entitlements and grievances becomes the endeavor of political activists and academics as part of their agenda to gain political power and influence.

Two documents capture our particular attention when considering the claim that equitable income distribution is one of the "basic human rights." I refer to the U.S. Bill of Rights, and France's 1789 Declaration of the Rights of Man and Citizen. Both are notable statements that have stood the test of time, representing humanity's shared ideals and aspirations. The right proclaimed by these documents to pursue happiness and strive for certain benefits for oneself and one's family without discrimination or interference from others is a very different right than being entitled to something someone else has. In other words, I have no right to take some of what you produce through your labor solely to assure my own personal satisfaction.

However, people in a free society can and do decide to collectively provide certain welfare benefits for members in need through democratic processes; our natural inclination, as individuals and communities, is to provide for others but as we the electorate choose, not as commanded by an unelected, unchallengeable authority. This natural inclination still does not make all such benefits bestowed by voters inalienable entitlements for the recipients, much less a fundamental "human right."

The amount of one's income obviously matters in terms of what one can acquire, possess, and do. However, as previously observed, poverty is not a matter of relative income, with those on the low end of a statistical distribution categorically "poor." Individuals and families, of course, are likely to change their relative income position at different stages of life. The primary question is instead: Is one's income life-sustaining and enough to provide the possibility for advancement? What constitutes the "necessities of a life with dignity" can be argued at great length. Yet having what it takes to sustain life and pursue one's further wellbeing, be it food, shelter, medicines, or educational opportunity, is an entirely different proposition than insisting that everyone deserves and should receive a certain determined amount of money and personal property.

Consider a family that has free access to K-12 education for the children, libraries and literature, playgrounds, police and fire protection, hospitals and vaccines, that has heated and often air-conditioned housing, electric lighting, potable water and indoor plumbing, that has a color TV, cell phones, oven, refrigerator, automobile, and multiple sets of clothing, and that still has enough money left over for ample food and even entertainment. Should such an individual or family be thought "poor?" If poverty were relative, this picture is one of tremendous wealth, not poverty, for more than three billion people on planet earth! In Soviet Russia during the 1920's, a family with comparable possessions would have been considered wildly rich, and like the modestly successful kulak farmers, would have been deemed class enemies. They would have had their belongings confiscated by the State, been sentenced to a Siberian work camp, or simply executed.

Thomas Paine was perhaps the first to propose a social policy to reduce the risk of poverty without destroying liberty. Recall that the Babeuf's "Conspiracy of Equals" movement during the French Revolution planned to abolish and confiscate all private property, eliminate money and commerce, distribute equal amounts of whatever is produced regardless of work, and murder any who stood in their way. Reportedly horrified by this assault on an individual's freedom to own and use property for one's own benefit—so fundamental to the functioning of any society—Paine presciently proposed a system of tax on land, not the production from it, as well as universal public education and insurance pools to protect the poor from income loss due simply to severe misfortune. This preserved one's right to own property and the fruits of one's labor even with a government's need to collect taxes. Various homestead laws later also protected land ownership even in the case of personal bankruptcy. In Rights of Man, Paine also proposed the use of tax revenue to help the poor, children, the old, sick, injured and military veterans.[10]

Ideas like Paine's have long been incorporated into democratic societies. There is recognition that the very idea of liberty in a civil society must include help for those in need supplied by those who can afford it, not only because morality demands it, but because freedom and democracy cannot long endure in a society where many who are hungry or otherwise unable to meet their needs receive no assistance and have no hope of ever becoming self-supporting. Such welfare is not optional; it is essential. Hayek also supported the need for such "social insurance" in The Road to Serfdom:

There is no reason why (in a wealthy society)...security ("the certainty of a given minimum of subsistence") should not be guaranteed to all without endangering general freedom. . . . (Also,) the case for the state's helping to organize a comprehensive system of social insurance is very strong . . . There is no incompatibility in principle between the state's providing greater security in this way and the preservation of individual freedom.[11]

On the other hand, seeking to eliminate material inequality instead of ameliorating poverty is destructive of the motivation to produce, and thus leads to economic decay. We might call it a "butcher's economy," after Victor Hugo's *Les Miserables*. published in 1862:

> By good distribution, we must understand not equal distribution, but equitable distribution. The highest equality is equity."
> [The word "equity" means fairness, justice, and impartiality.]
> "Communism and agrarian law think they have solved the second problem [distribution]. They are mistaken. Their distribution kills production. Equal division abolishes emulation. And consequently labor. It is a distribution made by the butcher, who kills what he divides. It is therefore impossible to stop at these professed solutions. To kill wealth is not to distribute it.[12]

Hugo was right. Economic leveling, which is a central tenet of socialism, can never vitalize and raise a society, only drag it downward by grinding human individuality into a foul sausage. The disastrous results of attempting to apply dysfunctional socialist theory to the real world have been amply documented and the reasons for its failure explained at great length. There is no need to rehash the reasons here. It is perhaps enough to paraphrase Michael Novak, that by forcing an equal distribution of wealth, socialism's "quest for security and equality" succeeds only in "creating a zero-sum society foredoomed to failure."[13]

Ibn Khaldun, considered by some the father of Sociology, lived in the 1300's, and he wrote of sociology and economics, long before either field of study had been defined. But Khaldun's insightful warning about the destructive consequences of misdirected social policy are clear. In his undisputed masterpiece *The Maqaddimah*, Khaldun made the following observations in the form of empirically-derived axioms:

> It should be known that attacks on people's property remove the incentive to acquire and gain property. People, then, become of the opinion that the purpose and ultimate destiny of (acquiring property) is to have it taken away from them. When the incentive to acquire and obtain property is gone, people no longer make efforts to acquire any. The extent and degree to which property rights are infringed upon determines the extent and degree to which the efforts of the subjects to acquire property slacken. When attacks (on property) are extensive and general, extending to all means of making a livelihood, business inactivity, too, becomes (general), because the general extent of (such attacks upon property) means a general destruction of the incentive (to do business). If the attacks upon property are but light, the stoppage of gainful activity is correspondingly slight. Civilization and its well-being as well as business prosperity depend on productivity and people's efforts in all directions in their own interest and profit. When people no longer do business in order to make a living, and when they cease all gainful activity, the business of civilization slumps, and everything decays. People scatter everywhere in search of sustenance, to places outside the jurisdiction of their present government. The population of the particular region becomes light. The settlements there become empty. The cities lie in ruins. [14]

It is Both Just and Fair to be Rewarded That Which is Deserved

To "deserve" is to do something or show qualities worthy of reward or punishment. Its synonyms are "merit," "warrant," or "justify." As with justice and fairness, human nature includes the instinctive concept of "just deserts," perhaps linked to our built-in drive to survive, inasmuch as for many millennia humans often fought over food sources, living space, mates and anything else advantageous, only gradually internalizing norms that facilitated the coexistence and cooperation needed for our species' success. And like justice and fairness, our understanding and appreciation of just deserts begins early and is sharpened by daily life. At a young age we are taught rudimentary lessons in constructive behaviors and the just deserts that accompany them from interactions with our parents and other family members. Little Johnny may complain: "It's not fair! My brother got more than I did!" Children typically expect equal treatment from their parents, but when we grow into adulthood, we come to realize that parents can have very good reasons for not always giving the same things and identical quantities to each child, though they are each being treated non-preferentially. This is where "just deserts" begins to enter the equation. For example, when a son is behaving in a lazy and defiant manner and fails to do his chores while his older sister completes hers, fairness demands that each sibling receive unequal rather than equal rewards from the parents. They both receive their just deserts.

Such lessons permeate our social fabric. They are taught in schools, athletic endeavors, workplaces, and in commerce. Certain students, athletes, and workers deserve greater rewards based on their relative efforts, achievements, and the value of what they provide to society. In the world of adults, we daily observe there are those willing to expend greater effort to improve themselves and who work much harder than others, while a few deserve only to be called lazy. Some individuals are naturally more talented, creative, or intelligent than others, more or less inclined to develop useful skills, and more or less willing to save and thereby accumulate wealth by deferring immediate gratification, as well as to take risks investing some of what they have saved. Sadly, there also are always some in society who choose to be indolent, reckless, irresponsible, and self-destructive, some who waste their talents and ignore opportunities for self-development, and still others who engage in criminal activity. In short, merit/demerit continua are recognized in all facets of society as a basis for reward or punishment. The reason for this is that guaranteeing an equal outcome for all "would run counter to both nature and justice."[15]

To illustrate this point, consider a 2x2 "Matrix of Justice" with Fairness and Unfairness on one axis, Equal Distribution of Rewards and Sanctions and Unequal Distribution on the other. Such a matrix would have four possible outcomes. Socialism's message focuses exclusively on two outcome quadrants: the Fair and Equal Distribution quadrant, and the Unfair, Unequal Distribution quadrant. Blinded by their dogma, socialists pretend that two other possible outcomes do not exist; namely, the Fair and Unequal Distribution outcome; i.e. one based on merit, and the Equal but Unfair outcome, which results from equal distribution irrespective of merit. It is this last outcome that is both most unjust and most likely under socialism. Indeed, socialism is determined to create justice for some through injustice to others, again the morally contradictory concept that lies at the core of its otherwise seductive message. Hayek explains this as one of the fundamental contradictions of socialism. Starting with differences among people, achieving its brand of equality requires that people be treated unequally, rather than equally.[16]

Treatment of people that is fair, equitable, and just should not be conflated with people being rewarded the same, whether in the form of test grades, promotions, pay, favors granted, playing time on a sports team, and so on. "Just deserts" means rewards based on achievements and outcomes to ensure that people are treated justly, receive honest feedback from the society in which they live, and are thereby motivated to improve as individuals, as a social unit, or as an organization. Collective institutions of society are almost always improved through the

work of individuals who are motivated to innovate and produce, redounding to everyone's mutual benefit.

Motivation is the reason we do what we do; it is what ac-
tivates, energizes and directs human behavior.[17] There are two
sides to it, both of which socialism destroys: on one side is the
hope of gain and fulfillment of desires, and on the other the
fear of loss or suffering. Socialism annuls both by depriving the
most productive individuals of the full measure of their just
deserts in order to achieve its version of "equality," while holding out the impossible promise of government fulfilling everyone's needs and desires, including of those who put forth little
effort and act irresponsibly, with no fear of loss or suffering.
Without the individual ambition that results from the incentive of gain or conversely suffering adverse consequences from
one's irresponsible actions, production is minimal and all facets
of society stagnate and decline.

No Two People are Exactly Alike, Attributes Naturally Vary Among Individuals

In the 1991 film *Enemy at the Gates*, a Soviet political commissar is in love with a woman who spurns his advances in favor of a war hero. Before sacrificing himself to a sniper's bullet
the commissar admits:

> We tried so hard to create a society that was equal, where there
> would be nothing about your neighbor to envy, but there is al-
> ways something to envy. The smile, the friendship, something
> you don't have and want to appropriate. In this world, even the
> soviet, there will always be rich and poor. Rich in gifts, poor in
> gifts, rich in love, poor in love." [18]

Self-evident from observation and now known from the
science of genetics, there is infinite variation among individual
humans. We know that each person is bequeathed genes from
ancestors that make each person biologically unique. The natural diversity resulting from this unique heredity and singular

life experiences that makes our world such a wonderfully rich place. At the same time, we also are unequal across every measure used to compare human capabilities. We are all genetically different from birth, except for those who are identical twins.

The real equality among human beings has not to do with our individual biological makeup. The only true equality is "political equality," a revolutionary ideal established by man with religious inspiration. This phrase gives a subtle but crucial nuance to equality. Political equality is not equality in any physically measurable sense. Rather, it is the idea of equal justice and equal liberty based on moral equality. That is, all souls, created equal, are judged in the same way. Every human life has the same intrinsic value.

Over centuries this abstract but revolutionary idea of moral equality became a fundamental precept of classical liberalism, incorporated in governmental and legal systems in the Western World. The same rules and laws are to be applied to all individuals equally, without discrimination; all persons possess and exercise equal rights, and therefore authority in society must flow upward from consenting, morally equal individuals rather than downward from a "superior." This profoundly important concept of political equality, in turn, is the basis for equal citizenship guaranteed to each member of a constitutional society governed by the rule of law.

Contrary to what some might assume, the idea of the political equality of individuals embodied in Western laws and institutions does not conflict with the reality of innate human differences, nor the differences that arise from humans' natural striving for their own betterment. Far from it, true political equality, with the equal human rights and freedom it engenders, enables individuals to develop and creatively use the different, unequal talents they are naturally endowed with to contribute much more to society than would be the case in an authoritarian society that attempts to force the equalization of material conditions.

Let's take the argument about human inequality a step further. It is readily observable that each human being is endowed with traits which impart different, unequal amounts of aptitudes, physical abilities, health, beauty, and natural talents across a wide continuum. In addition, each person has life experiences that shape them physically, mentally, and emotionally, yielding widely differing attitudes and abilities. Such innumerable biological and experiential differences can be advantageous or disadvantageous in different places, times, and societal contexts. In that respect then, complete natural equality of individuals never exists. Moreover, such natural inequality among individual human beings can never be eliminated, only politically suppressed by those also seeking to destroy liberty. On the other hand, the equality enjoyed by citizens in democracies is a political and legal construct that stems from cultural values refined over centuries which promote the justice and fairness necessary for social peace and stability.

An important caution: real differences among individuals' abilities should not be confused with the debunked assertion of "natural inequality" of intellectual capability among different races or ethnic groups, with one or another being inferior or superior. The natural inequality of individuals is just that; it is not determined by their race or ethnicity. Nor should the fact of real and natural differences between individuals be extended to justify a distinction between those comprising a "ruling class" and all others: patricians versus plebeians, aristocrats versus feudal serfs, Party members and non-members, and so on. We rightly reject any differentiation based on "birthright," heritage, or exercise of force. It is likely that in many cases the ruling class "nobility" are merely descendants of leaders of the bands of "stationary bandits"[19] who, like the bad King John and the Sheriff of Nottingham of Robinhood

294 <img

legend, repeatedly rob those they rule to support their lavish and privileged lifestyle.

In the end, human beings are endlessly differentiated in every trait and aspect of human life, and the broad natural variation of individual persons spans across the spectrum of mental and physical abilities. Where freedom exists, markets and other capitalist undertakings make a virtue of human variety to maximize the totality of benefits produced. This natural differentiation is harnessed through the division of labor, specialization, and trade for more efficient production and greater abundance. Because the spontaneous, voluntary division of labor and trade in open markets multiplies production to the benefit of all, it is the natural manner of cooperation amongst peoples.

Socialism, on the other hand, endeavors to supplant these voluntary mechanisms with authoritarian command, producing pathetic economic results along with the loss of freedom. Self-determined occupations and the natural division of labor based on talents, skills, and interests are not "problems" that invite social engineering to correct. They are worthy things recognized as such from ancient to modern times. Consider the arguments of the French sociologist Emile Durkheim in his 1933 classic *The Division of Labor in Society,* or Adam Smith's *Wealth of Nations,* and David Hume's *Treatise of Human Nature.* The division of labor is so fundamental that Smith devoted the entire first three chapters in Wealth of Nations to explaining the origins of labor specialization and its significance in society. Regarding humans' natural acquisitiveness, in the chapter "Accumulation of Capital" he went on to observe:

> The principle which prompts us to save is the desire of bettering our condition, a desire which, though generally calm and dispassionate, comes with us from the womb, and never leaves us till we go into the grave...[20]

According to Brown's *Human Universals,* some degree of division of labor, inequality, and envy are found in every human society, even those very primitive and isolated, and thus must reflect traits inherent in human nature.[21] It has been obvious for almost all of recorded history that spontaneous human specialization and its corollary, division of labor, are key to effective human cooperation, dramatically multiplying the invention and production of what economists appropriately call "goods."[22] With its infinite web of interrelationships and interactions, such cooperation is essential to the development of human societies if not their very survival.

It is not only every individual's natural inclinations and abilities, but also the acquisition and honing of specialized skills that advances expertise and state-of-the-art practices in all endeavors, and consequently enables greater productivity and innovation. Yet because such differences undercut their scheme for justifying social leveling, Socialists treat division of labor and the different values placed on unequal levels of professional attainment as an unnecessary manipulation of the economy by the capitalist Bourgeoisie.

Rather than being a friend to the working class, socialists actually view people who seek to be rewarded for improving themselves in any occupation with mistrust, and workers as mere interchangeable cogs in a machine. On the other hand, their leaders who are miraculously endowed with an infallible utopian formula for transforming society are exceptions deserving the special privileges they are able to obtain for themselves using their governmental position.

Because every person is naturally distinct in his or her abilities and such specialization is required in all social systems, no amount of governmental coercion, regardless of how ruthless and oppressive, can ever fully negate the uniqueness of human beings and the singular roles they play. Unless they are enslaved or otherwise deprived of freedom humans instinctively pursue enterprises and positions within social organizations that match their skills and interests and provide them maximum benefit. Organizations in all walks of life also naturally provide greater incentives for individuals who possess unique and scarce talents and lesser incentives for those with skills more broadly available and easy to master.

Along with natural and experiential influences, we each possess a free will and will persistently exercise it unless intimidated and brow-beaten into submission or otherwise coerced. The free choices we make likewise differentiate one person from another and condition our personal successes and rewards.

"Just deserts" cannot be totally separated from freedom and still be just. Most human beings instinctively desire freedom from control of their lives by others, though some may willingly submit to being continually told what to do rather than struggle against various forms of authority. According to the Western view of universal human rights, we own our life as individuals, and each human life has value and should be treated with dignity. Our life is not the property of anyone else, and through our actions and behaviors even in collective endeavors we continually differentiate ourselves individually for better or worse. We give shape to our own individual development and future by the innumerable choices we make throughout our lives, including those which elicit differential rewards or punishments. An individual's choices may be constructive, or they may manifest numerous vices, destructive tendencies, dishonesty and other gross character weaknesses. In either case, we are not bound by any pseudo-scientific and related socialist determinism. We have a rightful say in our own individual destinies.

Sadly, certain people take a darker view. Arendt points out in *Origins of Totalitarianism* that despite obvious natural differences among human beings, where there is political equality, the social and economic differences among outcomes become more visible. For some this becomes a source of intense resentment. This is a very dangerous perversion of equality from a fundamentally political concept turned social, which because of the many actual differences among people, is never workable.[23]

Free will is not the only basic human trait; pride and envy also enter the equation. In democracies, resentment can lead Leftist sympathizers to assert a dangerous non-sequitur that political equality must be accompanied by complete economic equality, that social differences are abnormal and intolerable, and that it is the duty of government to provide a cure using any means whatsoever.

The Less Fortunate

One often hears that life is not fair, and indeed, to those without some sort of moral compass, it can easily resemble a giant wheel of fortune. Of course, the world itself is not fair because nature does not make choices. Nature does not involve a conscious human choice between outcomes. Accidents occur; we call it misfortune. Some men and women are born with mental or physical disabilities while others are free from them. Bad things happen to good people, and good things happen to bad people. It is human nature and a sign of civilization to want to help people who are unable to help themselves, particularly children and those who are old, sick, or injured.[24] Sympathy and compassion often lead to a degree of self-sacrifice on our part, contrary to the impulse to apply our resources entirely for our own benefit.

Research now suggests that concern for others, especially those we encounter within our own social circle is actually "wired" into our makeup. For example, most parents teach their children to share with others, and to think of their well-being. Some would call this natural sense of sympathy, concern, and compassion a social conscience, not to be confused with the vague but nice-sounding phrase "social justice." Sharing with and caring for those who are in need has been a central tenet of many religious traditions throughout history. Archaeologists have discovered an ancient Egyptian ethical code that instructed the people to share their bread to feed the hungry, to clothe the naked, and to not mock those who are malformed.[25] Such ancient ethical precepts or innate social conscience seem to reflect the fundamental human attribute of caring about the fate of our fellow human beings. Moreover, a "reciprocity norm" exists in all societies.[26] Because of the myriad interdependencies in human life, it may be part of our survival instinct for persons to care about and bestow favors on others, knowing that we ourselves may at some point in time depend on the corresponding good will of those we have helped. Caring for the collective "us" includes organizing the means to provide for the basic needs of the hungry and the infirm, and all those who are unable to care for themselves because of illness or disability, particularly those bereft of family support. It is instinctively human to think: "That could be me…"

In the U.S. the dominant cause for an individual's inability to reach higher levels of prosperity, locked into a cycle of multigenerational crime and poverty, is not an uncaring society but personal and parental behaviors.[27] Destructive personal behaviors and their outcomes arise from individuals' bad choices. However, we know that the choices a person makes especially early in life are heavily influenced by their parents and other authority figures, as well as their peer group, and other behavioral models, good and bad. Examples of parental behaviors that can have grave consequences for their children include the well-known litany of pathologies: physical abuse and negligence, failure to teach their children the norms of acceptable social behavior, a fatherless family unit in which the mother is left alone to support her children, mothers raising out-of-wedlock children by multiple fathers, addiction to alcohol or drugs, untreated mental illness, engaging in deviant or criminal activity, exposing children to violence, failure to see that children obtain even a basic education that enables a person to function in society, simply deciding to work less or not at all even when jobs are available, and to have more than two children if the family is impoverished. Physical deprivation, such as failure to provide adequate food, clothing, and shelter, can negate what might otherwise be healthy parenting, but in Western societies has been largely, but not entirely ameliorated by governmental and charitable welfare safety-nets, including schools providing free meals to children. It is well established that early childhood development deficits are a major factor in lowering lifetime human potential, and that impoverished households are more likely to raise children with such deficits. Therefore, addressing their poverty and the proximate causes of these deficits must be an important public policy goal.

It should come as no surprise to even the casual observer that much of the economic "inequality gap" is caused by pathologies in the family and immediate community, more so than by the influence of broader society and "the system." Also, far too little attention has been given to the potential adverse effect of welfare programs on parental incentives which influence individual behaviors, and that of cultural norms at the family and community level. Instead, politicians focused on income inequality have too often blithely continued to promote governmental policies that fail to realistically account for human nature and are repeatedly proven to cause more harm than good for those who are at the social and economic bottom. Simply providing ever greater amounts of money from the government's treasury to people in certain low-income categories may provide virtue-signaling cover for politicians, but unless used by the recipients to gain valuable skills or for better childrearing, fails to improve the prospects of its recipients and their dependents, including of course those who are idlers or engage in anti-social behaviors. Instead, we know from long experience of experimenting with transfer payments of many kinds that for some people, "income inequality" is more of a consequence than a cause of their irresponsible decisions and destructive behaviors, even though they may be statistically associated; lower income is rarely proven to be an actual cause of social pathologies, even though such behaviors may be more prevalent in lower income groups. In fact, though it cannot be proven one way or the other, it seems more likely that the reverse is true. We know that destructive behaviors cause individuals and their children to quickly drop in economic and social status and hinder their climb back up. As few are immune to the effects of their behaviors, this is almost a tautology. Moreover, some of those at the highest income levels at times exhibit the same social pathologies as those at the lower end of the spectrum. In each group thankfully they represent just a small percentage. We often see that wealth does not fully immunize those who possess it from the crash and burn consequences of a pattern of bad life choices, though it may cushion their fall for a time. Although unearned money bestowed by government can help low-income people in some ways, more cash by itself is neither a preventive nor a cure for social ills.

Even if it does not help, one would hope that the government's actions would not be destructive. Nevertheless, a half century of so-called "Urban Renewal" and "Great Society" programs, and the exponential growth of new regulations in the United States, while certainly well-intended, have often contributed to greater dependency, hardships, and despondency. Examples of government programs with unintended consequences at a community level include: so-called "slum clearance" which destroyed minority communities, displacing the poor from their homes, churches, and businesses; restrictive zoning and rent control which discourage investment and greatly increase the cost of urban housing; people trapped in notorious crime-plagued, decaying public housing "projects;" law enforcement policies that fail to suppress criminal activities affecting the safety of inner city residents, their property, school children and small business viability; and social welfare policies that undermine the family unit by making fathers who earn low wages superfluous as providers. Add to this list nice sounding but counterproductive "minimum wage" laws, which may benefit some, but actually destroy job opportunities for those in the labor market most in need of entry-level employment from which they can start to climb the ladder to greater prosperity over time. While there are some instances of success, despite the expenditure of many trillions of dollars, there can be little doubt that more than fifty years of Great Society welfare in the U.S. did not achieve its goal of eliminating poverty, and some of its programs arguably have contributed to worsening social problems such as low labor force participation and nuclear family disintegration in the communities the initiative was designed to help. This has resulted in an enormous ongoing loss of human capital affecting all of society, not just those being "helped!"

Throughout history, laziness has been rewarded with hunger. But not all hunger is the result of apathy or irresponsibility. When a person is in a true state of need, even if the need is self-inflicted, it is both a moral and social imperative for others who make up a society to collectively help those not in a position to help themselves. In so doing, however, it must also be recognized that even when poverty and basic needs have been addressed, the "destructive social passion of envy" may remain for some. Such resentment can and will be exploited by socialist propagandists. Their claim is always that those less fortunate were locked into a world of inescapable misery as a result of being victimized and oppressed by those more fortunate, the very people providing them physical aid and financial assistance.

302 Some Call it Utopia

Competition, Cooperation and Compassion is the Natural State of Human Affairs

The competition among individuals and groups which stimulates human's desire for betterment is a part of the social dynamic in all societies, even those that espouse socialism. Humans evolved as acquisitive creatures. Competition for resources, territory, status, and mates is a universal trait; it is a part of our evolved nature, not simply a learned behavior. Parental attention, potential mates, fame, political power, prestige, and social status are all areas where humans compete individually and in groups, motivated by the hope of exceling to advantage themselves and their progeny. Economic competition among human beings is as natural and unavoidable as any other form, not somehow an artificial social construct imposed by certain greedy people. It is however true that some compete by fully using and building upon their natural abilities, according to rules established by society, whereas there are those who compete by undercutting others in hidden or overt ways, such as cheating and violence. Thus, humanity invented laws. Despite being a committed socialist, H.G. Wells made this observation about competition in society:

> There must be competition in life of some sort to determine who are to be pushed to the edge, and who are to prevail... Whatever we do, man will remain a competitive creature, and though moral and intellectual training may vary and enlarge his conception of success...no Utopia will ever save him completely from the emotional drama of struggle for exultations and humiliations, from pride and prostration and shame. He lives in success and failure, just as inevitably as he lives in space and time.[28]

But while competition naturally occurs, so does cooperation in many forms, sometimes motivated by the prospect of mutual benefit but often out of a sense of shared humanity. Humans successfully evolved as social not solitary animals, and we rely on complex webs of collaborative interdependencies to supply food and other necessities. From time immemorial, trade with resultant markets enabling mutually beneficial exchanges, also known as "commerce," has been the natural, spontaneous means of economic cooperation amongst human beings. Collaboration also occurs within organizations of all types, but is fundamental to productive enterprises from the largest to the smallest in free market economies. I speak here of the cooperation that is voluntary in free societies. Such cooperation is vital to producing the goods necessary for human survival in ways that are efficient, fair and just, and not dependent on the threat of force.

Markets provide continuous feedback from the mass of consumers concerning what others in our society want, value, appreciate, and need. They signal the amount, where, and when, essential information that guides continuous adjustments in the production and distribution of goods. This is essential to successful human cooperation, exchange, and collective undertakings. Markets also provide two other vital functions: they stimulate innovation, leading to new and improved products and services, and help prioritize investment to meet society's wants and needs.

We produce what others want and need in exchange for what we ourselves require, resulting in mutually beneficial outcomes. These exchanges include creation and transmission of new knowledge as well as tangible goods. Archaeological evidence proves that trade among geographically disparate peoples possessing different resources and talents has been a feature of human societies from prehistoric times. For example, from the dawn of recorded history there was a vigorous long-distance commerce in grain and metals between Mesopotamia and southern Arabia. Going back even further, archaeologists have found evidence of prehistoric conveyance over long distances of strategic materials such as obsidian and stone tools, some even dating transport and exchange of goods to around 100,000 years ago.[29]

On the other hand, rather than produce goods themselves and engage in trade, bandits have found ways throughout recorded history to take by outright force or by surreptitiously stealing from others. Whether these bandits ride horses or issue dictates while seated in positions of government authority, they are parasitic bandits who take from society without contributing toward their own needs or the collective needs of their fellow citizens.

This does not imply that markets or Adam Smith's "Invisible Hand" alone are the complete answer to every human need, nor that unlimited individualism lying at one end of the continuum is any more a viable societal model than the socialist model lying at the other end. On the contrary, mankind has learned the hard way over millennia that along with individual rights and the liberty to own and use property or participate in the market economy must come a system of laws. The Durants noted: that "Individual freedom contains its own nemesis; it tends to increase until it overruns the restraints necessary for social order and group survival; freedom unlimited is chaos complete."[30] Laws that set rules equally applicable to all are necessary to ensure order and justice and foster productive voluntary cooperation. The alternative to a common set of rules and properly constituted governmental authority to ensure they are followed is predation by the powerful and violent or the chaos of mob rule. Recent episodes of prolonged rioting in certain U.S. cities vividly illustrate the social imperative of maintaining civil order and protecting private and public properties and the institutions they house against destruction or intimidation by mobs comprised of anarchists, looters, and violent criminals who are not simply peaceful protestors. Societal cooperation, compassion, and justice are immediate casualties of mob rule and intimidation; indeed, real liberty cannot exist without the rule of law.

I am referring, of course, to laws democratically enacted by the people and the application thereof that treats people equally. That is the great caveat. Civil authorities exist to enforce laws in a color-blind manner without bias by strictly adhering to the traditional egalitarian principle of equal treatment of all individuals; that is the genuine social justice humans universally crave. Government treating people differently can only result in mistrust of authority and corrosive resentment of those wielding power by those treated unjustly. Rather than being champions of equal treatment, because they are motivated by their desire to create substantive equality socialists always demand and try to contrive laws that advantage particular social groups and disadvantage others. For socialists the primary purpose of government is to seek and enforce such group advantage so they can even the score as they see it. They endeavor to secure the political power needed to determine who will get how much of whatever is produced by the economy, in order to counter the naturally uneven distributional effect of individuals' actions in the competitive marketplace which they consider illegitimate.

To live in true freedom, humans require laws that permit successful cooperation to occur and that deter predation and prevent intimidation. Laws are necessary to assure fair competition and place boundaries on what individuals may do to satisfy their own wants in situations where their actions would otherwise endanger or harm others, including sociopathic behaviors where the strong prey upon the weak. The problem with the politics of extreme individual libertarianism lies in the blindness of its enthusiasts to the reality that a prosperous society, in Reinhold Niebuhr's words "requires community as much as liberty."[31] Moreover, while we naturally live for our individual selves, seeking to satisfy our own personal interests, we are also naturally social beings who seek to harmonize our actions with those of others for mutual benefit and sometimes even act out of selflessness. A system of laws that apply equally to all helps maintain the balance between both spheres, individual and social, that engenders genuine cooperation without infringing on the rights of any individual. According to Lord Acton, the object of a constitution is "not to confirm the predominance of any interest, but to prevent it, to preserve with equal care the independence of labour and security of property; to make the rich safe against envy, and the poor safe against oppression."[32] Such a system is necessary to set the stage for what one might call "responsible freedom." Again, in order to be just, laws must be legitimately enacted by true representatives of the people, not imposed by a supreme human authority.

Speaking of unconstrained individualism, one might argue that by rejecting all forms of law and lawful authority, anarchists themselves become utopians of a sort, even if they lack the usual manifesto containing the recipe for a perfect world. Indeed, both socialism and anarchism share the extreme conviction that present society and its incumbent structure of rules should be utterly destroyed – burned to the ground, so that mankind's intrinsic goodness will miraculously bring about a crime-free, shining new world of perpetual harmony.

Along with natural compassion for the less fortunate, cooperation in free societies also typically entails collective action to provide certain cost-shared services recognized as essential to public health, safety and welfare. One might ask where the circle is to be drawn that encompasses the legitimate domain of governmental and collective social involvement. To begin with, government representing the people collectively must supply those services which a free competitive market cannot. Such services include military protection from external threats, programs to help the poor, aged, and unemployed, public safety and internal security, operation of courts, administrative and legislative functions, tax collection, money supply, utilities, dams, canals, and aqueducts, public schools, roadways and other transportation systems, and environmental protection. Nor is strong temporary intervention by the central government into areas outside its normal domain in the case of crises (e.g., wartime defense manufacturing, depression, pandemic) a form of socialism. Given civic evolution and development, this circle cannot remain etched in stone.

For example, as the historian Samuel Huntington notes in Political Order in Changing Societies, in certain rural settings protecting existing communal ownership and use of productive land and water resources instead of breaking them up into individual private holdings may be preferable from a socioeconomic perspective.[33] However, pooling resources contractually or through democratic processes to supply protection and essential common services is fundamentally different from the involuntary collectivization of individually-owned farms that was demanded by socialism's theoreticians and enforced by its henchmen, leading to disastrous famines.

With surrendering ever greater power to the State being the solution to all societal ills, socialists either want to ignore, trivialize or completely do away with the significant role of voluntary Christian and other faith-based charities. Together these represent a clear example of an alternate pathway people have used for centuries to exercise their natural proclivity for compassion – a pathway lying far outside the domain of coerced governmental wealth redistribution. There are numerous other voluntary organizations and cooperative initiatives that stand to serve the needy a free society, including even programs funded by private endowments and corporations, if they are allowed opportunity and aren't squashed by an authoritarian socialist agenda.

Socialism's Very Essence Conflicts with Religious Beliefs and Human Spirituality

Historians, archaeologists, and anthropologists have documented at great length that in nearly every part of the globe, transcendent theistic spirituality in one form or another has always been a prominent and potent feature of human existence. Moreover, belief in the supernatural is one of the "universals" of our inherited human nature cutting across all cultures.[34] As I pointed out earlier, humanity's innate craving for meaning in life has at times perversely given rise to temporal Theocratic Utopian movements. Nevertheless, a most basic flaw of the socialist creed lies at the other extreme; namely, its endeavor to supplant the spiritual side of our nature by elevating humans to god-like status.

Certain ancient pharaohs and emperors indeed tried to assume god-like status, but of course, in the end, they too died. Socialists attempt thereby to create a spiritual void to be filled by socialist indoctrination, as though the human soul and mind are merely blank sheets of paper having no innate nature. As previously noted, making morality whatever one wants it to be in any situation destroys the cultural and institutional strictures on human behavior, making it easier for regimes to find and use people to commit demonic atrocities. Matthew 16:26 warns: "What good will it be for a man if he gains the whole world but forfeits his soul?" But if man has no soul, why worry about morality?

Attempts at elevating man to supreme status while at the same time suppressing religion may create a spiritual wasteland for a time, but history shows such attempts are doomed to fail. After the fall of the Soviet Union, churches quickly reopened throughout Russia and Eastern Europe and were one of the first signs of the freedom regained by a long-suppressed people. Still today, people tenaciously hold fast to their religious traditions in the face of intimidation and outright persecution in remaining communist countries of Asia. They willingly put themselves at considerable risk while practicing their faith in secret. It is simply impossible for socialism to slake the human thirst for spirituality and replace religion with personality cults and conformity to an atheistic, immoral doctrine.

Moreover, a complete spiritual vacuum in the human soul can never truly exist.

Some Socialists who identify themselves as Christians would like to believe the two religions they purport to espouse can coexist. Nothing could be further from the truth. Make no mistake about it, Marx sought not to understand and coexist with theistic religion, but to destroy it by revolution.[35] It is clear from his writings that he saw the forceful elimination of religion (he described religion as nothing but "superstition") from society as a necessary step in changing the world to accord with his "scientific" utopian theory. Statements and protestations to the contrary, true Socialists do not really believe in a supreme being or in absolute moral laws and teachings under which every individual will be held accountable for their behavior toward others, even those laws and teachings that arose from timeless truths about how to maintain fruitful mutual relationships. In the socialist concept, human beings are simply another manipulatable part of nature, not a separate and special creation of God possessing immortal souls.

Hitleresque statements about the divine may be made for political convenience, but the belief system of the utopian socialist places man at the center of an anti-theistic universe; since in the world of socialism humans have no eternal soul, the notion of "sin" and its eternal consequences is meaningless. The lives of human beings are not intrinsically important, and human life can be extinguished for the State's convenience. Depravities become simply a sociological matter rather than a fundamental evil that infects our subconscious and produces many repulsive actions. From this view also comes the belief that superior intellects have the natural right to rule over others. Alas, without the benefit of religion and its moral absolutes, those who in the abstract most righteously claim to care for others are the very ones to instigate the greatest cruelties once in control.

It is therefore important to understand that socialism is not simply a matter of political preference. Nor is it just an issue of competing economic systems outside of the political and religious realms. It is an exclusive, all-encompassing belief system with an insatiable appetite for power. The secular, godless religion of socialism seeks to supplant Christianity and all other religions with a man-centered cosmology and an arrogant vision of a utopian secular world brought into being by human will and imposed by force when necessary. Ironically, socialism, while it pretends to be "scientific," is analogous to the medieval doctrine of an Earth-centered celestial universe debunked by Galileo; only in this case, the "infallible" authority of the socialist State replaces that of the medieval Church in proclaiming man to be at the center of the cosmos. As stated by the admittedly irreligious philosopher John Gray, "For the utopian mind the defects of every known society are not signs of flaws in human nature. They are marks of universal repression – which, however, will soon be ended. History is a nightmare from which we must awake, and when we do we will find that human possibilities are endless."[36]

Judeo-Christian Ethical Tradition vs. Socialism

Those of Judeo-Christian heritage are generally pessimistic about prospects for a utopian, human-created heaven on earth. The failure of early Christian attempts to "have everything in common" (Acts 2:44), the many wars pitting Christian against Christian, mass slaughters during the Crusades, horrors of the Spanish Inquisition, and other sad facts of Church history have led most Christians and Jews today to a greater appreciation of the harsh truths contained in Biblical writings:

> Mankind is born headed for trouble, just as sparks soar skyward. Job 5:7

> For there is not a single righteous man on earth who practices good and does not sin. Ecclesiastes 7:20

"For the poor you will always have with you." John 12:8

Recognizing such truths, Judeo-Christian teachings none-theless continue to press for peace, justice, and more generally, to make things better for all peoples and societies in the world – but without socialist illusions of creating an earthly utopian paradise. These teachings are put into practice in a great many ways. Witness, for example, the extent of Christian health, edu-cational, and emergency response activities sponsored by agen-cies like Catholic Charities, Lutheran World Relief, and a host of other Christian faith-based organizations.

There are stark differences in the underpinnings of Chris-tian and socialist doctrine and in their respective belief systems. In the Judeo-Christian ethical tradition all people are created equal in the eyes of God. Each must be judged according to one's own individual choices and actions rather than the ac-tions of any group or group identity, be it ethnicity, heredity, or social class. Inspired by Judeo-Christian ethics and the legacy of the Anglo-Lockean legal tradition, American laws are intended to guarantee each citizen equal rights and equal treatment by government, as well as other now universally recognized rights.

Furthermore, inherent in Judeo-Christian commandments is the belief that no person or persons are entitled to confis-cate the fruits of another's work in whole or in part, and that every human being has a natural right to defend life, liberty, and property against all such threats. This too is underscored in the Biblical injunction against envy; the commandment "do not covet your neighbor's house or any of his other posses-sions" forbids believers from even desiring the property of oth-ers, much less wanting to deprive them of their property out of envious spite.[37] Envy is a ubiquitous and socially destructive impulse that is restrained by our reason and morality, while so-cialism ostensibly claims that in the end envy will disappear, in contradiction it legitimizes envy by treating it as an acceptable motivation for "correcting" the supposed injustice of differing material conditions among people. In so doing, socialism is tapping into one of Mankind's most primitive and harmful instincts.

Whereas covetousness is considered a vice, compassion for others is a virtue. Biblical doctrine says, "Whatsoever you would have others do for you, do you even so for them" or, "Do unto others as you would have them do unto you." A society pooling resources through democratically self-imposed taxes to assure collective needs are met is something people of faith everywhere can agree upon. However, as I have noted before, meeting collective needs, including caring for those in poverty or unable to care for themselves, is entirely different than the socialist commandment compelling wealth to be redistributed.

From its earliest manifestations, in both its theoretical development and practice, socialism has been anti-religious and rejected any notion of peaceful coexistence with religion. Warring against belief in God is considered one of the ideological hallmarks of socialism. Disciples of this secular religion engage in relentless attacks on religious institutions. Two centuries ago, the Jacobins of the French Revolution conducted a murderous campaign against clerics and the Catholic Church. Similar atrocities were carried out against the Church during the Spanish Civil War. Bolsheviks in Russia, and other communist organizations actively repressed religion for being a source of spiritual freedom, thinking, and moral authority contrary to their ideology.

Lenin's Bolsheviks murdered hundreds if not thousands of Orthodox priests. Brutal persecution of religion is still being carried out by the Chinese Communist Party against the Falun Gong, Uighur Muslims, and Chinese Christians, after having persecuted Buddhists starting in the 1950's. Religion, even where tolerated for a time, is viewed as a part of a conservative social structure whose compassionate aims are to be cunningly manipulated by the Party to help achieve socialist goals. After its usefulness has been exhausted, any religion remaining among the people can then be rooted out. In the opinion of communism's would-be messiah, Karl Marx, "religion is the opiate of the people," and "there can be nothing more abominable than religion."[38]

The Soviet socialist dictatorship created generations of children who were taught that Marx, Lenin, Stalin, and Mao were the anointed prophets of a new "modern" religion, the source of all truth and meaning in life. However, instead of this new religion fulfilling the need shared by all humans for spirituality, it created a spiritual nullity which led those under its spell to engage in vast, pitiless, and absolute evil. For example, the new religion asserted that all human history is determined by inescapable hate-filled class struggle, and any actions taken by the proletariat against property-owning capitalists are unbounded by morality.

All manner of horrific crimes against humanity have consequently been carried out in the name of establishing social equality, whereas Christians believe God created every human being to be free and to exercise free choice, accept moral responsibility for those choices, and to use the natural abilities he or she is endowed with for humanity's good. It also recognizes that everyone is capable of evil as well as good. In addition to fostering base impulses like envy, socialism dangerously embraces the notion of collective versus individual guilt, and consequently uses hate to incite violence against persons because of their group identity, including members of religious faiths. True Christians believe that all are children of God and equal in His eyes, whether rich or poor, servant or master, and regardless of race or ethnicity. That is the belief in moral equality I described earlier in this work. For these and other reasons, totalitarian states are antithetical to true Christian beliefs and teachings.

To gain moral high ground in the West, some on the Left compare use of governmental power to reduce "income inequality" with Biblical references to sharing wealth. It is true that in both Old and New Testaments one can find exhortations concerning sharing one's possessions with the needy. For example, Acts 4:32-35 is often cited:

> There were no needy persons among them [the early Christians in Jerusalem]. For from time to time those who owned lands and houses sold them, brought the money from the sales and put it at the Apostles' feet, and it was distributed to anyone as he had need.[39]

However, there is a difference between this practice and socialist doctrine; in Biblical citations, as in others, the context provides the meaning. First, if some Believers had not been able to become relatively wealthy, there would have been little or no wealth available for them to share with others. Second, although the group of the Believers wanted to share everything they had with the others they first must have owned private property (land, houses, goods, or other material) before being able to sell a portion of it to help those in need. Specifically, Peter asks Ananias in Acts, "Didn't it [the land] belong to you before it was sold? And after it was sold, wasn't the money at your disposal?" According to this passage Ananias and his wife dropped dead because they had lied to the Holy Spirit about the true, limited extent of their charity, not because they had held back a portion of the sale proceeds. Third, the purpose of pooling resources was to help the truly poor among them, not those who simply had less wealth and wanted more. (Writing to Christians in the Greek city of Thessalonica, St. Paul stated flatly: "If a man will not work, neither shall he eat.") Fourth and finally, becoming a Believer was a wholly voluntary act and no distributions were coerced, which gives the sharing its true moral significance.

Similarly, the famous quote from Matthew 19:21-24: "go, sell your possessions and give to the poor, and you will have treasure in heaven...Again I tell you, it is easier for a camel to go through the eye of a needle than for a rich person to enter the Kingdom of God," This passage again makes clear that choosing to generously share one's private wealth with the poor is virtuous, but was not a commandment to do so. Further, Matthew 6:24 warns that accumulating wealth as an end to itself is impossible for those who want to devote their lives to God: "You cannot serve both God and money." Inspired by these teachings, people who devote their lives to religious works often eschew personal wealth, just as Jesus instructed the young man, "If you want to be perfect, go, sell your possessions and give to the poor, and you will have treasure in heaven, then come, follow me." Likewise, many others who have become wealthy heed this message by devoting much of their wealth to philanthropy. These passages are not a Biblical injunction against becoming highly successful in one's chosen livelihood. Far from it. Rather, they teach Christians not to hoard their wealth, accumulating it for its own sake. There is no virtue in merely doing what one must; any claim of moral virtue requires the freedom to choose altruistic actions, rather than to merely obey government's commands.

As Winston Churchill wryly observed at a 1908 meeting of the England's National Liberal Club, socialism flipped the Christian altruistic ideal of "All I have is yours" into the covetous "All you have is mine."[40] Note that this statement by Churchill was made less than a decade before the ideological regimes inspired by Marx and other false prophets of Utopia began callously destroying millions upon millions of lives under the doctrine of their godless pseudo-religion. How could anyone, even someone without the least religious convictions, believe there are any social justice ends that could justify the death of innocent millions as the means? By revealing its hideous nature as it festered and spread, the false religion of socialism once and for all slammed the door shut on its sanctimonious claims to moral virtue.

Yes, there are "useful idiots" in religious garb, not just in secular institutions, who are willing tools for channeling religious energy and passion into socialism's secular utopian crusade. Permit me now offer a few observations on a specific socialist pseudo-religion called "Liberation Theology." Liberation Theology is a Marxist misinterpretation of Christianity that became popular in certain parts of Latin America, particularly from the 1950's to the 1970's. It twisted the Christian Gospel message into a seductive siren's song, preaching that God calls us to resort to violence, if necessary, to eliminate economic inequality in human societies since capitalism and capitalists are manifestations of evil. It was this very notion that was seized upon by the 20th Century's most evil men in order to justify horrific mass murders and totalitarian oppression, including, of course, suppression of all religions.

The ironic perversion of Christian dogma here lies in its tag of "liberation." This is nothing more than Orwellian double-speak. The revolutionary "liberation" from dictatorships in Central and South America led to merciless political oppression, economic enslavement and murder under new socialist rulers. Thinking of Cuba, Venezuela, and Nicaragua, millions found themselves "liberated" into anti-religious, socialist regimes since their liberators believed only in a secular religion and a salvation that came through a secular utopian society.

In *Post-Capitalist Society*, social commentator Peter Drucker argued, "The collapse of Marxism and communism brought to a close two hundred and fifty years that were dominated by a secular religion. What I called the belief in salvation by society. The first prophet of this secular religion was Jean-Jacques Rousseau. The Marxist Utopia was its ultimate distillation – and apotheosis."[41] Alas, as proven by Liberation Theology and the resurgence of socialism now underway in the West, it did not.

Socialism and the Catholic Church

Being in no way an expert on Catholic Church doctrines

and teachings, and with much humility in that regard, I nonetheless believe some very brief commentary specifically on the Church's evolving views concerning socialism should be included here.

In the past two centuries, while not unconditionally embracing free market democracy, Catholic Popes issued a series of encyclicals that analyzed and consistently condemned socialism and communism, understanding that they represent a unitary political philosophy replete with moral contradictions leading to the greatest of evils. See Pope John Paul II's 1991 encyclical *Centesimus Annus* – On the 100th Anniversary of Pope Leo XIII's *Rerum Novarum*, Pope Pius XI *Quadragesimo Anno* encyclical in 1931, and long before that, Pope Leo XIII's 1878 encyclical *On Socialism*. These and other papal statements condemning socialism could be extensively quoted here but are best read in their entirety to get the benefit of the reasoning and arguments they present in detail, but in *On Socialism* Pope Leo XIII set the stage for the Church's vigorous opposition to socialism. This encyclical reflected Church views that would last until recent times:

> Socialists, stealing the very Gospel itself with a view to deceive more easily the unwary, have become accustomed to distort it so as to suit their own purposes...in accordance with the teachings of the Gospel, the equality of men consists in this: that all, having inherited the same nature, are called to the same most high dignity of the sons of God, and that as one and the same is set before all, each one is to judged by the same law and will receive punishment or reward according to his deserts...the Church recognizes the inequality among men, who are born with different powers of body and mind, inequality in actual possession, and also holds that the right of property and of ownership, which springs from nature itself, must not be touched and stands inviolate.[42]

Despite past papal condemnations, in more recent times several social agendas have come to infiltrate and sometimes even dominate Catholic teachings and religious pronounce-ments. I begin with an account of then Cardinal Ratzinger's (later Pope Benedict XVI) rebuttal of so-called Liberation Theol-ogy is taken and paraphrased from an article found in Catholic publications.[43]

In 1984 Ratzinger issued official condemnations of certain elements of Liberation Theology, rejecting as Marxist the idea that class struggle is fundamental to history, and the interpreta-tion of religious events such as the Exodus and establishment of the Eucharist in exclusively political terms. Ratzinger saw a ma-jor flaw in attempting to apply Christ's Sermon on the Mount teaching about the poor to present-day social situations. Rather than preaching a communal responsibility, Christ's teaching in this case focused on individual responsibility, meaning that we will be judged as individuals when we die with particular at-tention to how we personally have treated the poor.

Ratzinger also argued that Liberation Theology did not originate in a "grass-roots" movement among the poor, but rather was a creation of Western intellectuals, i.e., "An at-tempt to test, in a concrete scenario, ideologies that have been invented in the laboratory by European theologians." He saw the emergence of this Marxist movement clothed in Christian garb as a reaction to the demise or near demise of the Marxist myth in the democratic West. It should be noted that Cardi-nal Ratzinger did acknowledge Liberation Theology in some respects, including its ideal of justice, its rejection of violence, and its stress on "the responsibility which Christians necessar-ily bear for the poor and oppressed." I suspect that many of those churchmen who embraced Liberation Theology's social justice theme did so in an attempt to atone for and wash away the past sins of Spanish colonialism.

Pope John Paul II, in his 1991 encyclical was also con-cerned about "capitalism unbounded by law and a healthy cul-ture." He had the life experience of being subjected to the Nazi occupation, then years of communist rule imposed by Stalin on his native Poland. Like Benedict, John Paul strongly supported "human rights to private initiative, to ownership of property and to freedom in the economic sector."[44] He felt compelled to write this most insightful critique of socialism:

> The fundamental error of socialism is anthropological in nature. Socialism considers the individual person simply as an element, a molecule within the social organism, so that the good of the individual is completely subordinated to the functioning of the socio-economic mechanism. Socialism likewise maintains that the good of the individual can be realized without reference to his free choice, to the unique and exclusive responsibility which he exercises in the face of good or evil. Man is thus reduced to a series of social relationships, and the concept of the person as the autonomous subject of moral decision disappears, the very subject whose decisions build the social order. From the mistaken conception of the person there arise both a distortion of law, which defines the sphere of the exercise of freedom, and an opposition to private property. A person who is deprived of something he can call "his own," and of the possibility of earning a living through his own initiative, comes to depend on the social machine and on those who control it. This makes it much more difficult for him to recognize his dignity as a person, and hinders progress towards the building up of an authentic human community.[45]

Clearly, John Paul saw no conflict between the Church's championing the downtrodden through strong laws and a culture of caring for the poor and oppressed, and its support of human freedom and the right to private property over ideologies rooted in Marxism.

Despite the collapse of communism in the former Soviet Union and Eastern Europe in the early 1990's, the Church has said little about the 100 million lives sacrificed to the Utopian god of socialism, nor has it condemned the corresponding moral complicity of Western intelligentsia. Perhaps to current Church leaders, the past is the past. Maybe the Church fears retribution with forced closure of churches, and imprisonment of clerics in the remaining communist countries of Asia and Latin America (millions of Christians live in China itself), and thus is practicing a form of silent religious "realpolitik." Or more ominously, perhaps by viewing human freedom under capitalism as "unbridled license," (an odd phrase considering the extent of laws regulating Western economies) sympathy for a more authoritarian form of government is growing among certain circles within the Church.

It is most likely, I personally believe, that in order to gain greater recognition as a champion of the world's poor, some Church leaders wish to align with socialism's beguiling appeal to the underprivileged, despite the reality of its inhumane underlying ideology. But for whatever reason, in the years since John Paul II and Benedict XVI the Church has had relatively little to say about the fundamental evils of socialism. It seems heedless of the admonitions of its many victims who have borne witness, to socialism's insidious progression toward a moral abyss.

Under the current Pope Francis, the Church has continued its silence concerning socialist ideology, the root cause of the most significant human catastrophe in history and a continuing threat to the Church around the world. It is impossible not to contrast the silence on the evils of socialism with Francis' ongoing strident condemnation of income inequality in Western free market economies. This implies a moral comparison favorable to socialist totalitarianism. It also tends to put socialism in a different category than communism despite being simply the other side of the same ideological coin. Most incredibly in terms of the Church's future, the intense focus on income inequality plays into the socialist agenda of class warfare, overlooking socialism's strident attacks on religious institutions it is unable to neuter and manipulate.

Making simplistic attacks on the "evils" of money, markets, and wealth inequality in Western societies a centerpiece of his papacy, Francis ignores the dramatic uplift in freedom, prosperity, and overall well-being achieved by the West's liberal market economies and departs from the moral guidance offered by his predecessors. He remains inexplicably silent concerning socialism, which, if we have learned anything at all from the last 100 years, offers only a hell on earth for its victims during life, and for its victimizers, surely a hell to come after death. As a result, Pope Francis's messages on social justice are being interpreted by some as moral ambivalence toward or even a preference for socialist ideology. This flies in the face of the Church's repeated and unequivocal condemnation of socialism's teachings and those who espouse them. I refer again to Pope Leo XIII's 1878 encyclical *On Socialism* in which he speaks of the "Plague of Socialism...also called Communism and Nihilism...a poisonous doctrine being spread by bad men, like an evil seed that bears fatal fruit," and John Paul's critique cited above.[46]

In contrast to Pope John Paul's important role in lifting the Iron Curtain in 1989 to free Eastern Europe, today's leaders of the Catholic Church hierarchy are mostly silent. The Church must not fail to give a voice to the many millions crushed and murdered by socialism, and attest to its extant evils. It must instead wake up and bear witness to the truth about socialism it previously articulated for over a century. If the Church does not, it would be making a most profound error in moral judgement by giving tacit support for socialism's Faustian vision of a new "Socialist Man" who triumphs over and replaces God.

An endorsement, alignment, or even a modus-vivendi with socialism would plunge the Catholic Church into spiritual darkness that would undermine and could ultimately destroy one of the world's most important institutions. The implications reach farther than any single religious institution; it is no coincidence that the most recognizable socialist leaders were and would remain fervent atheists hostile to religion of any sort. If all the world's governments embraced socialist doctrine, how long would any religion based on morality survive? To answer, one need only look at the pattern of deadly religious persecution that everywhere accompanied the spread of the atheistic "secular religion" of modern socialism. To repeat, the anti-religious policies carried out by such regimes flow directly from the dogma proclaimed by its highest authority, Karl Marx, that "religion is the opiate of the people," articulated by his dedicated disciple Lenin as "there can be nothing more abominable than religion."

The real path to shared human dignity, prosperity, and morality does not lie in Liberation Theology or any other "gospel" of socialism. These benefits to humanity derive from spreading the liberal democratic model that promises individual freedom, rights, and respect based on what one does rather than on one's class or origin. If the Church shrinks from perhaps its greatest moral duty and becomes uncomfortable with the West's heritage of genuine liberalism, then one must ask whether this ancient institution is a true friend of freedom. One would have to wonder whether the blood flowing through its veins might instead still harbor the authoritarian germ of an intolerant theocratic medieval world that, thank God, no longer exists in the West.

Notes

1. George Lichtheim, *The Origins of Socialism*, Frederick A. Praeger, 1969, Chapter 10, "The Marxian Synthesis, Theory and Practice," p. 192.

2. Karl Marx, *Karl Marx and Frederick Engels Collected Works April 1845-April 1847*, Vol. 5, *The German Ideology*. "I. Feuerbach," p. 50, Lawrence & Wishart Electric Books, 2010, transl. W. Lough and C. P. Magill.

3. Steven Pinker, *Blank Slate*, 2002, Penguin Books 2016 edition, Chapter 3, "The Last Wall to Fall," pp. 52-56.

4. Max Eastman, former member of the U.S. Socialist Party, in the "Biographical Introduction to his Reflections on the Failure of Socialism," Devin-Adair Company, 1955, pp. 24-25. Eastman, an American, had spent a great deal of time in Russia in the early 1920's during the formative years of the Soviet Union, came to know and was much impressed by both Lenin and Trotsky, and wrote extensively singing the praises of the Bolshevik dictatorship in books such as *Marx and Lenin; The Science of Revolution* (1927), as he had previously in magazines he edited between 1912 and 1922, the *Masses,* and the *Liberator.* In his subsequent works he began to raise doubts about the philosophical basis of Marxism, and as a socialist, critiqued the Soviet regime, but with sympathy for the ideals he then thought it represented. His support for the Soviet Union ended when his disillusionment with "the socialist idea" became complete in 1940, and he broke away from Socialism altogether. He began to see Marxian socialism as a global totalitarian threat to political and economic freedom, and spent the rest of his life writing against it.

5. Alexander Solzhenitsyn, quote of a character named Nerzhin (Solzhenitsyn's alter ego) in his novel *In The First Circle,* Chapter "Secret Conversation," p.340, this work was composed from 1955 to 1958, translated by Harry Willets for the 2009 Harper Collins version. "We were born with a sense of justice in our souls; we can't and don't want to live without it."

6. F. A. Hayek, The Collected Works of F. A. Hayek, *The Constitution of Liberty,* University of Chicago Press, 1960, 2011, "Introductory Essay," p. 15.

7. Ronald Bailey and Martin L. Tupy, Ten Global Trends Every Smart Person Should Know, pp. 9-10, 33-34, 55-56, and 97-98, Cato Institute, 2020; sources of these trend data noted by the authors include: the World Bank, Angus Madison Project Database, American Economic Review, and The Conference Board Total Economic Database; very similar data are found in Steven Pinker's Enlightenment Now, pp. 85, 116, and 246, Penguin Books, 2018.

8. Deirdre McCloskey, *Bourgeois Equality: How Ideas, Not Capital or Institutions, Enriched the World,* 6 "Inequality is Not the Problem," 9 "The Great International Divergence Can be Overcome," pp. 1621 and 2089 of 18935 respectively in Kindle e-version.

9. F. A. Hayek, *Road to Serfdom,* University of Chicago Press, 1944, 1994 edition, Chapter 9, "Security and Freedom", p. 133.

10. Thomas Paine, *The Rights of Man* at pp. 576-582 9 (e-version) In *Rights* Paine proposed the use of tax revenue to help the poor, children, the old, sick, injured and military veterans, and even estimated the amount of money such a proposal (in England) would require.

11. Hayek supported the need for social insurance in *The Road to Serfdom*, p. 133, University of Chicago Press, 1944, 1994 edition.

12. Victor Hugo, a contemporary of Marx and Engles, from his classic novel concerning justice, *Les Miserables*, 1862, translated by C. E. Wilbur, Chapter 3 (4) "Cracks Under the Foundation," pp. 505-506.

13. Michael Novak, *The Spirit of Democratic Capitalism*, V. "Providence and Practical Wisdom," 5. "Zero Sum Society," pp. 122-23, 1982, Madison Books.

14. Ibn Khaldun, from his masterpiece *The Muqaddimah*, Book One, "Kitab al 'Ibar," Chapter III, No. 41. "Injustice Brings About the Ruin of Civilization," translated by Franz Rosenthal.

15. Michael Novak, *The Spirit of Democratic Capitalism*, "The Ideal of Democratic Capitalism," IV. "Sin," 1. "Freedom and Sin," p. 85, Madison Books, 1982.

16. F. A. Hayek, *The Constitution of Liberty*, 1960, University of Chicago Press, 2011 edition, Chapter "Equality, Value, and Merit," pp. 149-150, and "Individualism and Economic Order," 1948, "Individualism: True and False," No. 4 pp. 15-16.

17. This definition is taken from *Human Augmentation – The Dawn of a New Paradigm*, p. 12, May 2021, a report issued by The UK Ministry of Defense with the Bundeswehr Office for Defense Planning.

18. Envy is a ubiquitous human impulse that when controlled is controlled by reason; for more on the role envy plays in societies see Helmut Schoek, *Envy: A Theory of Social Behaviour*, Liberty Press, 1966, English translation 1970, and Donald Brown *Human Universals*, Kindle Edition, 1991, 2017.

19. Mancur Olson described a historical phenomenon he called "roving bandits" and "stationary bandits" in his paper "Dictatorship, Democracy, and Development," *American Political Science Review*, Vol. 87, No. 3 September 1993, p. 568.

20. Adam Smith, *The Wealth of Nations*, 1776, Penguin Books, 1970, "Book I," Chapters I-III, pp. 107-126, and "Book II," p. 441.

21. Donald E. Brown, *Human Universals*, 1991, 2017 Kindle edition, Chapter Six, "The Universal People," location 880 and 888 of 6032 in Kindle e-version.

22. Ibid, Chapter Six, "The Universal People, Demonstrating Universals," Kindle e-verson, location 2960 of 6032.

23. Hannah Arendt, *The Origins of Totalitarianism*, Second Edition, 1958; this is a paraphrase of a key point Arendt makes about the grave dangers of trying

to make conditions instead of political rights equal for all, in Chapter Three: "Jews and Society," pp. 54-55.

24. Adam Smith, the great social philosopher and political economist, pointed out in *The Theory of Moral Sentiments*, and *Wealth of Nations* (see Andrew Skinner "Introduction," "Section 1," pp. 25-29 of 1984 Penguin edition) it is human nature and a sign of civilization to have a sympathetic reaction, to want to help people who are unable to help themselves, particularly children and those who are old, sick, or injured. Smith was referring to his theory that a positive morality must be shared by those comprising society in order for it to be beneficent, and not simply guided by rules of justice that discourage actions that may hurt one's neighbors. For Smith, both rules of justice and a shared morality are indispensable for a society to flourish.

25. These and many similar ethical precepts are found at http://oaks.nvg. org/egyptian-proverbs.html, along with a very extensive bibliography. Other such sources are "Precepts and Teachings of Ancient Egypt," by Dr. Keith Seddon, Lulu Publisher 2011, and "The Forty-two Precepts of Maat," and" Ancient Egyptian Proverbs" by Muata Ashby, published by the Sema Institute of Yoga 2002

26. The reciprocity norm is part of what makes us human. It is "a key element in their (the universal people's) morality." Both positive and negative reciprocity are found in all human societies. It is therefore one of the "human universals" as explained by anthropologist Donald E. Brown in *Human Universals*, at locations 2960 and 2984 of 6032 in Kindle Version 1991, 2017.

27. Sawhill and Haskins, *Work and Marriage: The Way to End Poverty and Welfare*, Brookings, 2003, one of many such works leading to this conclusion.

28. Hertzler, Joyce O. quotes from the H. G. Wells book *Modern Utopia*, p. 135, in her *The History of Utopian Thought*, Chapter X, "Limited Perspective of Utopians," pp. 304-305, FN No.2, George Allen & Unwin, Ltd., London.

29. William J. Bernstein, *A Splendid Exchange: How Trade Shaped the World*, p. 8, 2008, Grove Press.

30. Will and Ariel Durant, *The Age of Napoleon* – "Life Under the Revolution," Chapter VI, p. 153.

31. Reinhold Niebuhr, essay critical of extreme libertarianism titled *The Limits of Liberty*, January 24, 1942.

32. John E. E. Dalberg-Acton, First Barton Acton, essay "The History of Freedom in Antiquity," 1877, p. 39 in *Essays on Freedom and Power* (1949), Chapter I "Inaugural Lecture on the Study of History."

33. Historian Samuel Huntington, *Political Order in Changing Societies*, see Chapter "Revolution and Political Order," pp. 264-343.

34. Donald E. Brown, *Human Universals*, 1991 Kindle edition, Chapter Six e-version, location 2995.

35. Karl Marx and Frederick Engels, *Collected Works, Vol. 5, Marx and Engels 1845-1847*, Lawrence & Wishart Electric Books, 2010, "Preface," p. XV prepared by Lev Churbanov, referring to Marx's *Theses on Feuerbach*.

36. John Gray, *Black Mass: How Religion Led the World into Crisis*, 2007, Anchor Canada, "Death of Utopia" p. 21. In *Black Mass* Gray has written extensively about the influence of the French Revolution and the Great Terror of the Jacobins on the formation of secular utopian "religions."

37. The 10th Commandment from Exodus 20, the Biblical injunction against envy "Do not covet thy neighbor's house or any of his other possessions" forbids believers from even wanting the property of others.

38. Karl Marx's famous quote about religion is in the introduction to his work *A Contribution to the Critique of Hegel's Philosophy of Right*, 1843, published separately in 1943 in Marx's *German – French Annals*. Lenin discussed religion in "Socialism and Religion," No. 28, December, 1905, *in Lenin Collected Works*, Progress Publishers, 1965, pp. 83-8.

39. *The New Testament* of *The Bible, Acts 4:32-36, and 4:2-11* is a passage cited by those who attempt in vain to reconcile Christianity with socialism.

40. Andrew Roberts, *Churchill: Walking with Destiny*, Viking Peguin Random House, 2018, pp. 115-116.

41. Peter Drucker, *Post-Capitalist Society*, Harper Collins, 1993, *The Shift to a Knowledge Society*, p. 7.

42. Pope Leo XIII's 1878 encyclical *On Socialism*, Source: the Vatican.

43. Cardinal Ratzinger's (later Pope Benedict XVI) rebuttal of Liberation Theology is taken and paraphrased from an article found amongst Catholic publications.

44. Pope John Paul II encyclical *Centesimus Annus – On the 100th anniversary of Pope Leo XIII's Rerum Novarum*, May 1, 1991, Source: the Vatican.

45. Ibid, n. 12.

46. Pope Leo XIII's 1878 encyclical *On Socialism*, Source: the Vatican.

CHAPTER SEVEN

True Believers Tenaciously Cling to Power

"Turning our backs or abandoning Marxism means that our Party would lose its soul and direction."
—Xi Jinping, General Secretary of the Chinese Communist Party

In the Western world, we can easily find columnists, authors, bloggers, and even entertainment celebrities serving as socialist apologists. They routinely tout achievements of totalitarian countries, whether it be the high-speed rail systems in China or medical clinics in Cuba. Universal free education in socialist countries might resonate with many, but its real purpose is more effective indoctrination and obedience, and suitability for jobs designated by the state. This creates a pool of true believers with capabilities the Communist Party can use for its ends, rather than teaching students to think freely for themselves and do what they want with their lives. But the truth of socialist societies is not hard to see. The shiny buildings of Shanghai and the medical clinics in Havana cannot hide the stifling social and economic conditions of socialist dictatorships that persist behind the facade of lies erected by their governments.

China "Backslides" from Reform to Repression

Because of modern communication technologies, information can more easily spread beyond national borders, making the lies embedded in socialist propaganda less effective. The People's Republic of China (PRC) and some other socialist governments have responded to this threat to their control of their citizenry by somewhat loosening their prohibitions on private property ownership and by allowing their citizens to establish businesses, save and invest money, own land, and accumulate wealth. What led to this change in policy?

The easing of some controls during the past 40 years follows a terrible history under the leadership of Chairman Mao and the Chinese Communist Party (CCP), which came to power by defeating Chiang Kai-shek's Kuomintang (KMT) Army in 1948. It is difficult to exaggerate the full extent of the horror visited on the Chinese people by Mao's government since that time. Although exact numbers will never be known, as many as 65 million people may have died under Mao's Socialist Utopia, exceeding even Lenin and Stalin's ghastly toll, and making Mao's 28-year rule certainly the most deadly regime in all of human history.[1] With little or no value placed on individual lives, it should come as no surprise that to the "Great Helmsman" Mao, people were a problem to be "managed" using guns, starvation, and gruesome forms of torture.

Between 1959 and 1961 the collectivism and forced labor of Mao's "Great Leap Forward" resulted in mass starvation and a complete breakdown of the Chinese economy. The next State-sponsored disaster, Mao's "Cultural Revolution" of 1966-'76, attempted to reinvigorate the original revolution and led to a decade of murderous violence and chaos. The product of Mao's socialist policies over almost three decades was a generation hardened with revolutionary fervor, but also little education and dire economic prospects. Finally came Mao's demise in 1976 and then the downfall of his self-selected successors including Mao's wife, known as the "Gang of Four."

In order to stay in power after years of repression and catastrophic policies, the CCP began a somewhat different approach to the economy. The revamp in strategy was hastened by the Western democratic capitalist model having taken root in other parts of Asia, giving rise to the undeniable economic success of Japan and the so-called "Asian Tigers," Hong Kong, South Korea, Taiwan, and Singapore, in stark contrast to the nightmare experienced by the Chinese people. In the late 1970's under its new supreme leader Deng Xiaoping, China's long-ruling Communist Party began departing from socialist ideological orthodoxy without repudiating their outmoded Marxist doctrine, instituting what Deng called "socialism with Chinese characteristics." The popular steps that allowed a certain measure of economic freedom, including previously forbidden market-based elements, have in the decades following led to rapid economic growth. Some Chinese citizens, especially those well-connected to the CCP, have achieved significant wealth, and many more a level of prosperity undreamed of under Mao. A similar path has been taken by the Party leaders of the Socialist Republic of Vietnam.

But let there be no mistake, whatever prosperity the Chinese and Vietnamese enjoy today is not from the Marxist central planning and the intrusive social control that the CCP still clings to. Rather, it is the result of their governments' partial embrace of market principles which by creating a degree of economic freedom has allowed their millennium-spanning culture of hard work and commercial prowess to flourish. Notwithstanding recent economic reforms, basic human liberties are still being trampled underfoot in China, and we now see a frightful reversal of the more lenient political trends that author Malia labelled "Reform Communism."[2]

Current Chinese leader Xi Jinping, son of one of Mao's followers and a so-called "red aristocrat," appears determined to resume crushing dissent and whitewashing history.

Consider the plight of the Uyghur people. It is here where we most clearly see the true face of the CCP's totalitarianism. There are reportedly more than 10 million Uyghurs in the Xinjiang province of China. Primarily Muslim, they speak a Turkic language, and tend to resemble other peoples of Central Asia. Since at least 2014, Xinjiang has been the target of some of the most restrictive and comprehensive security measures ever deployed by a state against its own people. They include the large-scale use of new technologies: ubiquitous surveillance cameras with facial recognition capability, monitoring devices that read the content of mobile phones, and mass collection of biometric data. Uyghurs are prohibited from practicing Islam, from attending mosques, and from fasting during Ramadan. Use of the Uyghur language is forbidden in schools.

Rumors that China was operating a system of internment camps for Muslims in Xinjiang began to emerge in 2017. Satellite photos published by the BBC confirmed that huge complexes had sprung up virtually overnight in remote locations, but when investigative journalists tried to visit these locations, they were constrained by Chinese authorities and told the camps were "schools." One such camp was thought to house as many as 130,000 "students" and featured 18 watchtowers, discrediting official statements. The few local people willing to talk referred to them instead as re-education camps. In the words of one local, the camps' inhabitants were there because "They have some problems with their thoughts." Not wanting to "waste" this human resource, the Uyghurs are subjected by the CCP to what some refer to as "modern slavery" to produce vast amounts of cotton products.

Even more horrifying to any normal person is the extensive evidence of widespread organ harvesting by the CCP from live prisoners ending in their murder, that has recently been brought forward and presented to a People's Tribunal.[3] If the data and witness reports are true, such acts are so heinous they can be compared to the gassing, starvation, and torture of Jews by the Nazis, the massacres by the Khmer Rouge, and the butchery of the Rwandan Tutsis. This is not an isolated rogue undertaking. The CCP has apparently built an entire infrastructure around its organ harvesting.

Talk by Mr. Xi and other CCP leaders about communist China being a superior model of development for the less developed nations are belied not just by their history but also by their efforts to destroy the Uyghurs. The CCP's genocide of the Uyghurs is finally being recognized, studied and condemned by governments and human rights organizations around the world. There is substantial evidence that the CCP's inhumane actions, including systematic rape, torture, forced abortions, and mass internment, have been taken with the approval if not at the direction of Xi Jinping.[4]

Looking back twenty-five years, Western elites naively assumed that opening markets to freer trade with China and importing massive amounts of inexpensive Chinese goods would encourage China to liberalize and become more respectful of the rights of its people. As the Chinese people became more prosperous, they then would also eventually democratize, essentially doing away with the CCP's monopoly on power. Western belief that democratic economies could expand freedom by expanding economic prosperity in China was little more than a delusion.

The committed Marxists of the CCP leadership have not wavered from their belief that basic freedoms and rights taken for granted in the West must be politically suppressed. The CCP proudly proclaims its firm adherence to the "four cardinal principles" on which debate is not allowed.[5] The Principles are:

1. Upholding the socialist path.
2. Upholding the people's democratic dictatorship.
3. Upholding the leadership of the Communist Party.
4. Upholding Mao Zedong thought and Marxism–Leninism.

Xi strongly defended the Party's unwavering commitment to Marxism despite the horrendous human toll from its past, in a speech to the Communist Party Central Committee on January 5, 2013:

> There are people who believe that communism is an unattainable hope, or even that it is beyond hoping for – that communism is an illusion…Facts have repeatedly told us that Marx and Engel's analysis of the basis contradictions of capitalist society is not outdated, nor is the historical-materialist view that capitalism is bound to die out and socialism is bound to win. This is an inevitable trend in social and historical development. But the road is tortuous. The eventual demise of capitalism and the ultimate victory of *socialism* will require a long historical process to reach completion.[6] [emphasis added]

He reinforced this view at a 2016 event marking the Chinese Communist Party's 95th anniversary:

"Turning our backs or abandoning Marxism means that our Party would lose its soul and direction."[7] The Marxist "soul", if there is one, has no sense of morality, and it is a strange metaphor for a person to use while also reminding Party members to be "unyielding Marxist atheists." More recently, Mr. Xi is quoted as having said "Socialism with Chinese characteristics is *socialism*, not any other 'ism.'" Unquestionably, ever since the armed takeover by the Party's army in 1948, China remains today a Communist, Marxist *and* socialist totalitarian state, one which governs by the ideology of the Unholy Trinity as now interpreted by its President for life, Xi Jinping. It is a state intent on aggressively expanding its economic and military power to ward off liberalizing influences, assure the CCP's iron grip on China continues indefinitely, ultimately creating a socialist and non-Western New World Order.

Mao attempted to completely transform Chinese society from a peasant economy with a small industrial proletariat directly into a fully communist one. He failed, having skipped a vital step in the historical process described in Marx's doctrine. The Marxist dream of the revolutionary dictatorship creating prosperity shared equally by all eluded him. Mao's response to disappointing results was continuous destructive upheavals such as the "Cultural Revolution." Recall that Marx wrote that industrial capitalism would be the necessary predicate for socialism, and socialism would then evolve into communism. Recognizing this as an essential step in the development of a socialist state, Deng placed China on the true Marxian path by first stimulating capitalism, including Western foreign investment, to give China the technologies, industrial strength, wealth, and military power from which socialism could successfully emerge. All the while, he kept it on a leash through the CCP's undemocratic monopoly on political power, setting strict terms under which foreign businesses could invest and operate in China without recourse to independent courts of law in the case of governmental abuse of such power.

The CCP's strategy differed from Marx's expectations by adhering to Deng's Four Cardinal Principles, able to maintain full political control to block or squash any incipient social unrest, as they did in Tiananmen Square and are doing now. The Party would guide the national transition without a second revolutionary phase needed to establish socialism, and Chinese society becoming unhinged from the Party's control by a rise in democratic sentiments.

This approach is sometimes referred to as "birdcage socialism," a policy concept initially put forward in response to widespread famine in 1961-62 by Chen Yun, then a vice-chair of the CCP and member of its politburo. Chen was later punished for doing so during Mao's Cultural Revolution. It is an apt metaphor. How can people consider themselves to be free when they are perpetually "caged" by a single party possessing a monopoly on political power. In what kind of insane world is being caged considered "freedom?" The answer: a socialist one.

Looking at China's recent history though a Marxian lens, it appears that Xi is now dutifully fulfilling the next step of China's transformation to full socialism. Driven by the desire to tap into China's vast market and labor potential and blinded by the hope for peaceful co-existence with a potential behemoth, elites in the West mischaracterized Deng as a "reformist" committed to Western openness and freedom in the long run. Foolhardy Western companies who invested heavily in China after drooling over its low labor costs, culture of unquestioning hard work, and large potential market, now find themselves inside the CCP's invisible, but very real cage. They are trapped financially and thus subject to forced transplantation of their proprietary know-how and inclusion of CCP operatives within their organizations. Perhaps they were unaware of or failed to take seriously Deng's Cardinal Principles, and later, Mr. Xi's socialist zeal.

As China turns sharply away from its market-based reforms, we now recognize again the fuller application of the dangerous tenets of socialism in the CCP's actions. No one should be surprised by this, given that in Mr. Xi's words, the Party is building China into a "modern socialist power."[8]

In another version of Nikita Khrushchev's infamous 1956 Moscow challenge to Western diplomats the arrogant and boastful CCP leadership recently declared the superiority of their system over a supposedly declining United States and liberal international order. Despite its massive human rights abuses, the CCP not only celebrated its successes in overseeing China's transformation into a formidable power on the world stage but also presented its authoritarian model to the world as superior to democracy and capitalism. General Secretary of the CCP, Xi Jinping marked the CCP's centennial celebration at a speech, ironically given at Tiananmen Square, the scene of the 1989 massacre of pro-democracy demonstrators, claiming the CCP had used Marxism to "seize the initiative in history" and create a "new model for human advancement."

The U.S. has recently concluded after years of futilely hoping that freedom and democracy would start to take hold in China:

> Beijing is increasingly attempting to curb the aspirations of a rising generation of entrepreneurs, leaders, and advocates of democracy. The message is clear. National sovereignty along with constitutional rights, civil and human liberties, and free market economic values are impediments to the CCP's goals of a 'community of common human destiny' which in simplest terms is the Party's ever-expanding control over its own people and other nations' citizens as well.[9]

Even more committed to fully totalitarian socialism is a neighboring client state, the Kim regime in North Korea (a.k.a. The Democratic People's Republic of Korea). Kim's fully militarized state continues to menace South Korea, and now poses a nuclear missile threat against Japan and the U.S. Ten years after assuming power following his father's death at a meeting of his Politburo, the supreme leader Kim Jong-un reportedly warned of significant food shortages but proclaimed "self-confidence in a fresh victory of our own-style socialism."[10]

Returning to the CCP, its continued suppression of organized religions, the many years of a "one child" policy, the "disappearing" of authors, publishers, and booksellers of literature who criticized the regime, and the emerging social scoring" of its citizens using modern technology make it abundantly clear that despite limited economic reforms, the, one-party Chinese Socialist State is determined to remain firmly in control of its people. Moreover, we now have seen the CCP under Xi's leadership lying to the world about the Wuhan origin of coronavirus, COVID-19, which has proved catastrophic to world economies. Despite the collapse of the Soviet Union and its other massive failures everywhere else, socialism's current leaders in China remain unrepentant in their full-hearted embrace of Marx's doctrines. In China socialism has a powerful new standard-bearer, controlling 19 percent of the world's population, harboring nine out of ten World Communist Party members, and possessing ever increasing economic and military power. What might this portend for humanity? Nothing good to be sure, but the year 2020 provides an example.

As the COVID-19 virus spread from Wuhan, China, to the rest of the world, some of the ramifications of foolishly trusting China's regime to respect norms of international trade, information exchange, and intellectual property became all too apparent. The virus revealed China's utter disregard for such norms, and its suffocating control of vital global supply chains, including especially rare earth materials used in high-tech products and the supply of numerous pharmaceuticals. It also brought to the fore China's campaign to dominate global institutions like the World Health Organization, control critical trade routes, and infiltrate Western research and educational institutions. The worldwide influence of China and its Communist Party in Beijing already surpasses the grandest dreams of previous Soviet dictatorships. All doubt has been erased. The monster of Marx's totalitarian ideology lives on behind the shiny façade of economic liberalization.

Castro's Cuba: Exporter of Dystopia

Since the revolutionary Popular Socialist Party led by Fidel Castro and Che Guevara seized power from the military dictator Fulgencio Batista in 1959, over a million Cubans, or greater than 10% of Cuba's current population, have fled the island. Cuba's regime has been abandoned in favor of the U.S. or Mexico via a steady exodus in leaky boats, home-made rafts, and even floating inner-tubes! It is a short journey to freedom in most cases, but very risky; over 75,000 are believed to have perished in the attempt. An estimated 60,000 successfully fled in just the two-year period of 2016 to 2017, and many more since then. Cubans who have fled the Island could be considered the Western Hemisphere's "Boat People," like the refugees who fled Vietnam after U.S. involvement ended and the Communists from the North took over the entire country.[11] Boat people around the world have chosen a perilous journey to freedom over a stifled life in the unproductive economy of a socialist police state.

Paralleling the ongoing immiseration of the Island, this exodus has continued unabated in recent years. According to the New York Times the U.S is currently experiencing the largest Cuban immigration ever. ("Since October, the start of the federal government's fiscal year 2022, nearly 79,000 Cubans have arrived at the southern border of the United States, more than in the previous two years combined.").[12] In addition to makeshift rafts, Cubans were until recently flying to Guyana (no visa required for Cubans), and trekked from there through Columbia, the Darien Jungle, Panama, Honduras, Guatemala, and Mexico where they could finally cross the Rio Grande River into the U.S. Now discontented Cubans instead seek to travel to Nicaragua (no visa required for Cubans) where they arrange with "coyotes" (smugglers) for transit to the U.S. By whatever route and means, the trip to the U.S. is extraordinarily costly and risky for the poor emigres, but their motivation to escape Cuba's totalitarian misery remains incredibly strong. What Castro began as political exile to push out freedom-seeking dissenters has become a continual political and economic exodus.

After jailing and murdering tens of thousands and driving many more of his dissenting countrymen to an escape by sea, Castro set his sights on becoming a major international figure; he began exporting his socialist ideology and revolutionary expertise both overtly and surreptitiously. Provocateurs and armed militants were sent throughout Latin America in search of fertile ground in which to sow the seeds of socialism. Che Guevara was executed after being caught while attempting to cultivate a Cuban-style revolution in Bolivia. Planting socialism proved more successful in Venezuela and in corrupt post-colonial regimes such as Nicaragua that were previously ruled by incompetent strongmen.

From the beginning, to help maintain control of his dissatisfied populace Castro used hatred and brave defiance of the "Yankee Imperialist" boogieman to justify "sacrifices essential to the peoples' revolution." As a Western Hemisphere surrogate for the USSR during its heyday, he thrilled at the notoriety gained from hosting Soviet nuclear missiles on Cuban soil, thereby almost triggering a cataclysmic military exchange between the USA and USSR in October 1962. From Soviet archives we know that Fidel Castro sent an urgent message to Khrushchev during the night of October 26 at the height of the Cuban Missile Crisis urging the Soviet Union to launch *a nuclear first strike* attacking the United States if the U.S. embarked upon an invasion of Cuba. Khrushchev told the top Soviet leadership "We were completely aghast," and promptly sent a blunt reply to Castro turning down his "suggestion." Khrushchev went on to criticize Castro for being "blinded by revolutionary passion" and "failing to comprehend the true nature of war in the thermonuclear age." Castro "made clear his extreme displeasure with the Soviet Union's handling of the crisis," including the removal of their missiles and troops from Cuba. Following the "Armageddon letter" exchange, the Soviet Presidium concluded that the Cubans were "unreliable allies."[13]

Although of questionable loyalty to his Soviet benefactors, Castro was never lacking in socialist zeal. During the 1960's he also sent his armed forces to foment and support communist revolutions in far-away African states such as Angola, Zimbabwe, the Congo, and Ethiopia where they aided the Marxist government of Mengistu Haile Mariam, which launched a campaign of terror that killed thousands.

Despite Cuba's relatively small size, with heavy Soviet aid and a large, effective network of spies and covert operatives Fidel Castro's regime openly projected the doctrine of socialist revolution on the world scene until the collapse of the socialist regimes in the USSR and Eastern Europe. Today, Cuba's subversive agents operate mostly in the shadows in countries like Venezuela. His family members have surreptitiously funneled many millions of dollars (Forbes has estimated Fidel's family wealth at $900 million) into overseas bank accounts. Castro's heirs enjoy the good life of successful capitalist tycoons while the Cuban people earn an average of only about $25 per month. Fidel's son, Antonio, reportedly cruises the Mediterranean in his own 160 ft. yacht, enjoying fine dining and luxury resort suites![14] The legacy of Socialist Cuba is straight out of George Orwell's allegory, *Animal Farm*: "All animals are equal, but some animals are more equal than others." Meanwhile in Cuba, despite Fidel Castro's demise, the socialist regime he and his brother Raul created continues to have its own version of Stalin's gulag system; the whole island remains a vast prison for anyone who would dissent. It is now headed by Raul Castro's appointee Miguel Diaz-Canel. Most recently, The U.S. State Department reported "it has received credible evidence of unlawful killings, forced disappearances and torture of political activists in a scorching assessment released of the Cuban government's record."[15]

Beguiling Promises and Betrayal: Venezuela, Nicaragua, Zimbabwe, and Others

In societies emerging from a history of undemocratic colonialism such as Venezuela, Nicaragua, and Zimbabwe, socialist regimes may be voted into office when they tap into public frustration with widespread poverty and unjust conditions by promising to bring order, do away with upper class privilege and power, and provide cradle to grave welfare. During the dangerous transitional period from colonialism socialists, often with help from the likes of Cuba, Russia, or China, may gain sufficient political power to do away with free elections and transform the elected regime into a totalitarian state. Amid the chaos of political transition, tightly organized and secretive socialist paramilitary forces will act quickly to take control of the police, courts, elections, and news media unless strong public support arises to defend these institutions. Democratic legislative, judicial, and electoral processes, especially in those countries lacking deep historical and cultural roots, become weaknesses that can be exploited by more ruthless and aggressive factions. Once purged of dissent and co-opted, these processes become a façade of legitimacy the new regime can hide behind. Corrupted elections become nothing more than a smoke screen. Those who think democratic processes will protect them against this fate need to be warned: democracies can vote themselves into socialism, but not out!

How do countries emerging from colonialism and newly on the road to democracy so easily become hijacked by socialism? Unfortunately, socialism is put into actual practice by methods of which reformist socialists, inhibited by their ideals, would disapprove.[16] Without a public voice and lacking the protection afforded by the rule of law, these reformists soon start "disappearing." Take the illusion of elections and voter preferences as an example. Would this not normally be evidence of a budding democratic state? Yet as Stalin said, "It's not who votes, but who counts the votes that matters."[17]

Rather than safeguarding the voting rights of its members, socialist regimes ensure individual citizens gradually become *subservient* to the State and Party cadres, with democratic recourse to voting in open elections choked-off once the levers of power, particularly the police, military, election supervision, and news media, are in their hands.

For that reason, and from its intellectual roots, socialism points in the direction of communism with its need to destroy all competing political factions. The State determines who is "qualified" to stand for office, and the public is put through the charade of voting in "democratic" elections. It is not by accident that communist regimes often incorporate the word "socialist" into the label they themselves adopt to describe their governments. As noted previously, Lenin, Stalin and Mao each wrote at length about the "socialist State" they were endeavoring to create and saw to it that their people were indoctrinated accordingly. Hence, the assertion by some that there is a moral difference or fundamental chasm between a socialist political party and a communist party bent on assuming power in a newly formed national government is utterly preposterous.

Much like the allegory of the docile frog that will not try to escape from a pot of slowly heated water that finally boils and kills it; so too is the effect on the public of the guise created by socialist propaganda and the incremental appeasement of its adherents' political demands. History confirms that as socialists take power under the banner of achieving greater social equality, it's difficult for pacifistic, more democratic elements to see and believe what is really happening to their freedom and rights. By the time they are sufficiently aroused to action it is already too late. Solzhenitsyn observed that "Modern society is hypnotized by socialism. It is prevented by socialism from seeing the mortal danger it is in. And one of the greatest dangers of all is that you have lost all sense of danger, you cannot even see where it's coming from as it moves swiftly towards you."[18] Perhaps he was thinking about Lenin who said: "It is true that liberty is precious, so precious that it must be carefully rationed."[19] Increasingly tight rationing of liberty is exactly what happened in nations like Venezuela, Nicaragua, and Zimbabwe.

Regardless of lingering discontent, once socialists gain control of a government's security apparatus, together with other branches of government and the media, a tipping point is reached where they cannot be peacefully ousted. In carrying out their agenda and further cementing unchallengeable political positions in newly emerging states, they use the law itself as an instrument of oppression. The law becomes a means of persecuting any opposition and dissenters, rather than serving as guarantor of rights and freedom. Instilling the fear of arrest, jail, torture, or even murder enables the new rulers to tighten their grip. Widespread surveillance by secret police and informant networks leading to the arrest of opponents becomes the order of the day. Fear for oneself and one's family becomes pervasive.

Over time, fundamental rights are nullified, including due process, jury trials, free speech, and other basic civil liberties. Once there is censorship control of news, literature, educational institutions, and even the arts and entertainment, these basic features of freedom become twisted into organs of indoctrination. An alternate reality is created and sustained by official lies that become indisputable truths disseminated by Orwellian-like "Ministries of Public Enlightenment." These regimes may be voted into office, but not out. Through ceaseless propaganda, tight control on public communications, intimidation, and fixing of elections, such new regimes themselves can soon only be challenged by a violent coup d'etat or massive civil disobedience organized at great personal risk.

Let us consider the plight of the people in Venezuela, Nicaragua, and Zimbabwe, examples where socialist true believers came to power in modern times.

Venezuela

It appears that the struggle the Venezuelan people are currently in with the Hugo Chavez/Nicholas Maduro "United Socialist Party" may at some point end in open violence or even civil war. The Party took power through elections in 1999 with Fidel Castro's help. It then began nationalizing industries in 2007, and over time succeeded in destroying Venezuela's economy by appropriating its oil industry and vast oil wealth to fund financially unsustainable increases in social spending. They put Chavez/Maduro loyalists of dubious competence and honesty in charge of all state-owned enterprises, including the massive oil company Petróleos de Venezuela SA. This quickly led to a precipitous drop in production of Venezuela's most valuable commodity while their cronies were busy looting the company's coffers, making many in Venezuela's socialist leadership rich. Having helped Chavez create this mess, Maduro, a Communist hand-picked by the Castro regime and clandestinely supported by Cuban agents inside Venezuela, now blames the nation's problems on "counterrevolutionary elements" in society and sinister meddling by the U.S. He argues he must have even more powers to combat them, including the suspension of remaining civil liberties. Reminiscent of the tactics employed by Lenin, Stalin, and Mao, he began arresting opposition politicians at gunpoint, firing dissenting government employees en masse, and ordering his army to seize and distribute food so people must rely on his regime to avoid hunger and starvation. Maduro has now been accused by the UN of crimes against humanity.[20]

Venezuela is modern day confirmation that to fully implement socialism once it is in control of the machinery of government, there must be only one political party. Opposition must be eliminated. This should sound very familiar: first put nearly everyone on the government dole so they become dependent and compliant, and rig "elections;" next, take over industry and weed out those managers not loyal to the new regime; then as the economy begins to collapse, tighten control of the people through goon squads and by controlling the necessities of life such as their food, medicine, and fuel. Although Hugo Chavez died in 2013, his Marxist daughter Maria Gabriela, a close associate of Maduro, has been able to loot a country where 96 percent of the people now live in poverty, twice the level of 20 years ago. She reportedly has one or more billion dollars held in foreign accounts.[21] Meanwhile, since 2014 over five million desperate Venezuelans – roughly 15 to 20 percent of the population – have fled their collapsing socialist society, and the poorest of them have become a large and growing refugee burden in neighboring countries. Meanwhile, Chinese state-sponsored companies are busy investing in Venezuela's strategic energy assets, but with a great many strings attached.[22]

Nicaragua

"How did we not realize they were becoming monsters? How did we let them get away with so much?" These are the questions of a former Sandinista in 2018.[23] Nicaragua demonstrates that creeping socialism can take years to metastasize into its full deadliness. Recently, we have witnessed Nicaragua's revolutionary strongman Daniel Ortega the previous leader of the Sandinista National Liberation Front (FSLN) throwing off the sheep's cloak of democratic government he wore to get elected President. Ortega had been hiding beneath this cloak for years, but now has come his bold wolf-like move to seal Nicaragua's fate as a totalitarian police state. Ortega's initial attempt to take power by violence in 1989 having failed, he bided his time while quietly consolidating the external support of Cuba, Venezuela, and China to bolster his internal forces. One may rightly think of the situation in Nicaragua as the "Cuban Curse," fueled by Venezuelan oil, Russian and Chinese money, and Castro's agents. To this day the unrepentant Socialist Strongman of Nicaragua continues to strengthen his grip on power, arresting and imprisoning after farcical "trials" those in political opposition to his dictatorial regime, even former revolutionary Sandinista rebels as his regime begins to "eat its own."

Zimbabwe

Another example of the "one-time, for-life" election style of Socialists is that of Zimbabwe's ruthless Marxist dictator Robert Mugabe. Mugabe was elected as a "Democratic Socialist" prime minister and president in 1980. He then engaged in tribal genocide, torture, terror and political murder to keep his regime in power for over 35 years. His regime nationalized agriculture, seized land from private farmers, redistributed wealth, and controlled prices, along with inflicting widely publicized human rights abuses. Mugabe's regime ended in 2017 via a military coup d'etat, but any transition to truly democratic government in Zimbabwe remains highly uncertain. History has shown how hard such a transformation is to accomplish. Once a society has been caught in a socialist-drugged utopian dreamland, awakening to take a different political path can be painful.

What will be Venezuela, Nicaragua, and Zimbabwe's fate, as well as that of other countries such as Argentina, Bolivia, Peru, and Chile where the monster of socialism is again on the loose? In the long run, without secure property rights and assured rule of law, what will be the outcome for their economies? Who will invest in any developing nation-state engulfed by socialism? There is a very worrisome answer in some cases. Private investors may certainly shy away from a country like Venezuela, but there are others lurking in the shadows. Venezuela's oil and mineral wealth is the Western Hemisphere's "biggest possible prize" for the United States' powerful adversaries according to former CIA Cuba analyst Brian Lattel.[24]

While Venezuela struggles to repay massive oil-backed loans from China, the CCP with its state-controlled banks and industrial enterprises could easily intervene to gain political leverage against the U.S. in the Western Hemisphere. Indeed, Russia has already slipped into Venezuela with military supplies and military personnel on the ground, much as the Soviet Union did in "aiding" Castro's regime in Cuba, which in turn supported Hugo Chavez's rise to power and the creation of his police state in Venezuela. Perhaps the abject failure of Venezuela's current regime and disintegrating economy will signal the approach of socialism's demise in the Western Hemisphere. At this point in time that favorable scenario seems doubtful given the elections of a radical Mexican President Andres Manuel Lopez

Obrador, who is now beginning to appropriate and re-nationalize American investments in Mexico's oil, gas, and electricity supply energy infrastructure, substituting historically corrupt and ideologically driven state control for the open market,[25] the Marxist leader, Pedro Castillo in Peru, and Gustavo Petro, the former M-19 guerrilla, now President of Colombia. These and a number of other struggling democracies in Latin America could follow the same path to ruin as Cuba and Venezuela. History shows that the lingering traces of socialism, like a pathological disease, can mutate and spread anew among diehard advocates in transitioning states that have yet to develop a political culture which places a high value on protecting freedom.

Notes

1. Jean-Louis Margolin, "China: A Long March into Night," in *The Black Book of Communism: Crimes, Terror, Repression*, by Courtois et al, in the Chapter "Communism in Asia," pp. 463-464.

2. Martin Malia et al, *The Soviet Tragedy: A History of Socialism in Russia, 1917 – 1991*, The Free Press, 1995: "Reform Communism," pp. 315-350; Malia describes "Reform Communism" as a break from Stalinist War Communism, which "was generated from the very moment of building socialism...an effort to humanize and liberalize the Stalinist legacy without abandoning its integral socialist nature, that is to say, planning, collective property, and the leading role of the Party" (p. 317). This phenomenon was not unique to the Soviet Union. From necessity, all communist states have tried to go down this path to one degree or another. Deng Xiaoping's moves away from the Maoist system is an example. However, it is still an open question whether it is possible to have it both ways, with liberalization and introduction of incentives on the one hand, and censorship, and strict state planning and control on the other through a one party, non-democratic system that relies on brutal repressive force (such as the Tiananmen Square massacre of pro-democracy protestors in 1989) whenever dissent rattles the leadership.

3. Evidence pro and con regarding the CCP's alleged systematic program of organ harvesting from live people is documented in a report titled "The Independent Tribunal into Forced Organ Harvesting from Prisoners of Conscience in China: JUDGEMENT, dated 1 March, 2020.

4. Examples of this recent condemnation are the Uyghur Tribunal Summary Judgement, issued December 9, 2021, Church House Westminster, of the United Kingdom, research reports by Robert Zenz, senior fellow in China Studies at the U.S.-based Victims of Communism Memorial Foundation, and passage on December 8, 2021 of bills in the U.S. House of Representatives including the Uyghur Forced Labor Act (H.R. 1155) and another condemning the ongoing genocide and crimes against humanity being committed against the Uyghurs, the Uyghur Human Rights Protection Act (H.R. 317).

5. Paramount Leader Deng Xiaoping's March 30, 1979 speech to the Chinese Communist Central Committee, *Uphold the Four Cardinal Principles* (exerpt); source: academics.wellesley.edu.

6. Matt Pottinger article in *Wall Street Journal Opinion*, March 27-28, 2021 entitled "Beijing Targets American Business," The article was adapted from a speech by Mr. Pottinger at the Hoover institution in which he quoted previously secret remarks from an important policy speech in 2013 by Xi Jinping.

7. President Xi Jinping's remarks concerning the Party's Marxist roots at an event marking the Chinese Communist Party's 95th anniversary, as reported in the July 2-3, 2016 *Wall Street Journal*: "Turning our backs or abandoning Marxism means that our Party would lose its soul and direction." In 2018 Xi later described Marxism is "totally correct" and said "the party must not forget its socialist roots" in a speech in Beijing on May 4, 2018 marking Marx's 200th birth anniversary, now referred to as the "Marx Was Right" speech. Xi also instructed all party members to read Marx's works and understand his theories as a "way of life" and a "spiritual pursuit". Those who claim to be Marxists can now see in Xi's communist dictatorship a living example of the implications.

8. Lingling Wei "Xi's Goal: Restore Mao's Economic Vision" article found at pp. A1 and A10 of September 21, 2021 *Wall Street Journal*.

9. The primary source of these quotes is *Xinhua*, Xi Jinping: Speech at the Centenary of the Founding of the Chinese Communist Party, July 1, 2021, which is discussed in *2021 Report to Congress of the U.S.-China Economic Security Review Commission, Executive Summary and Recommendations*, November, 2021, "Introduction," p. 1.

10. Timothy W. Martin, "U.S. and South Korea Recalibrate Wartime Plans for North Korea," article found at p. A9 of the December 3, 2021 *Wall Street Journal*.

11. An estimated 60,000 have successfully fled in 2016-17 according to a November 28, 2016 article in the *Wall Street Journal* written by Jose de Cordoba and Dudley Althaus, titled "Castro, in Death, Casts Long Shadow Over Cuba." These are the Western Hemisphere's "Boat People."

12. Article by Maria Abi-Habib and Eileen Sullivan in the May 4, 2022 *New York Times*, "Cuban Migrants Arrive to U.S. in Record Numbers, on Foot, Not by Boat."

13. These statements are recorded in the following Soviet archives: document 115219, the October 30, 1962 Minutes of Conversation between the Delegations of the CPCz and CPSU, The Kremlin (exerpt) which contain a summary by Nikita Khrushchev of the entire Cuban Missile Crisis episode; and document 115094 December 03, 1962 Central Committee of the Communist Party of the Soviet Union Presidium, Protocol 71; these documents are found at the Wilson Center Digital Archive – International History Declassified, http://digitalarchives.wilsoncenter.org/document/115219 and 115094; another source is Nikita Khrushchev, leader of the Soviet Union from 1953-1964, *Memoirs of Nikita Khrushchev*, Volume 3 *Statesman [1953-1964]*, Edited by Sergei Khrushchev, translated by George Shriver, 1999, 2007, The Pennsylvania State University Press, "The Cuban Missile Crisis," pp. 345 and 348.

14. January 4, 2019 article in *The Miami Herald* reported by Mario J. Penton.

15. Reported by Nina Gamez Torres in *The Miami Herald*, April 15, 2022 article "State Department says Cuba has killed, disappeared and tortured July 11 protesters."

16. F. A. Hayek, *The Road to Serfdom*, Chapter 10 - "Why the Worst Get on Top," pp. 148-167, University of Chicago Press, 1994.

17. Quote attributed to Stalin in *Memoirs of Stalin's Former Secretary*, Boris Bazhanov's memoirs published in France in 1980. This quote is not found in Stalin's published writings. Despite its unverifiable source, this thinking is entirely consistent with Stalin's and the Bolshevik's methods to create the illusion of following a democratic process, and his utter distain for honest elections to select from among competing candidates and ideas. The language quoted by Bazhanov is: "I consider it is completely unimportant who in the party will vote, or how; but what is extraordinarily important is this – who will count the votes and how." This is obviously a dictator's distain for any sort of democratic process.

18. Alexandr I. Solzhenitsyn, *Warning to the Western World*, BBC Interview March 1976, pp. 43-44 Bodley Head and British Broadcasting Corp., 1976.

19. Sidney and Beatrice Webb, *Soviet Communism: a New Civilization?*, Sribner and Sons, published in 1936, Chapter XII "The Good Life," p. 1036; Vladimir Lenin "is said to have observed in his epigrammatic way: 'It is true that liberty is precious – so precious that it must be rationed.'"; in a footnote the Webb's attempt to draw a parallel between Lenin's reference to rationing liberty to Britain's use of sugar ration cards in WWI; however, it is quite a stretch

to compare government rationing of scarce essential commodities during a wartime emergency that assures everyone gets an equal share, to the socialist idea of rationing liberty. We can never know for certain the full intent of Lenin's statement, but perhaps the idea is that under socialism it is the government's intent to make liberty scarce, so that it can "ration" it, reflecting its fulsome control of its subjects.

20. On September 16, 2020 the United Nations released a report prepared by a UN-appointed human rights panel; It concluded that grave rights violations by Maduro security forces against anti-government protesters in Venezuela "amounted to crimes against humanity." The panel, the Independent International Fact-Finding Mission on Venezuela, appointed by the Human Rights Council in Geneva on September 27, 2019, cited evidence of unlawful executions, enforced disappearances, arbitrary detentions, and torture. The panel accuses Maduro of personally giving orders to his Bolivarian National Intelligence Service (SEBIN) as to who to target, and to ensure the commission of crimes. They "investigated or reviewed 140 operations which resulted in 413 people being killed, sometimes shot at point blank range." The news report urging accountability, and detailed findings released on September 16, 2020 can be found respectively at www.news.un.org, September 16, 2020, and www.ohchr.org/EN/HRBodies?HRC/FFMV/Pages?Index.aspx.

21. *Daily Mail*, U.K., reporting on statement in *Diario las Americas* August 11, 2015 by Pete D'amato, titled "Being the ex-President's Daughter pays off: Hugo Chavez's ambassador daughter is Venezuela's richest woman." At the time of that article, she reportedly had assets in Andorran banks worth almost $4.2 billion.

22. Stephen B. Kaplan and Michael Penfold, "China and Russia have deep financial ties to Venezuela. Here's what's at stake," February 22, 2019 *The Washington Post*, Analysis.

23. Words of a former Sandanista reported by BBC News on September 6, 2018 referring to Daniel Ortega's Socialist dictatorship.

24. Brian Lattel, former CIA Cuba analyst, *Castro's Secrets: The CIA and Cuba's Intelligence Machine*, p. 73 and 81, Palgrave Macmillan, 2012.

25 Mary Anastasia O'Grady, "Mexico Moves to Seize American Assets," found at p. A15 in October 18, 2021 *Wall Street Journal*.

CHAPTER EIGHT

Monster on Our Doorstep

*"We will ask a man (any man) are you for us or against us?
If he says against us, we will stand him up against a wall."*

— Vladimir Lenin

The Epochal Struggle for Hearts and Minds

The seeds of modern socialism were sown in Revolutionary France. After a long gestation period that included Marx and Engel's decisive influence and the stillborn socialist revolution of the Paris Commune in 1871-72, it violently burst forth in 1917 Russia. In that vast autocratic czarist empire, socialism was transformed from a radical political and economic ideology into a totalitarian non-democratic revolutionary movement where men of great ambition, will to power, and passion for force seized control of the apparatuses of governmental authority. There, the Marxian synthesis of socialism's two hereditary strains described by Lichtheim, ideological theory with revolutionary activism,[1] finally manifested itself in a paroxysm of blood, death, and destruction that shook the world. Lenin, as Robespierre before him, no doubt believed that what he did was somehow justified because "the spirit of the nation" demanded it.[2] Instead it was his totalitarian self-deification that allowed the dark side of his nature and that of his Marxist followers to be released.

So, have the demons supplying socialism's primal energy now been spent? Are there no more tyrants lurking on the horizon? We would do well to remember John Maynard Keynes' admonishment that: "The ideas of economists and political philosophers, both when they are right and when they are wrong, are more powerful than is commonly understood...Madmen in authority, who hear voices in the air, are distilling their frenzy from some academic scribbler of a few years back."[3]

They are certainly *not* finished. Mankind will continue to wrestle with this monster of our own creation, a struggle that will mark an epoch of history. Advocates and apologists for socialism in the West continue to propagate their influence from the institutions they occupy, even as their societies are threatened externally with the prospect of a new cold (or hot!) war with the forces of resurgent socialism under national banners. Unless Russia's Putin manages to reconstitute the USSR, socialism's principal sponsor on the world scene will be an ideologically regressive, quite powerful, and highly nationalistic China. A malevolent and aggressive anti-democratic alliance of socialist China, fascist-like Russia, totalitarian North Korea, and theocratic Iran is even possible. The West's will and the means to defend its free institutions are simultaneously being undermined internally by the alignment of socialists with racist demagogues and challenged internationally by regressive national powers with global agendas inimical to individual freedom and rights.

Although socialist/Marxist/communist ideology has been entirely discredited by the actual events of history, there are many in democratic capitalist societies who continue to make excuses for its crimes against humanity. These zombie dreamers cling to the fantasy of a utopia in the face of the overwhelming atrocities that socialist ideologies have engendered. Some proponents do so from ideological purity, some because of vested interests, and some through self-deceit and an "ends justify the means" rationalization that makes them unwilling to admit their long-held beliefs are in horrific error. Others, soft socialists of a good heart filled with idealism, suffer from a blind faith that socialism still could be reshaped into a force for good in the "right hands," a conviction that allows them to live in denial of its actual, well-documented history of terror and mass murder. But for hardcore socialists, truth does not primarily stem from objective facts and reason. To them, there is always justification for coercion and always enough money for government to appropriate without being unfair or harming the economy.

Hannah Arendt referred to such thinking as "conspicuous disdain of the whole texture of reality."[4] Truth must be shaped to accord with political ideology and prophecies about the world; words and the thoughts they comprise have no veracity of their own, they must only serve the ends being sought, thus debasing language. Everywhere the Left makes inroads, the meanings of words such as freedom, equality, and justice are disfigured beyond all recognition. Human expression in any form is censored by the State. Intimidation soon gives way to punishment and violence against the innocent who possess the temerity to speak out. People are subject to arbitrary extrajudicial arrest, torture, and murder. They are rounded up and herded into prison camps for "re-education," a form of indoctrination which is like being forced to swallow toxic, polluted water from a hose jammed down one's throat.

Instead of a voluntary quest for learning, their brand of education is force-fed brainwashing for obedience, excising religious faiths, and assuring "social reliability" so that the masses are useful to the state. In such a system only the collective entity matters, not the individual people who comprise it.

Language manipulation, as an ideological craft, was highly developed in the world's totalitarian regimes over the past 100 years. It has been practiced with great skill by an invasive political vanguard, guided by socialism's tenet that reality and the truth are whatever they can be contrived to represent.

Socialists have found that their alternate reality is easier to sell to the public with a drumbeat of big, loud lies, nice sounding but deceptive half-truths, and censorship to stifle dissenting opinions and control election outcomes; it is a key to socialists' recent political gains as well as their continuing grip on power in other countries. History has shown this to be one of the first steps on the road toward institutionalized totalitarianism, whether of the socialist, fascist, racial, or theocratic kind. A frightening example is the proposal to create a "Disinformation Governance Board" in the U.S. to investigate and police speech, determining what is false or unchallengeable truth. Those who say they want to "build socialism" begin with government "cancelling" debate and censoring expression of ideas, opinions, and values, which they describe as harmful disinformation spread with evil intentions. Free speech is intolerable in the new and "better" world these utopian ideologues wish to create. Socialist reality is very much like Orwell's fictional dystopian world in 1984, a world dependent on the language of doublespeak and lies with a "Ministry of Truth" to hold it together. Their goal is to achieve complete conformity of thought and behavior supporting the new order they oversee.

Even without indoctrination, the cognitive bias that allows the long record of socialism to be ignored and the wishful thinking about the perfectibility of human nature are not easily overcome. Those with historical amnesia or plain ignorance of the past steadfastly cling to the idea that a model society can be engineered to produce perfect human beings, in Stalin's words, to "reform the human soul."[5] Ludwig von Mises wrote that every true socialist is a "disguised dictator" masking "self-deification" and love of power with a phony idealism.[6] More difficult, to acknowledge any mistake now would require errant believers to admit their political views represent a lie, and that they have been spiritually complicit in a global-scale catastrophe of inhumanity and terror, buying into the diabolical manipulation of group envy and hate justifying a world of systematic state-sponsored murder. Theirs is a landscape where the dark side of our human nature roams unchecked by reason. Maybe, as Arthur Koestler wrote in *Darkness at Noon*: "...they know there is no way back for them. They are too deeply entangled in their own past, caught in the web they had spun themselves, according to the laws of their own twisted ethics and twisted logic..."[7]

Equally sad, other victims in this social fraud, people of Russia, China, and Cuba, having lived their entire lives under socialism, were subject to its totalitarian indoctrination and thus have great difficulty in freeing themselves from a belief system force-fed to them from early childhood. For those who had actual opportunity to choose freedom but zealously embraced socialist ideology instead, no avenue exists for exculpation, so they reject their guilt or cover it with excuses and attempts at distorting history.

Lastly, the young, who have begun to experience the world outside their family but have little knowledge or appreciation of the true history of socialism, often become susceptible to alluring sirens lurking in academic institutions and entertainment who take advantage of their access to mass audiences and the trappings of intellectual or moral authority to peddle the socialist utopian vision as the way to transform a world they condemn as "all screwed up." Of course, their remedy must include taking down anyone who gets in the way.

Lenin's "useful idiots" still abound despite overwhelming evidence disclosed by survivors, dissidents, and existing archives of mind-boggling evil now carefully documented by historians following the collapse of the Soviet Union.[8] Socialist regimes have a long history of actively recruiting, co-opting, duping, or bribing malleable Western news media, writers, and intelligentsia to ignore or parrot their lies, and for use in destabilizing activities.

One example is the story of Gareth Jones. A British journalist, he fought against co-opted and compromised Western journalist colleagues and a news media mostly sympathetic to socialism. Jones revealed the horrific Holodomor famine that killed millions in the Ukraine from 1932-1933 despite hostility of the Soviet Union and its denial by a co-opted Western press corps, most notably Walter Duranty reporting in the *New York Times*. This is but one example out of thousands of the manipulation of people by socialist regimes.

Until Mikhail Gorbachev's policy of "glasnost" (openness) took effect and public access was gained to the official records of the Soviet Union in 1991 following the collapse of the USSR, the honest but absurd truth of socialism's insanity could never be publicly uttered by Left-leaning news sources lest it erode the blind faith and loyalty of their audiences to their cause! But even with the horrific revelations uncovered by those who have researched the records, what followed was a deafening silence, rather than a public accounting of that shameful history. Where are the Gareth Jones' of today who will risk telling the truth to the outrageous lies told by the Left? They are few and far between. It seems that journalism in the U. S. and much of Europe has been overrun by apologists for the Left, driven by their ideological fervor to distort and ignore the facts instead of presenting the truth.

It must be understood that the likes of Lenin, Stalin, Mao, Pol Pot, and other communist dictators did not seize power all on their own; they each had a supporting cast of ardent disciples including: dedicated ideologues, propaganda artists, and sadistic henchmen, perhaps with a lesser will to power but still possessing the same "passion for violence," to repeat a phrase from Paul Johnson.[9] We must also remember that their path to power was paved by sympathetic journalists, and intelligentsia. All these useful idiots needed was a strong, charismatic leader with bogus theories to point them in the "politically correct" direction. Journalists who either because of their egos, gullibility, flightiness, or ideological bias turned a blind eye and failed to publicly expose and condemn these gangster regimes bear a special responsibility for these crimes and today's rebirth of socialism.

As Lenin casually observed, "Classes are led by parties and parties are led by individuals called leaders...This is the ABC. *The will of a class is sometimes fulfilled by a dictator.*"[10]

In addition to the Liberation Theologians, numerous other enablers and intellectual co-sponsors should be included among the cast of useful idiots; I speak of arrogant, morally supple Western academics, celebrities, and other notable figures who think it fashionable to wear Che Guevara tee shirts, honeymoon in communist countries, and explicitly or implicitly cheer on the likes of Kim Il Sung, Ho Chi Minh, Pol Pot, and Castro, not to mention lesser known 'little Stalins" of the recent past like the Albania's, Enver Hoxha, Nicolae Ceausescu in Romania, and Erich Honecker in East Germany

It is truly frightening that yet today, ignoring uncomfortable truths about the past now more fully revealed, new movements are gaining strength in Russia itself, glorifying the reign of history's most heinous totalitarian dictators. Decades have passed, and the murdered millions cannot speak directly to the living. Regrettably, many Russians and some who are ignorant of their own actual socialist history now yearn for the past and their lost national pride, not having themselves experienced the deadly purges, induced famines, and gulags. Certainly, there are some among Russia's leadership who would even favor reconstituting the USSR, reestablishing its former empire by force. They may only be aware that Stalin led "Mother Russia" to victory in the "Great Patriotic War" (i.e., WW II), a cataclysmic crucible that largely defined their nation for the generations since. A report by James Marson in the *Wall Street Journal*, "Russian Fights For Stalin's Victims" revealed recent polling of the Russian public that shows nearly a quarter now believe Stalin's repressions were justified, and half of the population do not consider his ordering the murder of millions of their countrymen, women, and children to have been a crime because it was some-how "necessary"![11] Although public opinion is indeed elusive and constantly shifting, a growing and willful moral blindness, or simple historical ignorance indicated by this recent trend in Russia should frighten us all, especially since this mass amnesia is not constrained to that country alone.

Those who love liberty should most fear the new socialism in Western democracies in the early 21st Century—the power-seeking, media-savvy professional activists, propagandists, and organizers of utopian political movements and violent protests. Recall the Bolshevik boast: "With an iron fist we'll chase humanity into happiness."[12]

As the new progressive Left gains a political following, rioters and henchmen with iron fists wearing black hoods and masks looking for people to attack are not far behind. In Hannah Arendt's words, "We should be fearful of those who believe in human omnipotence, who think everything is possible if one knows how to organize the masses for it."[13]

Garry Kasparov, once a subject of the Soviet Union and now chairman of the New York-based Human Rights Foundation explained his concern this way: "The story of human progress is striving, dreaming and sacrificing for a better future. Instead of believing that happy successful individuals make for a successful society, socialism insists that a perfectly functioning system will produce happy individuals. When the system comes first, the individual is an afterthought. When the system fails, individuals are blamed for not surrendering enough."[14] Then we and all other shirkers, reactionaries, and enemies of the people must be pounded into malleable clay, driving out our individuality, so that we can be reformed to fit into the compulsory socialist mold.

Unmistakable Signs of the Undead Monster's Approach

There is a pacifistic utopian assumption prevailing in some quarters that the World's democracies needn't defend their way of life from the onslaught of totalitarian ideologies. Because most of revolutionary socialism's manifestations occurred before 1990 and its most infamous cult figures have now passed into history, one might assume that the era of socialist dystopias is also quietly vanishing. So, why be concerned about a revival? Let me once again quote Alexandr Solzhenitsyn's warning to all humanity:

> Modern society is hypnotized by socialism. It is prevented by socialism from seeing the mortal danger it is in. And one of the greatest dangers of all is that you have lost all sense of danger, you cannot even see where its coming from as it moves swiftly toward you.[15]

Despite the superiority and recent spread of liberal democracy and capitalism with their incumbent political equality and open markets, it would be foolish to make the Marxian mistake of believing in historical inevitability.

History gives little reason to put trust in the natural ascendency and global embrace of democratic principles and the final demise of socialism, racial ideologies, and theocracies. It is true that democracy's overwhelming success has raised much of humanity from a hand-to-mouth existence in just the past 200 years. However, the spirit of such a pluralistic, practical, and natural system where better ideas flourish, Michael Novak has observed, is not easily described by a lofty turn of phrase on the order of socialism's phony "equality for all."[16] In the final analysis, as Voltaire put it, we must deal with the world as it truly is, a world on no certain immutable track to betterment or worsening. That means we must continually "tend to our garden" of liberty and human dignity if we desire to keep it.[17]

There are many clear signs of the approaching danger of socialism's reincarnation.

China's Plan for a New World Order

A large swath of Asia including China, North Korea, Vietnam, and Laos, along with parts of Latin America and Africa, are still in the iron grip of totalitarianism. There is little freedom of expression or civil rights and no truly open elections. Today in China a class of political elites representing a mere 6.6 percent of China's population determine the fate of the other 93.4 percent, or 1.25 billion people.

Clearly, in our 21st Century world, slavery has not been extinguished. It is not only evident in their brutal treatment of disfavored groups like the Uyghurs, but continues in the institutionalized forms of ubiquitous State surveillance and coercive control of people, including their labor, what they can read and communicate to others, the practice of their religion, and even their reproduction. But China's aims are by no means limited to China. It wishes to shape a world along the lines of its totalitarian model in which it becomes dominant and there is no place for democracy and capitalism. Despite the Soviet Union's failure, the CCP now plans to make Marx's vision of international socialism a reality.

Also consider the significance of the CCP now extending its intolerance of dissent into previously free Hong Kong, where its police now boldly abduct and punish anyone it considers disloyal to comrade Xi's Party and the inviolate "Four Principles" of Chinese Marxism. To apply Mao's analogy, one of every fifteen Chinese is therefore a "seed" while the rest, the dehumanized masses, are treated as mere "soil" to be commanded and exploited at will by the Party with its unchallengeable monopoly on political power.

While China regresses toward totalitarianism, several Latin American countries such as Venezuela, Bolivia, Chile, Nicaragua, and even Mexico, with a weak or non-existent legacy of political liberalism, have political parties that are openly Marxist-Leninist. As collective memories fade and are suppressed by a Left that has re-infiltrated education and media institutions, a resurgence of socialism certainly cannot be ruled out in those countries as well.

China is Dramatically Ramping-up Both Soft and Hard Espionage Against Western Nations

Since the ascendance of Xi Jinping in 2012, the CCP has had a massive surreptitious campaign underway to undermine the West, particularly the United States, by poisoning those institutions which guard the values and transmit the information critical to the functioning of democracy. In so doing, the CCP has taken advantage of the dreamy notion of many among the West's intelligentsia that through "constructive engagement" China would liberalize and behave less aggressively. The expectation was that China would then become a happy member of the family of nations, embracing shared norms of open exchange and free trade. Instead, with the growing financial and trade power they possess the dedicated Marxists in Beijing, true to their creed and taking a page from the Communist International (Comintern), use their leverage to support Leftist organizations worldwide, quietly infiltrating Western universities, news media, entertainment, corporations, non-profits, and even governmental institutions. They have for example set up numerous so-called "Confucius Institutes" at American universities to spread Chinese propaganda and discourage any questioning of the CCP's human rights abuses and geopolitical aggressiveness. Key international organizations like the World Health Organization are also included in the CCP's strategy. The Party's strategy is to essentially bribe these organizations and institutions to whitewash or at least turn a blind eye toward China's increasing hostility and aggression, and to mask China's extensive engagement in industrial and research espionage. Placing all nations and their populations within their orbit of control is the CCP's obvious goal, requiring that it unceasingly multiply its power until nothing remains that can oppose its aggression.

This growth in power is predicated on it taking control of the "truth," of words, of internal ethnic and religious groups (e.g., the Tibetans, Uyghurs, adherents of Islam, Falun Gong, and Christianity), and even changing the facts of history itself. The hybridized quasi-capitalist regime in China has renewed its commitment to its totalitarian roots and is intent on expanding its power and influence into other parts of the world. We are all now beginning to feel its weight on our backs. Like it or not, China now possesses enormous economic and miliary power with which to back up its ambitions.

Marxist Insurgent Groups are not a Thing of the Past

There still exist numerous violent insurgent groups in third-world countries aiming to emulate Fidel Castro's transformation of Cuba into a communist police state. These include the National Democratic Front in the Philippines, FARC and ELN in Columbia, the Zapatista (ELZN) in Mexico, and smaller groups in Paraguay and Bolivia. Such Latin American insurgent groups and their cousins in Somalia, Nigeria, Congo, and other places appear immune to reason and are more than willing to terrorize their fellow citizens. These groups are applauded by radical Leftists who, while comfortably enjoying the freedom and prosperity of democratic capitalist societies, resolutely undermine any attempts to aid those resisting Marxist revolutionaries.

The Dark Side of Technology

Technology has provided new tools that enable governments and other powerful organizations, along with the socialist "virtucrats" embedded in them, to gather and process data with which to monitor and control the behavior of individuals and functioning of whole economies, recalling Dostoevsky's view that the Enlightenment has a dark side as well. The same can be said of the present era of powerful, low-cost, integrated video, telephone and internet surveillance and location tracking, computing, communications, and software including artificial intelligence. Certainly, as these technical innovations have progressed and come to function together they have resulted in enormous social and economic benefits throughout the world. But by the same token, integrated modern technologies now enable a whole new level of state control of citizens and interference in the affairs of other nations. We are rapidly approaching the point at which every corner and crevice of human activity can be remotely monitored, tracked, and evaluated for signs of individuals' disloyalty or disobedience by large state-run organizations dedicated to shaping human thoughts and controlling their interactions and behaviors.

Consistent with socialist doctrine, the purpose of such deep intrusion by governmental authorities into people's lives is to deter or destroy any potential threat to their authority and encourage obedience to their diktats. Far from discouraging government, private tech corporations are complicit in this intrusion when they find it advantageous and enable it to a great degree. Gone is any distinction between a person's private and public life. During the last century secret police were forced to rely far more on human systems of physical surveillance, manual record-keeping, and networks of spies and informers, aided only by wiretapping. Electronic systems today are not only a great aide to socialist police states such as China, North Korea, and Cuba, but are also increasingly being used in democratic nations, though hopefully with less sinister goals such as finding and apprehending true criminals and terrorists, rather than suppressing political dissent.

But it is not government actions alone that we need be concerned about. In the West certain politically unaccountable leaders of mega-corporations in the communications, financial, and tech sectors have been manipulating public information, and in some cases using their corporate leverage to greatly magnify the Left's ability to achieve a socialist political agenda.

These technologies can be abused in yet other ways, that is, surreptitiously used as an offensive weapon. In addition to all-encompassing and continuous surveillance, powerful cyberweapons can be used strategically to quietly tilt or otherwise compromise democratic elections, or to attack infrastructure systems such as electrical grids to cause social discord, if not outright chaos. The open internet and social media also provide perfect vehicles for organizing and activating underground agitation-propaganda ("agitprop") operations aimed at destabilizing government, spreading misinformation about people and events, and playing dirty tricks on political targets. With their sources of funding hidden by various front organizations, activist groups are using social networks to engage in violent protests and media-promoted events that involve quickly planned gatherings and "spontaneous" attacks on any opposing their Leftist agenda. These groups sprout up overnight like "poisonous mushrooms" from the socialist rot inhabiting our academic and media institutions, long sheltered from the cleansing forces of truth, intellectual honesty, and reality. Now these radical groups are empowered by new technologies and the amplifying bullhorn of globally connected social networks.

Leftist Alliances and Networks are Proliferating and Becoming Bolder

Still deeply rooted within the relatively stable and prosperous Western democracies, socialism is being nurtured and perpetuated by a vast network of progressive and radical Left-wing organizations. Some are overt, such as the admittedly socialist political parties that have formed their own alliances with the hostile regimes in China, Cuba, and other totalitarian countries, dedicated enemies of freedom and democracy. This is reminiscent of the fondness shown to North Vietnam's communist regime by anti-war activists during the Vietnam War.

For example, one can see from their publications that the U.S. Marxist-Leninist Workers World Party has aligned itself with both Kim Jong-un's North Korea, communist Cuba, Daniel Ortega's Nicaragua dictatorship, and the Chinese Communist

Party (CCP). The Freedom Socialist Party supports the communist regime in Cuba. The Communist Party USA considers the CCP a fraternal comrade in their shared goal of promoting Marxism to create "world socialism in the 21st century." The Democratic Socialists of America Party was listed in 2015 as a full member of The Socialist International, an organization headquartered in London. They all explicitly or tacitly embrace the idea expressed in the slogan that "capitalism is the disease, and socialism is the cure."[18]

Some are more surreptitious in their efforts to delegitimize and otherwise subvert their freely elected democratic governments. These include socialist front organizations that try to poison rational debate in a democracy and give themselves patriotic or compassionate-sounding names for the sake of respectability[19] while demonizing those who resist the radical Left. Campus "safe-spaces," another Leftist debasement of language, are only safe for socialist propaganda, not for alternative views. The honest debate upon which democracy depends has become impossible in such places.

There are many older advocates of socialism who have preached the overthrow of governments and destruction of capitalism while singing the praises of totalitarian Marxist regimes but have never acknowledged an intellectual comradeship with the immense socialist-caused carnage of the 20th Century. Some have risen to positions of influence, assuming prominent leadership roles in key organizations and institutions. This includes many senior college faculty, particularly in the social sciences, journalists, and editors in news media, those in literature and entertainment, staff of well-funded non-governmental organizations (NGOs), and even some of those within capitalist enterprises.

Left-wing activist NGOs have proliferated like noxious weeds with the help of funding from the likes of the Ford Foundation and the Hewlett Foundation, whose most recent funding goal is to "reimagine capitalism" at leading academic institutions, and the Open Society Foundations.[20] These and numerous other non-profits quietly pour many millions into anti-capitalist Left-wing causes. The Ford and Open Society Foundations ironically use their multi-billion-dollar "philanthropic" endowments from capitalist benefactors to strategically support NGO partisan advocacy that influences election outcomes, and otherwise promote their agenda to transform society according to the wishes of the small group of people who control them.

Cultivating a Mindless Will to Goodness

We are now seeing that after a thirty-year hiatus following the demise of the Soviet Union and fall of the Iron Curtain, many true believers have been able to secure positions from which they are able to propagate socialist ideology without being challenged by contemporaries as they would have been during the Cold War era. Some of the younger generation who have been indoctrinated proudly self-identify as "social justice warriors," no doubt possessing what former Communist Party member Bella Dodd called a mindless "will to goodness."[21] Indignant, motivated by emotional idealism, and armed with sanitized interpretations of Marx, they are thrilled at the prospect of militant activism for the cause of a better world, but blind to all the harm they may cause. Because the complete story of socialism was withheld from them, these latest disciples rarely demonstrate any knowledge of past socialist debacles nor any doubts outside their own fervent enthusiasm. With a few exceptions like China and North Korea, reports of the most horrific atrocities committed by socialist regimes have faded into a distant past. In blissful ignorance, new socialists are prone to ignore the signs around them and abundant historical evidence of what Koestler rightly called "the moral and intellectual debauch" of socialism.[22]

Then again, many of the younger adherents who came to

adulthood in the 1990's or afterwards are intellectual offspring of the 1960's revolutionary generation. This remnant, some now entrenched in tenured educational positions, or retired, are holdovers who continue to passionately believe in their "Power to the People" slogans even after their communal "Love Generation" movement was discredited by drug use, rioting, and the revelations of massive atrocities. Such vestiges of the late 1960's and early 1970's may consider themselves true intellectuals, but their scholarly development and moral discernment appears to have been frozen long ago, perhaps a lasting side effect of the emotionally driven causes implanted in their hearts a half-century ago.

Included among these elderly sympathizers are well-educated people who are or were once teachers, college professors, lawyers, news writers, community and "public interest" group organizers, entertainers, and even clergy of various religious denominations. In effect, a great many value-shaping institutions in America and Europe have been "colonized" by the Left since the 1960's to a point where Leftist doctrine, completely intolerant of other views, is now dominant.

At least some of such long-time true believers fit the description penned by author and former 1960's radical David Horowitz of "arm-chair revolutionaries" who "project their self-hatred and their contempt for the privileges of democracy—which allow them to live well and think badly—onto people who would be only too grateful for the luxuries they distain."[23]

Patiently waiting on the sidelines with little political influence during the Cold War, they became deeply embedded in Western institutions, and gradually bolder. The meaning of "Power to the People" subtly changed. The goal became an ever-expanding welfare state to be run by bureaucrats, justified by new rights for self-defined victims of society's privileged few. Now the new mantra should become "Power *Over* the People," representing an arrogant desire for both the political and cultural power to dictate what people should want, do, say, and even think. They surely count themselves among society's intellectual elites. Socialism's utopian promise appeals to both a craving for social justice, and the idealist's love of a formula for curing human frailties, both of which should result from their superior intelligence and will to "get things done."[24]

Language and Speech Control

Free speech is under attack and language is being debased into doublespeak as the Left consolidates its gains from capturing the "commanding Heights" of the West's cultural institutions in the last five decades. From the time of Lenin's Bolsheviks, controlling the use of words and speech has been a predicate for socialism's ascendancy, as it is for all totalitarian ideologies. Not bound by any concern for truth and reality, many organs of communication, education, and entertainment in the West have been colonized by an elite intelligentsia and used to intimidate and censor, then to propagandize and indoctrinate the unsuspecting public. Celebrities and those in positions of influence in these fields are also being employed to impose language control and quash dissenting views, destroying the reputations and careers of any who stand in their way. Dominating culture and communication, now including social media and the internet, socialists and their fellow travelers can spread clever falsehoods that hide their agenda and destroy the lives of those who oppose. Vicious and obscene language is also employed to intimidate voters and politicians, and to attack those few in media or academia who have the temerity to publicly speak out. Great lies and great evil go hand-in-hand; should any dishonesty be exposed or factual claims discredited, they are protected by a "deafening silence" from allies in the media.

Divide to Destroy

As predicted by Malia, socialists in positions of influence in Western democracies have been successful in fracturing their societies by extending the Marxist paradigm of working class oppression and victimhood to other groups that define their identity primarily by ethnicity, gender, or sexual orientation, rather than national citizenship, and can easily be convinced they are "deprived, humiliated, offended, exploited, or victimized."[25] Such "social justice" groups have proliferated in the West where they take advantage of the multiple freedoms citizens enjoy, undermining social unity and the very institutional arrangements that protect freedom. Their answer to redress all identity-based grievances, of course, is transformation of society into a much more powerful, centrally managed welfare state in which the government controls all important aspects of life, and those of the "wrong" racial identity and business owners who are not left-leaning are treated as the enemy. Their ultimate goal is for the wealth and the fruits of individual success to be pooled for redistribution through a variety of government programs to their most loyal supporters and members of such "victimized" identity groups, whether or not particular recipients in the group have themselves truly experienced oppression of any kind. To that end, progressives and socialists, or by whatever label they use, are now actively seeking to undermine norms that foster social cohesion, and to transform institutions that help secure the normal functioning of society into instrumentalities of the Left. This includes educational, public health, prosecutorial, police, social service, border security, and tax collection agencies. We have even seen the Left boldly attacking the independent judiciary so vital to citizens' equal rights, by intimidation and threats of legislative court "packing" possible in a democracy only when Tocqueville's dreaded "tyranny of the majority" has come about.

Re-emergence of Racial Socialism

The most dangerous example of divide to destroy is what I have termed "Racial or Tribal Socialism" which has begun to take root in ethnically diverse nations. Latent racial animosities can be aroused and "weaponized" in diverse communities by racist demagogues, much like Hitler blamed the Jews for most of Germany's ills. When fused with the envy and hate-based doctrine of class oppression, these smoldering animosities form an explosive mixture and have the potential to blow society completely apart. A deformed history such as the 1619 Project, and the teaching of Critical Race Theory, are but two of the latest examples in the United States.

The totalitarian-minded posing as advocates of social justice emulate the Nazi strategy by portraying members of ethnic or racial groups who enjoy somewhat greater wealth and status as perpetrators of economic unfairness, seeking to sow and politically manipulate racial divisions in hope the resulting disorder will create opportunities to take power. They promise to fundamentally transform society by stripping the targeted racial group of its privileges and ill-gotten gains.

Pitting one racial group against another to produce mutual mistrust and antipathy is not only Hitleresque, but also one of the strategies prescribed by the Comintern for use by communist cells in the West to undermine capitalist nations through social conflict. Worse, in addition to disabling and unravelling democratic societies, racially-based wealth redistribution would soon destroy the hard-won, race-blind ethical principles and laws upon which human rights, freedom, and democracy depend.

The seeds of Tribal Socialism and its claims about which lives especially "matter" are now bearing poisonous fruit of racial discord, along with the frightening reappearance of pseudo-scientific "race theory," a concept first developed by certain racist European intellectuals.

True Believers are Immune to Facts

History has demonstrated that belief in a cause often trumps factual knowledge and reason. As Goethe's Faust says,

"A man sees in the world what he carries in his heart," a sentiment echoed by philosopher Michael Novak.[26]

> Ideas, always a part of reality, have today acquired power greater than that of reality. One of the most astonishing characteristics of our age is that ideas, even false and unworkable ideas...rule the affairs of men and run roughshod over stubborn facts. Ideas of enormous destructiveness, cruelty, and impracticality retain the allegiance of elites that benefit from them...The class of persons who earn their livelihood from the making of ideas and symbols seems both bewitched by falsehoods and absurdities and uniquely empowered to impose them upon hapless individuals.[27]

Equipped with cleverly presented ideas, arrogant and unrepentant true believers found a haven within the West's political, academic, and other value-shaping institutions. With zombie-like immunity to the facts about their creed they march on. The academic Left has now succeeded in establishing college campuses as "safe places" that protect only the propaganda of Leftist ideology, obliterating universities' historical commitment to free speech, genuine scientific inquiry, and critical thinking. Merely repackaging Marx and Lenin to appear fresh, these people constitute another generation of hard-Left activists seducing the ignorant, insecure, or impressionable young through orchestrated, incessant intellectual debauchery. Having never actually lived under a truly socialist regime, these apologists maintain that by concentrating more power in the State, their doctrine will peacefully demolish then reconstruct society from the ground up according to a "holistic social blueprint."[28] Their goal is to fundamentally transform mankind's future into the vastly better social order, despite the logical impossibility of any evidence whatsoever of the promised outcome.

Completely undeterred by the socialist disasters of the past century, for them government with greater power to intervene is the remedy to society's ills and will finally transform mankind's future into a new and perfect world order. Belief in their righteous cause is impervious to rational argument and contrary facts. All that is required to achieve the Socialist Utopia is political power, whether gained through elections or not. As one of China's Communist Party newspapers insisted: "The human will is the master of all things," while Party henchmen were indeed dutifully imposing Mao's will, pitilessly starving to death tens of millions in the Great Leap Forward. Utopian ideals and the power of ideas still impel today's socialist apostles to proselytize from positions of growing influence in Western societies. Their effort to legitimize and revive the *failed* socialist ideas of the past century continue wherever such ideas can find receptive ears.

Elites Openly Declaring Their Marxism are Gaining Political Influence in the Capitalist West

Self-proclaimed Socialists are emboldened by their ideological gains and eager to take concrete power and control the levers of government. In orchestrated "townhalls" or debates and nightly cable news programs they boldly proclaim the benefits of a larger and more powerful government while seeking high-level legislative and executive public office, and key bureaucratic appointments. In Europe, Latin America, and even in the United States, socialist political candidates have managed to score victories unthinkable only a few years ago. Reinhold Niebuhr observed of human nature, there are always going to be messianic ideologues lurking in society who are tempted to play God and "dream of mastering history."[29] Indeed, support for such earthly messiahs often comes from ordinary citizens who can be so anxious about the future that they wish, in Eric Fromm's words, to "escape from freedom."[30]

Like many victims before them, citizens in democratic societies are now being duped into giving more and more control over their lives in exchange for promises of a secure future in which they will be well taken care of and provided with "free stuff" by the government. Some want to be cared for from the cradle to the grave by society-at-large, living like dependent children who never grow up, rather than relying on themselves as free individuals.

The observation by American author S. P. Orth in his 1913 book *Socialism and Democracy in Europe* is as true today as it was then: "Socialism has organized the largest body of human beings that the world has known. Its international organization has but one rival for homogeneity and zeal—the Church." Orth attributed this growth to the quasi-religious zeal of its devotees and effective use of propaganda.[31] We have seen how socialism is, for all intents and purposes, a perverted secular form of religion for its adherents. The psychological appeal of socialism to humanity's weaknesses has not diminished and in fact has increased in recent days.

Thus, the history of socialism did not end with the collapse of the Soviet Empire. The stench of death from socialist utopianism once again began to seep from parts of the globe while Westerners were busy celebrating the end of the Cold War and the fall of communism. Unfortunately, within the Western World's institutions, particular universities, news media, non-profit and non-governmental organizations, reason and memory have largely been on holiday since 1990 as they increasingly promote left-wing ideas. Take for example the left-friendly *New York Times*, *Washington Post*, *The New Yorker*, *Atlantic*, and *The New Republic*, a plethora of cable news networks including CNN and MSNBC, and powerful tech media giants such as Facebook and Twitter. In academia, prominent New Left-Socialist intellectuals such as Herbert Marcuse, Noam Chomsky, and Howard Zinn, had an impact extending far beyond the confines of the institutions they were part of as their teachings have been absorbed and echoed by each new crop of true believers. Many of the U.S. top-tier universities either had or now have faculty who identify with the radical Left. The list includes institutions such as Columbia, Princeton, MIT, Brandeis, and Boston University, to name just a few. Today the breadth of socialism's influence can be seen virtually everywhere in the American academic scene.

Various surveys taken over the last 20 years have recorded that the number of faculty who count themselves as left-leaning outnumber those who are conservative by ratios from 10:1 to 30:1. The Left's influence is particularly strong in the social sciences and humanities. In 2006 it was found that over 20 percent of American social science and humanities faculty members considered themselves radical activists, and over 25 percent of those in sociology identified as Marxist.[32] A 2018 survey of political affiliations in the faculty of top-tier liberal arts colleges found that nearly 40 percent had no conservatives at all on their faculty.[33]

An example of Marxist programming offered at universities is the University of Maine's Socialist and Marxist Studies Series that draws upon faculty in History, Philosophy, Anthropology, and Political Science. A summary of one of its 2021 programs is titled "Development: Modern Capitalist Perspectives and Gandhi-informed and Marx-informed Socialist Perspectives:"

> What does it mean to submit that an individual, economy, society, culture, religion, civilization, nation, or world is at a high level of development? Why are modern capitalist perspectives structurally exploitative, amoral and immoral, violent, alienating, dehumanizing, destructive, and unsustainable? We'll present creatively formulated Gandhi-informed and Marx-informed perspectives offering a higher level of human and global development.

Another is titled "Karl Marx in 2020:"

> How does Marx help us to understand conflict-based theories of change?... How can an updating of Marx's social vision inform a defense of worker-managed market socialism? How can

Marx's vision of 'from each according to his work' to 'each according to need' inform recent work on basic income? How can Marx's historical dialectical approach provide the most insightful analysis of class relations, exploitation, oppression, corporate domination, globalization, and imperialism? How does Marx allow us to understand alienation and meaninglessness today, and how we can express social and moral development and unalienated human flourishing?[34]

The United Kingdom has experienced a similar marked leftward political tilt in its academic institutions since the 1960's.[35] The UK has a network of university students named the "Marxist Student Federation," which claims membership of roughly 3,500 students at 48 leading universities, including Cambridge and Oxford. On their website they call themselves "Marxists" and "revolutionaries," and refer to each other as "Comrade." They teach Marxist theory, echoing Lenin's "without revolutionary theory there can be no revolutionary movement," with a call to "Unite and Fight!"[36]

To undertake a serious research survey to determine the dominant ideologies at universities across all capitalist Western nations is well beyond the scope here, but anecdotal observations suggest that academic institutions in other countries in Europe and the "Anglosphere" are also experiencing a decades long ideological slide to the left. In short, despite all the horrific examples of the past century documented in *The Black Book of Communism* and many other sources, neo-Marxists in academia, news media, and publishing throughout much of the West persist in spreading the gospel according to Marx and Engels.

Many who characterize themselves as neo-Marxists promote resurgence of a seemingly "kinder and gentler" socialism. If only such socialist leaders had been true to Marxist theory, they say, and not taken a detour into totalitarianism, the experiment would have turned out well. If only they had not been seduced to evil by their exercise of unlimited power, they would have found the key to change human nature and engineer perfected people who think and act only for the common good. Neo-Marxists are at times bold enough to claim that socialism in practice can be democratic.

In truth, socialism and democracy are fundamentally at odds. Over the long run, government under "democratic socialism" is impossible where the practice of democracy includes the rule of law and constitutional protection of economic freedom, property, and human rights. At some point it becomes clear that socialist ends cannot be achieved through democratic means, and so democracy must be choked off.

Though oft repeated, such claims by advocates of socialism that a more humanitarian leadership will avoid a repeat of its dark history are obviously not credible. With its consistent record of mass murder and terror, giving credulity to socialism's central assumption of beneficent great leaders and idealistic followers without envy and wanting only an equal share for all and nothing more for themselves alone is, to paraphrase Karl Popper, "like believing in unicorns."[37] The god of socialism brings out not the best in people but the very worst, releasing monsters within humanity from reason's control. It is a tragic paradox that as socialism destroys existing moral frameworks, it imparts an alternate, absolute moral certitude leading even the most well-intentioned to "desire the good, but create evil."[38]

It's the Ideology Stupid!

Noted historian Stephen Kotkin concluded that Stalin and his fellow Bolsheviks truly acted on the same radical ideological beliefs they proclaimed, and not simply to exercise power or out of sociopathic insanity.[39]

Lenin, Stalin, Mao, Pol Pot, the Kims, and the others who emulated them did not necessarily begin their lives predestined to become monsters. Once in power, they didn't "detour" from a noble, humane ideology in order to demand the suffering and death of millions upon millions of innocent people. On the contrary, it was socialism's ideology that required all power to be concentrated in their hands so they, like Plato's self-selected Guardians, could enforce "whatever was necessary on behalf of the proletariat."

The ideology was the brew that helped make them drunk with power, and once inebriated, each successive "shot" came easier. Many have recognized this danger. To Bertrand Russell the desire for power, like vanity, is insatiable and addictive. Nothing short of omnipotence can completely satisfy the human desire for power, and our love for power is greatly increased by the experience of it.[40] Hannah Arendt echoed this sentiment when she wrote that "Power left to itself can achieve nothing but more power, and violence administered for power's (and not for law's) sake turns into a destructive principle that will not stop until there is nothing left to violate."[41]

Movements based on using political power to achieve absolute economic equality to better the human condition in fact destroy human life, freedom and equality absolutely, degrade the human soul, and make the very justice, prosperity and peace that human beings universally crave unattainable.

In one of his lesser known quotes, Lord Acton wrote that "passion for equality makes vain the hope for freedom."[42] It is abundantly clear from the past 100 years that attempting to achieve the goal of material and social equality necessarily requires forfeiture of our natural freedom and rights, a quite predictable result of concentrating absolute power in the hands of those eager to impose their will on society no matter what.

Common experience has confirmed that government as a guarantor of an equal portion, rather than of equal rights and freedom, guarantees only shared misery.

Humanity's struggle against the utopian beast continues to haunt both history and contemporary society. What will it take to eradicate this insidious ideological disease? What will it take to inoculate society against this scourge that afflicts the entire body politic and feeds off envy, ignorance of the past, naivete, dreamy idealism, and above all, a lust for limitless all-corrupting power? Can we ever stop Man's narcissistic attempts to play God? Can this conceit ever be eradicated? Whether we want to acknowledge it or not, we remain locked in a struggle with utopian evil for the very survival of democracy, true liberalism and the freedom of mankind.

Liberty and reason must prevail in this struggle, but not through the nihilistic class struggle taught by the likes of Marx, Lenin, Mao, and others of their ilk. This epochal confrontation is not one of class versus class prophesied by Marx; it is more fundamental than that. We fight not against classes, nor against races or true religions, but against an inhuman secular religion that believes the human will is the master of all things, including the ability to transform and perfect human nature itself, remaking men and women into entirely selfless beings. Our battle therefore is one of good against an evil that is insidious and all-encompassing, with roots in utopian idealism, arrogance, and a perverted concept of justice and human nature. We have every right, and even an obligation to be worried. In the end, the outcome for society depends upon what actions we, as individuals, do or do not take.

The essence of the confict, then, is defending "ownership" of your own life and the products of your efforts, instead of gradually relinquishing them to a soulless state. It demands humility and realism while opposing pretense and delusional hubris to avoid becoming "an accomplice in men's fatal striving to control society—a striving which makes him not only a tyrant over his fellows, but which may well make him a destroyer of a civilization which no brain has designed, but which has grown from the free efforts of millions of individuals."[43]

Cold Facts and Delusion's Warm Embrace

It is hard for us to wrap our minds around the fact that

close to 100 million innocent people died as a result of utopian experimentation in the 20th Century alone. The very magnitude can leave any person feeling numb and powerless. But the whole socialist-Marxist-communist movement is a cult of irrationality, and as such, impervious to any honest inquiry into its true nature. Its believers must attack and destroy all those who dare question their "jealous god" because the world has seen that their utopian promises and plans inevitably backfire. There is no fact or logic that can support their delusions. All they can argue is that there is a continuum of material well-being in the current reality which they promise to radically change. Freud noted that "No one, needless to say, who shares a delusion ever recognizes it as such."[44] *Folie à deux* is not synonymous with truth.

Stalin may very well have been right when he cold-heartedly offered, "If only one man dies of hunger, that is a tragedy. If millions die, that's only statistics." He, like Mao, held that the smaller the population, the lesser the problem, so mass death can be of benefit to the cause! Unfortunately, all governments, even good ones, tend to focus on statistics, not on individual humans and their individual needs, aspirations, joys, and tragedies.

It is crucial that we not become complacent in our Western democracies and view the suffering of those in Chinese internment camps, North Korean gulags, or Cuban prisons as mere data to be viewed and analyzed. If we do, we ourselves are likely to accelerate a long slide down the slippery slope that leads to a perpetual lure of "free" health care, "free" college education, and a promise of so-called social justice, income "security," and income equality. Rather than life, liberty, and the pursuit of happiness being our legacy, we, our children, and our grandchildren could well join the tragic statistics in a future history book.

Some today try to trivialize objections to socialism by

characterizing it as a narrow question of economics, a comparison of the relative material efficiency of an economic system based on state command and control on the one hand and laissez faire markets and private ownership on the other. But this is a delusion. As Eastman saw clearly, there is no moral distinction possible between the socialist economy and "its depraved politics."[45] It is a holistic and indivisible ideology.

Intended or not, merely relegating the subject of socialism to an argument about economics during an election campaign is the kind of deception that conveniently ignores the oppressive and ruthless nature of a socialist State. Yet, a limited, shallow discussion is all that one typically encounters in the world of liberal media, academia, and progressive politics.

We must oppose well beyond any election year an evil that insists that all people are mere creatures of the State and exist to serve it, rather than the State existing to protect the rights of its people. Human life has intrinsic value far beyond just economic utility to the State, which contends that democratic values such as impartial treatment under the law, an equal say in government, and support for those truly in need are not enough. Rather, socialists hold that all people automatically deserve, should demand, and are entitled to take an equal share of what is produced, be it money or property, no matter their choices, skills, talents, or behavior, and regardless of their contribution to society. It is a small step from the poisonous seed of envy masquerading as economic justice to righteous anger, then to politically instigated group hate, and finally to murder and plunder.

Heed the words of an 87-year-old Communist recorded by Svetlana Alexievich in *Secondhand Time:*

"First you shot the aristocrats and the priests. That was 1917. And then, in 1937, you all shot each other."[46]

Recent Danger Signals in the United States

Over a very short span of time, signs of peril and approaching danger have accelerated and confronts us now, on our doorstep where we live, not in some distant future or far-off land. Two major developments have taken place which are the latest signs of how shockingly pervasive and widely accepted the Left's influence has now become within the United States, once considered a granite-like bastion of freedom and democracy.

Pandemic Gives License to Government by Edict

The Covid pandemic brought home the growing determination of those in government with authoritarian tendencies to use administrative decrees to exercise increasing collective control of individual citizens. instead of seeking the consent of the governed expressed in democratically enacted laws. At the heart of this contest is the question of whether each person owns their own life, or does a bureaucratic authority controlled by left-leaning politicians own and direct it as they wish even when its goal is ostensibly to protect public health. That is, if there is an unavoidable trade-off between individuals' rights and freedom, and collective wellbeing, where is the line that cannot be crossed, who is empowered to make that determination, and how strong must the evidence of public benefit be?

In response to the pandemic, several Western nations ignored the right of each person to control what is done with their own body, compromising this fundamental human right by issuing blanket decrees requiring universal vaccination, physical tests, and mask-wearing. Using menacing threats of job loss, negation of health insurance, and even imprisonment, as well as denial of access to schools and other public services even against people who are not ill, and then requiring them to carry papers documenting proof of obedience. These "emergency" decrees, undertaken without the approval of legislative bodies have even been extended to children over the objections of some parents.

While vaccination may prove to be the wise choice for most adults to make, there are undoubtedly sizable segments of the population for whom it is unnecessary (e.g., existing immunity or youth), and others for whom it may even be dangerous, outweighing the risk of the disease itself. For Covid, the data currently tells us that while it is highly contagious, the average death rate for all those infected by the disease appears to be no more than one percent; for children it is virtually zero; while for those over 65 it is much greater.[47]

In an emergency such as a pandemic, people will generally accept a degree of temporary curtailment of their liberty. But in free societies, those in which people are not conditioned to automatically bow to authoritarian decrees, many are less inclined to accept commands which are not essential to crisis management, especially if they entail indefinite encroachment on their freedom and rights. Furthermore, rather than only restricting their liberty, the edicts issued in this case go a step further by prescribing certain physical actions everyone must take, a crucial distinction well-recognized in thought about human rights for centuries. Direct control of one's behavior by government threat of force is generally justifiable only in the extreme cases of public security and safety, such as legislatively approved wartime conscription for military service and incarceration of criminals arrested and convicted in a court of law. Even in genuine emergencies decrees that ignore such checks and balances smack of tyranny.

Then there is the justification that contagious viral diseases can be completely "eradicated." This implies that pure, virus-free public spaces will be created if everyone is forced to be vaccinated and their behavior controlled. This is scientifically sloppy utopian thinking at its worst, based on the false notion that government can completely master the micro-biological environment everywhere around us through sufficiently powerful acts of human will. One must ask, even if it were scientifically achievable, would people want to create and live within a bubble that is continuously sanitized? Rather than eradicating a virus microbe, we could instead be arresting the healthy development of children's immune systems and ruining human lives in a vain attempt to achieve zero disease mortality.

Yet, trade-offs are inherent in all public policy decisions involving protection of health and safety, such as air travel, road design, traffic management, building codes, food inspection, and pollution control. In other words, the full consequences, not just the targeted benefits, must be explicitly identified and weighed, especially when there is conflicting information and considerable uncertainty about the benefits. Side-effects should be carefully analyzed and never be excluded or completely discounted without due consideration in policy deliberations.

It is also impossible to ignore that these sweeping edicts are being justified with half-truths and contradictory evidence of benefits (efficacy of wearing masks indoors and outdoors, and of "social distancing"), ignoring some important facts such as the role, strength, and persistence of natural immunity, while distorting others, particularly the disease transmissibility among those vaccinated and those who have previously been infected by the disease.

It is a characteristic of a dictatorship that no one is allowed to question the basis for its commands. That is perhaps the most telling aspect of the Covid controversy. Unwilling to admit they do not have the answers to important questions, for political reasons these authorities have gone a step further toward the manner of social control found in totalitarian societies, by demanding the censorship of contrary views even as the science and the disease itself are rapidly evolving, and by publicly shaming and condemning those who resist their mandates or raise questions about their scientific justification. The state of California, a Left-wing bellwether state with a population of nearly 40 million, has passed a law that will use its Medical

Board to punish any physicians whose patient treatments or advice departs from the State's official pronouncements regarding Covid. Once again, we see the Left's pretense of being "scientific" and the final authority on facts so it can spew unchallengeable declarations and edicts and destroy any person who does not become subservient.

The Racializing of Education

Starting in the 1950's, the U.S. education system underwent a massive social reform known as school "desegregation." This paralleled the outlawing of discriminatory racial segregation in residential communities and public places. The basic goal of school desegregation was mixed race student bodies to assure that education offered to Black and White students would be comparable.

Today, regrettably, with the support of teachers' unions educational institutions from kindergarten through college are being intentionally re-racialized, but with a crucial difference. Now schools are bringing racial differences to the forefront instead of de-emphasizing students' different racial identities, but not for the purpose of achieving fair and equal treatment of all students. Rather, it is for their indoctrination in a political ideology described earlier as a re-emergent, highly toxic form of "Racial Socialism." This includes teaching a version of American history warped by neo-Marxist historians into an ideological argument.

The central theme of this new version of history is that racism, slavery, and genocide caused by the capitalist greed of European colonists made America what it is today. Under this narrative (example: the 1619 Project), the whole American economy and way of life depended upon slavery, a by-product of capitalism and, as a consequence, American society has been fundamentally evil from its very beginning. With this idea gaining strength, America is steadily drifting away from the hard-won racial integration of the Civil Rights movement toward a dark future of cultural and racial separation with an unstable truce existing between waring identity groups. But this interpretation of American society, one that calls for rejecting its very founding on moral grounds, bears only a faint resemblance to the actual, far more complicated truth of America's beginnings, its evolution toward a more just society, and today's reality.

Furthering this Marxism-inspired interpretation of history, and looking for redress, in certain parts of America a sociological/legal doctrine known as Critical Race Theory (CRT) is being introduced in educational institutions. One should not be confused by proponents' use of the word "theory." CRT is really an ideology. Students are taught to focus on their racial identity, and that of others around them, and that Black people continue to be subjected to subtle, even invisible racial discrimination by White people, an injustice Whites must change their lives to rectify. To be clear, CRT is not simply a descriptive academic theory that merely purports to better our understanding of race in society. Rather, it is a racial ideology based on Marxist principles, with the stated aim to fundamentally alter American culture and politics. By using their cultural influence and access to the educational system, its "theorists" seek to accomplish their aim without their vision and programs being subjecting to any democratic process of debate by duly elected representatives to determine if the transformation they desire accords with the will of the people.

Although initially developed by Black Marxists specifically to address their racial grievances, the theory has numerous "theorists" and adherents from other races as well, having been broadened to encompass all "victimized" groups, following Marx's socialist model as Malia foresaw. According to this theory, the way the American economy and society work is rigged against Black people, and others "of color," regardless of White peoples' intent and a system of laws assuring equal civil rights and forbidding racial, ethnic, or gender discrimination, enforced by the federal Department of Justice.[48]

Over time other groups—self identified or not— have been added to the mix. Sexual orientation was added to this list which now includes transgenders, who seem to have sprung up from nowhere as an organized "group" after years of being attached to the Gay and Lesbian movement.

In fact, Critical theory can be expanded to almost any other group who insists that their marginalized status as victims be acknowledged and accepted.

The theory's adherents invented an authoritative-sounding term, "intersectionality," to refer to their assertion that such social categorizations such as race, sex, class, and national origin overlap in systems of discrimination or disadvantage for all such groups. According to this concept, even if there is little or no actual discrimination by the standards set forth in the law, it is nonetheless pervasive. It permeates American society because White people, especially White males, have from the beginning maintained a special privileged place in society for themselves. Use of statistical data comparing the White population's average socio-economic outcomes to the averages for Black Americans and others whom the Left likes to refer to by its umbrella label, "people of color," imply that all such people should have a negative view of the United States, and join with Black activists in a class struggle to disempower White people, sharing in the political common cause of taking down a system designed, built, and controlled to maintain White advantage. It is worth noting that this kind of attack on America is not new. Racially motivated efforts to undermine and destabilize the United States by attacking its culture and open market economic system date back to Lenin's Comintern in 1922, a point I will return to later.

Creating terms like "intersectionality" to rationalize and try to legitimize a political ideology is reminiscent of use of the term "Klassenkampf," which refers to Karl Marx's fundamental premise that above all else, an ongoing struggle over material outcomes between dominant and victimized social classes shapes society. However, with the growing prosperity of democratic capitalist societies, the much-ballyhooed class struggle he prophesied emerging from the grass roots failed to materialize. There were no spontaneous popular revolutions in the industrialized nations back then, nor since, seeking to break the chains of "wage slavery." In a word, his theory flopped. But Marx's followers could not admit its empirical falsification in the real world. They continued the lie because it was the cornerstone of his entire political-philosophical framework, including his envy-based supposition that people not only seek the justice of being treated equally, but in doing so also crave enforced social leveling, what Marxists term, "social equity."

With their Klassenkampf prediction utterly discredited, Marxists have been trying ever since to find a new term of art and idea they can use to help them gain popular support in their struggle for power. Adding racial antipathy to lesser economic status and a call for "equity" as they have redefined it appears to be at the heart of their strategy for gaining the political empowerment to force a further leveling of society. By broadening the Marxist grievance landscape beyond race to include majorities among all peoples of color, homosexuals, and women they hope to ultimately create a much larger political coalition and permanently unchallengeable majority. But doing so is a long-term project, which requires a cultural transformation focused on today's children who are tomorrow's followers and voters.

Another term of art used by race theorists is "microaggressions," which given their examples, are instances of discourteous, antisocial, exclusionary, unpleasant, and sometimes even menacing behavior in social interactions, especially among youth, where different races intermingle.

A CRT educational program starts with indoctrination of all the teachers to change their behavior toward their students and enable them to incorporate critical theory's lessons within various standard subjects in a school's curriculum. Whether taught as a subject itself or worked into other subjects, it is a recognizable doctrine in educational materials schools select and teacher training.[49] Once a person is "trained" he or she is obliged to campaign against "institutional racism" and "White supremacy," and for radical social change that eradicates "implicit biases" in all walks of life, to achieve greater "equity" for aggrieved groups. They are even asked to submit their plans for doing so. This can include actions such as constructing "narratives" that support leftist political goals, actively backing organizations such as Black Lives Matter, which is openly Marxist. and adopting codes of conduct that punish what activists consider "hate speech," racist language, and other words and expressions they seek to outlaw.

Clearly, as a factual matter, immutable physiological characteristics do not determine a person's natural abilities and achievement. Laws in the U.S. and other Western nations also forbid outright racial discrimination. However, that does not rule out the possibility of subtle discrimination and cultural differences playing an important role in economic success. Race and culture are different constructs, culture being broadly defined (according to the Oxford Dictionary) as the ideas, customs, and social behavior of a particular people or social group.

Although we must acknowledge that racial prejudices remain, institutionalized racial discrimination against minorities has, thankfully, diminished considerably over time with the enactment of civil rights legislation.

Furthermore, trends in poverty, income, and welfare data also do not support the narrative of *systemic* racial inequity. If American society were truly structured around White oppression of Blacks and other racial minorities, one would expect to find that "people of color" have been making little or no economic progress, but that is simply not the case. U.S. Census data dating back to the 1970's (see *Income and Poverty in the United States: 2019*) document a dramatic *decrease* in poverty rates for the U.S. Black population as well as people labelled Hispanic and Asian, along with *increased* real incomes. The White poverty rate on the other hand, while it remains lower than the others, has not improved at all. Notably, Asian Americans as a group have now reached parity with White Americans' poverty rate and attained much higher median household income.

Even though it is not, and will never be a racial utopia, America is not systematically discriminating against its Black citizens or other minorities in the financial assistance it provides to those in need. On the contrary, consistent with its anti-discriminatory laws, needs based merit holds sway instead of racial apportionment, a fact all Americans should be proud of.

Until recently, few would have argued that race relations had not improved over the past sixty years in parallel with the economic progress of the Black population. Of course, progress, or lack of it, is not the real point the race theorists are trying to make. Under their neo-Marxist view any remaining statistical disparity in achievement and incarceration between Blacks and Whites from whatever causes, must point to injustices to be remedied by governmental intervention in the economy and peoples' lives. It is the modern-day version of Marx's proletariat of minorities oppressed by a despicable bourgeoisie that is both economically domineering and racist. Thus, poverty and class differences among Blacks and Whites represent a social evil that must be eliminated by any means necessary, including instituting measures such as quotas and reverse discrimination, fully socializing wealth and income, and payment of "reparations" by the guilty White population, as well as the "reeducation" of White people as to their sometimes unconscious deep-seeded racism, beginning with the most malleable segment, their children. It is this nexus of CRT with Marxist politics that gives rise to the twisted ideology of Racial Socialism described earlier.

To the contrary, most would probably agree that it would be vastly better for any person in the lower economic echelon to achieve greater relative prosperity and improved social status through talent, skill, and diligence, as many have done, instead of government redistributing wealth based on one's group identity. Americans would stand to benefit from a stronger society if that were to occur. A greater portion of Americans becoming better educated, more prosperous, treated equally, freed from dependency on government, and taking leadership roles in society's institutions, is indeed the hope, and should be the aim shared by all.

But how can such betterment ever be achieved if a racial theory is taught to children in which skin color determines what one deserves, either as a victim deserving special treatment by society or as a hated oppressor who must make sacrifices necessary to level society? Within its doctrine it holds that American history, including the socioeconomic differences among racial groups, has been shaped by subtle but deeply rooted institutionalized racism and oppressive race-based hierarchies favoring the White population.

Sadly, in the 21st century Marxists have melded together race theory with socialist dogma to create a volatile political weapon that is being aggressively implanted into the U. S. educational system by its Leftist administrators and teachers' unions in concert with national organizations. By indoctrinating impressionable youth in this racial ideology they are doubling down on the resentment, if not the racial hatred it summons forth. This is not education. Teaching a racist political doctrine is different from teaching about racism.

Like other Marxist teachings, CRT sows social discord, and is activist, not merely academic, with plans to change the world. And like Marxism, its ideological dogma is taught as proven, non-debatable fact in educational settings, with significant moral overtones. Accordingly, everyone, students and teachers alike, who reject this doctrine as a fallacious "theory" are not merely in error, they must be shunned and treated as evil racists who ignore all the racial inequities that it claims permeate America's capitalist society.

While purporting to occupy the moral high ground, CRT's emphasis on group identity versus personal responsibility undermines the moral foundations of civil society. Under a mantle of righteousness, its teachings imply that collective, heritable guilt for slavery and the racial discrimination of prior generations should be placed on all whites, not just descendants of America's colonists, based on the presupposition that they are all benefiting from the evils of that era, and perpetuating it in some measure.

Heritable guilt, a vestige of tribalism and form of collective guilt, is antithetical to the West's legacy of legal precepts and moral judgments that are based on an individual's actions alone.

The Civil War was America's dearly purchased and powerful atonement for slavery. The forging of a slavery-free nation came with an enormous cost measured in both blood and treasure. Speaking of the War in his famous Second Inaugural Address on March 4, 1865, President Abraham Lincoln described it "as the woe due" for the "offense" of "American slavery," and that God's justice might require the War to continue until "every drop of blood drawn with the lash, shall be paid by another drawn with a sword." Frederick Douglass, the most powerful Black voice of that era, at an event honoring Lincoln in 1876, spoke of "rejoicing in our blood-bought freedom."[50] In the end, on the Union side hundreds of thousands of White soldiers and nearly forty-thousand Black soldiers died, and many more were maimed in an incredibly brutal conflict to free four million Blacks from slavery and create a stronger unified nation of all-free states. With many centuries of interracial slavery around the world there may be other instances in history where a racial majority fought a protracted and bloody civil war to eliminate the practice of enslaving members of another race within its society, but I have been unable to find any such case. By giving short shrift to the moral gravity of the American Civil War, CRT disregards and disrespects the legacy of Lincoln and the great many soldiers who died in it as well as the enormous sacrifices endured by their families.

Embracing the retrograde tribal notions of collective guilt associated with group identity, and inherited guilt transmitted by one's blood over generations as the basis for racial justice not only means that a person living today would be deemed guilty of any past crime of any long-deceased ancestor, but also of any past crime committed by persons merely of the same race, even though the actual perpetrators were unrelated to that person.

To act on such thinking is not only unjust, but also antisocial, immoral, and a logical absurdity. This crosses a line that cannot be crossed or compromised upon.

Certainly, the iniquity of Black slavery, its abolition, and the subsequent civil rights struggle within a White majority nation to achieve the justice of equal treatment is an important part of America's history that should be straightforwardly taught, not glossed over. At the same time, the achievements of Black Americans must also be celebrated. But those with a Marxist political agenda are instead now craftily turning that history into a source of racial hatred and unwarranted collective shame, to the detriment of current and future generations. This is not about civil rights, that is, about unequal treatment of citizens. Instead, it draws upon the socialist principle that the unequal results often achieved by individuals are necessarily unfair and must be corrected by placing the irresistible hand of government on the scale to level the outcome so all of its citizens "end up at the same place."

Its ambition is to begin indoctrinating children at a very

young age. Inflammatory ideology is being taught to impressionable children starting in kindergarten, not just in high schools and universities. Both the Marxist Bolsheviks (later "Communists") and the Nazis prided themselves on their ability to shape the hearts and minds of their youth with propaganda to carry out totalitarian programs.

Lest anyone escape from it, it is also being being incorporated into many mandatory governmental and corporate employee "training" programs. Rather than consisting of useful knowledge that can help individuals advance in society, it is based on sorting everyone into categories by their racial identity in order to invoke a moral judgement about themselves, as either victims with grievances or oppressors perpetuating injustice, and thus justify the "hand on the scale" i.e., preferential or discriminatory treatment based on racial identity. This of course rejects the principle of non-discriminatory treatment and equal ("color-blind") rights for every citizen regardless of their racial identity, which Western societies have established, fought for, and sought to inculcate in generations of students through liberal civics and history education.

Promotion of this latest regressive form of racial ideology is another step in the Left's migration of Marx's paradigm of a zero-sum struggle between two opposing classes to an economic struggle between races. It is not just a warped history lesson, and not just about money. It's more about transforming culture in order for certain groups to gain status and power over others whom they attack. It is the fusion, once again, of an ideology of class conflict with racial identity-based ideology, each of which righteously demand radical social change and control of the levers of power to redress grievances.

No one should doubt that in rejecting the civilizing principle that racially neutral reason applied through the rule of law should govern over visceral passions, Racial/Tribal Socialism can tear apart the fabric of ethnically diverse societies. This is hardly a step forward on a path toward greater racial comity and a stronger unified society. Instead, it destroys the liberal political ideal of a non-racial society. It is a socially regressive manipulation by the radical Left of the understandable resentment of some Black people for the historical oppression suffered by their ancestors. But because there are no guilty individuals still alive to punish, guilt and victimization must be transferred in a time-warp to the present and collectivized according to racial identity.

As noted elsewhere, since Lenin's creation of his subversive Comintern, using latent racial antipathy to foment social division and chaos in capitalist democracies that are multi-racial has been a key part of the Left's game plan for destroying them and achieving the goal of world socialism.[51]

No, the United States is not a perfect place, a utopia. Nor will it ever be. But it does carry within its historical and constitutional makeup and culture the seed of self-criticism and continual improvement that encourages each generation to make it a better, more equitable place for people *regardless of their race*. When one considers the history of modern socialism, it would be foolhardy to assume that American education, once it becomes indoctrinated with racial ideology, will lead to a peaceful revolution that achieves greater distributive justice and racial amity.

Intrusive government decrees that set aside individual freedoms and the mandated teaching of highly divisive race theory in institutions do not make for a better, more equitable society. Rather, they are two of the latest "red flags" signaling socialism's increasingly strong hold on the key institutions of liberal Western societies such as the United States and its advance into every nook, cranny, and crevice.

Socialists have long recognized that in achieving their goal to abolish capitalism and build a socialist society, control of public education is equally important to fomenting class conflict. Building the ideological infrastructure to promote instruction in CRT is a strategy enabling them to do both using the massive influence of society's educational institutions.

To prevail in the contest of ideologies socialism must capture the children and will take only them into utopia to assure they are not taught the virtues of individual initiative and racially neutral merit but the opposite instead, while deliberately leaving behind and silencing the old who know better. With a political outlook warped by Marcuse-like thought, an increasing proportion of American educators have sacrificed rational inquiry, deliberation, and debate about important social issues to the intolerance of their ideology. They betray the nation's sacred trust when given custody of its youth by seeking to implant retrograde ideas of social justice, cleverly packaged with half-truths, into their students' impressionable hearts and minds. One should expect vicious personal attacks to be waged against any who pose a threat to the Left's growing hegemony over education. In this real-life drama there will be no *Deus Ex Machina* coming to the rescue to assure a happy ending.

Stepping back for a moment from the focus on these signs of immediate danger on our doorstep, to the bigger picture, perhaps those who have never lived under totalitarian regimes fall prey to what Dostoyevsky called the seductive "emotional ideal side of socialism."[52]

Consider the *Wall Street Journal* in 2016. A headline reads: "Is Communism Cool? Ask a Millennial."[53] It is easy to understand how the well-meaning young who are often ignorant of the past and who certainly have never observed or experienced first-hand what socialism really is are particularly susceptible to phony promises of engineering a better world. Only one part of the promises is kept, that of a radical transformation. Those who lived through the subsequent reality had their lives dramatically altered to be sure, but it was not from finding themselves in a better world. Instead, they had "a special relationship with death."[54]

Notes

1. The Marxian synthesis of socialism's two hereditary strains, German and French, is described by George Lichtheim in *The Origins of Socialism*, Frederick A. Praeger, 1969, Chapter 10 "The Marxian Synthesis, Theory and Practice," pp. 185, 197; it is the synthesis of ideological theory with revolutionary activism.

2. Will and Ariel Durant describe Robespierre's belief in "the spirit of the nation," or in Rousseau's language, the "general will of the nation" in *The Age of Napoleon: A History of European Civilization from 1789 to 1815*, Chapter II "The National Assembly," p. 14, Simon and Schuster, 1975.

3. This quote of Keynes is taken from *Soviet Tragedy: A History of Socialism in Russia, 1917-1991*, by Malia, p. 109, The Free Press, 1994; the original language Malia quoted is found on the final page of Keynes' *The General Theory of Employment, Interest, and Money*, Palgrave Macmillan, 1936.

4. Hannah Arendt at p. viii of her Preface to the First Edition of *The Origins of Totalitarianism*, The World Publishing Company, 1951 described totalitarian movements' "conspicuous distain of the whole texture of reality" in their "fictitious world."

5. J. V. Stalin speech at home of the writer Maxim Gorky in preparation for the first Congress of the Union of Soviet Writers in October 1932; full quote as follows: "The production of souls is more important than the production of tanks...And therefore I raise my glass to you, writers, the engineers of the human soul." The importance of this as a Marxist/Stalinist ideological tenet is discussed by John Garnaut in *"Engineers of the Human Soul: what Australia needs to know about ideology in Xi Jinping's China"* reported in an article by Bill Bishop January 16, 2019 in *Sinocism* (at sinocism.com).

6. Ludwig von Mises, *Human Action: A Treatise on Economics*, The Ludwig von Mises Institute, 1949, Chapter XXV "The Imaginary Construction of a Socialist Society," p. 689 that every true socialist is a *"disguised dictator"* masking his or her "self-deification" and love of power with a phony idealism.

7. Arthur Koestler, *Darkness at Noon*, p. 179, transl. by Daphne Hardy, Signet books, The New American Library, Macmillan Company, 1941.

8. The phrase *"useful idiots"* has been widely attributed to Lenin although it is not to be found by searching his written *Collected Works* (at least by me), and may have been invented by Ludwig von Mises. However, the phase is "useful" in characterizing Lenin's and Stalin's cynical view of those who report the "news." Indeed, it is very plausible that Lenin said exactly those words in a fit of candor! Lenin and Stalin were known to have actively recruited and often duped, bribed, or otherwise co-opted malleable Western news media, writers, and intelligentsia, so they would echo Soviet lies, and

could be used as a subversive Soviet tool in furthering their ambitions for a truly international Socialist movement. Notable examples would include the passionate American Harvard-educated journalist and communist John Reed, for whom according to Victor Sebestyen (page 462 of his 2017 biography, *Lenin*), Lenin authorized $1 million for propaganda in the U.S. Reed spent a great deal of time with Lenin, Trotsky and other Bolsheviks in 1917-18, then authored *10 Days That Shook The World* in 1919, a book praising Lenin's Bolshevik revolution as a model for America and the world to follow. Another is American Left-wing journalist Lincoln Steffens who after a brief visit to Russia in 1919 made his famous and lamentable misstatement "I have seen the future, and it works." Others, later in the 1930's who came under Stalin's influence included George Bernard Shaw, and Walter Duranty the Moscow bureau chief for the New York Times, who ignored and helped to suppress growing evidence of the horrific Soviet-caused Holomodor famine of 1932-33 in Ukraine, which starved to death an estimated four million. After all, that could not be true because the USSR was a utopia in the making! Sadly, to this day there seems to be an almost endless supply of such "useful idiots" posing as providers of reliable information among America's and the rest of the West's news, educational, and cultural institutions.

9. Paul Johnson, *Modern Times: The World from the Twenties to the Nineties*, Harper Collins Publishers, 1991, p. 51 "The First Despotic Utopias," referring to V. I Lenin as embodying both an extraordinary "will to power," and "passion for force."

10. V. I. Lenin, *Collected Works of Lenin*, Volume XXI, Lawrence & Wishart, 1959, p. 243; Lenin has been quoted as saying in an echo of Rousseau and Robespierre: "Classes are led by parties and parties are led by individuals called leaders...This is the ABC. The will of a class is sometimes fulfilled by a dictator. Soviet socialist democracy is not in the least incompatible with individual rule and dictatorship. What is necessary is individual rule, the recognition of the dictatorial powers of one man. All phrases about equal rights are nonsense."

11. James Marson, December 17, 2016 *The Wall Street Journal* article "Russian Fights For Stalin's Victims", recent polling of the Russian public reveals that nearly a quarter now believe Stalin's repressions justified, and half do not consider his ordering the murder of millions of their countrymen, women and children, to have been a crime because it was somehow "necessary"!

12. The Bolshevik motto was quoted from the statement of an 87-year old former Communist Commissar, Vasily Petrovich N, in the Chapter "On a Different Bible and a Different Kind of Believer" in *Secondhand Time: The Last of the Soviets*, by Svetlana Alexievich, Random House Publishing Group, 2016, p. 175.

13. Hannah Arendt, *The Origins of Totalitarianism*, p. 387 in Chapter "The Totalitarian Movement", Meridian Books: The World Publishing Company, 1951.

14. Gary Kasparov, December 17-18, 2016 article in *The Wall Street Journal* titled "The USSR Fell – The World Fell Asleep."

15. Alexander Solzhenitsyn, *U.S. Congressional Record* – Senate, S 4873, April 5, 1976; copied into in the Record an April 4, 1976 Washington Post article by Alexander Solzhenitsyn under title *Solzhenitsyn's Warning:* "...socialism of any type and shade leads to a total destruction of the human spirit and to a leveling of mankind unto death...All Communist parties, upon attaining power, have become merciless. But at the stage before they achieve power, it is necessary to use disguises...Modern society is hypnotized by socialism. It is prevented by socialism from seeing the mortal danger it is in. And one of the greatest dangers of all is that you have lost all sense of danger, you cannot even see where its coming from as it moves swiftly toward you...The solemn pledge to abstain from telling the truth was called 'socialist realism'...The simple step of a courageous individual is not to take part in a lie...violence can conceal itself with nothing except lies, and lies can be maintained only by violence. Violence...demands from us only obedience to lies, and daily participation in lies...You imagine you see danger in other parts of the globe and hurl the arrows from your depleted quiver there. But the greatest danger of all is that you have lost the will to defend yourselves."

16. Michael Novak, *The Spirit of Democratic Capitalism*, "Introduction", pp. 13-28, and Part One: "The Ideal of Democratic Capitalism," pp. 29-186, Madison Books, 1982; also see William Kristol's review of Novak's book, *Defending Democratic Capitalism*, in *The Public Interest*, pp. 101-102.

17. Voltaire, *Candide*, 1759, Boni and Liveright, Inc. publisher, 1918, pp. 280-282 of 297 in e-version; through the character Candide, Voltaire presents the message that we must eschew Panglossian optimism and deal with the world as it truly is, on no certain immutable track to betterment or worsening. We must continually "tend to our garden" of liberty and dignity.

18. The list of such groups and their affiliates in just the USA is almost endless. The Socialist Party USA (SPUSA) reference at www.socialistpartyusa.net contains this quote "most members envision a sweeping or revolutionary transformation of society from capitalist to socialist through the decisive victory of the working class in the class struggle;" SPUSA has 13 chartered local parties, and 2 chartered state parties; the UK-based Socialist International reference is at found at www.socialistinternational.org; the parties mentioned in the text are the Communist Party USA CPUSA) at www.cpusa.org; the Workers World Party (WWP) at www.workers.org which has 16 affiliates in 13 states; the Party

for Socialism and Liberation (PSL) at www.pslweb.org; the Revolutionary Communist Party, USA (RCPUSA) at www.revcom.us; and the Progressive Labor Party (PLP) at www.plp.org which effusively praises Stalin and calls for "burning down capitalism;" There are others as well, such as the Green Party of the US (GPUS) co-founded by a labor union activist, and the World Socialist Party (US) at www.wspus.org which states that "Our aim is world socialism. A worldwide system of society based on common ownership and democratic control of the means for producing and distributing wealth by and in the interest of the whole human community;" the Democratic Socialists of America (DSA) www.dsa.org boasts of over 94,000 members and 239 chapters as of July 2021. Its student wing is the Young Democratic Socialists of America (YDSA) www.y.dsausa.org, which claims 84 chapters, and publishes a newsletter titled "The Red Letter;" the Working Class Party (WCP) www.workingclassfight.com, and The Socialist Alternative which is Marxist.

19. In crafting names the Left uses virtue-signaling words like: democratic, freedom, liberty, law, poverty, justice, progressive, open, and green. And to create an aura of credibility they often call themselves an Institute, Foundation, Center, or Congress; Numbering in the hundreds, and perhaps thousands, such entities are far too numerous to catalogue here.

20. Ken Braun article "Big Media Ignores Ford Foundation's Big Left Influence," in *Capital Research*, January 2022, p. 23-29.

21. Author's transcription of an audiotape recording of a speech by former Communist Bella Dodd delivered in Utica, NY in 1953, during which she relates a 1944 talk by Alexander Trachtenberg to a group of fellow Communist leaders in NYC.

22. Arthur Koestler, "Part I - The Initiates," in *The God That Failed*, Richard Crossman Editor, 1949, pp. 55-56. The book is a collection of biographical essays written by a famous group of six disillusioned former communist writers, each of whom describes their first-hand experience with communism.

23. David Horowitz, *The Black Book of the American Left, Volume 1: My Life and Times*, Encounter Books, 2013, 2016, "Goodbye to All That," p. 166, "My Vietnam Lessons," p. 172.

24. Paul Johnson, *Intellectuals*, Chapter 13 "The Flight of Reason," Harper & Row Publishers, 1988, p. 306.

25. Predicted by Martin Malia in *Soviet Tragedy: A History of Socialism in Russia*, Chapter 13 "The Perverse Logic of Utopia, Socialism After Sovietism," p. 517, The Free Press, 1994.

26. While translations may vary, this is the most commonly found wording; the quote is from Johann Wolfgang von Goethe, in *Faust*, "First Part, Prelude-

At-The-Theater," line spoken by Merry Andrew the comedian. The e-artnow (2019) version is translated as "each beholds what in his bosom lurks," p.49.

27. Philosopher Michael Novak in his 1982 tour de force, *The Spirit of Democratic Capitalism*, Chapter 2 "From Practice to Theory," pp. 19-20, Madison Books, 1982.

28. Philosopher Karl Popper, *The Poverty of Historicism*, Routledge, 1957, Part III, "Criticism of the Anti-Naturalistic Doctrines," see Section 20 "The Technological Approach to Sociology," p. 184, Section 21 "Piecemeal versus Utopian Engineering," p. 170, and Section 24 "The Holistic Theory of Social Experiments," p. 204.

29. Reinhold Niebuhr, *Major Works on Religion and Politics*, Chapter IV "The Irony of American History;" paraphrase of his ideas found at p. 699 of 1339 in Kindle version of Library of America, 2015.

30. Eric Fromm, *Escape from Freedom*, 1941.

31. S. P. Orth, *Socialism and Democracy in Europe*, 1913, Chapter I, "Introduction – Why Does Socialism Exist?" location 252 of e-version.

32. Bryan Caplan, *Prevalence of Marxism in Academia*, Mach 31, 2016 report on a 2006 survey of American professors.

33. Mitchell Langbert, paper titled *Homogenous: The Political Affiliations of Elite Liberal Arts College Faculty*, National Academy of Sciences, Acad. Quest. (2018) 31:186-197; published online: 19 April 2018; https://www.nas.org.

34. Found at https://umaine.edu/socialismandmarxiststudiesseries/, January 30, 2022, The University of Maine Socialist and Marxist Studies Series Menu, Fall 2021, and October29, 2020 Virtual Zoom Lectures.

35. Noah Carl, paper titled *Lackademia: Why Do Academics Lean Left?* Briefing paper. Adam Smith Institute, March 2, 2017; found at https://www.static1.squarespace.com.

36. Reference to the Marxist Student Federation can be found at www.socialist.net/spectre-universities-marxist-student.html; accessed February 1, 2022.

37. This is paraphrased from Karl Popper, *The Poverty of Historicism*, pp. 198-199 of 396 in e-book version, Routledge, 1957, 1961 edition.

38. Italian socialist and disillusioned former Bolshevik Angelica Balabanova (aka Balabanoff) describing Lenin by a Goethe phrase, quoted by Victor Sebestyen in his biography *Lenin; The Man, the Dictator, and the Master of Terror*, "Introduction," p. 3, and repeated in Chapter 37 "Power-At Last," p. 346-347. Balabanova worked alongside both Lenin, and Benito Mussolini (then a

Marxist), later the leader of Italian Fascism. No one will ever know if Lenin truly "intended the good" in his heart, but we do know he was responsible for creating great evil!

39. Stephen Kotkin, *Stalin: Paradoxes of Power*, see "A Trip to Siberia", and "If Stalin Had Died," pp. 462, and 723-739 respectively.

40. Bertrand Russell, December 11, 1950 Nobel Prize-Literature lecture *What Desires Are Politically Important?*

41. Hannah Arendt, *The Origins of Totalitarianism*, Second Edition, Meridian Books: The World Publishing Company, 1958, Chapter Five: "The Political Expansion of the Bourgeoisie," p. 137.

42. The English historian Lord John Acton famously wrote in 1887 that "power tends to corrupt, and absolute power corrupts absolutely" in a letter to Bishop Mandell Creighton. He also expressed a statement concerning the relationship between equality and freedom found at Lord Acton (John Emerich Edward Dalberg-Action), *Essays on Freedom and Power*, Chapter III, "The History of Freedom in Christianity" (1877), The Free Press, Glencoe, IL, 1949, p. 84.

43. Friedrich Hayek, last paragraph of *The Pretense of Knowledge*, his lecture accepting the Noble Prize in economics, December 11, 1974.

44. Historian Paul Johnson cited this Freud statement in *Modern Times: The World From the Twenties to the Nineties*, Harper Collins Publishers, 1991, Chapter One "A Relativistic World," p. 8. Johnson's footnote #18 cites Sigmund Freud, *The Future of an Illusion* (1927) p. 28.

45. Max Eastman, a former socialist and early supporter of Lenin in the U.S. wrote *Reflections on the Failure of Socialism*, Devin-Adair Company, 1955, Chapter Five "The Delinquent Liberals," pp. 63-64 and 67.

46. Svetlana Alexievich, *Secondhand Time: The Last of the Soviets An Oral History*, 2013, Random House Publishing Group, English translation by Bela Shayevich 2016, "On a Different Bible and a Different Kind of Believer," p. 170.

47.See Johns Hopkins University's site: www.coronavirus.jhu.edu; this site compiles data sets for corona virus demographics, including death and case rates by age among other categories. The conclusions stated here concerning the overall death rate of those infected, and dramatically different death rates by age cohort are obvious from these data (accessed February 3, 2022). The U.S. Center For disease Control publishes this data as well; see "Case and Death Demographic Trends" at www.covid.cdc.gov.

48.While in order to respond to Critical Race Theory I use the historically common terms "Black" and "White" to refer respectively to people generally of Sub-Saharan African and European origins, I neither endorse nor ascribe to any form of racial labels or categorization, which I believe are conceptually fraught with problems. In my opinion it is scientifically dubious to create and use official racial and ethnic identity types. Such typologies are far too amorphous. Forcing all people to designate their racial type raises ethical questions as well. Government should refrain from using any categorization of citizens by racial identity. My misgivings extend to all government actions, such as for example the racial and ethnic categories used by the U.S. Census Bureau.

49. Data concerning the prevalence of CRT in colleges across America can be found at www.criticalrace.org, a website created by William A, Jacobson, a Cornell U. law professor who opposes CRT.

50. Diana Schaub, "Lincoln Did It Better," *National Review*, May 2, 2022, pp. 18-19; Schaub draws these quotes from Abraham Lincoln's famous March 4, 1865 *Second Inaugural Address*, and Frederick Douglass' *Oration in Memory of Abraham Lincoln*, delivered on April 14, 1876.

51. V. I. Lenin introduced the topic of racial conflict in the aid of world socialism at the Second Congress of the Comintern in June 1920 in V.I. Lenin's *Preliminary Draft Theses on the National and Colonial Questions for the Second Congress of the Communist International*. It was revisited at the Comintern Fourth Congress in 1922 with its publication of *The Black Question* on 30 November, which describes the U.S. Civil War as "not a war for the emancipation of the blacks, but a war for the preservation of the industrial hegemony of the North," which led to Black "wage slavery." At the 1930 Comintern Congress it was much more fully addressed in the *Resolution on the Negro Question in the United States*, which, after describing oppression of Blacks, discusses how their cause can become useful to the cause of communism. It directs the Communist Party of the USA to lead the charge for racial equality by, among other things seeking "*Confiscation of the landed property of the white landowners and capitalists for the benefit of the Negro farmers*" [emphasis added] in the so-called southern Black Belt of the U.S.; "All national reformist currents ...which are an obstacle to the revolutionisation of the Negro masses, must be fought systematically and with the utmost energy;" the " constant call to "the Negro masses" must be: *revolutionary struggle against the ruling white bourgeoisie, through a fighting alliance with the revolutionary white proletariat!;*" [emphasis added] "Enslavement of the Negroes is one of the most important foundations of the imperialist dictatorship of U.S.A. capitalism;" "The more American imperialism fastens its yoke on the millions strong negro masses, the more must the Communist Party develop the mass struggle for Negro emancipation, and the better use it must make of all conflicts which arise out of national differences, as an incentive for revolutionary mass actions against the bourgeoisie.;" "to win over to our side these millions of Negroes as active fellow fighters in the struggle for the overthrow of bourgeois power throughout America." The Resolution can be

found at www.marx2mao.org at which a copy is included within The 1928 and 1930 Cominterns' *Resolutions on the Black National Question in the United States,* Revolutionary Review Press, Washington D.C., 1975.

52. F. Dostoyevsky, *The Possessed (The Devils)* aka *Demons,* Chapter 2: "Prince Harry. Matchmaking," p. 73, trans. Richard Pevear and Larissa Volokhonsky, First Vintage Classics Edition, 1995.

53. Andrew Clark, December 22, 2016 *Wall Street Journal* article titled "Is Communism Cool? Ask a Millennial."

54. Svetlana Alexievich, *Secondhand Time: The Last of the Soviets An Oral History,* 2013, Random House Publishing Group, English translation by Bela Shayevich, 2016, "Remarks of an Accomplice," p. 3.

Chapter Nine
Conclusion

"Happiness is the fruit of freedom, and freedom that of valor."
—Pericles, 453 B.C.

What is to be done? Will there be continued freedom under a restrained government or a perhaps a transformational shift toward a domineering system of omnipotent state power, that history shows always brings out the very worst in human nature? How can we ensure the socialist monster is kept at bay and freedoms are preserved for future generations? Sadly, there is no magic wand or cookbook of well-proven lessons of history we can follow. I would argue that complete belief in a simple, glib solution to man's continued search for a more perfect world only leads into a trap, ensnared by over two thousand years of naive utopian models, and in more recent times horribly misguided experiments with socialism that have destroyed many millions of lives.

Like ships at sea, socialists have followed false prophesies and absurd promises onto the sharp rocks of reality. Those who have thus far managed to stay afloat have done so only by turning away from the precepts of Marx's modern socialism in deed, if not in word, though they still cling to its evil methods in their futile attempts at expunging the desire for freedom from the human soul.

The hard lessons of history and the realities of our human nature tell us that vain is the hope of finding an earthly Eden just over the horizon. Nonetheless, the peoples of the world must not fearfully seek refuge from an inherently uncertain future in socialism's grandiose and phony promises. Doing so imperils liberty, justice, and life itself.

If there are no ready solutions that would take care of all life's problems in a grand stroke irrespective of mankind's inherent frailties, I would nonetheless argue that there is at least a hopeful path forward. Utopian schemes are a dangerous misdirection. Real progress in human affairs has resulted from the difficult work of incrementally improving valuable institutions that organize and moderate human activity, inventing new and better ones to meet the challenges of the future, and discarding those which become dysfunctional. The path is revealed by, and results from, the hard work and creativity of individuals behaving responsibly with respect to one another in seeking to better themselves, their families, communities, and nation, while freely joining hands in cooperative undertakings as they do so. There is no reason why this cannot continue, if we honestly transmit the truths and wisdom hard won from past experiences to others and the next generation.

Concluding our discussion without a definitive, sure answer to the significant threat of Socialism/Marxism/Communism and other militant ideologies may disappoint. It is axiomatic that one cannot oppose something with nothing; it is not enough to simply critique and contest those who wish to impose utopian schemes. If it is true, as Paul Ricoeur argued in his lecture series, Ideology and Utopia, that any critique of a utopian ideology necessarily rests upon an alternative utopian construct, then disparagement of utopianism could be considered self-contradictory. Simply contesting and replacing one utopian ideology with another cannot be the solution, otherwise humanity could become subject to what Paul Johnson called "the Gresham's Law of political morality," under which frightfulness drives out humanitarian instincts, and the contesting visions of what society ought to become "corrupt each other into ever greater profundities of evil."[1] This is precisely what occurred in brutal contests between Nazism, Fascism, and Communism during the last century.

Indeed, the many ideological forms of utopianism have all been a scourge upon humanity. Any prescription for a heaven on earth is simply a seductive song alluring to careless listeners and ambitious would-be political leaders looking for a path to supreme power. It will destroy an otherwise triumphal chorus of human progress in which free people everywhere are a part. Replacing one utopian system with another is certainly not the answer. For example, the liberal, tolerant, moral basis of Western civilization is also today under assault not just from socialism, but also from theocratic Islamic fundamentalism, an offshoot of Islam that will stop at nothing to impose its totalitarian theocracy and Sharia law on the world. It is due to Islamic fundamentalism, not socialism, that we recently witnessed women in the Middle East enslaved and raped, children starved and abused, and people beheaded or burned alive in cages. However, it is a very hopeful sign that some parts of the Islamic world are actively supporting the principles of peaceful coexistence and mutual respect among the religions of the world and have issued formal declarations to that effect.

In our search for more humane and acceptable models of government, we must not allow ourselves to be seduced by any ideology that invariably leads to a dark place that strips us of the better part of our humanity. The victims of history's numerous utopian schemes continue to scream warnings to us from their graves.

Is there any ideal prescription for how people should govern themselves? There is no perfect answer for all times, all places, and all peoples. We have learned that utopias in our temporal world are a frightening impossibility, but there is yet something hopeful we can learn from a vision of utopia. Perhaps, as Ricoeur suggests, instead of becoming a destructive ideology, utopia can still be the non-ideological nowhere place or "Erehwon" of our imagination, providing a vantage point from which we can view collective shortcomings and from which pathways may be revealed for creating and continually improving institutions to better protect freedom, individual rights, and civil society at large.[2] Martin Luther King's "I Have a Dream" speech, which goes to the heart of what it means to be a human being, exemplifies such an inspiring but non-ideological vision.[3] Moreover, when free from the arrogant desire to command society through political power, unfettered thinking about our current situation and future possibilities by those who are restless can identify pathways to betterment indispensable to human progress; for example, to name a few: laws setting environmental, health, and safety standards, civil rights laws, and scientific advances such as the "green revolution" in food production that have done much to remove the dark shadow of starvation in much of the world, better and more accessible medical treatments, safer transportation, and cleaner energy technologies.

Absent the militancy and arrogance of past utopian movements, we can be encouraged by long-term prospects for a better future in which freedom, democracy, equal human rights, life-bettering prosperity, and the rule of law are universal. When anchored in the realism of our human nature, dreams and yearnings, and serious thought, together with humility, can help us in our never-ending voyage to discover improved ways of living together and adapting to an ever-changing world.

The need to use facts, morality, and reason to defend existing freedoms is another key element that must be present. Rather than positing a perfect end structure for human society, is seems reasonable to regard the alternative liberal democratic model of an open, self-adaptive society as a non-utopian framework for living collectively—a model in which power is diffused among politically equal and free individuals. Joseph Schumpeter expressed it this way: "Democracy is a political method, that is to say, a certain type of institutional arrangement for arriving at political—legislative and administrative—decisions and hence incapable of being an end in itself."[4]

Instead of rigid doctrines, an open, democratic model embodies an unending process of reconciling the wants, needs, and aspirations of a free people across the entire socio-economic spectrum. In that sense it is anti-ideological, adapting as civilization develops and self-correcting over time without claims to being the perfect end state. It is a inherently messy, forever-evolving process of sustaining liberty for everyone, a model in which collective decisions are made through the ballot box on how people will govern themselves. Societal decisions are debated and made from the bottom up, not by those seeing themselves as guardians. When all voices are heard, decisions are made by free people constantly struggling to keep the darker forces of human nature in check so they can follow the higher calling of virtue, conscience, and morality. This earnest aspiration should not be discounted. Throughout the centuries human beings have been able to invent institutions that better account for their fallibility and as Steven Pinker and others have documented, have made considerable real progress on that score.[5]

In considering the benefits of this alternate self-adjusting model, however, the tragedies of history show that: institutions established for noble purposes can suddenly crack and fall apart. Human beings do not readily become wiser and more moral from one generation to the next. For example, it took millennia to banish slavery in certain societies and yet human bondage still exists in the shadows.

"Human nature, if it changes at all, changes not much faster than the geological face of the earth," Solzhenitsyn writes in *The Gulag Archipelago*.[6] Natural resistance to change and mistakes along the way must therefore be expected and considered even in a pluralistic, open model.

If we dare not become overly optimistic, let us also not become excessively pessimistic about our ability to create change for society's good. The Ten Commandments, Code of Hammurabi, Buddha's Eightfold Path, Christ's Sermon on the Mount, and the United States' Declaration of Independence all testify to laudable efforts to improve society by memorializing the wisdom needed to guide our decisions so it may be faithfully transmitted from one generation to the next.

Considering its record of enabling human betterment over two centuries, the open, democratic and adaptive paradigm, probably best labeled democratic liberalism, is arguably one of mankind's most remarkable inventions. Michael Novak and others have labelled it as democratic capitalism. The core principles the West's institutions are based upon are democracy in which all power flows upward from individual citizens, each with equal civil rights, the rule of law over arbitrary fiat, legal states over ethnic nations, and the protection of the individual no matter his race or religion.[7]

Although Winston Churchill was a product of Great Britain's age of empire-building with its assumed racial superiority, he saw very clearly the price humanity would pay if subjected to either racial or socialist totalitarian regimes. History records that he resisted giving in to such evils with every fiber of his being. While his nation was under attack by the Nazis in 1941, as Britain's Prime Minister, he painted a vision of a world future for President Roosevelt's visiting wartime emissary Harry Hopkins:

> We seek no territorial gains, we seek only the right of man to be free; we seek his right to worship his God, to lead his life his own way, secure from persecution. As the humble laborer returns from his work when the day is done, and sees the smoke curling up from his cottage home in the serene evening sky, we wish him to know that no rat-a-tat-tat of the secret police upon

his door will disturb his leisure or interrupt his rest...only government by popular consent, freedom to say whatever one wishes, and the equality of all people in the eyes of the law.[8]

These proven liberal principles reflect the best of humanity's accumulated wisdom concerning how we can govern ourselves to live together in peace and happiness.

There exist in many nations today well-proven, democratic forms of government that are founded on the rule of law, equal citizenship, and realistic principles of genuine human decency rather than originating from religious, racial, or class divide, hatred, and envy. They are not all the same, but taken together, they are proof that true liberal democracy can enable people to freely cooperate in the mutual pursuit of prosperity and the greater good while respecting each other's beliefs and civil rights. Integral to their success in defending freedom is the redress of legitimate social grievances of hunger, unearned privilege, and prejudice where they exist, and the creation of more just and stronger societies based on individual merit and basic human rights shared by all and protected by government.

Capitalism, an economic system based on equal rights and voluntary exchanges and moderated by a system of citizen-enacted laws, is an essential element of this positive, adaptive model. As seemingly messy, flawed, and unpredictable as a capitalist system may be, it is undeniable that the introduction of the open market and its predicated human freedoms in places where socialism has begun to retreat has led to a dramatic decline in poverty with increased economic opportunities. To be sure, nothing about human beings is perfect and completely pure, least of all our thoughts, intentions and behaviors, and neither is capitalism a perfect expression of democratic liberalism. Capitalism with its open markets is a natural outgrowth of the universal practice of engaging in market exchanges for mutual benefit whenever people are free to do so, and therefore also to some extent of human self-interest.

Of course, taken to an anarchistic extreme it can challenge reason and morality; absent a system of laws that nurtures "responsible freedom," it can endanger individuals and society, but our experience with capitalism over hundreds of years now has led to reforms and the imposition of many important constraints in the law. Philosopher Michael Novak pointed out in 1982 that democratic capitalism is "Neither the Kingdom of God nor without sin." But he goes on to observe:

> Yet all other known systems of political economy are worse. Such hope as we have for alleviating poverty and for removing oppressive tyranny – perhaps our last, best hope – lies in this much-despised system...exactly tailored to the difference between the human being's highest aspirations for human unity and his limits of insight and purity of heart. Too low a system for angels, it seems not too high for humans as they are. It stretches them a bit.[9]

There will always be a better way, so we must continually improve upon our legacy. If the militancy, misdirection, and arrogance of utopian movements are negated, we can be encouraged by the long-term prospects for a future in which freedom, democracy, human rights, and the rule of law are universal. We must, however, always recognize and respect our own fallibility. True humility can help in our voyage to discover better ways of living together and adapting to an ever-changing world. We should be humble enough to recognize that we are not sovereign over a diverse world of more than seven billion people, and that we are subject to our own imperfections and folly. There is no magic key that will unlock the door into any ideal world utopians may envision, or reveal the secret to building an earthly Eden in which re-engineered humans do not act from their natural impulses. Events of the past, from the distant to the most recent, certainly belie any notion of human nature achieving saintly moral perfection.

Three important lessons of history should be kept it mind:

The only sureties are human imperfectability and our inability to know what the future holds; while information and knowledge may rapidly accumulate, the wisdom needed to fashion better human institutions lags far behind; and bad ideas, especially what Keynes termed the "mad scribblings" of arrogant political philosophers, repeatedly resurface under different labels and different masks to plague us.[10]

Considering the current state of human affairs, a "common sense realist," might honestly ask if rather than steadily accumulating wisdom, understanding has been draining out of our collective consciousness! Can the propensity to forget the past, combined with the willful distortion of it by those seeking to control the present, and to shape the future according to their will, outpace our learning from past human experience? One wonders how much historical truth is being willfully distorted and destroyed by untrustworthy custodians of future generations who in betrayal of that sacred duty have burrowed into our educational and cultural institutions like poisonous ticks.

My intent in this final chapter has been to tread the fine line described by Hannah Arendt between the "reckless optimism" of Candide's Pangloss on the one hand and the "reckless despair" of Martin on the other.[11] Both attitudes are irresponsible. While warning against complacency and ignoring the resurgence of evil utopian ideologies threatening to "destroy the essence of man" I am also not making a Marxian-like prediction that another such catastrophe is inevitable.[12]

Democracy is by no means inevitable, but I take heart from the fact that the people of the world have been voting with their feet in favor of Western liberal democracies whenever and wherever possible. This is not because the Western democracies are perfect, but because they are much better places in which to live, with equal civil rights for all their citizens and abundant opportunities for their new citizens to prosper. These include, non-discriminatory laws, voting in honest democratic elections to select and replace those who will govern, the ability to acquire and own property, the freedom to pursue opportunities to work to take care of their own needs and their children, to move about freely, and to share in the enormous benefits which arose from the prosperous and uplifting legacy of democratic capitalism noted herein.

There is still reason for optimism. Good ideas have taken root in many new parts of the world. In fact, wherever true liberalism prevails, the fortunes of the average person measured in political freedom and economic prosperity has improved at an astounding rate. As Deirdre McCloskey has extensively documented, "Ordinary men and women do not need to be directed from above, and when honored and left alone become immensely creative ... Liberty and dignity for ordinary people made us [humanity] rich, in every meaning of the word."[13]

I have maintained throughout that to prescribe what others should do in governing themselves is inherently arrogant and dangerous; it mirrors the socialist's desire to become one's own God. The world has had enough of self-proclaimed absolute rulers, kings and aristocrats, racial supremacists and demagogues, slave masters, fascist dictators, fanatical mullahs, self-righteous clergy, egotistic social engineers, brutal secret police, and little bureaucratic Napoleons. Louis Fischer, the former socialist, wrote in *The God That Failed*: "Dictatorship rests on a sea of blood, an ocean of tears, and a world of suffering - the results of its cruel means. How then can it bring joy or freedom or inner or outer peace? How can fear, force, lies, and misery make a better man?"[14] To preserve and encourage the spread of our cherished democratic institutions, it is also necessary for large numbers of peace-seeking "non-activists" to abandon the comfort of passivity and apathy. All must rally together and bravely challenge the false prophets of failed utopian ideologies wherever they take advantage of public forums in our open societies to insinuate themselves into the body politic. All must stay alert to demagogue claims that theirs is the only true path to an earthly paradise.

Almost 2,500 years ago Pericles defended Athens's democracy: "Happiness is the fruit of freedom, and freedom that of valor."[15] Valor in defense of freedom is not restricted only to the battlefield. The call of Pericles also encompasses the valor of many thousands of heroic voices of dissent such as Andrei Sakharov, Vladimir Bukovsky, Dimitri Muratov, Alexei Navalny, Lin Zhou, the brave martyrs of the 1989 Tiananmen Square massacre, the notable human rights activist who publicly criticized communist one-party rule, Nobel Peace Prize winner Liu Xiaobo, who died in 2017 after a lengthy imprisonment, and those challenging the Chinese Communist Party at great personal risk in Hong Kong such as Jimmy Lai, Gwyneth Ho, Lee Cheuk-yan, Chow Hang-tung, Joshua Wong, Agnes Chow, and Ivan Lam. Let us also not fail to recognize as well the imprisonment of hundreds of "counter revolutionaries" during Cuba's widespread anti-government protests on July 11, 2021 triggered by continuing impoverishment of the Island. Then there is the Venezuelan opposition leader, Juan Guaido, who could face arrest by the Cuban-trained henchmen of the socialist dictator Nicholas Maduro for protesting rigged elections and his nation's near apocalyptic conditions. In addition to such well-known cases, the list of those whose often quiet deeds are worthy of the world's respect and honor encompasses many thousands of lesser-known heroes in Africa, Asia, Europe, Latin America, and the Middle East, who, following the example of these notable heroes, championed and continue to champion freedom and democracy despite great risk of ruination, imprisonment, torture, and death. Criminal regimes in nations such as Cuba and Nicaragua have arrested and imprisoned hundreds in their efforts to stifle political opposition.

What must we do? It is my view that because thirty years have now passed since the collapse of the Soviet Socialist Empire, a reckoning is long overdue. We now have the benefit of substantially more archival documentation, and witness testimony, as well as greater historical perspective. This reckoning must yield a clear-eyed and widely shared understanding of the true nature of Marx's utopian socialism, regardless of how it is disguised by clever political labelling. The free part of the world must come to terms with socialism's inherent and vast criminality or be complicit in living a great lie and perhaps itself succumb to the false premises of that lie.

It is truly shameful that the West was compromised for so long by its earlier wartime alliance with Stalin's Soviet Union, its eagerness to put the Cold War behind, and its determination to establish a modus vivendi with China and other remaining Communist regimes. Beyond such political expediency, the West has also clearly lacked the moral courage to convene a comprehensive tribunal that would formally compile and publicize now-abundant evidence and to formally try and condemn socialism's criminal regimes on the world stage. But it is not too late to do so.

The Soviet dissident author Vladimir Bukovsky describes the desultory denouement of the Cold War this way:

> We do not want to total up its victims. No monuments will be erected to mark this war, no eternal flame will burn on the grave of the unknown soldier...It was probably the most unpopular war of all those we know. At least from the point of view of the side that seems to have won it. But there is no rejoicing now it is over. The losers signed no instruments of capitulation. The victors received no rewards. On the contrary, it is the very ones who, for all intents and purposes, were the losers, who are now dictating terms for peace, writing history, while those who supposedly won maintain an embarrassed silence. And do we really know who the victors are? Who are the vanquished?[16]

Solzhenitsyn's admonition to not sweep the ugly history of socialism under the rug is being ignored in today's Russia as Vladimir Putin endeavors to rehabilitate Stalin's USSR. As of this writing there exists an organization founded in 1992 under Mikhail Gorbachev in Moscow known as International Memorial dedicated to studying political repression in the USSR and promoting moral and legal rehabilitation of persons subjected to political repressions. It opposes the return of totalitarianism, supports human rights, and promotes preservation of memory of victims of totalitarianism. Sadly, its continued existence is in doubt, having come under attack by the Putin regime, which is seeking to abolish it. At the regime's urging, Russian courts have revoked Memorial Human Rights Center's legal status, and declared it and its sister organization, Memorial, "foreign agents," forcing them to close.[17]

I would like to demonstrate the concept of initiating a formal "day of reckoning" in some detail. I believe the time is ripe for the world's democracies, acting together, to pass unequivocal judgement on the great evils of socialist totalitarianism. This should be done by publicly reciting and cataloging these enormous evils as part of an official proceeding that names the very real monsters and their henchmen, including those responsible for continuing communist regimes still in existence. The point is not to physically imprison such people, as deserving of removal and punishment as they may be. Rather it is to seek a judgment of moral force that condemns the socialist utopian ideology they stand for, finally sweeping it into history's ash bin where it belongs, by turning it and its remaining true believers into Nazi-like pariahs. These illegitimate regimes and the evildoers who have led them, both past and present, bear responsibility for the greatest holocaust of modern times and its 100 million victims.

What I am calling a "World Tribunal on Marxist-Communist Crimes Against Humanity" should be convened to create a comprehensive record for current and future generations. Undertaking a public repudiation and condemnation of demonic socialist regimes is a profound moral duty of free peoples. In my opinion, continuing to shrink from this duty of remembrance would be tantamount to admitting the West no longer possesses the fortitude it took for previous generations to win World War II and turn back the tide of communist expansion during the Cold War. Without a clear and consolidated public record, there is a definite possibility that the truth will gradually be lost in the mists of time as it is rewritten by enemies of freedom.

In offering this proposal, I also ask, "Why has the West until now lacked the courage to formally declare the criminality of Marx's socialism based on carefully researched and documented examples, just as it did Hitler's totalitarian racial Nazi creed?" I believe there are several explanations. For one, the socialist states were not militarily defeated, and powerful socialist regimes still control China and other countries in Asia and Latin America. Second, these regimes are highly secretive and have either hidden or destroyed as much evidence of their vast crimes as possible. They, and their many sympathizers in democratic nations would certainly object, boycott, and do their utmost to dispute and disrupt the kind of proceedings I am proposing. Third, as this book has many times warned, Western democracies still harbor significant numbers of radical socialism advocates in their educational, cultural, and political institutions. These people would strongly oppose, scorn and ridicule any historical reckoning that delegitimizes them. As Martin Malia has pointed out, they are the primary obstacle to such a public reckoning because any realistic accounting of crimes committed in the name of socialism "would effectively shut the door on Utopia." Leftist elites who base their world outlook and political activism on notions of a "social justice" that requires equalizing unequal socioeconomic conditions by any means, including the unequal treatment of citizens, will ferociously resist such truth-telling.[18] Nevertheless, only by a formal, open, unified and widely publicized declaration condemning the utopian monster created by Marx and his followers will the monster finally become a political pariah entombed for eternity...with a stake through its heart. The peoples of nations in which Marx's retrograde ideology remains deeply rooted may thus have a hope of someday living in freedom and justice.

To those who might want to say no to this proposal and shrink away from it because they see it as impractical, too difficult, too controversial, and maybe too risky, I have this to say: we are the lucky ones who have not yet experienced the worst. Although our freedom may be slipping away, we are not yet locked in a prison of lies. For now, we can freely wander about, breathe fresh air, and enjoy looking up at the heavens as we contemplate the future.

Millions upon millions of victims cry out from their graves for recognition of the horrific injustices done to them. And what of the unborn millions of future victims of socialism? Will generations hence curse us for the great cowardice of remaining silent as once discredited utopian ideologies again threaten humanity?

While such an undertaking would undoubtedly have many political ramifications, this cause is moral, not political. It arises not from partisan politics, nor from seeking any power whatsoever over others, but instead from the urgent duty of this generation to future generations to shine a disinfecting light on the vast crimes of socialism that will help prevent its further spread.

Although I came to this proposal in response to the rhetorical question "What is to be done?" I must acknowledge the efforts I later discovered, which were launched in the summer of 2019 by Vladimir Bukovsky and Renato Cristin to promote a worldwide campaign for a "Nuremberg-like" tribunal that deals with both the horrific past, and the real and present danger of Marxist ideology.[19] This campaign is now underway, and political support for it will hopefully gain significant traction, building on the European Union Parliament's resolutions of 2009 and 2019 which deal with the crimes against humanity of past communist and Nazis regimes.

In writing about the horrors of socialism Solzhenitsyn warned that silence can allow such evil ideas to become implanted and fester until they ultimately reemerge with greater force:

> It is unthinkable in the twentieth century to fail to distinguish what constitutes an abominable atrocity that must be prose-cuted and what constitutes that 'past' which 'ought not to be stirred up.
>
> We have to condemn publicly the very idea that some people have the right to repress others. In keeping silent about evil, in burying it so deep within us that no sign of it appears on the surface, we are implanting it, and it will rise up a thousand-fold in the future.[20]

As timely and important as such a global initiative is, it is equally important for we who recognize utopian ideological trends within our own individual countries and local communi-ties to speak out now. We must not remain complacent and silent in the face of approaching socialist-inspired evil. We are in a continuing, deadly struggle, beginning with the critical battle against the Leftist media's control of words and thoughts, and its corresponding debasement of language and truth in public discourse. We must speak greater truth to negate great lies, so people have no more room in their minds and hearts for the siren songs of socialists of all stripes, instead looking truth squarely in the eye, and not be seduced by the alchemists' magic of so-cialism's black arts. It is said that the verdict of history will be decided against the silent. Thirty years after the Berlin Wall was torn down, we are still at a pivotal point in history, not beyond it. Will our civilization become one in which individual hard work, risk taking, and genius are for naught, and any deviation from prescribed secular religion brings persecution from a faceless, soulless State abetted by a fatally corrupted culture? Solzhenitsyn warned that we must not lack a moral backbone and throw up our hands in capitulation such as the on-and-off socialist Bertrand Russell who remarked: "better red than dead."

A cardinal lesson derived from the 20th Century rise of the totalitarian ideologies of Communism, Nazism, and radical Islam is that remaining silent makes a citizen an accomplice in the tragedy that ensues. We as free people must speak the truth. It is a duty that we can no longer pretend is not necessary. Let us not be deterred by the fear of those who would attempt to destroy people who speak the unvarnished truth about socialist ideology. Let all who are blessed with freedom find the fortitude to spread the truth and have faith that in the end "right makes might."[21] If we remain passive, we shall surely one day be asked haunting questions by succeeding generations:

Where were you when socialists using various labels started infiltrating, co-opting, and corrupting the great institutions of our civil society? Where were you when they began to suppress free speech and intimidate those who dissented? Where were you when law enforcement, education, and news media became subordinated to a political ideology that made truth and justice unrecognizable? Where were you when both Reason and God were cast aside and supplanted by base passions—like the Monster from the Id—serving an evil cause? Why didn't you speak out against the lies before it became too late?

Before closing, a word of caution. I must reiterate that proclaiming absolute truth, as socialists tend to do, can be an incredibly arrogant act, particularly when well-intended but untested and unverified opinion is treated as incontrovertible fact. I am reminded of Will and Ariel Durant's observation: "Truth is seldom simple; often it has a right and left hand, and moves on two feet."[22]

Ludwig von Mises wrote about utopian authors who: "drafted schemes for an earthly paradise in which pure reason alone should rule. They failed to realize that what they called absolute reason and manifest truth was the fancy of their own minds. They blithely arrogated to themselves infallibility and often advocated intolerance, the violent oppression of all dissenters and heretics. They aimed at a dictatorship either for themselves or for men who would accurately put their plans into execution. There was, in their opinion, no other salvation for suffering mankind."[23]

Undoubtedly there is a great amount of truth bearing on the topics of utopianism and socialism I have failed to fully convey in this writing. It has not been my purpose to proclaim absolute truth or to insist that there is a single truth, my truth, which all must accept. Considering my own imperfections, it seems likely that this work contains some errors, though hopefully few. But I am convinced that if you take the time to examine at least some of the many references I have included and explore further the subjects I have covered here on your own with an open mind and heart, you will discern additional and perhaps fuller truths for yourself.

I will conclude with a few quotes I believe well summarize the truth about socialism. The first is from a work by Dostoyevsky regarding any who would seek to create a perfect human society:

> Having devoted my energy to studying the question of the social organization of the future society which is to replace the present one, I have come to the conclusion that all creators of social systems from ancient times to our year have been dreamers, tale-tellers, fools who contradicted themselves and understood precisely nothing of natural science or of that strange animal known as man.[24]

Finally, I end this with a few quotes taken from witness interviews recorded by Svetlana Alexievich in *Secondhand Time*.[25] They speak for themselves.

> The first Bolshevik I ever saw...made a speech on the square
> 'A wonderful time will come when your wives will wear silk

dresses and high-heeled shoes. There will no longer be rich and poor. Everyone will be happy.' 'How can you not fall in love with a dream like that!...They won the support of the youth.'

'We wanted to create Heaven on Earth. It's a beautiful but impossible dream, man is not ready for it. He is not yet perfect enough... Man will always dream of the 'City of the Sun.'

'There's nothing more terrifying than an idealist.'

'In 1937 my father was arrested [by the NKVD]...Soon my mother was also arrested, and I was taken into custody along with her...my mother recalled how often little children would die in there. . . they would collect the dead children in big barrels, and leave them like that until spring. By then their bodies would be gnawed away by rats...At the age of three, children would be taken away from their mothers and moved into the children's barracks. In the morning we would see our mothers through the barbed wire fence: They would be counted and led off to work'

And now the words of the final witness, a clear and profound warning from a former communist executioner:

We were always covered in blood, we'd have to wipe our hands in our hair...The axe will survive the master! Mark my words!

Notes

1. Paul Johnson, *Modern Times: The World From the Twenties to the Nineties,* Harper Collins, 1991, Chapter 8 "The Devils," p. 296.

2. Paul Ricoeur, *Lectures on Ideology and Utopia* (given at the University of Chicago in 1975) Columbia University, 1986," Introductory Lecture," p. 15.

3. Dr. Martin Luther King's 1963 speech "I Have a Dream" delivered August 28, 1963 at the Lincoln Memorial during the Freedom March on Washington, D.C.

4. Joseph A. Schumpeter, *Capitalism, Socialism, and Democracy,* 1942, Harper Perennial 2008 3rd Edition, Part IV "Socialism and Democracy," XX "The Setting of the Problem," p. 242.

5. Steven Pinker, *Enlightenment Now: The Case for Reason, Science, Humanism, and Progress*, Penguin Books, 2018. Pinker makes the case that humanity has made astounding progress, in sharp contrast to John Gray's disturbing assertion in *Black Mass: How Religion Led the World into Crisis* (Anchor Canada, 2007) that much of what humanists would generally consider progress has been illusory as a result of religion, including the rise of utopian "political religions" during the 19th and 20th centuries.

6. Aleksandr Solzhenitsyn, *Gulag Archipelago*, English translation 1974, Editions du Seuil, 1973, Part II "Perpetual Motion," Chapter 2 "The Ports of the Archipelago," p. 334 of e-version.

7. Robert D. Kaplan, May 2017 essay The Return of Marco Polo's World and the U.S. Military Response, "The Dispersion of the West," p. 2.

8. Erik Larson, *The Splendid and the Vile, A Saga of Churchill, Family, and Defiance During the Blitz*, Crown, 2020, p. 351.

9. Michael Novak, philosopher and former socialist, *The Spirit of Democratic Capitalism*, Madison Books, 1982, "Introduction: Capitalism, Socialism, and Religion – An Inquiry into the Spiritual Wealth of Nations," No. 2 "From Practice to Theory", p. 28.

10. Lord John Maynard Keynes, *The General Theory of Employment, Interest and Money*, Macmillan Cambridge U. Press, 1936, Harcourt, Brace and Company, Ch. 24, "Concluding Notes on the Social Philosophy towards which the General Theory might Lead," Part V, final page.

11. Hannah Arendt, p. vii of her "Preface to First Edition" of *Origins of Totalitarianism*, Meridian Books: The World Publishing Company, 1951, and Voltaire's *Candide*.

12. Ibid, p. viii of Arendt.

13. Deidre McCloskey, *Bourgeoise Equality: How Ideas, Not Capital or Institutions Enriched the World*, Exordium: "The Three Volumes Show That We Are Rich Because of an Ethical and Rhetorical Change," p. 17; McCloskey has written that the lot of the average person measured in political freedom and economic prosperity has improved at an astounding rate.

14. Louis Fischer, *The God That Failed*, 1949, Ed. by Richard Crossman, Harper & Row, p. 225.

15. Pericles, leader of Athens, Funeral Oration, 431 BC, from "Ancient Hellas" in Thucydides *History of the Peloponnesian War*, pp. 143-51 translated by Rex Warner, 1972 Penguin Edition, p. 77, lines 8 and 9.

16. Vladimir Bukovsky, *Judgment In Moscow: Soviet crimes and Western Complicity*, Ch. 1, "Phony War," 1.7 "So who won?," p. 52, transl. by Alonya Kojevnikov, Ninth of November Press, 1996, 2019.

17. Solzhenitsyn's admonition about sweeping past atrocities under the rug is being ignored. See the International Memorial's website (as of December 2021): https://www.memo.ru/en-us/memorial/mission-and-statute/ to learn of the Memorial's aims, objectives, and works. See stories in the December 29 and 30, 2021 issues of the Wall Street Journal titled "A Court in Moscow Orders Human-Rights Group to Close," and "Prominent Rights Group to Close," respectively.

18. Martin Malia, Foreword to *The Black Book of Communism*, "Uses of Atrocity," p. xx.

19. Renato Cristin, June 22, 2021 Interview with J. R. Nyquist (Blog); see also "Appeal for Nuremberg Trials for Communism" (info@ nurembergforcommunism.org); "Why Communism Should Be Tried For Its Crimes Against Humanity (a June 16, 2021 article by Stella Morabito in The Federalist newsletter at thefederalist.com/2021/07/16/why-communism-should-be-tried-for-its-crimes-against-humanity); the Witness Project of the Victims of Communism Memorial Foundation (info@victimsofcommunism. org); and Vladimir Bukovsky's book *Judgement in Moscow: Soviet Crimes and Western Complicity*, which, along with The Black Book of Communism by S. Courtois et al, sets the stage for a Nuremberg-like reckoning.

20. Alexandr Solzhenitsyn, *The Gulag Archipelago*, Vol. 1, Chapter 4 "The Bluecaps," pp. 70-71, trans. by Thomas P. Whitney and Harry Willets, abridgment by Edward E. Ericson.

21. Abraham Lincoln, future U.S. President, taken from the final sentence of a famous anti-slavery speech he gave at Cooper Institute (NYC) on February 27, 1860.

22. Will and Ariel Durant, *The Age of Napoleon*, Simon and Schuster, 1975, "Afterward," p. 778.

23. Ludwig von Mises, *Human Action: A Treatise on Economics*, The Ludwig von Mises Institute, 1998, Chapter III. "Economics and the Revolt Against Reason," I. "Revolt Against Reason," p. 72.

24. Same as footnote #5; Fyodor Dostoyevsky's 1872 masterpiece *Demons* (aka "The Devils,"or "The Possessed"), Part Two, Chapter 7 "With Our People," translation by Maquire, p. 446; also found at p. 1801 of 3260 in Vintage iBook version, translation by Pevar and Volokhonsky, 1994.

25. Svetlana Alexievich, recorded testimonials in *Secondhand Time The Last of the Soviets: An Oral History* (2013, translation copyright 2016), Chapters: "On a Different Bible and a Different Kind of Believer," pp. 169, 170 and 172, and "On the Little Red Flag and Smile of the Axe" pp. 250, 277 and 281. Alexievich won the Nobel Prize for Literature in 2015.

SELECTED SOURCES AND BIBLIOGRAPHY

Alexievich, Svetlana, *Secondhand Time - The Last of the Soviets, An Oral History*, 2013, English trans., Winner of the Nobel Prize in Literature, Random House Publishing Group, 2016.

Anonymous, *Nine Commentaries on the Communist Party (China)*, The Epoch Times, 2004.

Applebaum, Anne, *Iron Curtain: The Crushing of Eastern Europe 1944-1956*, Anchor Books, Random House, Inc., 2012.

Arendt, Hannah, *On Revolution*, Penguin Books 1963, 1965 edition.

Arendt, Hannah, *The Origins of Totalitarianism*, Meridian Books: The World Publishing Company, NY, 1951,1958 second edition.

Attanasio, Orazio, Cattan, Sarah, Meghir, Costas, *Early Childhood Development, Human Capital and Poverty*, Working Paper 29362, National Bureau of Economic Research, Cambridge, MA, October 2021.

Berneri, Marie L., *Journey Through Utopia*, Beacon Press, Boston, 1951.

Bloom, Allan, *The Closing of the American Mind*, Simon and Schuster, NY, 1987.

British Government, *A Collection of Reports on Bolshevism in Russia*, presented to Parliament by Command of His Majesty, April 1919.

Brown, Donald E., *Human Universals*, 1991, 2017 Kindle Edition.

Bryson, P. J., *Socialism: Origins, Expansion, Decline, and the Attempted Revival in the United States*, Xlibris, 2015.

Buber, Martin, *Paths in Utopia*, 1949, The Beacon Press 1958 edition.

Buckley, Walter, *Sociology and General Systems Theory*, Prentice-Hall, 1967.

Bukovsky, Vladimir, *Judgement in Moscow: Soviet Crimes and Western Complicity*, 1996, translated by Alonya Kojevnikov, Ninth of November Press, 2019.

Castro, Fidel, *My Life: A Spoken Autobiography*, Ignacio Ramonet interviewer, 2009.

Caute, David, *Communism and the French Intellectuals 1914 - 1960*, The Macmillan Company, NY, 1964.

Center for Urban Renewal and Education, *The State of Black America: Progress, Pitfalls, and the Promise of the Republic*, Ed. by W. B. Allen, Encounter Books, NY, 2022.

Chambers, Whittaker, *Witness, Regenery History*, 1952, pub. 2014.

Chang, Jung and Halliday, Jon, *Mao: The Unknown Story*, Anchor Books Division of Random House, Inc. New York, 2005.

Churchill, Winston, *The Great War*, Volume III, "Russia Forlorn" pp. 1314-1327, George Newnes Ltd. 1933.

Clark, Andrew, *Is Socialism Cool? Ask a Millennial*, article published in December 23, 2016 *Wall Street Journal*.

Conquest, Robert, *The Great Terror: A Reassessment*, Oxford University Press, NY, 1990.

Cooper, William E., *Socialism and Its Perils*, Eveleigh Nash, London, 1908.

Courtois, Stephane, Werth, Nicolas, Panne, Jean-Louis, Paczkowski, Andrzej, Bartosek, Karel, and Margolin, Jean-Louis *The Black Book of Communism: Crimes, Terror, Repression*, published in Germany in 1997, and by Harvard University Press in 1999.

Dalberg-Acton, J. E. E. (Lord Acton), *Essays on Freedom and Power*, late 1800's, 1949 Free Press Edition.

de La Boetie, Etienne, *The Politics of Obedience: The Discourse of Voluntary Servitude*, circa 1552-1553, Translated by Harry Kurz, Introduction by Murray Rothbard, 1975, published by Mises Institute, 2015.

de Tocqueville, Alexis, *Democracy in America*, 1835 and 1840.

de Tocqueville, Alexis, *Speech on Socialism before the Constituent Assembly of France by Alexis de Tocqueville on September 12, 1848*, in *New Individualist Review, Chapter: Tocqueville on Socialism*, trans.

Ronald Hamowy, Liberty Fund, Indianapolis, 1981, accessed at www.oll.libertyfund.org.

de Tocqueville, Alexis, *On Democracy, Revolution, And Society,* ed. John Stone and Stephen Memmell, U. of Chicago Press, 1980.

Derfler, Leslie, *Socialism Since Marx: A Century of the European Left,* St. Martin's Press, 1973.

Dikötter, Frank, *Mao's Great Famine: The History of China's Most Devastating Catastrophe, 1958-1962, The Tragedy of Liberation: A History of the Chinese Revolution 1945-1957, The Cultural Revolution: A People's History, 1962-1976, and China After Mao: The Rise of a Superpower,* Bloomsbury Publishing PLC, NY, published respectively in 2010, 2013, 2016, and 2022.

Dodd, Bella, Audiotape of a Dodd speech delivered in Utica, NY in 1953 concerning the U.S. Communist Party, available online.

Dostoevsky, Fyodor, *Demons, (aka The Possessed or The Devils)* 1872, trans. Richard Pevear and Larissa Volokhonsky, First Vintage Classics Edition, 1995.

Draper, Hal, *The Two Souls of Socialism,* a pamphlet published by the Independent Socialist Committee: A Center for Socialist Education, Berkeley, California, 1966.

Drucker, Peter, *Post-Capitalist Society,* Harper Collins Publishers, NY, 1993.

Durant, Will and Ariel, *Rousseau and Revolution,* Simon and Schuster, NY, 1967.

Durant, Will and Ariel, *The Age of Napoleon,* Simon and Schuster, NY, 1975.

Durant, Will, *The Tragedy of Russia: Impressions from a Brief Visit,* Simon and Schuster, NY, 1933.

Durkheim, Emile, *The Division of Labor in Society,* transl. by George Simpson, The Free Press, Collier-Macmillan, 1933.

Early, John F., *Reassessing the Facts About Inequality, Poverty and Redistribution,* Cato Institute Policy Paper 839, April 2018.

Eastman, Max, *Reflections on the Failure of Socialism,* The Devin-Adair Company, NY, 1955.

Engels, Friedrich, *Socialism: Utopian and Scientific,* 1878.

Ferguson, Niall, *Civilization: The West and the Rest*, Penguin Books, NY, 2011.

Gates, Robert M., *Duty: Memoirs Of A Secretary At War*, Alfred A. Knopf, New York, 2014.

Geoghegan, Vincent, *Utopianism and Marxism*, Methuen, London, 1987.

Glucksmann, Andre, *The Master Thinkers*, trans. Brian Pearce, Harper & Row, NY, 1977.

Gorky, Maxim, *Untimely Thoughts: Essays on Revolution, Culture and the Bolsheviks*, 1917-1918, first published in English in 1968, by Yale University Press, 1995.

Gray, John, *Black Mass: How Religion Led the World into Crisis*, Anchor Canada, 2007.

Gregor, A. James, *The Faces of Janus: Marxism and Fascism in the Twentieth Century*, Yale University Press, 2000.

Griffith, Ernest S. Director, *Communism In Action: A Documented Study and Analysis of Communism in Operation in the Soviet Union*, U.S. Library of Congress Legislative Reference Service, 1946.

Gutmann, Ethan, *The Slaughter: Mass Killings, Organ Harvesting, and China's Secret Solution to its Dissident Problem*, Prometheus Books, 2014.

Hardin, Garrett, *Tragedy of the Commons*, in Science 162 (1968) p.p. 1242-1249.

Harrington, Michael, *Socialism: Past and Future*, The Classic Text on the Role of Socialism in Modern Society, Arcade Pub., 1989, 2011.

Hawthorne, Julian, editor, *Ideal Commonwealths: Comprising More's Utopia, Bacon's New Atlantis, Campanella's City of the Sun, and Harrington's Oceana*, The World's Great Classics, Colonial Press, 1901.

Hayek, Friedrich A., *The Fatal Conceit: The Errors of Socialism*, The Collected Works of F. A. Hayek, Volume I, edited by W. W. Bartley III, University of Chicago Press, 1988.

Hayek, Friedrich A., *The Pretense of Knowledge*, lecture upon accepting the Nobel Prize in economics, 1974.

Hayek, Friedrich A., *The Constitution of Liberty*, Vol. XVII of Collected Works of F. A. Hayek, University of Chicago Press, edited by Ronald Hamowy, 1960, 2011 edition.

Hayek, Friedrich A., *The Road to Serfdom*, U. of Chicago Press, 1944, 1994 edition.

Hazlitt, Henry, *The Foundations of Morality*, D. Van Nostrand Company, Inc.,1964, Second Edition, The Foundation for Economic Education, NY, 1994.

Hearnshaw, F. J. C., *A Survey of Socialism: Analytical, Historical,* and Critical, Macmillan and Co. Ltd., London, 1928, 1929 edition.

Heilbroner, Robert, *"Socialism,"* essay from *"The World After Communism,"* Dissent (Fall 1990), p.p. 429-430, found in *The Concise Encyclopedia of Economics*, January, 2022.

Hertzler, Joyce. O., *History of Utopian Thought*, George Allen & Unwin, Ltd., London, 1922.

Hessen, Robert, *"Capitalism,"* essay in *The Concise Encyclopedia of Economics* online, January, 2022.

Hobhouse, L. T., *Liberalism and Other Writings*, edited by James Meadowcroft, 1994.

Horowitz, David, *Radical Son: A Generational Odyssey*, Bombardier Books, 2020.

Horowitz, David, *The Black Book of the American Left, Volume 1: My Life and Times,* Encounter Books, 2013, 2016.

Huberman, Leo, and May, Sybil, *The ABC of Socialism*, Monthly Review, NY, 1953.

Huntington, Samuel P., *Political Order in Changing Societies*, Yale University Press, New Haven, 1968.

Johnson, Paul, *Intellectuals,* Harper & Row Publishers, NY, 1988

Johnson, Paul, *Modern Times: The World from the Twenties to the Nineties,* Harper Collins Publishers, 1991.

Jones, Charles I., *The Facts of Economic Growth*, paper, April 6, 2015.

Kaplan, Brian, *"Communism,"* essay in *The Concise Encyclopedia of Economics* online, January, 2022.

Kautsky, Karl, *Thomas More and his Utopia*, 1888, English translation by Henry James Stenning published by A.C. Black, 1927.

Keat, Nawuth, *Alive in the Killing Fields: Surviving the Khmer Rouge Genocide*, National Geographic, 2009.

Kennan, George, The "Long Telegram" from Moscow to U.S. Secretary of State, February 22, 1946.

Kharas, Homi, The Unprecedented Expansion of the Middle Class: An Update, Brookings Global Economy and Development Working Paper 100, February, 2017.

Kiehr, Harvey, Haynes, John Earl, Firsov, and Fridrikh Igorevich, The Secret World of American Communism, Russian documents translated by Timothy D. Sergay, Yale University Press, New Haven, 1995.

King, Dr. Martin Luther, I Have a Dream, speech in Washington, D.C., on August 28, 1963.

Kirkpatrick, Jeane J., Dictatorships and Double Standards: The Classic Essay That Shaped Reagan's Foreign Policy, in Commentary Magazine, November 1979.

Koestler, Arthur, Darkness at Noon, 1941, translated by Daphne Hardy, Signet Book, The New American Library, The Macmillan Company, 1941.

Koestler, Arthur, Silone, Ignazio, Wright, Richard, Gide, Andre, Fischer, Louis, and Spender, Stephen, The God That Failed, edited by Richard Crossman, Copyright 1949, published by Harper & Row, 1963.

Kohn, Hans, Political Ideologies of the Twentieth Century, Harper & Row, NY, 1949, 1966 edition.

Kolakowski, Leszek, Main Currents of Marxism: The Founders – The Golden Age – The Breakdown, translated by P. S. Falla, W. W. Norton & Company, NY, 1978 and 2005.

Kotkin, Stephen, Stalin: Volume I: Paradoxes of Power, 1878-1928", and Volume II: Waiting for Hitler, 1929-1941, Penguin Press, NY, 2014 and 1917.

Krushchev, Nikita, Memoirs of Nikita Khrushchev: Volume 3 Statesman [1953-1964], 1999, edited by Sergei Khrushchev, Transl. by George Shriver, published by The Pennsylvania State University, 2007.

Lazear, Edward P., Arnold, Morris, and Cox, Nona Jean, Socialism, Capitalism, and Income, Hoover Institution, 2020.

Lee, Hyeonseo, with John, David, The Girl with Seven Names: Escape from North Korea, Williams Collins pub., 2015.

Lenin (Ulyanov), Vladimir Ilyich, *What is to be Done?* 1902; *In Memory of the Commune* 1911; *The Three Sources and Three Component Parts of Marxism* 1913; *Socialism and War (with Zinoviev, G.)* 1915; *April Theses*, 1917; *The State and Revolution*, 1917; found in Lenin's Collected Works, Progress Publishers, Moscow, at Marxists Internet Archive.

Lichtheim, George, *The Origins of Socialism*, Frederick A. Praeger, NY, 1969.

Lincove, David A., *Radical Publishing to "Reach the Million Masses": Alexander L. Trachtenberg and International Publishers, 1906-1966*, Left History, Fall/Winter 2004.

Litwak, Eric, *Epistemic Arguments Against Dictatorship,"* in the journal *Human Affairs* 21, 44-52, 2011, published by Institute for Research in Social Communication, Slovak Academy of Sciences.

Luzkow, Jack Lawrence, *What's Left: Marxism, Utopianism, and the Revolt Against History*, University Press of America, 2006.

Malia, Martin, *The Soviet Tragedy: A History of Socialism in Russia, 1917 to 1991*, The Free Press, NY, 1994.

Mannheim, Karl, *Ideology and Utopia*, Harcourt, Brace & Co., NY, 1954.

Manuel, Frank E. and Fritzie P., translators and editors, *French Utopias: An Anthology of Ideal Societies*, The Free Press, NY, 1966.

Mao Tse-Tung, *Quotations from Chairman Mao Tse Tung, "The Little Red Book"*, 1930's - 1960's.

Marx, Karl, and Engels, Frederick, *On the Jewish Question*, 1843; *Theses on Feuerbach*, 1845; *Wage Labour and Capital*, 1847; *The Coming Upheaval (from The Poverty of Philosophy)*, 1847; *Class Struggle and Mode of Production*, 1857-58; *Manifesto of the Communist Party*, 1848; *Inaugural Address of the Working Men's International Association*, 1864; *Against Personality Cults*, 1877; *The Possibility of Non-Violent Revolution (the Amsterdam Speech)*, 1872; *Critique of the Gotha Program*, 1875; *The Tactics of Social Democracy (Engels)*, 1895; *The Class Struggles in France*, 1850; *The Eighteenth Brumaire of Louis Bonaparte*, 1852; *The Civil War in France*, 1871; *Socialism: Utopian and Scientific (Engels)*, 1880; *On the Division of Labour in Production (Engels from Anti-Duhring)*, 1878; *On Morality (Engels from Anti-Duhring)*, 1878; *The Origin of the Family, Private Property, and the State*, 1884; found in Karl Marx and Frederick Engels

Collected Works, Lawrence & Wishart Electric Books 2010, at
Marxist Internet Archive; These works are in the order they appear
in The Marx-Engels Reader, Second Edition, Ed. Robert C. Tucker,
W. W. Norton & Company, NY, 1978.

Mathiez, Albert, *Bolshevism and Jacobinism*, Library of the Socialist
Party and Humanity, Paris, translated by Mitchell Abidor, 1920.

McCloskey, Deirdre Nansen, *Bourgeois Equality: How Ideas, Not Capital
or Institutions, Enriched the World*, The University of Chicago Press,
Chicago, 2016.

McLetchie, Scott, *Maximilien Robespierre Master of the Terror*, academic
paper, 1983-84.

McMeekin, Sean, *Stalin's War: A New History of World War II*, Basic
Books, Hatchette Book Group, NY, 2021.

Meisner, Maurice, *Marxism, Maoism, and Utopianism: Eight Essays*, U. of
Wisconsin Press, 1982.

Menken, H. L., *The Slav Utopia*, book review, 1933.

Mill, John Stuart, *On Liberty*, 1859.

Mill, John Stuart, *Socialism*, 1879, The Perfect Library, CreateSpace
Independent Publishing Platform, 2015 edition.

Morris, James M., and Kross, Andrea L., *The A to Z of Utopianism*, The
Scarecrow Press, Inc. 2009.

Mumford, Lewis, *The Story of Utopias*, Boni and Liverlight, NY, 1922.

Munger, Michael, *"Division of Labor,"* essay in *The Concise Encyclopedia
of Economics* online, January, 2022.

Muravchik, Joshua, *Heaven on Earth: The Rise and Fall of Socialism*,
Encounter Books, NY, 2002.

Niebuhr, Reinhold, Reinhold Niebuhr: *Major Works on Religion and
Politics, Moral Man and Immoral Society, The Children of Light and
the Children of Darkness, and other works*, The Library of
America, Elizabeth Sifton, Editor, 2015.

Novak, Michael, *The Spirit of Democratic Capitalism*, Madison Books,
1982.

Nozick, Robert, *Anarchy, State and Utopia*, Basic Books, 1974.

Olson, Mancur, *Dictatorship, Democracy, and Development*, article in
American Political Science Review, Vol. 87, No. 3 September, 1993.

Olson, Mancur, *The Rise and Decline of Nations: Economic Growth, Stagflation, and Economic Rigidities,* Yale University Press, New Haven, 1982.

Orwell, George, *1984,* Mariner books, Harper Collins Publishers, NY, 1949.

Paine, Thomas, *Agrarian Justice,* 1795-96, published in 1797.

Paine, Thomas, *Rights of Man,* 1791.

Parsons, Talcott, *The Social System,* The Free Press, The Macmillan Company, 1951.

Payne, Stanley G., *A History of Fascism 1914-1945,* University of Wisconsin Press, 1995.

Pericles, *Pericles' Funeral Oration,* 431 BC, from *Thucydides' History of the Peloponnesian War,* translated by Rex Warner.

Pinker, Steven, *Enlightenment Now: The Case for Reason, Science, Humanism, and Progress,* Penguin Books, NY, 2018.

Pinker, Steven, *The Better Angels of Our Nature: Why Violence Has Declined,* Penguin Books, 2011.

Pinker, Steven, *The Blank Slate,* Penguin Books, NY, 2002, 2016 edition.

Pope Leo XIII, *On Socialism (Quod apostolici muneris)* encyclical, the Vatican, 28 December, 1878.

Pope Paul II, *Centesimus Annus* encyclical, the Vatican, 1991.

Pope Pius XI, *Quadragesimo Anno* encyclical, the Vatican, 1931.

Popper, Karl, *Poverty of Historicism,* Routledge, London, 1957, 1961 edition.

Popper, Karl, *The Open Society and its Enemies,* Princeton University Press, Princeton, 1945.

Pottier, Eugene, *The Internationale,* original words of the anthem of socialism, 1871.

Pro Patria Union, *On Crimes of Communism,* Jarl Hjalmarson Stiftelsen Foundation, June 2000.

Prychitko, David, *Marxism,* essay in *The Concise Encyclopedia of Economics* online, January, 2022.

Ricoeur, Paul, *Lectures on Ideology and Utopia,* Columbia University, published 1986.

Robespierre, Maximilien, *The Political Theory of Terror*, speech by Maximilien Robespierre, Feb. 5, 1794; a.k.a. *Report on the Principles of Political Morality Which Are to Form the Basis of the Administration of the Interior Concerns of the Republic*, by Maximilien Robespierre, (Philadelphia, 1794); source: Modern History SourceBook, Paul Halsall, August 1997.

Rousseau, Jean-Jacques, *Jean-Jacques Rousseau: The Basic Political Writings* 1750-1762, Trans. by Donald A. Cress, Hackett Publishing Company, Inc., 1987.

Russell, Sir Bertrand, *A History of Western Philosophy: and its connection with political and social circumstances from the earliest times to the present day*, Simon and Schuster, 1945, 1966 edition.

Russell, Sir Bertrand, *What Desires Are Politically Important*, Nobel Prize acceptance speech, 1950.

Saez, Emmanuel, *Income and Wealth Concentration in a Historical and International Perspective*, research paper, UC Berkeley and National Bureau of Economic Research, February 21, 2004.

Samuels, L. K., *Killing History: The false Left-Right Political Spectrum and the Battle between the 'Free Left" and the 'Statist Left,"* Freeland Press, 2019.

Sanandaji, Nima, *Scandinavian Unexceptionalism: Culture, Markets and the Failure of Third-Way Socialism*, Institute of Economic Affairs, London, UK, 2015.

Sassoon, Donald, *One Hundred Years of Socialism: The European Left in the Twentieth Century*, L. B. Tauris & Co Ltd., London, 1996.

Sawhill, I. and Haskins, R., *Work and Marriage: The Way to End Poverty and Welfare*, Brookings Institute, 2003.

Schlesinger Jr., Arthur, *Forgetting Reinhold Niebuhr*, essay, September 18, 2005.

Schlesinger Jr., Arthur, *The Disuniting of America: Reflections on a Multicultural Society*, W. W. Norton & Company, 1992.

Schoeck, Helmut, *Envy: A Theory of Social Behaviour*, Liberty Press, Indianapolis, IN, 1966, English translation 1970, 1987 reprint.

Schumpeter, Joseph, *Capitalism, Socialism and Democracy*, Third Edition, Harper Perennial, 1950, 2008 edition.

Sebestyen, Victor, *Lenin: The Man, the Dictator, and the Master of Terror,* Pantheon Books, NY, 2017.

Shafarevich, Igor, *The Socialist Phenomenon,* 1975, Harper and Row, 1980.

Sharansky, Natan with Troy, Gil, *The Doublethinkers: In assessing my own liberation, I recall a conformity that feels terrifyingly familiar today,* in Arts & Letters, February 11, 2021.

Shermer, Michael, *Heavens on Earth: The Scientific Search for the Afterlife, Immortality, and Utopia,* St. Martin's Griffin, NY, 2018.

Short, Philip, *Pol Pot: Anatomy of a Nightmare,* A John Macrae Book, Henry Holt and Company, NY, 2004.

Skelton, Oscar Douglass, *Socialism: A Critical Analysis,* University of Chicago, The Riverside Press, Cambridge, Mass., 1911.

Smith, Adam, *An Inquiry into the Nature and Causes of the Wealth of Nations: Books I - III,* 1776, published by Penguin Books, 1970.

Smith, Adam, *The Theory of Moral Sentiments,* George Bell & Sons, London, 1802.

Solzhenitsyn, Aleksandr, winner of the 1970 Nobel Prize in Literature, *1978 Commencement Address at Harvard,* 1978.

Solzhenitsyn, Aleksandr, *In the First Circle,* by A. 1978, written in 1958, fully restored version published by Harper Perennial, 2009.

Solzhenitsyn, Aleksandr, *Live Not By Lies,* essay, 1974.

Solzhenitsyn, Aleksandr, *The Gulag Archipelago,* published by Editions du Seuil 1973, English translation by Thomas P. Whitney, 1974.

Solzhenitsyn, Aleksandr, *Warning to the Western World, BBC interview and radio broadcast with A. Solzhenitsyn,* March 1976.

Sowell, Thomas, *A Conflict of Visions: Ideological Origins of Political Struggles,* 1987, Basic Books, Revised Edition, 2007.

Sowell, Thomas, *Discrimination and Disparities,* Basic Books, Hachette Book Company, NY, 2019.

Spargo, John, *Socialism: A Summary and Interpretation of Socialist Principles,* Norwood Press, J. S. Cushing Co.- Berwick & Smith, Norwood, Mass, 1906.

Spence, Jonathan D., *The Search for Modern China,* Third Edition, W. W. Norton & Company, NY, London, 2013.

Stalin, Josef, *History of the Communist Party of the Soviet Union (Bolsheviks)*, edited by the Central Committee, International Publishers, NY, 1939.

Stalin, Josef, *Problems of Leninism*, 11th Edition English translation, 1954.

Starmans, Christina, Bloom, Paul, and Sheskin, Mark, *Inequality Isn't the Real Issue*, essay published in the Wall Street Journal, April 29-30, 2017, based on *"Why People Prefer Unequal Societies"*, Article 0082, Journal Nature Human Behavior, April 7, 2017.

Sumner, William Graham, *What the Social Classes Owe to Each Other*, Caxton Printers, Ltd., Caldwell, Idaho, 1883, 1974 edition.

Talmon, J. L., *The Origins of Totalitarian Democracy*, Mercury Books, London, 1951.

The Prague Declaration on European Conscience and Communism, initiated by the Czech government, signed June 3, 2008.

United Nations Office of the UN High Commissioner for Human Rights (OHCHR) Assessment of human rights concerns in the Xinjiang Uyghur Autonomous Region, People's Republic of China, 31 August 2022.

Uyghur Tribunal, *Uyghur Tribunal Judgement – Summary Form*, Tribunal Members: Chair Sir Geoffrey Nice, Vice-Chair Nick Vetch, Tim Clark, Raminder Kaur, Dame Parveen Kumar, David Lynch, Ambreena Manji, Audrey Osler, and Catherine Roe, Church House Westminster, issued December 9, 2021.

Voigt, Frederick A., *Unto Caesar*, Constable, London, 1939.

Voltaire, *Candide*, 1759.

von Mises, Ludwig, *Human Action: A Treatise on Economics*, The Ludwig von Mises Institute, 1949, Scholars' Edition 1998.

von Mises, Ludwig, *Liberalism In the Classical Tradition*, Third Edition 1985.

von Mises, Ludwig, *Socialism: An Economic and Sociological Analysis*, German edition 1922, new updated edition (English translation) 195, translated by J. Kahane, New Haven, Yale University Press, 1962 edition.

Walling, William English, *Socialism As It Is: A Survey of The World-wide Revolutionary Movement*, The Macmillan Company, NY, 1912.

Wang, Wendy and Wilcox, Bradford, *The Millennial Success Sequence*, AEI Institute for Family Studies, 2017.

Widmer, Kingsley, *Utopia and Liberty: A Bibliographic Essay*, from journal Literature of Liberty: A Review of Contemporary Liberal Thought, vol. IV, no. 4, Winter 1981, published by the Cato Institute and the Institute for Humane Studies under the editorial direction of Leonard P. Liggio, 1981.

Wikipedia, *Socialism, Utopia, Socialist International, Liberalism, List of Socialist States*, Khmer Rouge Killing Fields, April 2016 – May 2017.

William J. Bernstein *A Splendid Exchange: How Trade Shaped the World*, Grove Press, N.Y., 2008.

Wittmer, Felix, *The Yalta Betrayal*, Caxton Printers, Ltd. Caldwell Idaho, 1953, Third Printing, 1961.

Wooldridge, Adrian, *The Aristocracy of Talent: How Meritocracy Made the Modern World*, Skyhorse Publishing, 2021.

Working Group on Chinese Influence Activities in the United States, *Chinese Influence & American Interests: Promoting Constructive Vigilance*, Co-Chairs Larry Diamond and Orville Schell, Hoover Institution Press, Stanford, CA, 2018.

Yathay, Pin,with Man, Jon, *Stay Alive My Son*, Cornell University Press, Ithaca and London, 1987.

Yergin, Daniel, and Stanislaw, Joseph, *The Commanding Heights: The Battle Between Government and the Marketplace that is Remaking the Modern World*, Simon & Schuster, NY, 1998.

Zamyatin, Yevgeny, *We*, 1924.

Zenz, Dr. Adrian, *Coercive Labor in Xinjiang: Labor Transfer and the Mobilization of Ethnic Minorities to Pick Cotton*, Intelligence Brief, Center for Global Policy, December 2020.

APPENDICES

Table 1 - Great Catastrophes of History

Historical Catastrophes	Estimated Deaths
Black Death (bubonic plague)*	75-100 million
Mongol Horde Massacres	50-70 million
Taiping Rebellion 1850-64	20-70 million
Nazi Genocidal Holocaust	6 million
Communist Holocaust (non-combatants)	100 million
World War I (military and civilian)	38 million
World War II (military and civilian)	50-80 million

* Mortalities from 1918 flu pandemic, and among indigenes of Western Hemisphere from diseases following European contact, were of similar magnitude.

While mortality estimates for these episodes are understandably difficult to construct, and thus vary considerably, they tend to be of similar magnitude.

Table 2 - The "Butcher's Bill" of Communism

Communist State	Est'd Deaths Caused
China	65 million
Soviet Union	20 million
North Korea	2 million
Cambodia	2 million
Africa	1.7 million
Afghanistan	1.5 million
Eastern Europe	1 million
Vietnam & Laos	1 million
Rest of World	150,000+
Since 1990	Indeterminate
Approximate Total:	**100 million**
Source: Courtois et al Black Book of Communism	

"Bloodlines" of Modern Socialism: Key Figures, Selected Works & Events

Pre-Modern literary influences include Plato (360 BC), Thomas More (1516), Tommaso Campanella (1623)

Key Events	French or Francophone	German, British, American	Russian	Asian & Latin American
	J. J. Rousseau 1754-62 "Discourse on Inequality", "Principles of Political Right", and "The Social Contract"			
Socialism's early theorist "pioneers" gain a following	C. H. Saint-Simon 1817 "The Industry"; critical of parasitic idlers and inheritance; began "utopian socialism"	Note: Arrows indicate influences		
1789-95 French Revolution	Robespierre Feb 5, 1794 Speech to National Convention - "The Political Philosophy of Terror" (guillotined in July 1794)			
1794 France's "Reign of Terror"				
1796 first revolutionary (proto) Communist manifesto; "Conspiracy of Equals" in Paris	FN "Gracchus" Babeuf "Conspiracy of Equals" (Guillotined in 1797) Sylvain Marechal 1796 "Manifeste des Egaux" P. Buonarroti (teacher of Blanqui) 1828 "History of Babeuf's Conspiracy of Equals"			
	F. M. C. Fourier Utopian Socialist 1808 "Theory of Four Movements"	J. G. Fichte 1806-10 Nationalism fueled by idealism		
1830's "Socialism" creed forms, and enters public discourse as society industrializes	Louis Blanc 1840 "Organization du travail"	G. W. Hegel A new social order can be created by a deliberate act of will		
	C. Pecqueur Father of collective socialism	L. Feuerbach 11th Thesis: "The point of philosophy is not just to interpret the world, but to change it."		
	P. J. P. Buchez 1833-38 "History of Fr Revolution"	T. Carlyle 1843 "Past and Present" attack on market economy		
1840 and 1848 French uprisings	E. Cabet 1839 utopian "Voyage en Icarie" 1841 Mon Credo Communiste"	Hess 1843 "Philosophy of Action" Atheism and Communism are respectable		
	P-J Proudhon "What is Property" "property is theft" Anarchist	Robert Owen Utopian socialist "Revolution in the Mind and Practice of Human Race"	A. Herzen Emancipation of serfs 1861 "Liberty and Land"	
1871 abortive Paris Commune	A. Blanqui Advocated insurrection to create Communist dictatorship	K. Marx & F. Engels: 1848 "The Communist Manifesto" 1867 "Das Capital"	N. Chernyshevsky: 1863 utopian novel "What Is To Be Done?" with concept of "The New People" who create a better society	

Proudhon   Fourier   Hegel   Marx   Fichte   Chernyshevsky

M. Bakunin
Revolutionary Socialist
1870-76 "Statism and
Anarchy" critic of
authoritarian socialism

V. Considerant
"Le Destinee Sociale" and
"Democracy Manifesto"

H. George
1879 "Progress and
Poverty"

Emile Zola
Non-socialist; 1885
"Germinal" influential critique
of worker exploitation

E. Bellamy
1888 "Looking Backward:
2000-1887"

1917-20 Russian Revolution

V. I. Lenin
1902 "What is to be Done?"
1917 "The State Revolution"
1917 Led overthrow of Tsar

Sun-Yat-Sen
Led 1911 Chinese
Revolution
Proto-socialist

1930-48 Chinese Revolution, massive famines and Stalin's Purges

A. Hitler
1920 National Socialist
(Nazi) Party (aberrant form
of socialism); anti-capitalist,
and anti-individualist
1925-26 "Mein Kampf"

J. Stalin
1924 leader of Bolsheviks
after Lenin
1939 published "History of
the Communist Party,
"Catechism of Communism"

Mao Tse Tung & Zhou En Lai
1926-1963 Mao's "Little Red
Book", and other works

1950-52 Korean War, Famines, political torture & murder

H. Marcuse
1955-64 "Soviet Marxism: A
Critical Analysis" and "One-
Dimensional Man"
denounced markets as evil

Ho Chi Minh
Marxist; helped found Parti
Communiste Francais in
1920; led Vietnamese
against Fr and USA

1950-75 Communists prevail in Vietnam

Kim Dynasty
Begins in 1948 with Stalin's
designation; now evolved
into deformed communism

1953-59 Cuban Revolution;

F. Castro & Che Guevara
1959 Led Cuban revolution
J. Stalin dies (1953)

1956-79 Soviets invade Hungary, Czech. & Afghan.

Noam Chomsky
Anarcho-libertarian socialist;
1979 "The Political Economy
of Human Rights"

Khrushchev, Brezhnev & others
1956 & 1962 Stalin
denounced by Khrushchev

Pol Pot
Led Khmer Rouge; 1949-51
joined Fr Communist Party;

Ho Chi Minh dies (1969)

1975-79 Pol Pot K. Rouge creates Cambodian "Killing Fields"

Allies to Mao, Kim, Ho Chi
Minh, and Castro until
collapse of USSR in 1991

Mao dies (1976)
The terror of his "Cultural
Revolution dies with him

1989-91 Collapse of Communism in USSR & E. Eur.

Li Peng
1987-2012 China's Leaders
gradually institute "Reform
Communism"

2012 - ? China ends "Reform Communism" & reasserts Marxism

Xi Jinping
Ascendancy of China's new
Neo-Marxist "Great
Leader"?

2016 - ? Socialism repudiated in Venezuela

H. Chavez & N. Maduro
Ruled Venezuela
1999-2017?
Fidel Castro dies (2016)

Primary sources: Lichtheim's "The Origins of Socialism", Morris and Kross "The A-Z of Utopianism", and biographies; A. Gray